Ultimate Festival & Travel Guide Sicily

Unforgettable Experiences, Unmissable Events, Unique Destinations, Authentic Travel Itineraries and Best Times to Travel to Palermo, Taormina, and Beyond

Katerina Ferrara

Immersion Travel Publishing

Ultimate Festival and Travel Guide Sicily

© 2024 Immersion Travel Publishing

All Rights Reserved.

No part of this publication may be reproduced, distributed, or transmitted in any form or by any means, including photocopying, recording, or other electronic or mechanical methods, without the prior written permission of the publisher Immersion travel Publishing, LLC.

ISBN: (Paperback) 979-8-9915871-1-2

ISBN: (Hard Cover) 979-8-9915871-2-9

ISBN: (eBook) 979-8-9915871-0-5

DISCLAIMER

The author is not a travel agent. All opinions, experiences and views expressed are those of the author based on my personal travel experiences. Businesses and websites recommended in this book may change ownership, rebrand, or close. The author has received no compensation or sponsorship from any recommended business. Festival dates and events are the decision of the local comune, so take care to check local listings before booking travel.

Contents

Explore More and Stay Connected!	VIII
1. Introduction to Festival Travel	1
2. Arrive & Explore	15
3. Map of Sicily's Must-See Celebrations	20
Summer Celebrations	23
4. The Cannolo Craze of Piana degli Albanesi	25
5. Blooming Streets: The Art of the Infiorata of Noto	35
6. Wild Swimming & Tranquill Escapes	52
7. Honoring the Dragon Slayer in Ragusa	55
8. From Milk to Masterpiece	75
9. Celebrating the Warrior Madonna in Scicli	79
10. FestaFusion Taormina	99
11. Naro's Black Saint: The Miracles of San Calogero	121
12. Maletto's Strawberry Spectacular	133
13. FestaFusion Palermo	141
14. Sun, Sand and Splendor at Mondello	169

15.	The Magna Via Francigena	173
16.	Trapani's Street Food Extravaganza	179
17.	FestaFusion Erice	193
18.	Dive Into the Egadi Islands	205
19.	Macaroni Magic: A Taste of Tradition in Librizzi	215
20.	FestaFusion Piazza Armerina	223
21.	Crafted in Clay, The Art of Caltagirone	236
22.	FestaFusion Messina: Giants, Grace and Ferragosto	239
23.	Saints and Sea Breezes in Lipari	263
Fall Celebrations		275
24.	A Culinary Journey in San Vito Lo Capo	277
25.	Savoring Bronte's Green Gold at the Foot of Mt. Etna	287
26.	FestaFusion Militello	299
27.	Cesaro's Taste of Tradition: Porcini & Black Pig Festival	315
28.	Wine & Warmth in Castelbuono	323
Winter Celebrations		335
29.	Light of Syracusa: Celebrating Santa Lucia	337
30.	Experience Ancient Stories in the Greek Theater	360
31.	A Taste of Sicily	363
32.	Epiphany & La Befana in Cefalù	365
33.	Catania: Flames, Faith and Festivity	377
34.	Into the Lava, a 4x4 Ride on Mount Etna	397
35.	Monreale: Guarded by Gold	401
36.	Train Ride with Mt. Etna Vineyards & Views	419
37.	FestaFusion Agrigento	425

38. Scala dei Turchi	441
Spring Celebrations	445
39. Carnival of Acireale: Sicily's Spectacle	447
40. Saint Joseph's Feast in Salemi	461
41. Holy Week & Easter in Caltanissetta	469
Navigating Sicily	485
42. Understanding Sicily: History	486
43. Dining and Sicilian Specialties	492
44. Understanding Sicily: Pop Culture	497
45. Transportation Detail	501
46. Accommodation Detail	511
References & Resources	513
47. Calendar of Festivals	514
48. Alphabetical Index of Locations with Events	521
49. A Glossary of Key Terms	522
50. Patron Saints of Sicily in Alphabetical Order	526
51. Photo Credits	530
52. Thank You & Please Leave a Review	532
Connect with Me	534
About the Author: Katerina Ferrara	536
53. Select Bibliography	538

Explore More and Stay Connected!

Thank you for joining me on this journey through the wonders of Italy.

Allow me to be your personal guide, sharing insider tips, unique experiences, and essential information to uncover the treasures of Italy like never before.

Sign up for my newsletter today and receive your **FREE downloadable guides** filled with curated itineraries, expert advice, and practical tips to make your adventures across Italy unforgettable and stress-free! https://katerinaferrara.com/

KaterinaFerrara. com

With your complimentary subscription, you'll enjoy:

- Monthly updates with insider secrets for Italy, top experiences, hidden spots, and seasonal highlights

- VIP access to exclusive offers on festival tours, events, and limited-time promotions

Travel Italy Book Series

Available now:
Book 1: *Ultimate Festival & Travel Guide Sicily (Available in English, Italian, & Dual-Language)*
Book 2: *Rome 2025 Jubilee Year Travel Guide*
Book 3: *Ultimate Festival & Travel Guide Rome & Beyond*
Arriving in 2025:
Book 4: *Ultimate Festival & Travel Guide Puglia*
Book 5: *Ultimate Festival & Travel Guide Tuscany*
Arriving in 2026:
Book 6: *Ultimate Festival & Travel Guide Naples, Amalfi & Beyond*
Book 7: *Ultimate Festival & Travel Guide Venice & the Veneto*

Don't miss out on exclusive insights and bonus content to enhance your Italian journey! Sign up today and let's start exploring!

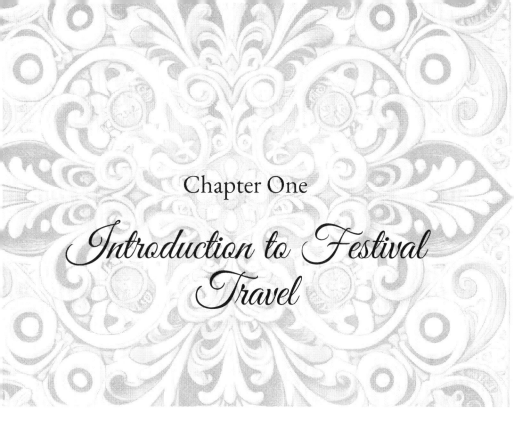

Chapter One
Introduction to Festival Travel

Discovering Hidden Sicily

Imagine standing in a medieval piazza as the evening air fills with the sound of drums. Locals in brilliant traditional dress sweep past, carrying centuries-old banners. The scent of festival specialties wafts from nearby stalls, offering treats made only for this celebration. This isn't just tourism, this is being part of a living tradition that's celebrated the same way for hundreds, even thousands of years. This is **Festival Travel**, where you don't just visit a destination—you become part of its story.

Welcome to a side of Italy that many travelers overlook—one of ancient traditions and unforgettable cultural heritage. As someone who has traveled to Italy for over 25 years and immersed myself in its vibrant culture, I've discovered that Italy's heart beats strongest during its festivals.

Whether small or large, each town comes alive with celebrations that unite history, local pride, and community spirit. These festivals are more than just events; they are living connections to the past, deeply woven into the identity of the people who celebrate them.

Finding Festival Culture

I didn't always know about this incredible world of Italian festivals. My husband and I started our international travels on our honeymoon in 1997, and we've made it a priority to return to Europe each year. But if I had my way, we'd always travel to Italy. There's something about it that draws me back, a deep connection that goes beyond the usual reasons to travel.

Like many travelers, my prior visits to Italy were filled with ticking off famous landmarks, tasting delicious food, and exploring beautiful sights. The rich culture, timeless art, and incredible depth of history drew me in. I was captivated by the warmth and kindness of the people, their traditions, and the stunning architecture that can be found in every corner of the country, from the northern Alps to the southern shores.

While each of these destinations left its mark, it was a journey to the southernmost reaches of Italy that would change everything. **Sicily,** with its unique blend of cultures, incredible festivals (the Feast of Saint Agatha in Catania is one of the largest festivals in Europe), and cherished traditions, truly captivated my heart. The vibrant energy of its celebrations, the warmth of its people, and the island's timeless beauty inspired this book–the first in my series of Festival and Travel Guides that will eventually cover all 20 regions of Italy. Sicily's beautiful architecture, deep-rooted history, and diverse cultural influences make it the ideal starting point for exploring the heart and soul of Italy's festivals.

Your Key to Sicily

This book is born from my experiences attending these extraordinary events. It's more than just a travel guide—it's a key to unlocking the heart of Sicily. While it includes all the essentials you'd expect, this guide offers something more. It invites you to feel the pulse of the island as you stand among locals during their most treasured celebrations, to connect with Sicily on a deeper level, discovering not just its sights, but its soul.

Sicily's rich tapestry of cultures, woven over millennia, is evident in every corner of the island. The ancient Greek temples of Agrigento and Selinunte stand in silent testimony to the island's classical past, while the Norman-Arab architecture of Palermo speaks to Sicily's unique position at the crossroads of civilizations. In Syracuse, layers of history unfold before your eyes, from Greek amphitheaters to Baroque piazzas.

But Sicily is more than its monuments. The island's vibrant traditions and festivals infuse every corner with energy, turning its streets into stages for celebrations that have been cherished for centuries.

Understanding Feste and Sagre

What Sets a Festa Apart from a Sagra?

As you explore this guide, you'll pick up some Italian along the way, starting with the words 'festa' and 'sagra.'

A festa (plural: feste) often stems from Roman Catholic traditions, like the Festival of Saint Lucy in Syracuse or Saint Agatha in Catania. However, not all feste (plural of festa) are religious; events such as the Jazz Festival in Palermo and the Art Festival in Taormina also fall under this category. Other notable feste include the Infiorata festival in Noto, where streets are decorated with intricate floral designs, and the Palio dei Normanni in Piazza Armerina, a historical re-enactment celebrating the Norman conquest of Sicily. These diverse celebrations showcase the rich cultural tapestry of Sicily, ranging from religious observances to artistic displays and historical commemorations.

While many of the festivals in Sicily are rooted in Catholic traditions, these celebrations are enjoyed by people from all walks of life, regardless of their religious background. You don't have to be Catholic—or even Christian—to immerse yourself in the vibrant atmosphere, cultural experiences, and communal joy that these events bring. Festivals in Sicily are a celebration of history, tradition, and the shared human experience, and all are welcome to join in the festivities and make unforgettable memories.

On the other hand, a sagra (plural: sagre) is an ancient tradition celebrating the harvest. The word comes from "sacro," Latin for "sacred." In ancient times, these events would take place in front of the temple yard to thank the Roman gods for the harvest. This tradition of celebrating the harvest has lived on in small towns and villages, often bringing money into the community for schools or other needs. All the citizens volunteer, making it a genuine community effort.

While a festa can celebrate various aspects of culture, a sagra is specifically focused on the culinary traditions of a town or region. From the Sagra delle Fragole (Strawberry Festival) in Maletto, where strawberries thrive in the rich soils of Mt. Etna, to festivals dedicated to chestnuts, sausages, gnocchi, wild rabbit, fish, wine, and other local delicacies, there's truly an event for every taste.

Recommendation number one: come to the sagra hungry. It's all about the food. When you arrive, you buy a ticket from the booth for the event, lunch or dinner. For between 12 and 15 euros, you'll enjoy an amazing zero kilometro meal, including local wine. "Zero kilometro" in Italy refers to food grown within approximately 150 kilometers (about 93 miles) of where you're eating it, emphasizing freshness and local production.

For feste, I always suggest a minimum two or three-night stay, as events often continue late into the evening (I list my recommendation by city/festival in the Accommodations section of the text of each chapter). However, overnight stays are not strictly necessary for sagre, which frequently occur in very small towns. In fact, some of these towns are so small they may not even have a single hotel. Many visitors choose to attend sagre as day trips, enjoying the local flavors and festivities before returning to their accommodations in larger nearby towns or cities.

Whether you're traveling solo, with family, or planning a multi- generational trip, Sicily's festivals offer something for everyone. Photographers will find endless opportunities to capture stunning moments, from colorful processions to intimate cultural celebrations.

Music and dance festivals showcase Sicily's vibrant performing arts, while craft fairs spotlight local artisans creating unique souvenirs. Many festivals feature interactive experiences where visitors can try traditional crafts or cooking techniques first hand.

Families particularly enjoy the kid-friendly atmosphere of many celebrations, where children can witness puppet shows, participate in workshops, or sample special festival treats. Best of all, many of these events promote sustainable tourism practices and directly support local communities, ensuring these cherished traditions continue for generations to come. This guide serves as your exclusive festival planner, helping you create memorable experiences that go far beyond typical tourist attractions.

An Insider's Perspective

Because of my love for Italy and our goal to move there one day, I started studying Italian in 2020 when our son Augustus left for university. I don't do anything halfway, so when I decided to learn Italian, I really committed myself to it and became fluent quickly (somewhat thanks to lockdowns). What began as a personal challenge soon opened up a whole extra dimension of Italian culture to me.

Every morning, I tune into Di Buon Mattino on TV2000, originally just to immerse myself in a few hours of Italian. What began as a language exercise quickly turned into a passion. The show, based in Rome, does more than just report the news—it travels across Italy, uncovering festivals, traditions, and local specialties. Between watching Italian TV series, talking to Italian friends, reading Italian newspapers and watching Di Buon Mattino, I stumbled upon festival after festival, each more enchanting than the last. Still today, almost every day, the show transports me to a new celebration somewhere in Italy, showcasing a different region's unique culture. It is like being invited into the heart of Italy itself.

As I explored deeper, I realized these festivals are a genuine reflection of Italian culture—a vibrant celebration of community, history, folklore, and tradition. This sparked an idea: why not experience these festivals first-hand? I began planning our travels around them several years ago, and fortunately, my husband, son, cousins, and friends were just as excited to join me on this adventure.

In the U.S., we have cultural festivals, but they are not quite like these. Italian festivals are more than celebrations; they are lifelong commitments, drawing people back year after year, even from far away. The festivals are a time to reconnect with family and friends.

Not surprisingly, a significant part of the allure in attending these festivals lies in savoring the special dishes and desserts prepared exclusively for these events—flavors that elude the menus of typical restaurants for the remainder of the year. As I delved into researching these festivals in preparation for our trips, the cuisine quickly emerged as an integral part of the experience, intricately woven into local lore and eagerly anticipated firsthand encounters.

I vividly recall searching out the Testa del Turco at the Festa della Madonna delle Milizie in Scicli. The anticipation built as I navigated the centro storico (historic center), following tantalizing aromas to their source. When I finally took my first bite, the delicate, crisp pastry harmoniously paired with its luscious, creamy filling offered a sensory experience unlike any I had encountered before. That inaugural taste didn't just please my palate; it transported me deeper into the festival's vibrant atmosphere—a flavor that encapsulated the very essence of celebration and tradition, leaving an indelible mark on my memory.

I'll never forget a conversation I had with my friend Annalisa. Like many Italians, she had moved to Rome for work, but every year, she returns to her hometown for the festival of her patron saint. When I asked if I could join her for one year, she laughed and said, "Katerina, you wouldn't be able to keep up! I run all over town just to see the procession of Sant'Ambogio at every important viewpoint!" Like that of so many other locals, her passion showed me just how deeply ingrained these festivals are in the lives of Italians.

Why Festival Travel?

- Experience cities at their most vibrant
- Participate in traditions rarely seen by tourists
- Taste foods made only for these special celebrations
- Immerse yourself in the history and culture behind each celebration
- Connect with local communities authentically
- Create unique photo opportunities
- Enjoy multi-generational activities
- Support local traditions and economies

What to Expect in This Book

In the chapters that follow, we'll delve deep into Sicily's most captivating festivals, exploring their origins, significance, and the best ways to experience them.

Whether you're planning a trip or simply armchair traveling, this book will be your guide to the heart of Sicilian culture through its vibrant celebrations.

Maximize Your Festival Experience with FestaFusion

Why see just one festival when you can experience several during one visit? I've coined the term FestaFusion to help you discover the magic of timing your visit to catch multiple celebrations. There are so many festivals in Sicily that you can visit more than one during your trip with a little planning. For example:

- FestaFusion in Palermo with the Palermo Jazz Festival and the Festa di Santa Rosalia.

- Visit the Catania for the Parade of Giants and then move the same week to Piazza Armerina for the Palio (medieval festival).

- Combine the Infiorata flower festival in Noto with the Festa della Madonna delle Millizie in Scicli, just 30 minutes south.

- During harvest season, experience multiple sagre (food festivals) along Mount Etna's slopes.

These festival combinations aren't just convenient—they're transformative. Each celebration adds new layers to your understanding of Sicilian culture, and the transitions between festivals often reveal hidden connections in traditions, foods, and customs. With a bit of planning, this guide makes it easy to experience several events in one trip—exactly what my husband and I plan to do in our retirement—una festa ogni settimana, a festival every week!

If you're concerned about crowds, don't be. While major events like the Festival of Saint Agatha in Catania, Santa Rosalia, Easter and Holy Week, Carnivale, and the Festival of Santa Lucia in Syracuse draw large numbers, most festivals featured in this book are more intimate, attended primarily by locals. These are relaxed, laid-back celebrations where you can soak in the culture without the hustle and bustle. Yes, I hope to inspire more travelers to join in and become Festival Followers, but rest assured, you won't find yourself in wall-to-wall crowds. In fact, many of these festivals are far less crowded than a typical morning inside St. Peter's Basilica in Rome, and they offer a much more authentic and personal experience. At many events, we have been the only tourists in attendance, which made me feel like I was discovering something special.

This guide to Sicily's festivals is just the beginning of an exciting journey through Italy's rich cultural landscape. It is the first book in the Travel Italy series, which aims to explore the festivals and traditions of all 20 regions of Italy. Each book in the series will delve deep into a different region, uncovering its unique celebrations, local customs, and hidden gems. By starting with Sicily, we set the stage for a grand tour of Italy's diverse cultural heritage, inviting readers to discover the heart of each region through its most cherished traditions.

Festival Travel transforms ordinary tourism into extraordinary experiences. Instead of viewing Sicily through the lens of a guidebook, you'll experience it through the joy of its celebrations, the warmth of its communities, and the depth of its traditions.

Join me in discovering the real Sicily—one festival at a time. Let's embark on this journey together, where every cobblestone street echoes with history, every local dish tells a story, and every celebration invites you to become part of Sicily's living heritage.

How to Use This Book

Sicily, with its rich tapestry of history, culture, and natural beauty, offers an abundance of treasures for travelers. Recognizing that most visitors have limited vacation time, this guide is designed to help you make the most of your Sicilian adventure, focusing specifically on **Festival Travel**. This book introduces a distinctive way to experience Sicily: through its vibrant sagre and feste. By timing your visit with local celebrations, you'll gain unparalleled insights into the culture, traditions, and community life.

The chapters in this book are organized chronologically by festival date, providing a year-round journey through Sicily's celebratory calendar. This structure allows you to easily find festivals that align with your intended travel dates. A comprehensive festival calendar is included to further assist your planning, offering a quick overview of events throughout the year. Chapter 47 has the Calendar of Festivals and Chapter 48 contains the Alphabetical Index of Locations included in the book.

To use this guide effectively, start by considering your travel dates. Consult the festival calendar to see which events coincide with your visit. Once you've identified festivals of interest, you can turn to the relevant chapters for detailed information about each celebration and its location. Each chapter provides not only festival details but also detailed descriptions of the host cities, including must-see attractions, local customs, and authentic experiences beyond the tourist track.

The guide offers more than just festival information. It provides historical context for each event, explaining their origins and why they remain crucial to Sicilian identity today. You'll also find practical advice on transportation, accommodation suggestions during peak festival periods, and language tips to enhance your interactions during these special events.

Embrace the spontaneity of Sicilian travel, particularly during festive seasons. While this guide offers well-researched information, the dynamic nature of festivals means schedules can evolve. To enhance your experience, we've included a variety of options and activities for each destination. This way, you're guaranteed an enriching adventure, with plenty of room for delightful surprises along the way.

It's important to note that festivals in Sicily fall into two main categories: fixed-date events that occur on the same date each year, and moveable feasts that are tied to specific weekends, religious calendars, or other variable factors. This guide indicates the timing for each festival to aid in your planning.

For those looking to create more comprehensive itineraries, visit the author's website. There, you'll find sample itineraries that can help you plan a trip combining multiple festivals or balancing festival experiences with general sightseeing across Sicily.

While this book emphasizes festival travel, it's also a valuable resource for general Sicily exploration. The city profiles, cultural insights, and practical tips are useful for any type of visit to this captivating island, whether or not you plan your trip around specific events.

As you embark on your Sicilian adventure, remember that this guide is your gateway to experiencing the island's vibrant soul. Whether you're drawn to the excitement of festivals or simply wish to explore Sicily's diverse offerings, you'll find a wealth of information to enrich your journey.

Allow yourself to be swept up in the warmth of Sicilian hospitality, savor the flavors of local cuisine, and immerse yourself in the island's millennia-old traditions. With this book as your companion, you're well-equipped to venture beyond the typical tourist path and create lasting memories in one of Italy's most captivating regions.

Festival Chapters – What's Included

Each Festival Chapter features the following elements:

1. Where, When, Festival Website, and Average Festival Temperatures

2. Town Snapshot

3. Festival Overview: Origin, Description, Events, Special Festival Treats

4. Self-Guided Walking Tour and Must-See Sites

5. Festivals Throughout the Year: Additional celebrations worth experiencing

6. Day Trip Options: Nearby cities and sites of interest

7. Logistics:

- Transportation
- Dining Recommendations
- Accommodation Options

Immersion Experience Chapters

While the festival chapters form the core of this book, Sicily offers a wealth of experiences beyond its celebrated events. That's why I have included special Immersion Experience chapters. These chapters are distinct from the festival sections, but near the town where the festival is occurring. They are designed to guide you towards unique, authentic encounters with Sicilian culture, special locations, nature, and traditions when you are not busy attending a festival. These

Immersion Experiences can be in town, near town, or a day trip option.

The Immersion Experience chapters showcase activities and adventures that allow you to engage more deeply with Sicily's essence. Unlike the festival chapters, which are tied to specific events, these experiences are available year-round and spread across the island. These experiences offer you the opportunity to:

1. **Connect with Local Traditions:** Participate in hands-on experiences like cooking classes where you'll learn to prepare traditional Sicilian dishes, or visit artisan workshops to observe centuries-old crafts such as pottery making in action.

2. **Explore Natural Wonders:** Embark on adventures that bring you closer to Sicily's stunning landscapes. This might include a 4x4 expedition up Mount Etna, hiking through the lush Nebrodi Mountains, wild swimming, or boat tours along the dramatic coastline.

3. **Engage with History and Culture:** Immerse yourself in Sicily's rich past with experiences like attending a classical Greek drama in an ancient theater, or visiting lesser-known historical sites.

4. **Discover Local Industries:** Get a behind-the-scenes look at Sicily's renowned products. Visit family-run vineyards for wine tastings, tour olive groves and learn about olive oil production, or take part in crafting traditional Sicilian cheeses.

5. **Live Like a Local:** Experience day-to-day Sicilian life by staying in an agriturismo (farm stay), taking a cammino, a historic walk, or taking part in seasonal activities at the sagre.

These Immersion Experience chapters complement your festival visits or stand alone as incredible Sicilian adventures. They provide opportunities for deeper cultural understanding, active exploration, interesting historical sites, and memorable encounters with the land and its people. Whether you're looking to fill the time between festivals or create a completely different kind of Sicilian journey, these experiences offer a way to connect more intimately with the island's heart and soul.

Each Immersion Experience chapter includes:

- Experience Description: What you can expect to see, do, and learn

- Practical Information: How to book, what to bring, best times to go, how to get there

- Insider Tips: Advice to make the most of your experience

By including these Immersion Experience chapters, this book aims to provide a comprehensive guide to Sicily - one that celebrates its festivals while also revealing the myriad of other ways to discover the island's unique charm and character.

Tour Guides versus Self-Guided Tours

While I've included over 25 self-guided walking tours, there's no substitute for the insights of a local guide. If it fits your budget, consider booking ahead through Tours By Locals or With Locals, especially in smaller towns. For example, in Militello in Val di Catania, we had an exceptional guide named Grazia Manuale, who arranged access to places typically closed to the public. Her connections allowed us entry into the museum of the diocese, Santa Maria delle Stella, and ancient ruins made our visit unforgettable.

Planning Your Festival Travel

When planning your trip to a festival, timing is crucial. It's recommended to arrive the evening before the festival begins. This early arrival serves multiple purposes: it allows you to explore the town at a leisurely pace, familiarize yourself with its layout, and secure a prime spot for the upcoming festivities. Take the time to locate the main piazza and the central church, whether it's a cattedrale, duomo, or chiesa madre, as these are often focal points of major events.

For major festivals, stay two or three nights. Hotels outside of the major cities in Sicily are not expensive (we stayed in Piazza Duomo in Ragusa for $100 a night). This lets you enjoy late-night events, especially in summer, without driving worries. It also helps you adjust to schedule changes. For food festivals, a night stay isn't always needed. These can be day trips, often in small towns with few hotels.

Arrive early? Use the time to explore. Follow my walking tour to visit the sites around town. Try local restaurants for regional dishes. Visit cafes to chat with locals, as they often share helpful festival tips.

As the festival approaches, it's wise to get a program of events if available (in my experience, they are posted on the doors of the cathedral and other important sites in town). This will help you plan which activities you want to attend and ensure you don't miss out on any highlights. Check if there's any traditional dress or color scheme for attendees.

Taking part in these customs can enhance your experience and show respect for local traditions. Don't forget to pack essentials like comfortable shoes, water, and any items specific to the festival, such as a picnic blanket for outdoor events or sun protection for daytime festivities.

During the festival, immerse yourself fully in the experience. Take part in activities, try local foods, and engage with the community. While it's natural to want to capture memories through photography, be mindful of local customs and any restrictions on taking pictures during certain events. Remember to stay flexible–some of the best experiences at festivals can be spontaneous and unplanned.

It's important to remember that each festival and town in Italy is unique. While this guide provides a general framework for planning your trip, always be prepared to adapt to the specific character and customs of your chosen destination. Embracing the local culture and going with the flow are key to fully enjoying the rich tapestry of Italian festivals.

Not Just Festivals: A Complete Guide to Sicily's Top Cities and Experiences

While festivals are a vibrant part of Sicilian culture, this guide offers much more than just a festival calendar. It serves as a comprehensive introduction to the key cities and experiences of Sicily, from the westernmost islands to Syracuse on the eastern coast.

Whether you're drawn by the allure of local celebrations or simply wish to explore this captivating island at your own pace, you'll find valuable insights to enhance your journey.

What This Guide Offers:

- **City Highlights:** Discover the unique character of Sicily's major cities and towns, from bustling Palermo to charming Taormina.

- **Self Guided Walking Tours:** Tours organized in an order to maximize your time and minimize your frustration.

- **Cultural Insights**: Delve into Sicily's rich history, influenced by Greek, Roman, Arab, and Norman cultures, and learn how it shapes modern Sicilian life.

- **Natural Wonders:** Explore Sicily's diverse landscapes, from the imposing Mount Etna to pristine beaches and lush nature reserves.

- **Local Experiences**: Uncover authentic Sicilian experiences, from bustling markets to quiet, off-the-beaten-path locations.

- **Transportation and Accommodation Information:** For each town and each even there are suggested accommodations and also transportation information.

- **Restaurant Recommendations:** Through our travels and our friends in Sicily, we have curated restaurants that specialize in Sicilian specialities and offer the best value.

- **Festival Focus:** While not exclusively about festivals, this guide does spotlight key celebrations across the island, helping you time your visit to coincide with these cultural events if desired.

Chapter Two

Arrive & Explore

A Quick Guide to Transportation and Accommodation

Sicily's Skyways: Getting to the Island

For more detailed information, see **Transportation Details Chapter towards the end of the book.

Picture this: you're standing in Sicily, surrounded by rugged landscapes and charming towns, ready for adventure. But how do you get around this enchanting island? Don't worry, I've got you covered! While exploring Sicily can sometimes feel like solving a delightful puzzle, you don't need to rent a car to piece it all together.

The Big Picture

- **Airports:** Sicily has three international airports in Catania, Palermo, and Trapani plus three other airports.

- **Trains:** Connect major cities and coastal towns.

- **Buses:** Reach smaller towns and rural areas.

- **Boats and Ferries:** Essential for island hopping and mainland connections.

- **Taxis and Private Drivers:** Great for specific routes or day trips.

- **Car Rentals:** Offer flexibility, but come with their own challenges.

In my travels, I've found that a mix of trains, buses, and hired drivers works best. It eliminates the stress of parking and navigating those narrow, winding streets. That said, car rentals are widely available if you're up for an adventure on four wheels.

Where to Stay: Sicily's Diverse Accommodation Options

*Find more information in **Accommodation Detail Chapter** toward the end of the book.

For accommodations, I've found a strategy that balances comfort and exploration:

- Stay put for 4-5 nights before moving on. This allows for a mix of "stay days" (local exploration) and "go days" (Immersion Experiences and day trips).

- Alternate between hotels and Airbnbs with washing machines. This gives you hotel comforts and the practicality of doing laundry and packing light.

- Search for accommodation within a one-mile radius of Piazza Duomo, the heart of most towns. You've struck gold if you can see the cathedral from your balcony! I provide accommodation ideas in each festival chapter.

Sicily offers a wide range of accommodation options to suit every traveler's needs and budget.

Hotels. Rated between one-star (basic) and five stars (luxury with full services), hotels are a great option for travelers.

Private Rooms and B&Bs. These offer a more personal touch and often provide insights into local life. They range from spare rooms in family homes to professionally run guesthouses.

Holiday Apartments. Self-catering apartments are magnificent for longer stays or for those who prefer more independence. They often provide better value for families or groups.

Rural Accommodations

Agriturismo: These are working farms that offer accommodation. They provide a unique opportunity to experience rural Sicilian life and often serve home-cooked meals made with farm-fresh ingredients.

Wineries: Some Sicilian wineries offer on-site accommodation, allowing you to immerse yourself in Sicily's wine culture.

Hostels. Hostels offer budget-friendly accommodations, often with shared rooms and communal facilities. They're great for solo travelers looking to meet others.

Campsites. Sicily has many campsites for outdoor enthusiasts, ranging from basic to well-equipped sites with amenities like pools and restaurants.

Booking Accommodations for Festivals

Remember, accommodation availability can vary greatly by season in Sicily, and this is especially true during festival periods. For the best experience, keep these tips in mind:

- **Book Early:** If you're planning to attend a festival, aim to book your accommodation at least 6 months in advance when possible. This is crucial for securing the best locations and rates.

- **Central Locations**: Getting a spot in the center of town is key for fully immersing yourself in the festival atmosphere. These prime locations fill up quickly, so early booking is essential.

- **Flexible Bookings:** Look for options with cancellation policies that allow you to modify your plans if needed. Many accommodations offer free cancellation up to a certain date.

- **Festival Periods:** Plan to stay more than one night. Be especially proactive about booking for summer festivals and other popular events. These periods see a significant influx of visitors.

- **Local Insights:** Some accommodations may offer special packages or insights for festival attendees. Don't hesitate to reach out directly and ask about any festival-related perks or information they might offer.

By planning and securing your accommodation early, you'll be well-positioned to fully enjoy Sicily's vibrant festival culture without the stress of last-minute booking scrambles.

Andiamo!

Enough with the introductions—it's time to dive into the heart of Sicily and talk about the vibrant traditions. Let's explore the festivals, sagre, and unforgettable events that make this island come alive throughout the year. Ready? Andiamo (Let's Go)!

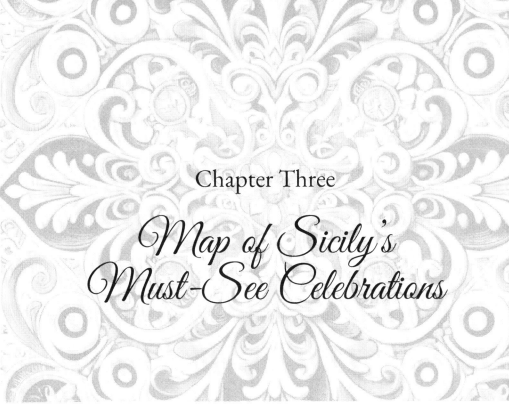

Chapter Three
Map of Sicily's Must-See Celebrations

Each city highlighted on this map is explored in a dedicated chapter, designed to provide everything you need for an unforgettable visit. Each chapter dives into the rich tapestry of local festivals, offering detailed information about their history, traditions, and unique appeal. You'll also find a curated walking tour of the city's top sights, helping you navigate its must-see landmarks and hidden gems. Beyond the major festivals, each chapter highlights other notable events and celebrations in the area, so you can make the most of your trip no matter the time of year. To enhance your experience, I've included carefully selected recommendations for restaurants and accommodations, ensuring your stay is as enjoyable as the journey itself. Plus, you'll discover ideas for nearby day trips and essential logistics information, from transportation tips to parking suggestions, making your travel planning seamless.

For a comprehensive Alphabetical Index of Cities and Festivals, refer to Chapter 48 for quick and easy reference. If the map appears difficult to read due to the 6x9 size, visit the book's page on my website at katerinaferrara.com. There, you'll find the same map in full color and with zoom functionality for a closer look at your chosen destinations. Thank you for understanding! https://katerinaferrara.com/ultimate-festival-and-travel-guide-sicily/

MAP OF SICILY'S MUST-SEE CELEBRATIONS

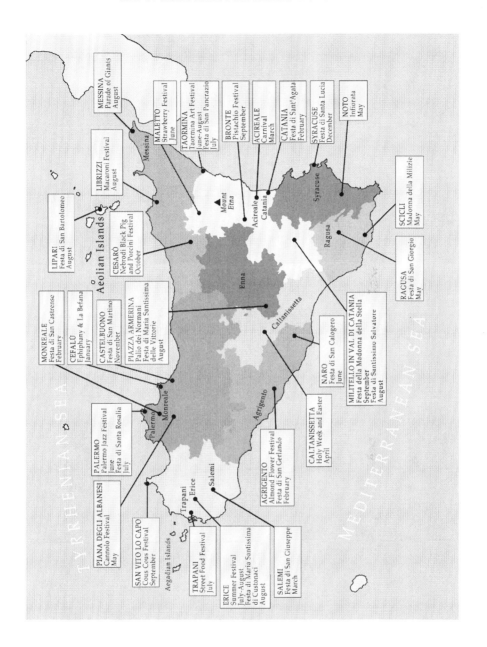

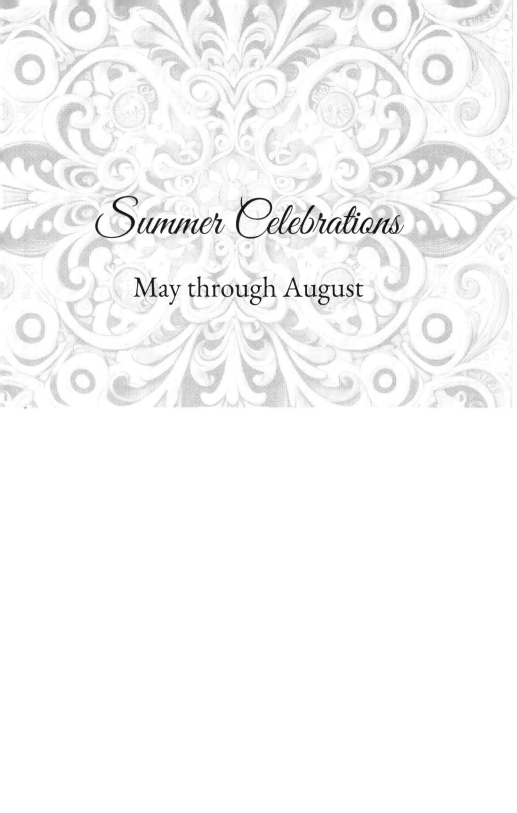

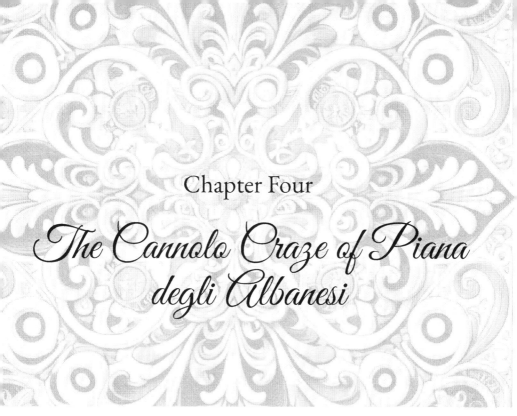

Chapter Four
The Cannolo Craze of Piana degli Albanesi

S agra del Cannolo

Where: Piana degli Albanesi

When: 2nd weekend in May, Saturday, and Sunday

Average Festival Temperatures: High: 21°C (70°F). Low: 13°C (55°F).

Discovering Piana degli Albanesi

Nestled in the verdant mountains just 24 kilometers (14 miles) southwest of Palermo, Piana degli Albanesi is a town where history, culture, and culinary traditions blend as seamlessly as the ricotta in their famous cannoli. This picturesque comune (village), with its population of around 6,000 residents, is a hilltop town that offers visitors a unique glimpse into a lesser-known facet of Sicily's rich multicultural tapestry.

The story of Piana degli Albanesi begins in 1488, amidst the turbulent times of the Ottoman expansion into the Balkans. As the Ottoman Empire advanced, a group of Albanian refugees fled their homeland, seeking sanctuary across the Adriatic Sea. They found a safe haven in Sicily, where the local authorities granted them permission to settle in this mountainous area, then known as Piana dei Greci (Plain of the Greeks).

These Albanian émigrés, known as Arbëreshë, brought with them their language, customs, and Eastern Orthodox Christian faith. Over the centuries, they've maintained their distinct identity while simultaneously embracing Sicilian culture, creating a fascinating fusion that persists to this day.

Perched at an elevation of 740 meters above sea level, Piana degli Albanesi enjoys a commanding view of the surrounding countryside. At the foot of the town lies the azure expanse of Lake Piana, an artificial reservoir that not only adds to the area's scenic beauty but also plays a crucial role in the local economy.

The Cannoli Festival

While the town's Albanian heritage is evident in many aspects of daily life, it's in the realm of cuisine where Piana degli Albanesi has truly made its mark on Sicilian culture. The town is renowned throughout Sicily and beyond for its cannoli–crisp, golden tubes of fried pastry filled with creamy sheep's milk ricotta.

It's said that the nuns of the town's Monastery of the Basilian Sisters were the first to perfect the recipe for cannoli filling, using fresh ricotta from local sheep. Over time, this sweet treat has become synonymous with Piana degli Albanesi, drawing food lovers from far and wide to taste what many consider to be the best cannoli in Sicily.

Picture this: It's the second weekend of May, and you find yourself on the bustling Piazza Vittorio Emanuele in Piana degli Albanesi. The air is filled with excitement, and everywhere you look, people are indulging in one of Sicily's most beloved culinary treasures: the cannolo. During this weekend, the town becomes the epicenter of this celebrated Sicilian pastry, with nearly 50,000 sold over the course of two days.

This festival, which began in 1998, celebrates not only the town's mastery of cannoli but also its unique cultural heritage. Started by local pastry chefs and the town administration, the festival showcases their exceptional cannoli and attracts visitors to this picturesque mountain town. Piana degli Albanesi is known for its particularly crispy cannoli shells and fresh, creamy ricotta filling, often garnished with candied fruit, chocolate chips, or pistachios.

The Making of the Perfect Cannolo

Cannoli may be enjoyed globally, but to truly understand the depth of their significance, let's take a moment to break down the making of this Sicilian masterpiece:

The Exterior: The Shell

The magic begins with the shell. Made from a dough of flour, sugar, and sometimes a splash of wine or vinegar for extra crispiness, the shell is rolled into thin circles and wrapped around metal or wooden tubes to form its signature cylindrical shape. It's then deep-fried to a golden brown, resulting in a crispy, slightly blistered texture that provides the perfect contrast to the soft, creamy filling inside.

The Filling: Sweetened Ricotta

Ah, the filling—the true heart of the cannolo. Traditionally, this creamy delight is made from sheep's milk ricotta, sweetened and often flavored with a touch of vanilla, cinnamon, or citrus zest. In some versions, you'll find bits of chocolate chips or candied fruit folded in, adding bursts of flavor. The balance of sweetness and richness makes every bite memorable.

Toppings and Garnishes

As if the crispy shell and creamy filling weren't enough, cannoli are often topped with crushed pistachios, chocolate chips, or candied fruit. Before serving, a light dusting of powdered sugar adds the finishing touch.

The Festival Experience

The Cannoli Festival is an immersive experience that goes beyond the pastry. As you stroll through the festival, you'll witness the pride of Piana degli Albanesi, a town that cherishes its heritage. Cannoli are more than a dessert here—they're a symbol of local identity and craftsmanship.

Visitors can watch skilled pastry chefs demonstrate the art of cannoli-making, join cannoli-eating contests, and enjoy performances celebrating the towns Albanian roots. Local bakers compete to create the largest or most unique cannolo.

Meanwhile, families share treats in the piazza, with musicians playing Sicilian tunes.

Cannoli are not just for dessert in Piana degli Albanesi. People often enjoy them with morning coffee or as an afternoon snack. Locals say there's no wrong time for a fresh cannolo, especially during the festival.

During the Cannolo Festival (Sagra del Cannolo), several cultural sites can be visited for free, including guided walking tours.

This annual celebration not only honors the town's culinary expertise but also serves as a testament to Sicily's rich, multicultural history and the enduring traditions of its diverse communities. The event has grown from a local celebration to a significant attraction, drawing food enthusiasts and cultural tourists from across Italy and beyond.

Walking Tour of Piana degli Albanesi

Our journey will begin at the city's cultural center, with the cathedral as our starting point.

#1. Piana degli Albanesi Cathedral

The cathedral houses Sicily's largest wooden iconostasis, created by the Cretan monk Manusaki. This ornate screen is adorned with intricate religious paintings and icons, serving as a visual representation of the divine realm.

The iconostasis not only separates the sacred space of the altar from the main body of the church, but also acts as a spiritual bridge between the earthly and heavenly spheres. Its presence in this cathedral is a testament to the strong Byzantine influences in Piana degli Albanesi's religious traditions.

The iconostasis adds to the cathedral's interior beauty, creating a striking contrast with the plain façade. When visitors enter, they are often surprised by the bright, colorful interior, dominated by this impressive wooden structure covered in vivid religious imagery.

#2. Parish of Saint George the Great Martyr (Chiesa Parrocchiale di San Giorgio Megalomartire or Famullia e Shën Gjergjit Dëshmor i Math)

A three-minute walk from the Cathedral is the parish church. Dating back to 1493, it is the oldest structure in the city center. A staircase that leads directly from the original mother church, which predates the adjacent convent constructed in 1716, provides access to the main square.

The fresco showing Saint George in glory dominates a single nave with a barrel vault. An apse featuring a neo-Byzantine fresco of Christ Pantocrator painted by Josif Droboniku encloses the western side.

Piana degli Albanesi Festivals and Sagre Throughout the Year

Sagra della Ricotta (Ricotta Cheese Festival)

Typically held on a weekend in late March or early April (exact dates vary yearly)

This sagra celebrates one of Sicily's most beloved ingredients: ricotta cheese. Local artisans and farmers take part, showcasing the importance of dairy production in the local economy. Visitors can taste fresh ricotta in various forms, from traditional cannoli to innovative dishes. The event often includes cheese-making demonstrations, cooking contests, and cultural performances that highlight the town's Arbëreshë heritage. Local shepherds bring their flocks to the town square, adding to the festive atmosphere.

Festa di San Giorgio Megalomartire (Feast of Saint George the Great Martyr)

April 23rd (or the nearest Sunday if it falls on a weekday)

This feast celebrates Saint George, revered in both Western and Eastern Christian traditions. In Piana degli Albanesi, the celebration blends Albanian and Sicilian customs. The day typically begins with a solemn liturgy in the Byzantine rite at the Church of San Giorgio. A procession through the town follows, with participants often dressed in traditional Arbëreshë costumes. The feast includes special foods, music, and sometimes reenactments of Saint George's legendary battle with the dragon.

Festa della Madonna Odigitria (Feast of the Patron Saint Mary Hodegetria)

September 2nd

This feast day is of great significance to the people of Piana degli Albanesi and draws pilgrims and visitors from across Sicily. Mary Hodegetria, whose name means "She who shows the way," is one of the most ancient titles for the Virgin Mary, particularly in the Byzantine tradition. The celebration includes a solemn Mass at the Cathedral of San Demetrio Megalomartire, followed by a procession carrying the icon of Mary Hodegetria through the town. The day often features religious hymns in Albanian, traditional dances, and a community feast.

Festa di San Demetrio Megalomartire (Feast of Saint Demetrius the Great Martyr)

October 26th

Saint Demetrius, known as a powerful protector and military saint, is celebrated with great devotion in Piana degli Albanesi. The day begins with a Divine Liturgy at the Cathedral of San Demetrio Megalomartire. A procession follows, carrying the saint's icon through the streets. The celebration often includes Byzantine chants, traditional Arbëreshë music and dance performances, and a communal meal featuring local specialties. This feast also marks the beginning of the autumn season in the town's cultural calendar.

Day Trip Options: Nearby Sites, Cities, and Towns

These locations provide a diverse range of experiences, from historical and cultural to outdoor activities, all within a short distance from Piana degli Albanesi.

Corleone: 40 kilometers (25 miles) south Corleone, infamous for its Mafia connections, offers a complex blend of history and pop culture. The town gained worldwide recognition through Francis Ford Coppola's "The Godfather" films, where it was portrayed as the hometown of the fictional Corleone family. While the movies weren't actually filmed here, the town's real-life Mafia history has made it a symbol of Cosa Nostra.

- The CIDMA (International Documentary Center of the Mafia and the Anti-Mafia Movement), which provides insights into the town's efforts to combat organized crime.

- Castello Soprano, a medieval castle with panoramic views of the surrounding countryside.

- The Church of San Martino, known for its beautiful frescoes and baroque architecture.

See my blog post Discovering the Godfather Filming Locations for more information: https://katerinaferrara.com/blog/

San Giuseppe Jato: 16 kilometers (10 miles) southwest. This small town is primarily known for its proximity to Monte Jato, an important archaeological site. The remains of an ancient city dating back to the 6th century BC. The site features: A well-preserved Greek theater, ruins of a marketplace (agora), remnants of residential areas, and fortifications.

Santa Cristina Gela: 5 kilometers (3 miles) southeast Like Piana degli Albanesi, Santa Cristina Gela is an Arbëreshë community, founded by Albanian refugees in the 15th century. Visitors can experience the Church of Santa Cristina, which follows the Byzantine rite, and enjoy traditional Arbëreshë cuisine in local restaurants.

Ficuzza Forest: 20 kilometers (12 miles) south. This vast nature reserve offers a refreshing escape into nature.

The Royal Palace of Ficuzza, built between 1799 and 1807, this hunting lodge was commissioned by Ferdinand I of the Two Sicilies. Ferdinand, also known as Ferdinand III of Sicily and Ferdinand IV of Naples, unified these two kingdoms into the Kingdom of the Two Sicilies in 1816. He chose Ficuzza as a retreat from the political turmoil in Naples and Palermo. There are extensive hiking and biking trails through the forest.

Logistics

Train: Palermo Centrale is the closest train station. It is 24 kilometers (14 miles) from Piana degli Albanesi.

Bus: There are regular bus services from Palermo to Piana degli Albanesi operated by AST (Azienda Siciliana Trasporti). The journey takes about an hour, and buses run several times a day.

Car: 24 kilometers (15 miles) from Palermo via SS624 (Stada Stratale 624) heading south.

Parking: Piana degli Albanesi does not have a ZTL (limited traffic zone) in the center. Parking is available on the street in the center or in public parking lots near Piazza Vittorio Emanuele or the Cathedral.

Dining Recommendations

Antica Trattoria San Giovanni. Address: Via G. Matteotti, 34

A long-established trattoria offering a cozy, traditional Sicilian atmosphere. Known for its rich history, this family-run restaurant has been serving locals and visitors alike with authentic Sicilian dishes for decades. Specialties include homemade pastas and the local delicacy, cannoli, which Piana degli Albanesi is famous for.

Osteria Le Volte. Address: Via Giorgio Kastriota, 49

A highly-rated restaurant known for its warm ambiance and exceptional service. Guests can enjoy an elegant yet cozy dining experience, featuring a menu of carefully curated Sicilian dishes made with locally sourced ingredients. Popular for both its traditional recipes and its modern takes on classic Sicilian cuisine, Osteria Le Volte is a favorite among food lovers.

Trattoria Sant'Isidoro. Address: Via XX Settembre, 8

A charming spot that offers hearty Sicilian fare in a rustic setting. Traditional Sicilian pasta and arancini served in a homey and inviting environment. Its laid-back, welcoming atmosphere makes it an ideal place for a relaxed meal after exploring the town's historical sites.

Accommodation

Agriturismo Sant'Agata.

Address: Just 16 minutes outside Piana degli Albanesi

A peaceful, family-run, 4-star hotel offering spacious rooms, a pool, and farm-to-table meals. It's perfect for those seeking tranquility and an authentic Sicilian countryside experience.

B&B Rampante.

Address: In the heart of Piana degli Albanesi. Address: 101 Via Francesco Crispi.

A cozy 3-star hotel/bed-and-breakfast, ideal for travelers looking for affordable comfort. The hosts are known for their hospitality and efficiency.

Rural Tourism Valle Himara (Agritourismo).

Address: Near the center of Piana degli Albanesi. Address: SP5, 113.

A charming agriturismo in a serene area, offering a swimming pool, beautiful surroundings, and authentic Sicilian cuisine.

Chapter Five
Blooming Streets: The Art of the Infiorata of Noto

The Infiorata of Noto

Where: Noto, in Val di Noto, on the Via Corrado Nicolaci

When: Celebrated the 3rd weekend in May. Open to the public on Sunday and Monday.

Festival Website: https://www.infioratadinoto.it/

Average Festival Temperatures: High: 24°C (75°F). Low: 18°C (64°F).

Discovering Noto: The Baroque Jewel of Sicily

Perched on a plateau overlooking the Asinaro valley in southeastern Sicily, Noto is a masterpiece of Baroque architecture and a testament to human resilience. This "stone garden," as it's often called, is home to approximately 24,000 residents and stands as one of the finest examples of Sicilian Baroque urbanism, earning it UNESCO World Heritage status.

Noto lies 32 kilometers southwest of Syracuse and 50 kilometers north of Italy's southern tip. Spanning 551 square kilometers, it's among Italy's largest municipalities. Despite its size, Noto's population density is low. Most residents live in the historic center and nearby areas.

Noto's modern story starts with disaster. On January 11, 1693, an earthquake devastated eastern Sicily, destroying Noto Antica. However, this tragedy paved the way for a new beginning. The city was rebuilt about 10 kilometers away, beside the River Asinaro. The Duke of Camastra, the Spanish Viceroy's top aide, led the effort.

The reconstruction of Noto became a grand urban project, attracting the finest architects, artists, and artisans of the time. They envisioned and created a city that would be a harmonious blend of urban planning and architectural beauty, adhering to the late Baroque style that was then in vogue.

The Infiorata Festival

The Infiorata is a festival of art demonstrated by a carpeted street artwork "painted" with flower petals. Each year, the event organizers hold the Infiorata along the Via Corrado Nicolaci, which is a narrow street on an uphill slant from the city center. They are on display only briefly because the flower petal scenes are vulnerable to wind and rain.

Art, religion, mythology, or Italian culture inspire the theme of the festival, which changes annually. Themes in the past have included Dante's Inferno, Italian Cinema, The Prince of Noto, and the last trip we made was a Tribute to Sicily that included a section of White Lotus and Montelbano images from the popular TV show and book series.

The idea of the Infiorata was first organized in 1625 in Rome by Benedetto Drei, the Vatican's head florist, and his son, Peter. They began using flower petals to create mosaics on the floors of churches during religious festivals, particularly on the feast of Corpus Domini. This idea later spread to other parts of Italy.

In Noto, the art festival was introduced in the early 1980s as a way to combine the town's Baroque artistic traditions with religious celebrations. Noto, renowned for its Baroque architecture, saw the Infiorata as a natural way to showcase its rich artistic and cultural heritage.

The locals pick and store the flower petals for months, organizing them by color in hundreds of barrels used in the designs and creations. They also collect other types of plants, like rosemary branches, basil leaves, as well as seeds, piles of sand, and grass.

The Infiorata

In the days leading up to the Infiorata, locals dedicate two full days to sketching intricate designs and filling them with flower petals. This cherished tradition has made Noto famous worldwide. The result is a stunning work of art covering 7,500 square feet of pavement, crafted from 400,000 flower petals gathered from the local countryside.

You will need a ticket to enter the Infiorata on Via Corrado Nicolaci. I recommend purchasing your tickets in advance because the entries are timed, and when I purchased ours, the only available entry times were early in the morning.

The art exhibit begins at the bottom of the hill. The exit is at the top of the street.

Also, at the top of the street, is the Chiesa di Montevergine. We entered the church, paid a small fee, and climbed the circular staircase to the top of the church tower. This spot offers a stunning view of the Infiorata along the alley and the historic center. We found the aerial view of the images to be just as vivid and interesting as walking next to the artworks in the alleyway.

But wait, this festival has more to offer! Everyone in the community is involved. There is a Baroque Parade with locals in period dress, local bands, and the tamburi (drummer groups) my favorite fill the street with the heartbeat of Sicily! Other events on Sunday include a market, flag throwing throughout the streets, bands, and other celebrations. I recommend 3 days in Noto for the event, with some time to visit nearby sites.

Arriving in Noto

The first piazza you will find when you enter from the Porta Reale gate (built in 1838 for the occasion of the arrival of King Ferdinand II of Bourbon) is the Piazza dell'Immacolata, and the Church of Saint Francis built between 1704 and 1745. When you continue straight, you will find the Piazza del Duomo. This is the central, most important square of the city, with the Cathedral, constructed between 1700 and 1776, and the Palazzo Ducezio, city hall. Palazzo Landolina serves as both the bishop's palace and the Cathedral Museum.

During the festival, reenactments take place here. This is also where the bands and drum groups will begin their parade. There will most likely be a bandstand setup and bleachers for seating. The locals will be milling around in period dress, waiting for their time to shine in the reenactment. From here, if you glance at Noto Cathedral, you'll spot a terrace beside the facade. A delightful spot for watching people and events as they unfold at Palazzo Ducezio, where parades gather and begin.

Walking Tour of Noto – Day 1

#1. Basilica Cattedrale di San Nicolo

The Basilica Cattedrale di San Nicolo (Cathedral Basilica of St. Nicholas) is one of the most striking landmarks in Noto, a beautiful baroque town in southeastern Sicily. Built in the early 18th century, the cathedral is a prime example of Sicilian Baroque architecture.

The cathedral is prominently at the top of a wide, grand staircase on Corso Vittorio Emanuele, Noto's main street. This elevated position adds to its imposing presence and creates a dramatic visual effect as you approach.

Exterior Features:

- **Façade:** The façade is made of local yellow limestone, which gives the building a warm, golden hue, especially during sunset or when illuminated at night. This color is characteristic of many buildings in Noto, earning it the nickname "the golden city."

- **Towers:** The cathedral features two symmetrical, short towers flanking the central façade. The left tower houses the church bells, while the right tower contains the town clock. This balanced design is typical of Sicilian Baroque architecture.

- **Staircase:** The wide, sweeping staircase leading up to the cathedral enhances its grandeur and serves as a gathering place for locals and tourists alike.

The current cathedral was built following the devastating 1693 earthquake that destroyed much of southeastern Sicily. It was part of the massive rebuilding effort that gave birth to the distinctive Sicilian Baroque style seen throughout the Val di Noto region.

The cathedral exemplifies the Sicilian Baroque style, characterized by ornate decorations, curved façades, and dramatic use of light and shadow. This style often incorporated sculpted figures, intricate stonework, and imposing staircases, all of which are present in the Basilica Cattedrale di San Nicolo.

As the mother church of the Diocese of Noto, the cathedral plays a central role in the religious and cultural life of the city. It hosts important ceremonies and festivals throughout the year, including the feast day of Saint Corrado in February.

The cathedral has undergone several restorations over the centuries. A significant renovation took place after the dome collapsed in 1996, leading to a careful reconstruction that was completed in 2007.

Interior Highlights:

- **Nave and Aisles:** The interior follows a Latin cross plan with a central nave and two side aisles separated by columns.

- **Dome:** An enormous dome sits over the crossing, allowing natural light to flood the interior.

- Artwork: The cathedral contains many paintings, frescoes, and sculptures, including works by notable Sicilian artists.

- Reliquary: One of the most significant features is the silver urn containing the relics of Saint Corrado Confalonieri (1290-1351), the patron saint of Noto. This reliquary is an important focus of devotion for local worshippers.

The Basilica Cattedrale di San Nicolo is not just a religious building, but also a testament to Noto's rich history, artistic heritage, and the resilience of its people in the face of natural disasters. Its stunning architecture and prominent position make it a must-see attraction for visitors to this beautiful Sicilian town.

#2. Seminario Vescovile

The Seminario Vescovile, or Bishop's Seminary, is a significant religious building located in the same piazza as the Noto Cathedral. This arrangement is common in many Italian cities, where important religious structures are often clustered together in the town center. As a seminary, it serves as an educational institution for training priests and other religious leaders in the Catholic Church.

The Seminario Vescovile's location in the main square of Noto places it at the heart of the town's historic center, alongside the famous cathedral. This positioning reflects its importance in the religious and cultural life of Noto. Given that Noto is renowned for its Baroque architecture, having been rebuilt in this style after a devastating earthquake in 1693, it's likely that the Seminario Vescovile also showcases Baroque architectural elements, fitting in with the overall aesthetic of the town.

The presence of the seminary in such a prominent location underscores its historical significance. As part of the religious complex in the town center, it has likely played a crucial role in shaping the spiritual and educational landscape of Noto for generations. Its proximity to the cathedral also suggests a close relationship between these two important religious institutions.

#3. Chiesa di Santa Chiara

The Chiesa di Santa Chiara, or Church of Saint Clare, is a stunning example of Sicilian Baroque architecture in Noto. Situated just down from the cathedral on the left along Corso Vittorio Emanuele. Construction of the church began in

1730 and was completed around 1758, rising from the ruins of the devastating 1693 earthquake that reshaped much of southeastern Sicily.

The church's exterior is a testament to the grandeur of Baroque design, featuring an ornate façade adorned with Corinthian columns and intricate stonework. Upon entering, visitors are greeted by an equally impressive interior, lavishly decorated with stucco, frescoes, and marble. The church houses many artworks from the 18th and 19th centuries, including a notable altarpiece by Vito D'Anna depicting the "Glory of Saint Clare."

Vito D'Anna was born in Palermo in 1718 and died there in 1769. He was one of the most important painters of the Sicilian Baroque period. While Palermo, in the northwestern part of Sicily, was his primary base of operations, D'Anna's work can be found in various churches and palaces across the island.

During his career, D'Anna received commissions for works in several Sicilian cities, including Noto, which was being rebuilt in the Baroque style following the 1693 earthquake. His presence in Noto and other parts of southeastern Sicily demonstrates the interconnectedness of the Sicilian artistic community during this period of extensive reconstruction and artistic flourishing.

#4. Chiesa di San Francesco d'Assisi all'Immacolata

This magnificent church, constructed between 1704 and 1745, is a prime example of Sicilian Baroque architecture. It stands as one of the most significant religious buildings in Noto, a city renowned for its Baroque urban planning and architecture. The church's facade features elegant curves and intricate decorations typical of the period.

The interior is equally impressive, richly adorned with artworks, including paintings, frescoes, and sculptures. Of particular note are the funerary monuments of Noto's noble families, which offer insight into the city's social history and artistic patronage.

Visitors can admire the harmonious blend of architecture and decorative arts, from the ornate altars to the detailed stucco work. The church also houses a valuable library containing historical texts and documents.

#5. Church of San Domenico

The Church of San Domenico stands as one of the most complete expressions of Noto Baroque style. Designed by prominent Sicilian Baroque architect Rosario Gagliardi, this masterpiece exemplifies the ornate decorations, theatrical facades, and elaborate balconies characteristic of the period. Construction began in 1727 and was completed in 1743. The church features a distinctive concave facade and an elliptical interior, showcasing the dramatic and dynamic qualities of Baroque architecture.

#6. Church of Santissima Annunziata

The Church of Santissima Annunziata is another notable Baroque structure in Noto. This church, dedicated to the Annunciation of the Blessed Virgin Mary, also plays a significant role in Noto's rich architectural landscape. While perhaps not as widely recognized as San Domenico, Santissima Annunziata remains an important piece of Noto's architectural heritage, further demonstrating the city's commitment to Baroque style in its post-earthquake rebirth.

#7. Palazzo Ducezio.

The final must-see building in the center is Palazzo Ducezio. Architects designed this municipal building in 1746, completed it in 1830, and added the second floor in the first half of the last century.

The second, and vital task, is to climb an interior set of stairs and to step onto the second-floor balcony. The balcony faces the Cathedral of Noto. It is a great opportunity to admire the town from this angle. It is a glorious spot for a photo op. We found it tranquil to be on the terrace, looking down at the groups preparing for the festival parade in the piazza.

Walking Tour of Noto – Day 2

#1. Palazzo Nicolaci di Villadorata

Located at Via Corrado Nicolaci, where the Infiorata takes place annually. On the facade, you'll see six balconies supported by intricately carved corbels featuring lions, children, and mythological creatures. Inside, explore ninety rooms, including the lavish "Salone delle feste" with painted ceilings and Sicilian tile floors. It's a must-visit for a glimpse into aristocratic life.

#2. Palazzo Castellucci

An exquisite example of an 18th-century noble palace, it dazzles with its warm golden stone exterior, painted ceilings, and period furnishings. The interiors are adorned with Sicilian tile floors and beautifully crafted décor. A reservation is recommended for both guided and non-guided tours to fully appreciate its splendor.

#3. Church of Santa Maria dell'Arco

Tucked behind Palazzo Ducezio on Via Viceré Speciale, this church was built between 1730 and 1749. Inside, you'll find the relics of the blessed Nicolò Morengia. Its location offers a serene stop to explore its Baroque architecture and religious history.

#4. Teatro Communale Tina Di Lorenzo

Known as a miniature version of Milan's Scala theater, it features a stunning neoclassical façade built in the 19th century. Enter with a combo ticket or purchase separately and enjoy the elegant design that continues to host performances.

#5. Belvedere Guastella

A scenic lookout point just a five-minute walk uphill from the Noto Cathedral. It offers breathtaking panoramic views of the town and the surrounding countryside. It's a perfect spot to pause and take in the area's beauty.

#6. Church of Santa Maria del Carmelo

With its beautiful concave façade, the church creates a dramatic backdrop to Via Ducezio. Inside, you'll find a precious statue of the Madonna del Carmelo attributed to the sculptor Antonio da Monachello, making it worth a visit for art lovers.

#7. Painted Staircase at Via Dante Alighieri

A modern art piece that adds a surprising pop of color and creativity to the historic center. Near the Infiorata, it's a fun and unexpected stop during your walk through Noto's vibrant streets.

#8. Noto Antica

Noto Antica is the ruin of the old town located 9 kilometers (5 miles) north of the current town center, on a heart-shaped rocky mountain, Mount Alveria. The terrible earthquake of 1693 razed ancient Noto to the ground, but it is still possible to visit. If time permits, consider a trip to explore this historical ruin.

Noto Festivals and Sagre Throughout the Year

Festa di San Corrado Confalonieri (Feast of Saint Conrad of Piacenza)

February 19th

In the Pizzoni Valley near Noto, San Corrado, a 14th-century hermit, passed away in 1351 in the cave he called home for many years. Today, the "Chiesa dell'Eremo fuori le mura" (Church of the Hermitage outside the walls) stands here, incorporating the saint's cave. On February 19th, the anniversary of his death, Noto celebrates its patron saint with great devotion.

The day begins with a solemn Mass at Noto Cathedral, followed by a grand procession through the city streets. The silver urn containing the saint's relics is carried on the shoulders of the faithful, accompanied by traditional music and prayers. Reaching the Church of the Hermitage, the procession allows pilgrims to visit San Corrado's cave.

The celebration also features food stalls offering local specialties, craft markets, and often concerts or theatrical performances depicting the life of San Corrado. This feast day not only honors the patron saint but also serves as a reminder of Noto's deep religious roots and the enduring connection between the city and its surrounding landscape.

Fiera del Crocifisso (Pentecost Fair)

50 days after Easter (date varies annually).

The historic Pentecost Fair, first held in Noto in 1427, takes place in the upper part of the city. This longstanding tradition celebrates local products, antiques, and crafts, offering a vibrant showcase of Noto's cultural and economic heritage. The fair features:

- Stalls selling traditional Sicilian food products, including local cheeses, olive oil, wine, and sweets

- Artisans showing and selling their crafts, from ceramics to lace-making

- Antique dealers offering a range of collectibles and historical items

- Cultural events such as folk music performances and traditional dance exhibitions

- Agricultural displays showcasing the region's farming traditions

The Pentecost Fair not only provides a bustling marketplace but also serves as a living museum of Noto's traditions, allowing visitors to experience the city's rich cultural tapestry.

Festa della Madonna del Carmine (Feast of Our Lady of Mount Carmel)

July 16th

Every year, Noto celebrates the Feast of Our Lady of Mount Carmel with a solemn procession. The venerated image of the Blessed Virgin of Mount Carmel is carried from her church through the city streets, accompanied by the faithful, clergy, and often a marching band.

The streets along the procession route are decorated with lights and flowers, and many residents place candles in their windows as a sign of devotion. This feast day is not only a religious observance but also a community event that brings together residents and visitors in a shared expression of faith and tradition.

Festa dell'Immacolata (Feast of the Immaculate Conception)

December 8th

Noto celebrates the Feast of the Immaculate Conception with a procession carrying the image of the Immaculate Virgin throughout the town. The route alternates each year between the lower and upper parts of the city, ensuring that all neighborhoods take part in this important celebration.

This feast day, which marks the beginning of the Christmas season in many parts of Italy, takes on a special significance in Noto. The city's Baroque architecture provides a stunning backdrop for the religious procession, creating a harmonious blend of spiritual devotion and artistic beauty.

Each of these festivals showcases a different aspect of Noto's rich cultural and religious heritage, offering visitors a chance to experience the city's traditions throughout the year.

Day Trip Options: Nearby Sites, Cities, and Towns

Modica: 35 kilometers (21 miles) southwest. Famous for its Baroque architecture and handcrafted chocolate, Modica is a UNESCO World Heritage site as part of the Val di Noto. The town is split into Modica Alta (Upper Modica) and Modica Bassa (Lower Modica), both of which offer stunning views, winding streets, and beautifully preserved historical structures. Highlights include:

- Cathedral of San Giorgio: A masterpiece of Sicilian Baroque architecture, this grand cathedral dominates the skyline of Modica with its imposing façade and dramatic staircase.

- Cathedral of San Pietro: Located in Modica Bassa, this beautiful church is equally notable for its Baroque style and statues of the apostles.

- Antica Dolceria Bonajuto: One of the oldest chocolate makers in Sicily, offering visitors the chance to try the town's famous Modican chocolate, made using ancient Aztec techniques.

- Historical city center: Wander through the town's winding streets, lined with local shops, artisan boutiques, and charming cafes.

Vendicari Nature Reserve. 15 kilometers (9 miles) southeast. A stunning nature reserve known for its pristine sandy beaches, wetlands, and rich wildlife, especially migratory birds. Vendicari is a peaceful haven for nature lovers and an ideal spot for outdoor activities. Highlights include:

Tonnara of Vendicari: The ruins of an ancient tuna fishery that sit on the edge of the beach, providing a glimpse into Sicily's fishing past.

- Birdwatching: Home to a wide variety of birds, including flamingos, storks, and herons, thanks to its wetlands, making it a popular spot for birdwatchers.

- Hiking trails: The reserve offers several walking paths that take you through unique ecosystems, from coastal dunes to forests, making it perfect for hikers of all levels.

- Beaches: The reserve is also known for its beautiful beaches, including Calamosche, one of the most pristine and tranquil beaches in Sicily.

Ispica. 20 kilometers (12 miles) south of Noto. A town offering a blend of Baroque and ancient heritage, Ispica is known for its Romanesque churches and proximity to the archaeological site of Cava d'Ispica. Highlights include:

- Cava d'Ispica: A scenic gorge 22 kilometers (17.5 miles) from Noto with ancient cave dwellings and rock-cut tombs, dating back thousands of years. The site includes remnants from both the prehistoric and Byzantine eras, offering a rich blend of history and nature.

- Basilica di Santa Maria Maggiore: An impressive Baroque church known for its grand colonnade and beautiful frescoes.

- Parco Forza: A well-preserved archaeological park within the Cava d'Ispica, showcasing ruins of ancient fortifications, a necropolis, and stunning rock formations.

Logistics

Train: Located just outside the town center, Noto's train station offers regional train services operated by Trenitalia. Trains connect Noto with other major cities in Sicily, including Siracusa, Ragusa, and Modica.

Bus: AST (Azienda Siciliana Trasporti) operates local bus services connecting Noto with nearby towns and cities, including Siracusa and Ragusa.

Intercity Buses: Several bus companies provide services to larger cities and towns across Sicily. The bus station in Noto is centrally located, making it convenient for travelers.

Car: To arrive in Noto by car, you would typically take the A18 motorway if you're coming from the nearest major city, which is Syracuse (about 32 kilometers away or 20 miles).

Parking: Noto has various parking options, but it's best to park near the historic center in designated lots, such as Parcheggio Via Napoli or Parcheggio Porta Reale. These parking areas allow easy access to the main sights and are just a short walk from the center of town. Note that some streets in the historic center may be limited to pedestrian access, so parking nearby is ideal.

Dining Recommendations

Caffè Sicilia. Address: Corso Vittorio Emanuele, 125

A world-famous pastry shop, known for its incredible granita, cannoli, and other desserts. A must-visit for those with a sweet tooth and perfect for a light bite while strolling through the historic center.

Caffé Sicilia has the best gelato, almond granita, and brioche in the world. Caffè Sicilia in Noto was prominently featured on the Netflix show Chef's Table in 2018. The episode highlighted the work of Corrado Assenza, the renowned pastry chef behind the café. His artistry with traditional Sicilian pastries and gelato, especially the famous granita, earned Caffè Sicilia global attention through the series and this is how we heard about it.

Granita is a type of frozen, slushy drink, a specialty in Sicily, made from fresh, local ingredients and a bit of sugar. Granitas come in many fruity flavors like strawberry, lemon, peach (when in season), coffee, almond, and so on. You eat a fresh, soft, sweet brioche along with the granita, dipping it in. Sicilians enjoy it for breakfast, but it's delicious anytime. Worth stopping by at any hour. Actually, we might have visited Cafe Sicilia twice in a single day while in Noto for the festival. No judgment!

Cafe Costanzo. Address: Via Silvio Spaventa, 7/9.

A charming local café in the heart of Noto. Known for: Traditional Sicilian coffee, pastries, and a welcoming atmosphere.

Looking for a cannolo? Head to Café Costanzo, located one block behind Caffé Sicilia. The cannolo is a Sicilian pastry comprising a tube-shaped shell of fried pastry dough, filled with a creamy fresh ricotta cheese filling. Often, in this area, they use local sheep's milk ricotta to make it. Cafe Costanza is an unassuming café that has the best cannoli in Sicily, according to my husband. Either way, Noto wins the prize for best coffee and fresh Sicilian breakfast.

Dammuso Noto - Ristorante, Baglieri. Address: Via Rocco Pirri, 10

Offers an intimate atmosphere and delicious traditional Sicilian dishes like pasta alla Norma and local seafood. This cozy restaurant has a perfect blend of elegance and local flavor.

Accommodation

If coming for the Infiorata, I recommend three nights in town that will give you time for the sites and the events.

*Hotel Q92.

Address: V3R9+JR Noto

4-star hotel offering modern comforts. It enjoys splendid views of Noto Cathedral, and it is a member of the prestigious international collection Small Luxury Hotels of the World™. Trendy, private, and unique, it is a luxury hotel that showcases the best combination of Italian and Sicilian design throughout its 9 lounges, guest rooms, and suites.

*San Carlo Suites

Address: Corso Vittorio Emanuele, 127

5-star hotel providing luxury accommodations.

Il San Corrado di Noto

Address: Contrada Belludia SP51

The 5-star resort features a variety of amenities, including a seasonal outdoor swimming pool, a fitness center, a spa center, and a restaurant offering gourmet cuisine.

The rooms are elegantly designed with modern comforts like air conditioning, flat-screen TVs, and private bathrooms. Some rooms even offer pool views and patios.

Gagliardi Boutique Hotel

Address: Via Silvio Spaventa, 41

Gagliardi Boutique Hotel is a charming and elegant hotel located in the heart of Noto, Sicily. Situated at Via Silvio Spaventa 45, this boutique hotel is housed in a late 19th-century historic building, offering a perfect blend of classic elegance and modern comfort.

The hotel features non-smoking rooms, a garden, free WiFi, and a terrace with views of the historic center. Guests can enjoy refreshments in the secret garden, relax on the terrace, or explore the vibrant streets of Noto.

Each room is equipped with a private bathroom, free toiletries, and a hairdryer. The hotel also offers concierge services, room service, and a paid airport shuttle service.

* For the Infiorata, these hotels will be closest to Via Nicolaci (street of the Infiorata) and Piazza Duomo (procession departure point).

Chapter Six

Wild Swimming & Tranquill Escapes

Immersion Experience: Laghetti d'Avola

Lagetti d'Avola

Tucked between Avola, Noto, and Syracuse in southeastern Sicily, the area known locally as "Laghetti d'Avola" (small lakes of Avola) is a natural gem nestled within the breathtaking Cavagrande del Cassibile Natural Reserve. This stunning reserve, spanning 2,700 hectares, is renowned for its dramatic landscapes and pristine beauty. At its heart lies the Cassibile River, which flows for ten kilometers, carving a deep canyon with walls soaring up to 300 meters. Over millennia, the river's gentle yet persistent erosion has created a series of freshwater pools and waterfalls, forming a picturesque oasis ideal for swimming and exploring.

Reaching the Laghetti d'Avola involves a 90-minute hike through rugged yet rewarding terrain, where you'll be greeted by awe-inspiring views of the canyon. The journey immerses you in Sicily's natural splendor, with lush vegetation and diverse wildlife accompanying you along the way. The reserve is home to an impressive variety of flora and fauna, including wild orchids—34 species, many endemic to Sicily—alongside plane trees, ivy, willows, oleanders, and vibrant ferns. It's also a haven for butterflies, while foxes occasionally make an appearance, adding a touch of wilderness to this serene location.

One of the most fascinating features of the reserve is the Grotta dei Briganti, a network of caves historically used as hideouts by bandits in the late 19th century. The caves are a testament to the area's rich history, adding a sense of mystery to your visit. Nearby, two striking azure pools await—crystal-clear waters that glimmer invitingly under the Sicilian sun, offering a refreshing reward after your hike.

Whether you're an adventurer seeking wild swimming spots, a nature enthusiast eager to explore Sicily's biodiversity, or simply someone looking to bask in the tranquility of untouched landscapes, the Laghetti d'Avola offers a truly unforgettable experience. Pack sturdy shoes, water, and a sense of wonder, and prepare for a journey into one of Sicily's most captivating natural treasures.

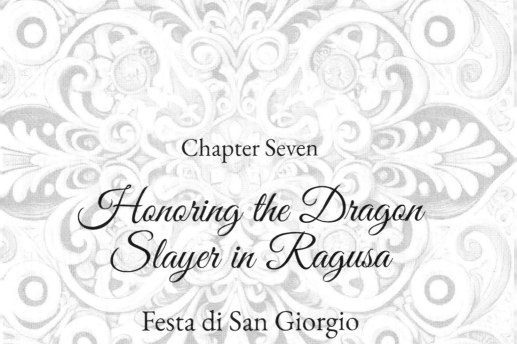

Chapter Seven
Honoring the Dragon Slayer in Ragusa
Festa di San Giorgio

Festa di San Giorgio

Where: Ragusa

When: Events throughout the 3rd week of May with the festival on the 3rd Sunday.

Comune Website: https://www.comune.ragusa.it/it

Average Festival Temperatures: High: 87°F (26°C). Low: 53°F (12°C).

Discovering Ragusa: A Tale of Two Cities

Perched atop the Hyblaean Mountains in southeastern Sicily, Ragusa is a city of striking contrasts and breathtaking beauty. Known for its distinctive split personality, Ragusa is effectively two towns in one - the ancient Ragusa Ibla and the more modern Ragusa Superiore. Together, they form a UNESCO World Heritage Site that captivates visitors with its blend of medieval charm and Baroque splendor.

Ragusa spans an area of approximately 442 square kilometers, making it one of the larger municipalities in Sicily. The city is dramatically situated across two hills separated by a deep valley, the Valle dei Ponti, which adds to its picturesque appeal.

As of the latest data, Ragusa has a total population of around 73,000 inhabitants. The population is distributed between the two main urban centers:

1. Ragusa Superiore: The "Upper Town" is home to about 50,000 residents. This newer part of the city, developed after the 1693 earthquake, sprawls across the higher of the two hills and serves as the modern administrative and commercial center.

2. Ragusa Ibla: The "Lower Town" has a population of approximately 3,000 people. This ancient core of Ragusa, with its maze of narrow streets and stunning Baroque architecture, is where most of the city's historical sites are located.

The remaining population is spread across the surrounding rural areas and smaller frazioni (hamlets) within the municipality.

History

Ragusa's history stretches back to the 2nd millennium BCE, with evidence of early Sicilian settlements. The city flourished under various rulers, including the Greeks, Romans, Byzantines, Arabs, and Normans, each leaving their mark on its culture and architecture.

The defining moment in Ragusa's history came on January 11, 1693, when a catastrophic earthquake devastated southeastern Sicily. This natural disaster reshaped not only the physical landscape of Ragusa but also its urban development and social fabric.

In the earthquake's aftermath, a significant debate arose among the citizens about how to rebuild their city. The aristocracy and wealthier inhabitants constructed a new town on the higher plateau, which became Ragusa Superiore. They designed it with wide, straight streets and elegant Baroque buildings, embodying the urban planning ideals of the 18th century.

In contrast, many common people rebuilt Ragusa Ibla on the old town's ruins.

They embraced the Baroque style for homes and churches but kept the medieval layout. This blend of architectural periods was captivating. This division created the unique dual nature of Ragusa that persists to this day. For nearly 300 years, Ragusa Superiore and Ragusa Ibla developed as separate towns, each with its own administration. It wasn't until 1926 that they were officially united into a single municipality.

Today, Ragusa stands as a testament to resilience and artistic brilliance. Ragusa Superiore, with its grid-like streets and more modern amenities, contrasts beautifully with Ragusa Ibla's winding alleys and Baroque treasures. The two parts of the city are connected by three bridges and a series of scenic steps, offering breathtaking views of the Hyblaean Mountains and the surrounding countryside.

The Festival of St. George

Religious festivals in Italy and Sicily, like the Festival of St. George, are deeply intertwined with local folklore, making them far more than solemn religious events—they are vibrant expressions of community spirit that unite people of all backgrounds. These festivals blend faith, culture, and tradition, becoming a shared celebration of local identity.

The Story of St. George

In 1063, the Normans defeated the Arabs in Sicily in a pivotal battle, where, according to tradition, St. George on horseback appeared by divine intervention to aid the Norman soldiers. Recognizing this heavenly sign, the Norman commander declared St. George the protector of Ragusa, and the city adopted him as its patron. In his honor, the townspeople built a grand Gothic-Catalan church in the lower part of town. Though the 1693 earthquake caused severe damage, the church's remarkable side portal, depicting St. George's victory over the dragon, still stands as a testament to his legend.

The tale of St. George and the dragon is a beloved story that has captured imaginations for centuries. According to the legend, a fearsome dragon terrorized a city in Libya, demanding sacrifices to appease its hunger. When the king's daughter was chosen as the next offering, St. George, a Roman soldier, happened upon the scene. Moved by the princess's plight and the city's suffering, he vowed to slay the dragon.

Armed with his lance and protected by his faith, St. George engaged in a fierce battle with the monstrous creature. Despite the dragon's terrifying size and strength, St. George's courage and divine assistance prevailed. He struck the dragon with his lance, subduing the beast. Using the princess's girdle, he led the now-docile dragon into the city, where he slew it before the astonished citizens.

This act of bravery not only saved the princess but also led to the conversion of the entire city to Christianity. The people, witnessing this miracle, abandoned their pagan beliefs and embraced the faith that had given St. George such strength and courage.

The story of St. George and the dragon became a powerful symbol of good triumphing over evil, faith overcoming fear, and the protection offered to the faithful. This same St. George was the one to save Sicily. It's this legendary tale that is commemorated in the side portal of Ragusa's church, serving as a constant reminder of the city's patron saint and his miraculous intervention in their history.

The Days Leading Up to the Festival

A few days before the official festivities begin, the organizers display the Holy Ark inside the Duomo di Ragusa. This marks the start of the preparations for the festival, and the town becomes infused with excitement. The Holy Ark, which symbolizes Saint George's triumph over the dragon, remains on display for devotees and visitors to admire.

The Day Before the Festival

On the day before the main event, a grand parade kicks off the celebrations. The parade features the banners of the Iblean brotherhoods, with participants dressed in traditional medieval costumes. They march through the streets, accompanied by lights, music, bands, and fireworks, bringing a lively atmosphere to the town. This festive parade highlights the start of the three-day event, as people gather to honor St. George.

The Iblean Brotherhoods

The Iblean brotherhoods, or "confraternite" in Italian, are religious lay organizations that play a crucial role in preserving and celebrating local traditions in Ragusa and the surrounding Iblea region. These brotherhoods have deep historical roots, often dating back centuries, and are named after various saints or religious concepts.

In the context of the Festa di San Giorgio, several brotherhoods take part in the celebrations, each representing different aspects of Ragusa's religious and cultural heritage. Some of the prominent brotherhoods involved in the festival include:

1. The Brotherhood of San Giorgio: Dedicated to St. George himself, this brotherhood often takes a leading role in the festival.

2. The Brotherhood of the Holy Sacrament: One of the oldest and most respected brotherhoods in many Italian towns.

3. The Brotherhood of Maria SS. Addolorata: Devoted to the Virgin Mary in her aspect as the Sorrowful Mother.

4. The Brotherhood of San Giovanni Battista: Honoring John the Baptist.

These brotherhoods serve multiple functions in the community:

Religious devotion: They organize prayers, processions, and other religious activities throughout the year.

Charitable works: Many brotherhoods engage in charitable activities, helping the poor and needy in their communities.

Cultural preservation: They play a crucial role in maintaining local traditions, costumes, and rituals.

Community: Brotherhoods provide a sense of community and belonging for their members.

During the Festa di San Giorgio, each brotherhood marches with its own distinctive banner, often centuries old and intricately decorated. Members wear traditional robes or costumes that distinguish them from other groups. Their participation in the parade not only adds to the spectacle but also shows the deep-rooted communal nature of the festival, linking present-day celebrations with centuries of tradition.

The presence of these brotherhoods in the parade symbolizes the unity of the community in honoring St. George and highlights the enduring importance of religious and cultural traditions in Ragusa's social fabric.

> **Special Festival Treat Celebrating San Giorgio**
> **Scaccia / Scacce (plural)**
> A regional delicacy featured prominently during the Festa di San Giorgio is the scacce, a type of savory pastry. These beloved treats are made especially for the celebrations of Saint George's feast day. The name "scacce" is derived from the Sicilian word "scacciata," meaning flattened or pressed, which aptly describes its preparation method.
> The process of preparing scacce involves using a dough similar to pizza dough. Bakers roll it out thinly and fill it with savory ingredients. Common fillings include tomato sauce, cheese (often caciocavallo or pecorino), and sometimes vegetables. The preparation begins by rolling the dough into thin sheets. Then, the baker spreads the filling evenly on one half of the dough and folds it over, sealing the edges. Finally, they bake the scacce until it turns golden brown and serve it warm.
> While the classic version features tomato, cheese, and vegetable fillings, various iterations of this dish exist. Some variations include fillings such as sausage or ricotta cheese. For those with a sweet tooth, there are even versions filled with chocolate or honey, offering a delightful contrast to the savory options.
> During the Festa di San Giorgio, the aroma of freshly baked scacce fills the air as local bakeries and food stalls offer this traditional treat to festival-goers. The scacce serves not only as a tasty snack but also as a tangible connection to Ragusa's culinary heritage, making it an integral part of the festival's gastronomic experience.

The Day of the Festival

The official feast day of St. George is celebrated on April 23rd, though the main festivities in Ragusa occur on the last Sunday of May, blending religious devotion with the warmth of late spring.

- **Morning Preparations:** As dawn breaks over Ragusa, the city stirs with anticipation. The air is filled with the scent of incense and freshly cut flowers as devotees gather near Piazza San Giorgio. The statue of Saint George, a masterpiece of local craftsmanship, is meticulously adorned with intricate floral arrangements and glittering ornaments. Participants, including clergy in their ornate robes, local dignitaries in formal attire, and musicians tuning their instruments, assemble to lead the solemn procession.

- **The Procession Begins:** The deep, resonant tolling of church bells signals the start of the procession. As prayers echo through the streets, the procession begins its journey through Ragusa's winding pathways. Clergy members carry ancient religious symbols and beautifully embroidered banners, while musicians play haunting devotional hymns that have been passed down through generations. The centerpiece of the procession is the statue of St. George and the Holy Ark, borne aloft on an ornate platform. As they wind their way through significant streets and landmarks, the air becomes thick with emotion. Bystanders, their faces etched with reverence, offer hushed prayers and blessings as the statue passes, many reaching out to touch the platform in a gesture of faith.

- **Evening Festivities**: As the sun sets, painting the Baroque facades of Ragusa in golden hues, the festival reaches its crescendo. The statue of San Giorgio is carried to Piazza Duomo, where an expectant crowd has gathered, their excitement palpable. The air crackles with anticipation as the bearers prepare for the most dramatic moment of the celebration.

Suddenly, to the thunderous cry of "Tutti Truonu!" (All Thunder!), the bearers make the statue "dance." This is no mere movement but a symbolic and electrifying display of faith and tradition. The statue seems to come alive, swaying and turning in a mesmerizing spectacle that leaves the crowd in awe. It's a moment of pure magic, where the line between the physical and spiritual worlds seems to blur.

As night fully descends, the festival culminates in a breathtaking fireworks display. The sky above Ragusa erupts in a symphony of light and color, perfectly synchronized to music that ranges from traditional Sicilian melodies to classical compositions.

The spectacular show illuminates the Baroque splendor of the city, casting an ethereal glow over the gathered crowds. As the final sparks fade and the music dies away, there's a moment of hushed reverence - a collective acknowledgment of the beauty and significance of this centuries-old tradition.

Walking Tour of Ragusa Ibla

#1. Duomo di San Giorgio, Cathedral of St. George

Our tour begins at the Duomo in the center of Ibla. The gates leading to the cathedral's front steps are typically closed, except for special occasions such as festivals, weddings, or funerals. The staircase is quite daunting, and I'm thankful it's not my task to transport the ark down it during the festival. Follow the signs and take the left staircase to enter the building.

The construction of the Duomo di San Giorgio, beginning in 1738, marked a turning point for Sicilian Baroque architecture. Its towering monumental façade, completed in 1775, is an intricate interplay of light and shadow, adorned with lavish Baroque details, carvings, columns, and statues. In Sicily, instead of having tall bell tower bells are incorporated into the facade of the churches. This was a lesson learned after the earthquake. The convex facades did not crumble, but the towers did.

A striking feature is the neoclassical dome, designed by Carmelo Cultraro of Ragusa. Inspired by the Pantheon in Paris, its full beauty is revealed only as you climb the stairs, with two rows of columns and distinctive blue-tinted windows. Illuminated at night, the Duomo becomes a breathtaking spectacle.

The Interior of the Duomo

Inside, you'll find exquisite statues crafted by the renowned Gagini family, a dynasty of sculptors and architects who were highly influential in Sicily during the Renaissance and early Baroque periods. Originating from northern Italy, the Gagini family, particularly Antonello Gagini and his sons, became famous for their delicate marble sculptures and architectural works throughout Sicily from the late 15th to the early 17th centuries.

The church also boasts an impressive organ constructed by the Serassi company between 1881 and 1882. With 3,368 pipes, it's considered their masterpiece and a testament to 19th-century craftsmanship.

Festival Displays

During San Giorgio's feast, two sacred items are carried in procession: a statue of Saint George on horseback by Palermo sculptor Bagnasco, and a large reliquary ark crafted in 1818 by Domenico La Villa. The ark, decorated with eight low-relief squares depicting Saint George's martyrdom, is usually on display above the church doors.

#2. Museo del Duomo / Cathedral Museum

Next to the cathedral, the museum houses a wealth of valuable artifacts, including remains of the ancient Church of San Giorgio and a stunning sixteenth-century Gagini altar in the sacristy.

The museum, the largest of sacred art in the province, offers a historical-devotional perspective of Ragusa's last millennium. It features artifacts recovered after the 1693 earthquake, a treasury of goldsmiths' work, silverware, and paintings from before and after 1693, and a Hall of Altar Frontals adorned in gold and silver.

The exhibits, featuring objects from both wealthy and poor locals, provide insight into the community's devotion to their saint and the sacrifices made to create these precious objects.

https://duomosangiorgioragusa.it/duomo-san-giorgio/

#3. Palazzo Arezzo Di Trifiletti

Palazzo Arezzo Di Trifiletti, an 18th-century baroque masterpiece, stands proudly across the piazza, offering a breathtaking view of Ragusa's duomo from its upstairs balcony. This architectural gem is a testament to Sicilian aristocratic elegance and a vital part of Ragusa's cultural heritage.

The palace opens its doors for intimate, owner-led small group tours from 11 a.m. to 5 p.m., by appointment only. During the 90-minute tour, conducted in Italian and English, the charismatic owner weaves fascinating tales spanning a millennium, covering family history, local lore, and the palazzo's evolution. Visitors can marvel at ornate frescoes, period furnishings, and a curated art collection that brings history to life.

The palace's romantic ambiance makes it a popular spot for wedding photography. Lucky visitors might catch a glimpse of newlyweds posing against the backdrop of baroque splendor.

Book in advance to ensure availability and immerse yourself in the rich tapestry of Ragusa's aristocratic past.

http://www.palazzoarezzo.it/en/home/

#4. Chiesa di San Giuseppe / Church of Saint Joseph

The Benedictine Chiesa di San Giuseppe, or Church of Saint Joseph, stands alongside its monastery in the same small piazza as Palazzo Arezzo in Ragusa Ibla. This church, together with the neighboring Monastery of San Benedetto, boasts a rich history dating back to around 1590.

It was then that Baron Don Carlo Giavanti, at the behest of his wife Violante Castilletti, transformed his palace into a convent. Though the devastating earthquake of 1693 inflicted significant damage, the church was meticulously rebuilt between 1756 and 1760, emerging as a beautiful blend of Rococo and Baroque architectural styles.

The Interior

The interior of the Chiesa di San Giuseppe is a testament to exquisite craftsmanship. Its oval-shaped design is crowned by an intricately decorated vault, while five stone altars, appearing to be crafted from marble, line the walls. The church's flooring is striking, featuring a unique combination of local limestone, black pitchstone, and ceramic tiles that adds a distinctive touch to the overall aesthetic.

Today, the Chiesa di San Giuseppe remains an active place of worship and reflection. The Benedictine Nuns of Perpetual Adoration continue to reside in the adjoining convent, maintaining the site's spiritual legacy. Visitors to the church may, as you experienced, encounter the sisters reciting the rosary, adding to the peaceful and contemplative atmosphere of this historic Ragusa landmark.

#5. Portale di San Giorgio (Portal of St. George)

This remarkable architectural remnant is one of the few surviving structures from the devastating 1693 earthquake that reshaped much of southeastern Sicily. The portal once served as the grand entrance to the original Church of San Giorgio, which was largely destroyed in the seismic event.

Today, this ancient stone archway stands as a testament to Ragusa's resilient past. Its most striking feature is an exquisitely carved Romanesque relief depicting St. George's legendary battle against the dragon. This masterful sculpture not only showcases the craftsmanship of medieval artisans, but also serves as a powerful symbol of the triumph of good over evil. The portal's enduring presence offers visitors a tangible link to Ragusa's pre-earthquake history and the city's rich cultural heritage.

#6. Giardino Ibleo / Iblean Gardens

Offering stunning panoramic views of the surrounding countryside, these gardens provide a peaceful retreat. The Giardino Ibleo, also known as the Iblean Gardens, is a beautiful public park located in Ragusa Ibla, the historic lower town of Ragusa. Created around 1858, these 19th-century gardens serve as a peaceful retreat for both locals and tourists, covering an area of approximately 15,000 square meters (about 3.7 acres).

One of the most striking features of the Giardino Ibleo is its panoramic views. Visitors can enjoy breathtaking vistas of the Irminio Valley and the surrounding Baroque architecture of Ragusa Ibla, making it a perfect spot for photography or quiet contemplation. The gardens are home to a variety of Mediterranean plants and trees, including distinctive palm trees, which add to the serene atmosphere.

The garden features three churches: San Vincenzo Ferreri, San Giacomo, and San Domenico. There are fountains and statues that enhance its historical and cultural value. Paths meander through the garden, with benches for relaxation.

The Giardino Ibleo is open to the public and free to enter, making it an accessible attraction for anyone visiting Ragusa. Its tranquil environment offers a stark contrast to the bustling city streets, providing a haven of calm. During the summer months, the gardens often become a venue for cultural events and concerts, further enhancing their role in the community.

Walking Tour of Ragusa Superiore

If you have a second day, you can visit Ragusa Superiore. You'll have to climb, but the views are absolutely worth it.

#1. Palazzo Cosentini

This palace is a prime example of Sicilian Baroque architecture, known for its elaborate balconies and ornate facade. On Corso XXV Aprile, this spot showcases the extravagant lifestyle of Ragusa Ibla's aristocracy.

#2. Santa Maria delle Scale (Saint Mary of the Stairs)

This place of worship is notable for its dramatic location on a steep hillside and its unique blend of Baroque and Gothic architectural styles. In honor of the stairs, it overlooks the 18th century church replaced a late gothic structure from the 15th century and kept the bell tower. The square in front of the church offers magnificent views of Ibla, looking down the steps. Spectacular frescoes and decorations adorn the interior.

#3. Ponte dei Cappuccini (Bridge of the Capuchin Friars)

As you continue walking toward the newer part of Ragusa, cross this modern bridge, which offers stunning views of the deep valley below. The contrast between Ragusa Superiore and Ibla can be appreciated from this vantage point, making it a perfect spot for panoramic photos.

#4. Palazzo Bertini

Known for its unique "mascheroni" adorning its balc#5. nies, this Baroque palace adds a touch of artistic humor and symbolism to your walk. The grotesque masks, representing characters like beggars and nobility, highlight the Baroque flair for contrast and caricature.

#5. Cattedrale di San Giovanni Battista (Cathedral of St. John the Baptist)

Before the 1693 earthquake, the church stood near the medieval castle in the western part of the old town. After the disaster, it was relocated to the "Patro" district in the new town of Ragusa. Remarkably, the sanctuary was completed in just four months, opening for worship on August 16, 1694. Expansion began in 1718, and the church was consecrated on May 30, 1778. The dome, added in 1783, was later covered with copper in the 20th century, and the flooring was updated in 1848 with pitchstone slabs and limestone inlays.

#6. Chiesa del Santissimo Trovato

This smaller Baroque church is a quieter stop but boasts a richly decorated interior with elaborate stucco work. It provides a peaceful, intimate space for reflection and admiration of religious art.

Ragusa Festivals and Sagre Throughout the Year

Festival of San Giovanni Battista

June 24th

The Festa di San Giovanni Battista (Feast of St. John the Baptist) is an important religious and cultural celebration held annually in Ragusa Superiore. This festival typically takes place on June 24th, which is the feast day of St. John the Baptist in the Catholic calendar. The celebration honors St. John the Baptist, who is the patron saint of Ragusa Superiore.

The festivities include a solemn procession through the streets of Ragusa Superiore, where a statue of St. John the Baptist is carried by the faithful. This procession is often accompanied by music, prayers, and the participation of local clergy and community members.

Besides the religious aspects, the festa often features cultural events, including traditional Sicilian music and dance performances, food stalls offering local specialties, and fireworks displays in the evening.

Sagra del Cinghiale (Wild Boar Celebration)

October/November

This festival is typically held in autumn, usually between October and November, in various towns throughout the Ragusa province. The exact dates and locations can vary from year to year. Key features of the Sagra del Cinghiale include:

1. Culinary focus: As the name suggests, wild boar (cinghiale) is the star of this festival. Various dishes featuring wild boar meat are prepared and offered to visitors.

2. Traditional recipes: You can expect to find classic Sicilian preparations of wild boar, such as wild boar ragù, wild boar stew, and sausages made from wild boar meat.

3. Local produce: While wild boar is the principal attraction, the festival often showcases other local products like cheeses, wines, and seasonal vegetables.

4. Cultural events: Many of these sagre (food festivals) also include cultural elements such as folk music performances, traditional dances, or historical reenactments.

5. Community gathering: These events are important social occasions for local communities, bringing together residents and attracting visitors from neighboring areas.

6. Hunting tradition: The festival often highlights the hunting traditions of the region, as wild boar hunting has been a part of Sicilian culture for centuries.

Some towns in the Ragusa province that have hosted this festival include Giarratana and Chiaramonte Gulfi, although the specific locations can change.

Ibla Buskers Festival

October

An international street artist festival that transforms the streets and squares of Ragusa Ibla into open-air stages. You'll find jugglers, acrobats, musicians, and performers from around the world. The festival creates a magical atmosphere, making it one of the most popular cultural events in the city.

Scale del Gusto (Stairs of Taste)

October

The Scale del Gusto is a delightful gastronomic festival held annually. It takes place over a weekend in mid-October; this event transforms the famous Santa Maria delle Scale, the staircase connecting Ragusa Superiore to Ragusa Ibla, into a vibrant food and wine-tasting route. Visitors can ascend the 242 steps, stopping at various points to sample a wide array of local Sicilian delicacies, from traditional street food to gourmet creations, all paired with excellent regional wines.

The festival showcases the rich culinary heritage of the Val di Noto area, featuring products like Ragusano DOP cheese, Cerasuolo di Vittoria wine, and local olive oils. Beyond the gastronomic offerings, the event includes cooking demonstrations, cultural tours, and music performances, all set against the stunning backdrop of Ragusa's UNESCO-listed baroque architecture. The Scale del Gusto not only tantalizes the taste buds but also offers a unique way to explore the town's history and culture, making it a must-visit for food enthusiasts and culture seekers alike.

Sagra della Scaccia

December

The sagra celebrates scaccia, a traditional Ragusan specialty that's deeply rooted in the local culinary culture and described above. Key aspects of the festival include tastings, cooking demonstrations, and a sciaccia showcase with a variety of flavors.

Day Trip Options: Nearby Sites, Cities and Towns

Vittoria. 25 kilometers (16 miles) west of Ragusa. Known for its wine production and agricultural heritage. Highlights include: Piazza del Popolo, the main square, surrounded by notable buildings including the Basilica of San Giovanni Battista. The Vittoria Wine Route, visit local wineries to taste Cerasuolo di Vittoria, Sicily's only DOCG wine. And the Museo Civico, a museum showcasing archeological finds and the local history.

Marzamemi. 70 kilometers (43 miles) east of Ragusa. A charming fishing village known for its picturesque setting and seafood. Highlights include:

- Piazza Regina Margherita: The main square, surrounded by charming buildings and the iconic Church of San Francesco di Paola.

- Tonnara: Visit the historic tuna processing plant, now partially converted into shops and restaurants.

- Harbor: Stroll along the quaint port, watching colorful fishing boats and enjoying sea views.

- Seafood restaurants: Sample fresh local catches at one of the many eateries, especially known for tuna dishes.

Marzamemi can be quite quiet during the off-season. The best time to visit for a lively atmosphere is typically during the summer months, especially July and August. However, if you prefer a more tranquil experience, the off-season can offer a peaceful retreat with fewer tourists.

Marina di Ragusa. 25 kilometers (15.5 miles) from Ragusa. This is the closest beautiful beach location from the Val di Noto and Ragusa cities. Great for a day at the beach, both free and paid amenities available. Highlights include: golden sand: Marina di Ragusa boasts a long stretch of fine, golden sand beach.

While Marina di Ragusa is the closest, there are other beautiful beaches in the area if you're willing to travel a bit further, such as Punta Secca (famous as the fictional Marinella in the "Inspector Montalbano" TV series) or Sampieri, both within 35-40 km from Ragusa.

Logistics

Train: The railway station, known as Ragusa Centrale, connects the city to other major cities in Sicily, such as Catania, Syracuse, and Gela. Trenitalia operates trains and provides a convenient way to travel longer distances. Ragusa has a train station, but the station in Ibla is closed. The station to Duomo is a 30-minute walk, with stairs included. I recommend a taxi or the free bus to Ibla if you arrive by train. The bus stop is directly in front of the station.

Bus: Ragusa has a network of local buses operated by AST (Azienda Siciliana Trasporti) that connect different neighborhoods within the city and provide links to nearby towns and cities. The bus station is near the train station (Ragusa Centrale).

Car: To reach Ragusa by car from Syracuse, you would take the SS115 highway, which connects the two cities. The drive takes about 1 hour and 30 minutes and is relatively straightforward, passing through scenic countryside and small towns along the way.

Parking: Access to Ragusa Ibla is restricted, so check parking options before approaching town. Hotels may offer parking. Options include: Parcheggio Piazza della Repubblica, Parcheggio Via Avv. Ottaviano (San Paolo area) or Parcheggio

Giardino Ibleo.

Dining Recommendations

Osteria Imperfetta. Address: Via Torrenuova, 27

A highly rated Sicilian restaurant offering a range of local dishes made with fresh, seasonal ingredients. Osteria Imperfetta is known for its cozy, rustic atmosphere and friendly service, making it a favorite among both locals and visitors. The menu features traditional Sicilian favorites with a modern twist, and the restaurant is wheelchair accessible, offering both dine-in and takeout options.

La Terrazza dell'Orologio. Address: Chiasso Arestia, 12/13

This popular Sicilian restaurant boasts a stunning terrace with panoramic views of Ragusa Ibla, making it an ideal spot for enjoying a meal while taking in the scenic beauty of the historic town. La Terrazza dell'Orologio specializes in Sicilian cuisine with a contemporary touch, featuring dishes made from locally sourced ingredients. The restaurant offers both dine-in and delivery services, allowing guests to enjoy the flavors of Sicily from the comfort of the terrace or their own home.

Duomo Ristorante. Address: Ibla, Via Capitano Bocchieri, 31

An award-winning fine dining establishment, Duomo Ristorante offers an upscale culinary experience in the heart of Ragusa Ibla. Known for its Michelin-starred chef Ciccio Sultano, the restaurant serves sophisticated Sicilian cuisine that celebrates the island's rich culinary heritage while incorporating innovative techniques. The elegant setting and attentive service make Duomo a top choice for those looking to indulge in one of Sicily's finest gastronomic experiences. Reservations are recommended for this highly sought-after dining destination.

La Piazzetta Ristorante. Address: Piazza Duomo

A beloved local restaurant in Every visit is memorable thanks to the staff's friendly and attentive service. the picturesque Piazza Duomo of Ragusa Ibla, La Piazzetta Ristorante is known for its focus on fresh, indigenous ingredients. The menu features traditional Sicilian dishes, including handmade pastas, fresh seafood, and locally sourced meats, all expertly prepared and beautifully presented. The staff is renowned for their friendly and attentive service, making every visit memorable. The restaurant also offers reservations through Google Maps, ensuring guests can secure a spot at this popular dining location.

Food Market: Antico Mercato. Address: Via del Mercato, 134.

For those curious about traditional cuisine, the Antico Mercato is a must-visit. Explore this lively market for an array of fresh produce, Sicilian delicacies, and more. It's an excellent place to experience local food culture and ingredients.

Accommodation

If arriving for the Festa di San Giorgio, I recommend 3 nights in town. There is a lot to see in and around Ragusa.

*The Duomo Relais. Address: Via Dottor Solarino, 61.

Il Duomo Relais is located in the heart of Ragusa Ibla, just a few steps from the Duomo of St. George and the former Parade Ground of the Military District, in one of the most photographed spots in Ragusa Ibla. You can almost "touch" the dome of St. George from its windows.

*San Giorgio Palace Hotel. In the heart of Ragusa Ibla. Address: Salita Mons. Salvatore Pennisi, 18.

Nestled in the heart of Ragusa Ibla, this boutique hotel is housed in a historic building with stunning views of the Santa Domenica Valley. Guests can enjoy modern amenities, including free Wi-Fi, air conditioning, and LCD TVs, all while being surrounded by charming Baroque architecture. The hotel's garden and panoramic terrace offer a serene escape, making it an ideal spot for a relaxing stay.

*Giardino Sul Duomo. Overlooking Cathedral of San Giorgio, Ragusa Ibla. Address: Via del Duomo, 66.

Giardino Sul Duomo: Overlooking the Cathedral of San Giorgio, this charming bed-and-breakfast is set in a picturesque location within Ragusa Ibla. The property features spacious, bright rooms with tiled floors and wood-beamed ceilings, some of which offer views of the cathedral or the garden. Guests can unwind in the garden-view conservatory, enjoy homemade cakes and fruit jams at breakfast, and explore the nearby historic sights.

De Stefano Palace Luxury Hotel. Near historic center of Ragusa. Address: Via Fontana, 7.

Near the historic center of Ragusa, this luxury hotel offers elegant rooms with modern comforts, such as LCD TVs and pillow menus. The hotel features a wellness center with an indoor pool, hammam, and relaxation area, providing a perfect retreat after a day of exploring the city3. With its strategic location and beautiful architecture, the De Stefano Palace is an excellent choice for a memorable stay in Ragusa.

*Best hotel options for the Festa di San Giorgio because they are on the procession route or have duomo views.

Chapter Eight

From Milk to Masterpiece

Immersion Experience: Ragusa

Cheese Factory Experience on a farm close to Ragusa, Azienda Bussello

We thoroughly enjoyed immersing ourselves in the local farm life. Cows filled the field while we worked and observed in the cheese factory.

The tour begins with a brief introduction to the factory, its history, and the types of cheese they produce. This includes a presentation outlining the cheese-making process and the company heritage.

The experience lasts for two hours and includes:

Milk Collection and Preparation

During the first part of the visit, the guide will show the area where they collect and store fresh milk. The owner explained the importance of the quality and type of milk used, whether it is from cows, goats, or sheep. He explains pasteurization, homogenization, and other processes the milk undergoes before cheese-making begins.

Cheese-Making Process

Curdling and Cutting: As you step into the heart of the factory, you'll see large vats of heated milk where the magic begins. Here, the guide will show how coagulants like rennet are added to transform the milk into curds. This process requires precision—timing and temperature are key to achieving the desired consistency. You'll hear about how these techniques have been passed down through generations, blending artisanal traditions with modern equipment.

Draining and Pressing: Witness the next stage, where the curds are cut, stirred, and drained to remove whey. You'll see how these curds are carefully pressed into molds to shape the cheese, each one destined for a unique texture and flavor. The owner will explain how factors like pressing time and the weight used during pressing can create anything from soft, creamy cheeses to firm, dense varieties. You'll also get to handle some tools used in this step, adding a tactile layer to the experience and perhaps taste some fresh, warm ricotta at this step (we did!)

Aging and Curing

During the tour, they will guide you to the aging rooms where cheeses mature. This area is often cool and humid, with shelves lined with wheels or blocks of cheese. The guide will explain the aging process, including the environmental controls and how factors like time, humidity, and temperature affect the flavor and texture.

Packaging and Quality Control

The tour includes a look at the packaging and labeling area. Here, you will see how they wrap, seal, and prepare cheeses for shipping. The guide discusses how quality control measures are important to ensure the cheese meets specific standards before selling it.

Cheese Tasting

A highlight of the tour is undoubtedly the tasting session. Gather around as the guide and his family present a beautifully arranged platter of cheeses made on-site. You'll sample everything from fresh, creamy ricotta to aged, nutty caciocavallo, each paired with thoughtful accompaniments like house-made red wine, sweet fruits, and crunchy nuts.

The guide will offer tasting notes, helping you identify subtle flavors and textures. You might even learn about traditional pairings specific to Sicily, such as honey drizzled over pecorino or scacce filled with seasonal ingredients. Beyond cheese, you'll enjoy freshly baked bread, local sausage, and perhaps even dessert and coffee to round off the experience.

For many, the tasting is a revelation, connecting the flavors of the cheese to the processes and care you've witnessed during the tour. It's an experience that deepens your appreciation for the artistry of cheese-making.

Booking ahead is essential to ensure a seamless visit to this hidden gem, often overlooked by tourists. The factory staff (aka the family) carefully plans for your arrival, which may include coordinating an English-speaking guide for non-Italian speakers upon request. Tours are intimate and personal, giving you a unique opportunity to delve into the world of artisanal cheese-making.

Visit their website at https://www.bussello.com/ to plan your trip and secure your spot. Whether you're a cheese enthusiast or simply curious, this tour offers an unforgettable blend of education, tradition, and flavor, making it a must-do experience in Sicily.

Other Cheese Factories that offer Tours and Tastings in Sicily

Caseificio Dei Nebrodi: Situated in Nicosia, this factory provides tours that showcase the production of traditional Sicilian cheeses, including the famous Piacentinu Ennese. https://www.caseificiodeinebrodi.com/

Caseificio Neve Dell'etna: Found in Fondachello, this factory offers tours that cover the entire cheese-making process, from milk curdling to the final product. https://www.caseificionevedelletna.com/

Casa Mia Tours offers tours in both Ragusa and Piazza Armerina. https://casamiatours.com/tours/ragusa-modica-sicily/cheese-farm-experience/

Chapter Nine
Celebrating the Warrior Madonna in Scicli
Feast of the Madonna delle Milizie

La Madonna delle Milizie (The Festival of the Madonna of the Military)

Where: Scicli

When: Last Saturday in May

Festival Website: The comune will update the information in the days before the festival here https://www.comune.scicli.rg.it/home

Average Temperature in May: High: 24°C (75°F). Low: 18°C (65°F).

Discovering Scicli: Baroque Gem of the Val di Noto

Nestled in the southeastern corner of Sicily, Scicli (pronounced "sheek-lee") is a picturesque town that exemplifies the Baroque splendor of the Val di Noto region. Located approximately 25 kilometers (16 miles) from Ragusa and just 8 kilometers (5 miles) from the Mediterranean coast, Scicli sits at the confluence of three scenic valleys: the San Bartolomeo and Modica valleys, and the Santa Maria La Nova valley.

With a population of around 27,000 inhabitants, Scicli maintains a charming small-town atmosphere while offering visitors a wealth of historical and cultural attractions. The town's unique geography, with its houses and churches dramatically perched on the slopes of rocky hills, creates a stunning visual impact that has earned Scicli a place on the UNESCO World Heritage list as part of the Late Baroque Towns of the Val di Noto.

Scicli Street View

Scicli's history includes Sicel, Greek, and Roman settlements. The town blossomed after the 1693 earthquake, leading to its Baroque architecture. Recently, Scicli gained fame as a filming location for "Inspector Montalbano." The town hall represents the fictional Vigàta police station (See Pop Culture section for more).

Traditionally, Scicli's economy relied on agriculture, focusing on carobs, almonds, and olives. Now, tourism is on the rise, attracted by the town's architecture, culture, and nearby beaches like Sampieri and Donnalucata.

The Festival of the Madonna of the Military

The Festival of the Madonna of the Military in Scicli is deeply rooted in the town's historical and religious identity. The miracle of 1091, which forms the basis of the celebration, symbolizes divine intervention and the resilience of Christian faith during a time of turmoil in Sicily's history. This event not only marked a turning point in the town's resistance against external threats but also solidified the Virgin Mary's role as a protective figure for the community.

The festival includes a dramatic reenactment of the miracle, with actors portraying the Virgin on horseback, Saracen invaders, and Christian defenders. This spectacle takes place in the town square, drawing visitors and locals alike into the story. The event is accompanied by processions, traditional music, and prayer services, creating a vibrant mix of faith and festivity. For Scicli's residents, the festival is not only a celebration of their patroness but also a reaffirmation of their cultural heritage and enduring connection to their past.

In the Days before the Festival

The festival kicks off with a procession, where the statue of the Madonna delle Milizie is carried from the Church of St. Bartholomew to the Church of Santa Maria (Holy Mary). In the days leading up to the event, the statue is displayed in the Church of San Guglielmo. Singers, musicians, and the faithful accompany the parade with music and prayers.

Friday afternoon

4:00 p.m. The events start at the Palazzo Comunale, where you'll also discover a vibrant Sicilian market. These markets are a cornerstone of local life and commerce, offering a diverse array of goods that transform the area into an open-air shopping paradise. As you wander through the stalls, you'll find clothing, leather goods, jewelry, home goods, local crafts, produce and regional specialities such as cheese, cured meat and gourmet items.

The atmosphere is lively, with vendors calling out their wares and shoppers haggling over prices. It's akin to a mobile shopping mall that has set up in the heart of town, offering both locals and visitors a chance to browse, shop, and experience a vital part of Sicilian culture. Whether you're looking for a unique souvenir, a stylish addition to your wardrobe, or just want to soak in the bustling ambiance, the market at Palazzo Comunale is not to be missed.

5:00 p.m. A significant gathering takes place at Palazzo Spadaro, where local officials, organizers, and key participants in the reenactment of the battle meet to finalize preparations. This meeting is an important precursor to one of the festival's central traditions, known as the Testa del Turco (Head of the Turk). Here's what typically happens:

Local officials, organizers, and participants gather to discuss the details of the upcoming reenactment. The event symbolizes the legendary battle between the Christian defenders of Scicli and the Saracen invaders, with the miraculous intervention of the Madonna delle Milizie. During the meeting, participants are briefed on their roles, the historical significance is reiterated, and final arrangements are made. It also serves as an opportunity for the community to come together, building excitement and anticipation for the upcoming festival events.

The reenactment of the Testa del Turco typically involves participants in medieval costumes, including Christian knights on horseback, staging the legendary battle. The culmination of the reenactment often involves the symbolic beheading of a Saracen figure, representing the victory of the Christians, with skill and precision in the display.

As the afternoon concludes, the atmosphere in Scicli becomes increasingly festive. Locals and visitors fill the streets, eagerly discussing the upcoming events of the Festa della Madonna delle Milizie.

You'll notice heightened activity around the town as preparations for the festival are finalized, with decorations going up and the community coming together to celebrate this important historical and religious tradition.

6:00 p.m. – 10:00 p.m. Events in Piazza Italia

Inauguration Ceremony: The official opening of the evening's events, often featuring speeches by local officials or festival organizers. This is a moment to celebrate the festival's rich history and traditions, marking the start of key festivities over the weekend. The ceremony may include the unveiling of special decorations, artwork, or banners dedicated to the Madonna delle Milizie.

Cooking Show: A lively cooking demonstration that showcases traditional Sicilian cuisine, especially foods connected to the festival or local culinary heritage. Chefs prepare iconic dishes from the region, allowing visitors to learn about the flavors of Scicli. These include local favorites such as scacce ragusane (a type of stuffed flatbread) or desserts like Testa del Turco (a pastry symbolizing the Saracen's head). The event provides an interactive experience for both locals and visitors, with the possibility of sampling the dishes after the demonstration.

Throughout this time, the atmosphere in Piazza Italia will be vibrant with music, lights, and the presence of vendors offering local crafts, food, and festival-related items. Families and visitors will enjoy strolling through the piazza, participating in various events, and getting ready for the reenactment and religious celebrations that will follow in the coming days.

The evening is a mix of cultural and culinary experiences, allowing people to enjoy the festive spirit leading up to the central religious and historical events of the weekend.

10:00 p.m. Concert and Dancing

The concert usually takes place in Piazza Italia, offering a lively and celebratory atmosphere to end the day.

These concerts often feature local or regional musicians, with performances that range from traditional Sicilian folk music to more contemporary styles, ensuring there's something for everyone to enjoy. The music acts as a prelude to the more solemn and historical events that will unfold during the rest of the festival.

The combination of the earlier cooking show, the inauguration, and the festive concert helps build excitement for the major events that will follow, including the iconic reenactment of the Madonna's miraculous intervention during the battle.The statue of the Madonna on horseback, will be display in the church for the days of the festival. It is normally kept in a special area behind her when not part of the procession.

Festival Day

8:00 a.m. Alborata (Dawn celebration)

The festival begins with the Alborata, a symbolic celebration that marks the start of the day's events. This involves the sound of bells ringing from the town's churches and fireworks illuminating the early morning sky, setting a tone of excitement and reverence for the day ahead.

9:00 a.m. Holy Mass

The day continues with a solemn Holy Mass at the Church of Santa Maria la Nova. This mass is a deeply spiritual moment for the community, where prayers are offered to the Madonna delle Milizie, asking for her protection and blessings. The church fills with locals and visitors, many dressed in traditional attire, creating a picturesque and reverent atmosphere.

10:00 a.m. – Solemn Procession with the Statue of Madonna delle Milizie

This is the key event of the festival, blending deep religious devotion with historical reenactments and vibrant community participation.

The procession begins after the Holy Mass, with the statue of the Madonna delle Milizie carefully carried through the streets. This statue holds immense significance as it depicts the Madonna as a warrior, mounted on a horse and holding a sword—commemorating her legendary intervention in saving Scicli from a Saracen invasion during the Norman period.

Highlights of the Procession:

Locals don elaborate medieval costumes, portraying various figures such as Norman knights, nobles, soldiers, and townspeople. The costumes are meticulously crafted, reflecting the attire of the 11th century, the time of the Madonna's miraculous intervention.

Marching bands play traditional music, interspersed with the dramatic rhythm of drummers, creating an exhilarating soundtrack to the procession.

Falconers accompany the procession, showcasing the medieval art of falconry. The sight of these majestic birds, often associated with nobility, adds a unique and historical touch to the event.

The streets of Scicli are adorned with flags and flowers, while locals and visitors line the sidewalks or gather on balconies to watch the procession pass by. Many join in the walk, creating a lively and inclusive atmosphere.

The statue of the Madonna is carried with great care and devotion through the streets, pausing at key locations where blessings and prayers are offered. The route includes a return to the Church of St. Bartholomew, the final destination of the procession.

This morning event is not only a religious ritual but also a powerful expression of Scicli's historical pride, community spirit, and cultural heritage.

The procession lasts several hours, immersing everyone in the town's vibrant history and faith.

4:00 p.m. – The Medieval Parco Giochi

In the afternoon, the Medieval Park opens, bringing to life the era of the Madonna's legendary intervention.

This lively area offers:

- Knights in armor demonstrate their skills in exciting displays of medieval combat.
- Activities for all ages, such as archery and games that would have been enjoyed during the Norman period.
- Artisan Demonstrations: Blacksmiths, potters, and other craftspeople showcase medieval techniques, offering visitors a chance to engage with history.

5:00 p.m. – The Medieval Parade and Testa del Turco Stands

The Testa del Turco, a sweet pastry filled with ricotta, is a culinary highlight of the festival. Stalls selling this treat open in the afternoon, inviting festival-goers to indulge in a taste of history.

Meanwhile, the medieval parade begins, featuring knights, nobles, and the medieval court making their way through Scicli's streets. This parade evokes the grandeur of a medieval pageant, complete with banners, flags, and fanfare.

Testa del Turco stands open, and the medieval court, knights, and army members make their way through Scicli's streets in a parade.

Special Festival Treat
Testa del Turco - A Sweet Taste of Victory

No visit to the Festa della Madonna delle Milizie is complete without indulging in its signature dessert - the infamous Testa del Turco, or "Head of the Turk." This delectable treat is more than just a pastry; it's an edible piece of history, commemorating Madonna's legendary triumph over the Saracen invaders.

Imagine biting into a crispy pastry shell, only to be surprised by a burst of flavor from within. Will it be velvety pastry custard or rich sheep's milk ricotta that greets your taste buds? The excitement lies in the discovery! These sweet delights come in various sizes, from dainty cream puffs perfect for a quick nibble to grand creations rivaling wedding cakes in their splendor. On the day of the festival, Scicli transforms into a battleground of bakers, with locals competing to create the most impressive Testa del Turco. As you wander through the festive streets, you'll witness an array of these pastries, each one a testament to the skill and creativity of its maker. From intricate designs to innovative fillings, the variety is astounding.

While there may be official winners in this sweet contest, don't be surprised if you find yourself unable to choose a favorite. Each Testa del Turco is a masterpiece in its own right, offering a unique blend of textures and flavors that will have you coming back for more.

So, whether you sample this treat once or make it your mission to try every variation you can find, the Testa del Turco is not just a dessert - it's an essential part of the Festa della Madonna delle Milizie experience. It's a delicious way to connect with the town's history, culture, and culinary prowess all at once. Go ahead, take a bite out of history!

9:30 p.m. As night falls, the town is illuminated for the evening procession of the Madonna delle Milizie. This procession mirrors the morning's solemnity but is heightened by the beauty of the statue lit by torches and candles.

The medieval court accompanies the Madonna's statue, creating a stunning visual as the procession moves through the darkened streets.

Fireworks light up the sky as the procession reaches its conclusion, marking the festival's emotional and spiritual high point.

Walking Tour of Scicli–Day 1

#1. Church of San Guglielmo (Church of St. William)

The Mother Church of San Guglielmo (formerly known as the Church of Sant'Ignazio di Loyola) dates back to the early 18th century. It was connected to the Jesuit college, which was destroyed in the mid-20th century. They erected something terrible there instead, impossible to miss as you enter the piazza (the building on the left. I know you are going to wonder what it is. It is an unfortunate build of a modern building next to the baroque church that seems completely out of place. It appears to be of the Mussolini era but it is actually even more modern).

When we arrived at the heart of the city, we discovered that the church was closed and there were no official hours available. Upon our return a while later, we found it open, and we were fortunate to encounter the Madonna of the festival. Among Marian images, this particular Madonna is commonly believed to be the only one depicted as a warrior riding a horse and wielding a sword.

The local deacon in the church repeatedly told us in Italian, "Ask me if you have any inquiries." I had the impression he would give us a tour, and my assumption was correct! He showed us around the church and mentioned we were in the church on a special day because Mary was on display only to prepare for the evening procession. As per our guide, the local Sicilian women graciously donated their hair to fashion the statue's black hair, giving her a captivating appearance. Genuine human hair used for non-blonde Madonna. Such a valuable treasure!

#2. Chiesa di San Giovanni Evangelista (Church of St. John the Evangelist)

Departing from the main church and going right, it takes just three minutes to walk through this scenic core and reach St. John the Evangelist. An 18th-century Baroque church is what you're looking at. Adorning the church front are exquisitely sculpted columns and pilasters, with the church bell sitting atop the tympanum. When the sun shines on it, the local stone transforms into a stunningly beautiful shade of sandy color. It is incredibly mesmerizing.

#3. Palazzo Spadaro

Just a few steps down the street, we arrive at Palazzo Spadaro, a true gem. If you're interested, you can purchase a combo ticket here, which grants access to several sites.

The Inspector Montalbano (Italian: Il Commissario Montalbano) is a popular Italian TV series based on Andrea Camilleri's famous detective novels. Though set in the fictional town of Vigàta, inspired by Camilleri's hometown, much of the filming took place in Scicli. The police station from the show is preserved here, just as it appeared on screen. As a fan of the show, I couldn't resist sending photos to my Italian friends, jokingly asking, "Where am I?" They replied, "Why are you in Montalbano's office?"

In Scicli, you can visit these sets. The police commissioner's desk, complete with documents, phones, and furnishings, is still intact. Having watched the 15 seasons and 37 episodes twice while learning Italian, I found this tour to be a fun and nostalgic experience.

Palazzo Spadaro, an 18th-century palace, is impressive even from the outside, with its beautiful facade and intricate balcony railings. Inside, you can imagine grand balls in the ballroom, featuring a stunning 19th-century fresco of Apollo and the Nine Muses.

The baron's bedroom, the only room preserved in its original condition, is also on display. The second-floor balconies offer a great spot for people-watching and provide a unique glimpse of the city.

#4. Palazzo del Seminario

A short distance away is the mayor's office from the Montalbano series. An impressive structure from the 18th century, this building served as a seminary for priests in its early days. Inside the palazzo, you'll discover a sizable room which is the office of the actual mayor and is designated for meetings and conferences of the town. The room is an excellent representation of Sicilian Baroque architecture, offering a captivating glimpse into Scicli's history.

#5. The Rocca (the rock)

Head up the hill, known as Rocca, to San Matteo, which offers a scenic view of the city. You won't come across a better perspective of the city than this. No muddy trails, just some uneven stairs.

Tower climbs, dome climbs, and terrazzo views are experiences I never pass up. Along the route to San Matteo, we come across these captivating little alleyways, stairways, and palazzi. Discover something incredible in every direction of this lovely town.

Along the route up the stairs, you will see cave houses sculpted into the rock in every direction. Once, people lived in these cave homes, and some still do today. The type of rock used in the house is identical to the stone found in the square caves they uncovered. You can enter some of these caves while hiking up.

Chiesa di San Bartolomeo

#6. Chiesa di San Bartolomeo (Church of St. Bartholomew)

Architect Rosario Gagliardi completed the construction of the church in 1752. Adorning the church's exterior are columns and pilasters, with Saint Bartholomew's statue adorning the tympanum. The interior of the plan has enchanting Rococo decoration with a central transept in a Latin cross plan.

Indoors, we found a Presepe Napoletano or a Napolitan nativity scene, though the term "nativity scene" doesn't do it justice, as it is a whole town filled with activity surrounding the birth of Jesus. This one is from 1776. Don't hesitate; simply pay a euro and switch on the light.

#7. Chiesa di San Matteo (St. Matthew)

Next, head up the stairs towards St Matthew. Take a moment to pause and appreciate the scenery. The views of the hills and houses are absolutely breathtaking. The photo stops will be beneficial as they provide a break from climbing.

Before the earthquake, the Chiesa di San Matteo served as Scicli's main church and also functioned as a protective stronghold for the citizens. In 1874, the citizens abandoned the church when the new mother church of St. William opened below (the first stop on the tour). According to the locals, many citizens opposed abandoning this church, even after its décor and treasure were moved to the new church.

Ultimately, the roof was removed by the church authorities, effectively blocking any additional masses from occurring. Some suggest that San Matteo was constructed in the Norman period. Based on evidence, it seems there was a three-aisled basilica with a bell tower in the Middle Ages. The genuine history remains a mystery.

Upon our arrival and after admiring the view, we learned we could enter because of ongoing construction work, including the installation of a new roof. What a delight! The church, although in ruins, remains remarkably appealing because of its remaining architectural features.

Also, since the church was open, it was possible to climb to the higher terrace for an even more breathtaking view. Very few people do both climbs, making it a quiet spot.

Walking Tour of Scicli – Day 2

#1. **Antica Farmacia Cartia.** Located on Via Mormina Penna.

Opened in 1902, this beautifully preserved antique pharmacy is a journey back in time. Its interior is filled with early 20th-century furnishings, medical equipment, and jars once used for remedies. It's a fascinating glimpse into Scicli's medical history and the art of pharmacy in a bygone era.

#2. **Palazzo Bonelli-Patané**

This elegant neoclassical palace is adorned with period furniture and rich decor, making it a perfect example of aristocratic life in Scicli. Visitors can tour the inside to experience its grandeur, which has remained untouched for decades.

#3. Palazzo Beneventano. Located on Via Duca degli Abruzzi

A baroque masterpiece, Palazzo Beneventano is one of Scicli's architectural jewels. Its grotesque masks and ornate balconies make it one of the most impressive buildings in town. The intricate carvings on the stone facade are a must-see for lovers of baroque architecture.

#4. Chiesa di San Giuseppe (Church of St. Joseph). Located in Piazza Italia

The Church of St. Joseph, built in baroque style, is another significant religious site in Scicli. The facade is elaborate, and inside, you'll find an impressive altar and religious art. It's a serene stop that adds to the town's spiritual history.

#5. Chiesa di Santa Teresa d'Avila (Church of St. Teresa of Avila)

This 17th-century baroque church is dedicated to St. Teresa of Avila and is a peaceful spot to reflect. Its elegant facade and simple yet graceful interior make it a charming stop.

It's located just a short walk from Piazza Italia.

#6. Chiesa di San Michele Arcangelo (Church of St. Michael the Archangel)

Another exquisite baroque church, this one is dedicated to St. Michael the Archangel. Known for its beautiful interior with frescoes and fine details, it's a peaceful stop to admire Scicli's religious art.

#7. Convento dei Cappuccini (Capuchin Monastery)

This monastery is in a more secluded part of Scicli, offering a tranquil atmosphere. It has a small church and serene cloisters where the monks once lived.

#8. Convento dei Francescani (Franciscan Monastery)

Near the Capuchin Monastery, this site is quieter but still integral to the town's monastic history. With its humble architecture, it represents the Franciscan values of simplicity and faith.

#9. Castle Ruins above St. Matthew's Church

Perched above the town, the ruins of Scicli's medieval castle offer breathtaking views of the town and the surrounding landscape. It's a bit of a hike but well worth the effort for the panoramic perspective. The ruins sit near the Church of San Matteo, which adds to the area's historic allure.

End your walking tour with this scenic climb, giving you a sweeping view of Scicli from above.

Scicli Festivals and Sagre Throughout the Year

La Cavalcata di San Giuseppe (The Ride of St. Joseph)

The Saturday closest to March 19th

This vibrant religious festival celebrates St. Joseph's feast day and the Holy Family's flight into Egypt. The highlight is a spectacular horse and knight procession that begins at the Church of San Giuseppe. Elaborately decorated horses, adorned with flowers, follow actors portraying the Holy Family through the town's streets in a candlelit procession. The event combines religious devotion with local tradition, creating a mesmerizing spectacle that draws both residents and visitors.

Il Gioia (The Joy)

Easter Sunday

Il Gioia is Scicli's joyous Easter celebration, marking the resurrection of Christ. The festival's centerpiece is a solemn yet jubilant procession where a statue of the risen Christ is carried through the town's streets. This event is a profound expression of faith and communal joy, often accompanied by music and followed by festive gatherings. The procession typically winds through the historic center, allowing the entire community to participate in the celebration.

Sagra del Pomodoro e Festa del Grappolino (Tomato and Grape Festival)

May 1st

This dual festival celebrates the first local harvest of tomatoes and grapes, along with the creation of cheeses and other local products. It's a gastronomic extravaganza that showcases Scicli's agricultural heritage. Visitors can sample a variety of tomato-based dishes, fresh grapes, local wines, and artisanal cheeses.

The event often features cooking demonstrations, wine tastings, and educational displays about local farming techniques. It's an excellent opportunity to experience the flavors of Sicilian cuisine and learn about the region's agricultural traditions.

Basole di Luce (Tiles of Light)

Throughout August

Basole di Luce is a month-long cultural festival that transforms the historic center of Scicli into a vibrant hub of artistic expression. Throughout August, the town hosts a diverse array of events, including musical performances, theatrical productions, art exhibitions, and literary readings. The festival's name, which translates to "Tiles of Light," refers to the way these events illuminate the town's beautiful Baroque architecture and cobblestone streets. It's a celebration of both contemporary culture and Scicli's rich heritage, attracting artists and audiences from across Sicily and beyond.

Taranta Sicily Fest (Music Festival)

August (specific dates may vary each year)

The Taranta Sicily Fest is a dynamic music event that brings the rhythms of traditional Southern Italian folk music to Scicli. Focusing on the energetic and hypnotic style of Taranta music, which originated in the Salento region of Puglia, this festival has become a significant cultural event in Sicily. Visitors can enjoy live performances by local and international musicians, participate in dance workshops, and experience the captivating blend of ancient and modern musical traditions. The festival often includes related cultural events, such as food tastings and artisan markets, celebrating the broader cultural context of the music.

Day Trip Options: Nearby Sites, Cities and Towns

Sampieri and Cava d'Aliga Beaches. 10 kilometers (6 miles).

- **Sampieri**: Known for its long sandy beach lined with dunes and vegetation, Sampieri is a tranquil destination perfect for relaxation. A must-visit site is the **Fornace Penna**, an abandoned 20th-century brick factory that has become an iconic ruin, locally referred to as the

"Mannara." This atmospheric site has been featured in the *Inspector Montalbano* TV series, adding a touch of cinematic allure. The town itself has charming lanes and seaside views that capture the essence of coastal Sicily.

- **Cava d'Aliga**: This quieter beach town offers rocky coves and crystal-clear waters that are perfect for snorkeling and exploring marine life. The rugged coastline provides a scenic backdrop, and the sunsets here are particularly mesmerizing. It's an ideal spot for those seeking peace and natural beauty.

Punta Secca. 30 kilometers (19 miles). Punta Secca is a charming seaside village best known as a filming location for the popular Inspector Montalbano TV series, attracting fans and travelers alike.

- Faro di Punta Secca: The village's iconic lighthouse is a landmark you can't miss. Its picturesque setting offers fantastic photo opportunities and sweeping views of the sea.

- Montalbano's House: Fans of the series will enjoy seeing the famous beachfront house used as the residence of the fictional detective. While privately owned, it's a popular spot for photos.

- Golden Sand Beaches: The beaches here are perfect for a leisurely day by the sea, with soft sand and gentle waves ideal for swimming or sunbathing.

- Piazzetta del Porto: This small square near the port is dotted with quaint cafes and restaurants, offering delicious seafood dishes and a chance to relax while soaking up the seaside atmosphere.

Pozzallo. 25 kilometers (15.5 miles). Pozzallo is a lively coastal town recognized for its Blue Flag beaches and historical landmarks, making it a perfect stop for beachgoers and history enthusiasts alike.

- Torre Cabrera: This 15th-century watchtower once protected the coast from pirate attacks and now serves as a symbol of the town. Visitors can explore its history and enjoy panoramic views of the surrounding area.

- Piazza delle Rimembranze: The town's main square is a vibrant hub with cafes, shops, and cultural events. It's a great place to experience local life and indulge in gelato or coffee.

- Blue Flag Beaches: Pozzallo's beaches, such as Pietre Nere and Raganzino, are renowned for their cleanliness and beauty. Both beaches offer golden sands, clear waters, and amenities for a relaxing seaside experience.

- Port Area: A stroll through the port provides views of ferries heading to Malta and the bustling activity of this vital transportation hub.

Note on Pozzallo / Malta: For those looking to expand their journey, Pozzallo is the main gateway to **Malta**, a separate country offering a wealth of historical and cultural experiences. The ferry ride takes about 3 hours and arrives in Valetta, Malta's stunning capital city. Highlights in Malta include the ancient city of Mdina, the dramatic cliffs of Dingli, and vibrant nightlife in St. Julian's. On one of our visits, we took the ferry to Malta and enjoyed a few days exploring its unique culture before flying back to the U.S. from Valetta. This extension is highly recommended for travelers wanting to combine the best of Sicily with Malta's distinct charm.

Logistics

Train: Scicli's train station, about 2 km from the town center, is on the Syracuse-Gela-Canicattì line with limited service (5-6 trains daily) connecting to cities like Syracuse, Ragusa, and Modica. To reach the center from the station, take a local bus or taxi.

Bus: Interbus and AST (Azienda Siciliana Trasporti) offer bus services linking Scicli with nearby towns such as Ragusa, Modica, and Noto. The main bus stop is in the town center, near Piazza Italia, with local buses connecting the station and other areas.

Car: Driving is a convenient way to explore Scicli, accessible via the SS115 highway. Approximate driving times: from Catania Airport (2 hours), Comiso Airport (45 minutes), and Ragusa (30 minutes). Rental cars are available at airports and major cities.

Parking: The historic center has limited traffic zones (ZTL), so it's best to park outside and explore on foot. Options include free parking at Parcheggio Via

Dolomiti and paid parking at Parcheggio Via Ospedale. Street parking is also available outside ZTL areas, but spaces can be limited. Always check for signs to avoid fines.

Dining Recommendations

Osteria Donna Luisa. Address: Via Francesco Mormino Penna, 72

This charming osteria offers a delightful dining experience beneath the trees, where you can enjoy views of the stunning baroque palazzi. The menu features traditional Sicilian cuisine with seasonal ingredients, and the atmosphere is perfect for a leisurely lunch, even on rainy days.

Ristorante Baqqalà. Address: Via San Bartolomeo, 4

Known for its focus on seafood, Ristorante Baqqalà offers a modern twist on traditional Sicilian dishes. The restaurant's creative menu, using locally sourced ingredients, is complemented by its cozy and rustic ambiance, in the heart of the historic center.

Osteria Tre Colli. Address: Via Guadagna, 2

Set near the scenic hills of Scicli, this osteria offers a menu filled with authentic Sicilian flavors. With a relaxed and welcoming atmosphere, it's a perfect spot for a family dinner or a casual meal, featuring traditional dishes like pasta alla norma and Sicilian caponata.

Accommodation

For the festival, I recommend three nights in town. There are enough places to visit and events to keep you busy.

Scicli Albergo Diffuso. Address: Via Francesco Mormino Penna, 15

A 3-star innovative hotel offering scattered accommodations across Scicli's historic center, combining modern comforts with traditional settings. The hotel includes amenities like free Wi-Fi, air conditioning, and breakfast.

An albergo diffuso in Italy is a unique type of hospitality accommodation that translates to "scattered hotel." It is designed to revitalize small villages or rural areas by offering guest rooms that are spread out in various buildings throughout a historic town or village, rather than concentrated in one central location. Guests stay in rooms housed in traditional or restored buildings, often centuries old, while central services such as reception, dining, and communal spaces are in a designated hub.

Hotel Novecento. Address: Via Dupré, 11

A 4-star boutique hotel housed in a restored aristocratic building, offering elegant rooms, free breakfast, and modern amenities in the heart of Scicli's historic center.

*Hotel Palazzo Conti - Camere & Suites. Address: Via Mormino Penna, 82

A 3-star hotel offering beautifully restored suites in a historic palace, with free parking, Wi-Fi, and breakfast, in Scicli's picturesque baroque district.

*Palazzo Montalbano

Address: Via Francesco Mormino Penna, 97

A 3-star hotel set in a charming baroque palazzo, offering luxurious accommodations that blend history and modern comforts, ideal for a stay in Scicli's historic center.

*These hotels are directly on the procession route for the Festa della Madonna delle Millizie.

Chapter Ten

FestaFusion Taormina

Where Artistic Flair Meets The Tradition of San Pancrazio

F estaFusion Taormina

#1 Taormina Art Festival: Set in the magnificent Ancient Theater, it offers a lineup of prestigious musical, theatrical, dance, and cinematic performances in partnership with the Taormina Film Fest, which kicks off the season.

#2 Festa di San Pancrazio: This festival honors Saint Pancras, the patron saint of the city of Taormina, with religious ceremonies, parades, and traditional music.

#FestaFusion means two or more festivals happen at around the same time in the same town, so visitors can enjoy multiple events during their visit.

Where: Taormina

When: Taormina Arte Festival runs June through August. San Pancrazio is on June 9th.

Event Website: https://festivaltaorminarte.it/

Average Temperatures: High: 31-32°C (88-90°F). Low: 22-23°C (72-73°F).

Discovering Taormina: Pearl of the Ionian Sea

Perched on a rocky hillside overlooking the azure waters of the Ionian Sea, Taormina stands as a testament to Sicily's rich and diverse history. This enchanting town, often referred to as the "Pearl of the Ionian Sea," has captivated visitors for centuries with its stunning vistas, ancient ruins, and Mediterranean charm.

Taormina's history stretches back to ancient times. Founded in the 4th century BCE by Andromachus, it quickly became an important Greek settlement. The town's strategic location made it a coveted prize, passing through the hands of various civilizations. Greek colonists established the initial settlement, which was later expanded by the Romans, who built many of its enduring structures. The Byzantine Empire incorporated Taormina into its territories, followed by an Arab conquest in 902 CE that brought new cultural influences. The Norman conquest in 1078 led to a period of medieval prosperity, and Spanish rule from the 15th to 19th centuries left its mark on architecture and culture.

Taormina is situated on the east coast of Sicily, approximately midway between Messina and Catania. Its elevated position, about 250 meters above sea level, offers breathtaking panoramas. To the east, one can admire the glittering Ionian Sea and the coastline of Calabria. The south is dominated by the imposing silhouette of Mount Etna, Europe's largest active volcano, while the rugged Peloritani Mountains rise to the north. The town is built on a terrace of Monte Tauro, with steep streets and charming alleyways winding their way up the hillside. Below, the beautiful beaches of Giardini Naxos and Mazzarò attract sun-seekers and water enthusiasts.

Taormina is a thriving tourist destination and cultural hub. As of 2024, the town has a population of approximately 11,000 residents. However, this number swells significantly during the peak summer season when tourists from around the world flock to experience its unique blend of history, culture, and natural beauty. The ancient Greek Theater, still used for performances and events, stands as a testament to the town's enduring appeal. Corso Umberto, the main street, is lined with shops, cafes, and historic buildings, offering a vibrant atmosphere for visitors and locals alike. The 13th-century Duomo di Taormina adds to the town's architectural splendor, while numerous luxury hotels and resorts cater to the discerning traveler.

Taormina's cultural scene is equally impressive, with events like the annual Taormina Film Fest drawing international attention. Despite its popularity, Taormina has managed to preserve its authentic charm, offering visitors a glimpse into Sicily's storied past while providing all the amenities of a modern resort town. It's this unique combination of historical significance, natural beauty, and contemporary comfort that continues to make Taormina a jewel in Sicily's crown, captivating the hearts of all who visit.

#1 Taormina Arte Festival

The Taormina Arte Festival is a prestigious cultural event that has been captivating audiences in Sicily for decades. Nestled in the picturesque town of Taormina, this festival has become a cornerstone of artistic expression, drawing talent and spectators from across Italy and around the world.

The festival's roots can be traced back to 1983, when it was established by a group of local cultural enthusiasts and government officials. Their vision was to create a multidisciplinary arts festival that would showcase the rich cultural heritage of Sicily while also bringing international talent to the region. The ancient Greek Theatre of Taormina, dating back to the 3rd century BCE, was chosen as the primary venue, providing a stunning backdrop that blends history with contemporary artistic expression.

Over the years, the festival has evolved and expanded its scope. In 1991, the Taormina Film Fest, which had been running separately since 1955, was incorporated into the Taormina Arte Festival, further enhancing its prestige and drawing power. This merger brought together the worlds of performing arts and cinema, creating a unique and comprehensive cultural experience.

The Taormina Arte Festival typically runs for several weeks during the summer months, usually from June to August. The program is diverse and eclectic, designed to cater to a wide range of artistic tastes and interests. Classical music concerts featuring renowned orchestras and soloists are a staple of the festival, often held in the atmospheric setting of the Greek Theatre.

Contemporary dance performances bring modern energy to the ancient stones, with both established companies and emerging choreographers showcasing their work. Theatrical productions range from reimagined classics to cutting-edge experimental pieces, often featuring multilingual performances that bridge cultural divides.

Art exhibitions are scattered throughout the town, transforming Taormina into an open-air gallery. These exhibitions often highlight both Sicilian artists and international talents, covering various mediums, from painting and sculpture to installations and digital art.

The Film Festival

The Taormina Film Fest, a significant component of the overall festival, screens a carefully curated selection of international films. It includes premieres, retrospectives, and competitions, attracting filmmakers, actors, and industry professionals from around the globe. The festival has hosted numerous celebrities over the years, adding a touch of glamour to the artistic proceedings.

Workshops and masterclasses led by visiting artists provide opportunities for local talent to learn and engage with international professionals. These educational components help to foster a new generation of artists and maintain the festival's relevance and vitality.

While the ancient Greek Theatre remains the crown jewel of the festival's venues, performances and events take place throughout Taormina. The Palazzo dei Congressi hosts indoor performances and exhibitions, while smaller theaters and outdoor stages are set up in various piazzas and scenic locations around the town.

The festival transforms Taormina into a vibrant hub of cultural activity. The narrow medieval streets buzz with energy as visitors and locals alike move from one event to another. Cafes and restaurants overflow with patrons discussing the latest performances, creating a lively atmosphere that extends well into the warm Sicilian nights.

The breathtaking views of Mount Etna and the Ionian Sea provide a constant reminder of the natural beauty that complements the artistic offerings. This unique combination of culture, history, and natural splendor makes the Taormina Arte Festival a truly immersive experience.

Over its four-decade history, the Taormina Arte Festival has significantly impacted the cultural landscape of Sicily and Italy as a whole. It has played a crucial role in promoting Sicilian culture to an international audience while also bringing world-class performances to local audiences who might otherwise not have access to such diverse artistic expressions.

As the festival continues to evolve, it remains committed to its founding principles of artistic excellence, cultural exchange, and the celebration of Sicily's rich heritage. Each year brings new challenges and opportunities, ensuring that the Taormina Arte Festival remains a dynamic and essential part of the international arts calendar.

#2 The Festa di San Pancrazio

The festival honors Saint Pancras, the patron saint of the city, and represents a rich tapestry of religious devotion, cultural heritage, and community spirit.

Saint Pancras: The Patron Saint

Saint Pancras, known in Italian as San Pancrazio, holds a special place in the hearts of Taormina's residents. Born in Phrygia (modern-day Turkey) around 290 AD, Pancras was orphaned at a young age and brought to Rome by his uncle. There, during the reign of Emperor Diocletian, he converted to Christianity.

Despite his youth–he was only fourteen years old–Pancras refused to renounce his faith during the widespread persecution of Christians. As a result, he was martyred in 304 AD, beheaded on the Via Aurelia. His unwavering commitment to his beliefs in the face of death quickly led to his veneration as a saint.

The connection between Saint Pancras and Taormina stems from a legend that diverges from the commonly accepted historical account. According to local tradition, Pancras was born in Antioch and traveled to Jerusalem with his parents during Jesus' ministry. After his family's baptism in Antioch, Pancras retreated to a cave in Pontus. It's said that Saint Peter discovered him there and later sent him to Sicily to become the first Bishop of Tauromenium (the ancient name for Taormina) in 40 AD.

This version of the story concludes with Pancras being stoned to death by pagans opposing the new Christian faith. While this account differs from the widely accepted Roman narrative, it underscores the deep connection felt by the people of Taormina to their patron saint.

The Festa di San Pancrazio has been celebrated in Taormina for centuries, with its origins likely dating back to the medieval period when the veneration of saints became a central part of Christian practice in Europe. The festival has evolved over time, incorporating various cultural elements while maintaining its core religious significance.

In the past, the celebration would have been a primarily religious affair, centered around the church and involving solemn processions and prayers. Over the centuries, it has grown to encompass more secular elements.

The festival's longevity and continued importance to the people of Taormina show the enduring influence of religious traditions in shaping cultural identity. It serves as a living link to the city's past, connecting modern-day residents with countless generations who have honored Saint Pancras before them.

Festival Events and Timeline

The Festa di San Pancrazio typically takes place on July 9th, the day traditionally associated with Saint Pancras's martyrdom. However, celebrations often extend over several days, creating a festive atmosphere throughout Taormina.

9 Days of Prayer

The festival begins with a novena, nine days of prayer leading up to the major celebration. During this time, the faithful gather each evening in the Duomo di Taormina (Taormina Cathedral) for special Masses and devotions to Saint Pancras.

July 8

On the eve of the feast day, July 8th, the excitement builds with the illumination of the city. Streets and buildings are adorned with elaborate light displays, creating a magical atmosphere that signals the approaching day of the festival.

July 9

5:30 a.m. Dawn Mass at Taormina Cathedral

The celebration begins with an early morning Mass at the cathedral, drawing local devotees and pilgrims.

7:00 a.m. - 12:00 p.m. Additional Masses

A series of masses take place throughout the morning to accommodate the influx of pilgrims from nearby towns.

4:00 p.m. - 5:00 p.m. Grand Procession

The highlight of the day, the grand procession featuring a statue or relic of Saint Pancras, begins in the late afternoon. The procession weaves through Taormina's historic streets, making stops at important churches and landmarks for prayers and blessings.

7:00 p.m. - 8:00 p.m. Return to the Cathedral

The procession concludes back at the cathedral, where final blessings are given.

8:30 p.m. Sicilian Music and Folk Dances

The Piazza IX Aprile becomes the focal point for traditional Sicilian music and folk performances, with local food vendors offering regional delicacies.

10:00 p.m. Fireworks Display

The day concludes with a spectacular fireworks display over the Ionian Sea, visible from various vantage points in Taormina.

As always, it's best to check locally closer to the event or with Taormina's tourist office for the most accurate schedule. This outline provides an estimate based on how similar festivals are typically structured in Sicily.

The Festa di San Pancrazio is both a religious event and a celebration of Taormina's culture and community. It showcases Sicilian traditions, making it unique.A highlight is the creation of flower carpets along the procession route. Local artists and volunteers collaborate to design these intricate displays, honoring the saint and showcasing their creativity.

The festival also serves as a homecoming for many who have left Taormina for work or other reasons. Families reunite, and the city's population swells as people return to honor their patron saint and reconnect with their roots.

For visitors, the Festa di San Pancrazio offers a unique opportunity to witness the living traditions of Sicily. It provides a window into the deep-seated faith, rich culture, and warm hospitality that characterizes this beautiful corner of Italy. The blend of religious devotion, historical reenactment, traditional music and dance, and culinary delights creates a multi-sensory experience that captures the essence of Sicilian life.

> **Special Festival Treat**
> **Cucciddatidi San Pancrazio**
> Food plays a vital role in the festival. Families prepare traditional recipes,reserved for this occasion. A standout is the "cucciddati di San Pancrazio," a sweet pastry prepared with a filling of figs nuts,and spices (with perhaps a splash of liquer or Marsala wine).
> The filled dough is rolled, sliced into individual cookies, and then glazed with icing and decorated with colorful sprinkles.
> This treat symbolizes the abundance and blessings from the saint's intercession.

Walking Tour of Taormina – Day 1

#1. Porta Catania and Palazzo Duca di Santo Stéfano

The Porta Catania gate is a key entry point to the historic center. Porta Catania is at the southern end of Corso Umberto, Taormina's main street and pedestrian thoroughfare. The 14th-century gothic gate is a stone structure with a wide archway spanning the street. The old town has two main gates: this one and Porta Messina. In medieval times, the locals constructed Porta Catania as a defensive measure, fortifying the town with walls and gates to repel invasions. While renovations occurred over the centuries, the current structure preserves its historical charm and significance.

#2. The Palazzo Duca di Santo Stefano

The palazzo is attached to the Porta Catania. Its distinct features, such as Gothic windows, fish-tail crenellations, and detailed stonework, make it easy to identify. Besides hosting concerts, The Great Hall displays sculptures by Giuseppe Mazzullo (1913-88) in two separate rooms. Giuseppe Mazzullo (1913–1988) was a Sicilian sculptor known for his expressive, abstract works that often reflected the natural landscape and cultural heritage of Sicily. Born in Graniti, a small town near Taormina, Mazzullo worked extensively with stone, particularly lava and sandstone, creating sculptures that evoke a deep connection to the rugged beauty of his homeland.

Once you pass through the gate, you'll be on the Corso Umberto. Follow this route for a minute, and you'll find yourself in Piazza del Duomo, where the gothic, renaissance Cathedral awaits on your right.

#3. The Duomo di Taormina

In the 13th century, the builders constructed the Cathedral, blending Romanesque and Gothic architectural features. The recycling habits of historical builders suggest that the columns in the naves probably came from the ancient amphitheater. Renaissance-style portals were added during a partial reconstruction in the 15th century.

The artisans in the 17th century transformed the building by adding a Baroque portal, placing marble tables along the walls, and constructing chapels in the side apses.

Duomo di Taormina

"The fortress cathedral" became the church's nickname because of its severe architecture and external fortification elements. Crown battlements adorn the façade of the church, while a bastion tower in the back served as the bell tower, beginning in 1750.

The tour carries on along Corso Umberto, a picturesque street where shops are brimming with locally produced goods like Sicilian pottery, pastries, gelato, shoes, and clothing. It's Taormina's own Rodeo Drive. Upon passing through another gate, you will find yourself in a piazza offering stunning views of the sea. The Clock Tower and Middle Gate are located here.

#4. Piazza IX April

Why was the Piazza named the 9th of April?

A rumor circulated in Taormina on April 9, 1860, claiming that Giuseppe Garibaldi had arrived in Marsala, Sicily, to begin his mission of unifying Italy. The Risorgimento movement sought to unify Italian states into a single nation, and this event played a role in it.

While the rumor turned out to be false (Garibaldi actually arrived on May 11, 1860), it caused a considerable stir and anticipation in the region, as many Sicilians were in favor of unification. The news sparked such enthusiasm and public response that the piazza in Taormina was later named after the date, April 9th.

This piazza features a viewpoint known as the Belvedere.

#5. Chiesa di San Giuseppe (The Church of St. Joseph)

In one of Taormina's picturesque plazas, the Chiesa di San Giuseppe stands as a testament to the town's rich religious heritage. Built during the 17th and 18th centuries by the Confraternity of the Souls in Purgatory, this church offers visitors a glimpse into Taormina's fascinating past.

The church's facade showcases a harmonious blend of materials, including Syracuse stone, local stone with white, gray, and pink tones, and muted plaster. This combination creates an elegant chromatic contrast that enhances the church's visual appeal. The Confraternity's focus on the souls in purgatory is reflected in the church's decorative elements. Throughout the building, you'll find inscriptions, coats of arms, sculptures, bas-reliefs, mottos, and allegorical figures, many incorporating imagery associated with fire or purification to symbolize the cleansing of souls.

#6. Ex-Church of Saint Augustine

The building with a yellow façade on this square used to be a church, but it is no longer consecrated or sacred. Enter and check out the exhibits. If you're feeling overheated, it's a perfect spot to refresh.

#7. Odeon

Odeon, a smaller version of, or a rehearsal space for, an open-air Greek theater from 21 BC, can be found behind the church. You can climb, sit, and stand wherever you want.

Head back to Corso Umberto, where you can find the Palazzo Corvaja.

#8. Palazzo Corvaja

Palazzo Corvaja, a historic building from the 10th century, embodies the rich blend of Norman-Arab architecture that defined medieval Sicily. Its sturdy stone construction and smooth, unadorned walls reflect the practicality and defensive nature of the time. One of its standout features is the tower, a symbol of both residential and defensive purposes for noble families.

The arched windows and doorways showcase the influence of both Norman and Arab styles, combining structural strength with aesthetic charm. Even a glimpse of the exterior offers a fascinating insight into Sicily's medieval heritage.

#9. Piazza Vittorio Emanuele II also called Piazza Badia.

Instead of going straight on Corso Umberto, we'll turn right at Piazza Badia and take the route via Teatro Greco. When the street ends, you are at the ticket booth and entry gate to the Teatro Greco.

#10. Teatro Greco di Taormina / Ancient Theater of Taormina.

If you're not doing a guided tour, it's highly advisable to buy tickets in advance for the Greek theater to avoid waiting in line. You can also opt for an audio guide. The Greek Theater offers breathtaking views of Mount Etna and the Ionian Sea, making it one of Sicily's most iconic and well-preserved ancient theaters.

Today, it serves as a venue for concerts, plays, and other events, blending its historical legacy with modern performances, including the Taormina Arte Festival.

During our visit, preparations for a show were underway, and it was inspiring to see such a historic site still actively in use. Dedicate an hour to the Greek Theater, specifically for photography. There is a café where you can indulge in breakfast, lunch, and aperitivo at the café, all while enjoying the scenic view.

The Greek Theater of Taormina, a magnificent relic of ancient times, stands as one of Sicily's most impressive archaeological sites. Constructed in the 3rd century BC, this remarkable structure is believed to be the work of ancient Greeks, possibly built on the site of an earlier Sicilian-Greek temple. True to Greek architectural practices, the theater was ingeniously carved into the natural curve of Monte Tauro, taking advantage of the hillside's natural acoustics and topology.

The theater's design is a testament to ancient engineering and artistic vision. With a diameter of approximately 109 meters (358 feet), it exemplifies the characteristic horseshoe shape typical of Greek theater architecture. The seating area is divided into three main sections: the diazoma, the lower cavea, and the upper cavea, collectively capable of accommodating up to 5,400 spectators. This layout not only provided ample seating, but also ensured that every member of the audience had an unobstructed view of the performances.

The Backdrop

One of the theater's most striking features is its breathtaking backdrop. As spectators face the stage, they are treated to a panoramic view of the Ionian Sea with the majestic Mount Etna rising in the distance. This natural scenery, combined with the theater's architectural beauty, creates an awe-inspiring setting that has captivated visitors for centuries.

The stage area (skene) and orchestra pit (orchestra) remain in excellent condition, allowing modern visitors to easily envision the grand performances that once took place here. The theater's exceptional acoustics, a hallmark of Greek architectural ingenuity, continue to impress. Even without modern amplification technology, sounds from the stage can be clearly heard throughout the seating area, a testament to the advanced understanding of sound propagation possessed by ancient Greek architects.

Today, the Greek Theater of Taormina stands not only as a remarkable archaeological site but also as a living venue. It continues to host various cultural events, including theater performances, concerts, and film festivals, bridging the gap between its ancient origins and contemporary use. This ongoing utilization of the space for artistic expression creates a unique connection between past and present, allowing visitors to experience the theater much as ancient spectators did over two millennia ago.

As one of Taormina's most iconic landmarks, the Greek Theater attracts tourists from around the world. It serves as a powerful reminder of Sicily's rich cultural heritage and the enduring legacy of ancient Greek civilization on the island. Whether one is a history enthusiast, an architecture buff, or simply a traveler in search of breathtaking views, the Greek Theater of Taormina offers an unforgettable experience that seamlessly blends historical significance with natural beauty.

Walking Tour of Taormina – Day 2

#1. Chiesa di San Pancras (Church of San Pancrazio)

Begin your day at the Chiesa di San Pancras, located in the heart of Taormina. This church, dedicated to Saint Pancras, a martyr from the early Christian period, is believed to have medieval roots, possibly dating back to the Norman era (11th-12th centuries). Take some time to admire its architecture and learn about its historical significance.

#2. Villa Comunale

From the Chiesa di San Pancras, take a short walk to the Villa Comunale. This public garden offers stunning panoramic views of the Ionian Sea, the Bay of Naxos, and Mount Etna, Europe's highest active volcano. Enjoy a leisurely stroll through the lush greenery, vibrant flowers, and exotic plants. This serene refuge in the historic center is free to access year-round and provides a perfect spot for a mid-morning rest or picnic.

#3. Madonna della Rocca and Via Circonvallazione (Ring Road)

After enjoying the Villa Comunale, prepare for a bit of a hike. Head towards the hill above Taormina to visit the Madonna della Rocca. This chapel is uniquely carved into the mountain rock. As you ascend, you'll be following the Via Circonvallazione (Ring Road).

If you're up for a more challenging hike, continue past the chapel on the path leading upwards to Castello di Taormina. Situated at an elevation of 398 meters on Monte Tauro, this castle on the ancient Greek Acropolis offers breathtaking views from its tower. The winding road from Circonvallazione extends further to the beautiful mountain village of Castelmola if you wish to explore more.

#4. Isola Bella

For the ultimate stop of the day, make your way down to Mazzarò Bay to visit Isola Bella, known as "The Pearl of the Ionian Sea." This small island is connected to the mainland by a narrow strip of sand at low tide, allowing you to walk across.

Isola Bella, a nature reserve known for its crystal-clear waters, diverse wildlife, and breathtaking landscapes, offers a variety of activities for visitors. The calm, turquoise waters are ideal for swimming, while snorkeling around the island reveals vibrant marine life and colorful underwater flora. Sunbathers can relax on the pebbly beach or rent loungers and umbrellas to enjoy the Sicilian sun. For those who prefer exploring, a short nature walk around the island offers the chance to admire lush vegetation and spot local bird species. Photography enthusiasts will find plenty of scenic views, from the coastline to the island's azure surroundings. Visitors can also explore a small museum housed in a 19th-century villa, which provides a glimpse into the island's history and former private ownership.

Boat tours departing from the beach offer the opportunity to discover nearby grottoes and hidden coves along the stunning coastline. Spend the rest of your afternoon here, enjoying the beach and the beautiful surroundings. As the day winds down, you might want to have an aperitivo at one of the nearby beach bars, watching the sunset over the Ionian Sea - a perfect end to your Taormina walking tour.

Note: The walk from Madonna della Rocca to Isola Bella involves a significant descent. You may want to consider taking a bus or cable car down to Mazzarò Bay if you prefer not to walk.

When visiting Isola Bella, it's a good idea to bring or rent water shoes, as the beach is pebbly and the water's edge can be rocky. If you enjoy snorkeling, pack your gear or rent some locally to explore the marine life. Be sure to bring cash for beach rentals, such as sun loungers and umbrellas, as well as for refreshments. Since Isola Bella is a protected nature reserve, remember to respect the environment and take any litter with you.

Taormina Festivals and Sagre Throughout the Year

Sagra della Mandorla (Almond Festival)

February (typically mid-month)

The Sagra della Mandorla, or Almond Festival, is a celebration of Sicily's rich agricultural heritage, particularly its famous almonds. Almonds have been cultivated in Sicily since ancient times, introduced by the Greeks and later expanded by the Arabs. The festival originated as a way to mark the end of the almond harvest and has evolved into a significant cultural event.

During the festival, Taormina's streets come alive with the sweet aroma of almonds. Visitors can enjoy tastings of various almond-based sweets, including the famous Sicilian marzipan fruits, almond pastries, and the refreshing almond granita. Local producers showcase their products, offering a chance to purchase high-quality almonds and almond-derived goods.

The festival also features traditional Sicilian folk music and dance performances, adding to the festive atmosphere. Cultural events, such as exhibitions on the history of almond cultivation in Sicily and cooking demonstrations of traditional almond-based recipes, provide educational elements to the celebration. The Sagra della Mandorla is not just a gastronomic event, but a vibrant expression of Sicilian culture and traditions.

Carretti Siciliani (Sicilian Cart Festival)

Fridays in May, September, and October

The Carretti Siciliani festival celebrates one of Sicily's most iconic symbols: the ornate horse-drawn carts. These carts, known as "carretto siciliano," have a history dating back to the early 19th century. Originally used for transportation of goods and people, they evolved into elaborate works of art, showcasing intricate paintings depicting historical events, folkloric scenes, and religious themes.

During the festival, Taormina becomes a showcase of Sicilian folk art. Colorful carts with intricate designs parade through the town. Horses, adorned with vibrant decorations and jingling harnesses, pull these carts. Drivers, in traditional Sicilian costumes, add to the spectacle.

The festival is also a feast for the ears. Traditional Sicilian music fills the air. Folk songs and the clip-clop of hooves create a lively atmosphere. Artisans demonstrate their skills in cart decoration and maintenance, offering a glimpse into this unique tradition.

The Carretti Siciliani festival serves as a vibrant reminder of Sicily's rich cultural heritage and artistic traditions, allowing both locals and tourists to step back in time and experience a piece of living history.

Taormina Jazz Festival

August (typically spans a week)

The Taormina Jazz Festival, established in the late 20th century, has become one of the most anticipated musical events in Sicily. It brings together renowned jazz musicians from Italy and around the world, creating a melting pot of musical styles and cultural exchanges.

The festival takes advantage of Taormina's stunning locations, with concerts held in various scenic venues throughout the town. The ancient Greek Theatre, with its spectacular backdrop of the Ionian Sea and Mount Etna, often serves as the main stage, providing an unforgettable setting for evening performances.

Throughout the week, visitors can enjoy a diverse range of jazz styles, from traditional to contemporary, fusion to experimental. In addition to the main concerts, the festival often includes jam sessions, masterclasses, and workshops, allowing aspiring musicians and jazz enthusiasts to learn from and interact with established artists.

Taormina Gourmet

October (typically spans several days)

Taormina Gourmet is a relatively recent addition to Sicily's festival calendar, but it has quickly become one of the most anticipated culinary events in the region. Launched in the early 2010s, this festival celebrates the rich gastronomic heritage of Sicily while also showcasing innovative approaches to traditional cuisine.

The festival brings together top chefs, food producers, winemakers, and food enthusiasts from across Italy and beyond. It features a wide array of events, including cooking demonstrations, wine tastings, food markets, and gourmet dining experiences. Visitors can watch acclaimed chefs prepare signature dishes, often with a focus on local, seasonal ingredients.

The festival also includes panel discussions and conferences on topics related to gastronomy, sustainability in food production, and the future of Sicilian cuisine. These events provide a platform for industry professionals to exchange ideas and for the public to gain deeper insights into culinary trends and traditions.

Day Trip Options: Nearby Sites, Cities and Towns

Giardini Naxos. Distance from Taormina: 6 kilometers (about 4 miles). Giardini Naxos is a seaside town located just south of Taormina, famous for its beautiful beaches and historical significance as one of the earliest Greek colonies in Sicily. This charming coastal destination offers a perfect blend of history and relaxation. Sites to see include the Archaeological Park of Naxos, Recanti beach, the Museum and Archeological Area of Naxos and the Schisò Castle, a 16th-century fortress overlooking the bay.

Castelmola. Distance from Taormina: 5 kilometers (about 3 miles). Castelmola is a picturesque medieval village perched on a hilltop above Taormina. Known for its breathtaking panoramic views of Mount Etna and the Ionian Sea, this charming town offers a glimpse into traditional Sicilian life. Sites to include: Castello di Castelmola, Piazza Sant'Antonio, Chiesa Madre di San Nicola di Bari and visit the Bar Turrisi, famous for its unique almond wine and quirky décor

Forza d'Agrò. Distance from Taormina: 16 kilometers (about 10 miles). Forza d'Agrò is another charming hill town that offers stunning views of the coastline and a glimpse into traditional Sicilian life. Like Savoca, it was also used as a filming location for "The Godfather" trilogy. Sites to visit include the Castello Normanno, Chiesa Madre, Piazza Carullo and the Convento Agostiniano, a 16th-century convent with a unique octagonal cloister.

Godfather filming locations in Forza d'Agrò:

- Town entrance: As you approach Forza d'Agrò, you'll recognize the iconic entrance featured in "The Godfather Part III." This is where Michael Corleone, accompanied by his bodyguards, is seen arriving in

Sicily. The scene, which establishes the location for subsequent Sicilian sequences in the film, captures the essence of a traditional Sicilian town and sets the stage for the unfolding drama.

- Church of Sant'Agostino: The striking exterior of the Church of Sant'Agostino plays a significant role in both "The Godfather" and "The Godfather Part III." In the original film, it serves as a backdrop for scenes featuring Michael Corleone (played by Al Pacino) during his time in Sicily. Later, in Part III, it's seen again when Vincent Mancini (portrayed by Andy Garcia) visits the town. The church's impressive facade and the surrounding piazza create a powerful visual connection to the Corleone family's Sicilian roots.

- Town streets: As you wander through Forza d'Agrò, you'll find yourself immersed in the same narrow, winding streets that served as a stand-in for Corleone, Sicily throughout the trilogy. These authentic, unspoiled thoroughfares, lined with traditional architecture, provided the perfect backdrop for various Corleone family members and associates as they moved through the town.

The timeless quality of these streets helped director Francis Ford Coppola create a vivid, believable Sicilian setting that was crucial to the film's atmosphere. These locations in both Savoca and Forza d'Agrò were chosen by director Francis Ford Coppola for their authentic, unspoiled Sicilian atmosphere, which helped to create the vivid sense of place that is so crucial to the Sicilian sequences in "The Godfather" trilogy.

Logistics

Train: The train station is in the coastal town of Giardini Naxos. It's approximately 3-5 kilometers (about 2-3 miles) from the center, depending on where you start your journey. It is a stunning train station, and the train line runs right along the ocean.

Bus: Interbus operates regular buses connecting Taormina to nearby towns and attractions like Catania, Messina, Giardini Naxos, and Mount Etna. Buses also provide convenient transportation to Catania-Fontanarossa Airport.

Local Buses: Buses run within Taormina and nearby locations, including Isola Bella and the Taormina-Giardini Train Station. ASM Taormina operates a shuttle bus service that connects key spots within the town, such as the historic center, the cable car, and the train station.

Cable Car (Funivia): The Taormina Cable Car connects the town to the beach areas below, particularly Mazzarò and Isola Bella. The ride takes just a few minutes and offers beautiful views of the coast. It's a convenient way to get from the beach to the town center without driving.

Car: To reach Taormina by car from Catania, take the A18/E45 highway towards Messina. The drive is about 45 minutes and offers stunning views of the coastline.

Parking: Porta Catania Parking–near the southern entrance of Taormina, this garage is convenient for accessing the historic center, including Corso Umberto and the nearby attractions. Lumbi Parking – at the northern end of the town, it offers a shuttle service to Porta Messina and the town center.

Dining Recommendations

The Bam Bar. Address: Via di Giovanni, 45.

The Bam Bar is a popular and colorful café nestled in the charming streets of Taormina. Known primarily for its exceptional granitas, this local institution has been serving up refreshing treats since 1967. The bar's vibrant, retro-style decor featuring hand-painted Sicilian ceramics creates a lively and welcoming atmosphere. While granitas are the star attraction, with flavors ranging from traditional lemon and almond to more unique offerings like peach and pistachio, Bam Bar also serves excellent brioche, gelatos, and coffee. It's a favorite spot for both locals and tourists to cool off on hot Sicilian days or enjoy a sweet breakfast. Despite its popularity, The Bam Bar maintains its authentic, family-run feel, making it a must-visit destination for anyone looking to experience a true taste of Taormina's culinary culture.

My husband and I visited daily for coffee, granita, and brioche, enjoying the lively atmosphere and outdoor seating perfect for people-watching. With its welcoming ambiance, friendly staff, and a range of drinks, including coffee and fresh juices, Bam Bar has become a beloved institution. It can get crowded, especially in summer, so arriving early is recommended.

Pasticceria Minotauro. Address: Corso Umberto, 7.

Pasticceria Minotauro is a beloved confectionery shop located on Taormina's main street, Corso Umberto. This charming pasticceria has been delighting locals and visitors alike with its array of traditional Sicilian sweets and pastries for decades. Known for its high-quality ingredients and artisanal approach, Minotauro offers a tempting selection of treats, including cannoli, cassata, almond pastries, and refreshing granitas.

The shop's interior exudes old-world charm with its classic décor and display cases filled with colorful confections. Whether you're looking for a quick espresso and pastry to start your day, or a box of sweets to take home as a souvenir, Pasticceria Minotauro provides an authentic taste of Sicily's rich culinary heritage in the heart of Taormina.

Ristorante Pizzeria Al Saraceno. Address: Via Bagnoli Croci, 84.

Ristorante Pizzeria Al Saraceno is a charming local establishment nestled in the heart of Taormina. Known for its authentic Sicilian cuisine and wood-fired pizzas, this restaurant offers a delightful dining experience with a view.

My husband and I enjoyed dinner at the Ristorante Pizzeria Al Saraceno, at the top of the hill above the town, on the way to the Castle of Taormina. The views are breathtaking no matter the time. On the night we arrived in Sicily my husband and I walked from our Airbnb in Piazza Duomo, which was 1.1 kilometers away and a 23-minute walk.

We assumed it would be no problem; we had been sitting on planes all day and needed to get some steps in. Unfortunately, I wasn't aware that the route to the renowned church includes steps that zig-zag. At approximately 500 steps, my husband reached the peak of his frustration, but there was no turning back. We worked hard to climb up here, and the food was well deserved. Upon finishing our four-course dinner, a seafood platter for my husband and pasta with pesto for me. And the staff called for a taxi to bring us back to the Porta Catania Gate.

The bay view from our table. Worth it, right?!

Accommodation

If arriving for the FestaFusion events I recommend three nights in town minimum.

*Hotel Metropole Taormina. Address: Corso Umberto, 154

A 5-star luxury hotel in the heart of Taormina offering elegant rooms with stunning sea views, a rooftop pool, and a full-service spa. It provides an unforgettable stay with amenities like free Wi-Fi and air conditioning.

Grand Hotel Timeo, A Belmond Hotel. Address: Via Teatro Greco, 59

This 5-star historic hotel sits next to Taormina's Greek Theatre, offering panoramic views of Mount Etna and the sea. Known for its luxurious accommodations, fine dining, and exquisite gardens, it's one of Sicily's most prestigious hotels.

Hotel Villa Paradiso. Address: Via Roma, 2

A 4-star hotel offering stunning sea views, a central location near the town's attractions, and excellent dining options. The hotel combines classic charm with modern comforts like air conditioning and free breakfast.

*Hotel Taodomus. Address: Corso Umberto, 224

A 3-star warm and welcoming hotel offering comfortable rooms with sea views. Its intimate atmosphere, combined with a rooftop terrace, makes it a favorite for travelers looking for a personal touch.

*These accommodations are located on the procession route for the Festa di San Pancrazio.

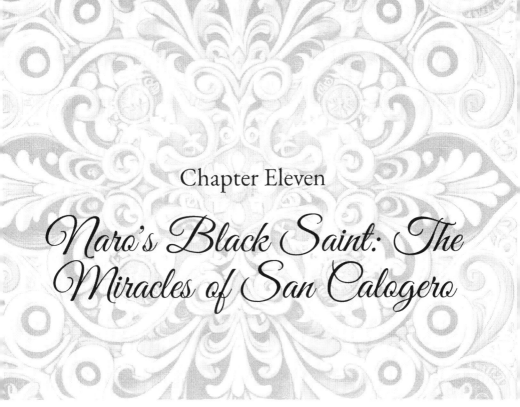

Chapter Eleven

Naro's Black Saint: The Miracles of San Calogero

Festa di San Calogero

Where: Naro

When: June 15-25

Average Festival Temperatures: High: 31°C (88°F). Low: 20°C (68°F).

Discover Naro: Baroque Gem of Agrigento

Nestled in the heart of Sicily's Agrigento province, Naro stands as a testament to the island's rich history and cultural heritage. This charming hill town, often overlooked by casual tourist, offers a glimpse into Sicily's authentic past, with its winding medieval streets, impressive baroque architecture, and panoramic views of the surrounding countryside.

The origins of Naro stretch back to ancient times, with some historians suggesting it may have been founded by the Sicani, one of Sicily's earliest indigenous peoples. However, its documented history begins in the medieval period. The town flourished under Arab rule in the 9th century, as evidenced by its name, believed to derive from the Arabic word "nahr," meaning river.

Following the Norman conquest of Sicily, Naro gained prominence as a strategic stronghold. The powerful Chiaramonte family left an indelible mark on the town during the 14th century, constructing the imposing castle that still dominates Naro's skyline. Throughout the centuries, Naro passed through various hands, including Spanish rule, each leaving layers of cultural and architectural influence.

Naro is perched on a hill about 520 meters above sea level, offering stunning views of the surrounding Sicilian landscape. The town is located approximately 20 kilometers east of Agrigento and its famous Valley of the Temples, and about 30 kilometers from the Mediterranean coast. This strategic position in the heart of Sicily's interior has shaped Naro's history and character. The town is surrounded by rolling hills covered with olive groves, vineyards, and almond orchards, typical of the Sicilian countryside. The Naro River, from which the town may take its name, flows nearby, contributing to the fertility of the land.

Naro is a small town with a population of around 7,000. Despite its modest size, it boasts an impressive array of historical and architectural treasures.

Festival of Saint Calogero

The Festa di San Calogero in Naro is a major religious and cultural event celebrated with immense passion and dedication. In Naro, the cult of the "Black Saint" is deeply revered, as San Calogero serves as the town's patron saint.

From June 15 to June 25, the Friends of San Calò committee hosts joyful festivities throughout the city. The celebration begins on June 15 when the statue of the saint is brought out from the crypt beneath the Sanctuary church, leading up to the major celebration on June 18.

On this day, the statue is transported using a "straula" or "Cart of Miracles". The faithful pull it with a rope over 100 meters long, from the Sanctuary of San Calogero to the city's Mother Church. Participants in the procession shout "Viva Diu e San Calò," and it's common to see them walking barefoot, occasionally even climbing the town's steep slopes to reach the Sanctuary.

As part of the event, bread is blessed to represent the body parts San Calogero has miraculously healed. Devotees bring the bread to the Sanctuary, keeping some to share and leaving the rest for distribution. This tradition symbolizes the saint's healing powers and the community's faith.

During the celebration, a fair and market are held on the city's principal streets, along with cultural events such as medieval theater performances, concerts, and other activities. The festivities culminate in a grand fireworks display in front of the Sanctuary of San Calogero on the night of June 17-18.

Besides the June festivities, there is a procession on January 11 to commemorate the Saint's protection of Naro during the powerful 1693 earthquake, further emphasizing the deep connection between the saint and the town.

Who is San Calogero?

Saint Calogero, also known as San Calogero or Saint Calò, holds a significant place in Sicilian Catholic tradition. He is often referred to as the "Black Saint" because of his African origins. Born in North Africa in the 6th century, San Calogero traveled to Sicily, where he became a hermit and renowned miracle worker. He settled in a cave near Naro, and his reputation grew through acts of healing and protection. San Calogero's legacy is defined by miraculous interventions, particularly in curing the sick and safeguarding the faithful from disasters.

The Saint's influence remains strong in Naro. His significance is further emphasized by two notable historical events. During the 1626 plague, Sister Serafina Pulcella Lucchesi, a Capuchin nun, experienced a vision of San Calogero while praying in his sanctuary cave. In this vision, the Saint assured her that God had heard her prayers and that the plague would soon end. Additionally, historical accounts credit San Calogero with saving Naro from the devastating earthquake of 1693, further cementing his role as a protector of the town.

These events have contributed to the enduring devotion to San Calogero in Naro and throughout Sicily, where he is revered as a powerful intercessor and guardian. The miracles attributed to him, along with his humble origins and dedication to serving others, have made San Calogero a beloved figure in Sicilian religious and cultural traditions, inspiring faith and hope for centuries.

Schedule of the Events during the Festa di San Calogero

Day 1: Saturday (The day before the major festival)

Morning: Naro's streets are vibrant, with market stalls and vendors offering traditional Sicilian food, crafts, and souvenirs.

Afternoon: Local bands and musicians perform in the main square, entertaining both residents and visitors.

Evening: Many devout individuals attend the Vigil Mass, a special religious service held at the church of San Calogero.

The Candlelight Procession is a solemn event where people carry candles, sing hymns, and walk through the streets in honor of San Calogero.

Day 2: Sunday (Main festival day)

Morning: The San Calogero church holds a high mass during which the priest blesses and distributes the bread to those in attendance, symbolizing the blessings of San Calogero.

Late Morning: The streets of Naro come alive with the procession of San Calogero. Dedicated followers carry the statue on their shoulders during the procession, which is a major focal point of the festival. Prayers, hymns, bells, and fireworks add to the atmosphere.

Evening: The procession continues, making stops in various areas of the town. The faithful lining the streets offer prayers and flowers.

Folk music, dance performances, and theatrical presentations are among the cultural events held in the main square and other venues.

A fireworks display ends the evening's festivities.

Day 3: Monday (The day after the big celebration)

Morning: People hold a mass of thanksgiving at the church of San Calogero to express gratitude for the successful celebration of the festival.

Afternoon: Community gatherings bring residents together to share meals, socialize, and reconnect with each other.

Evening: During the closing ceremony, local dignitaries give speeches, and there are final musical performances and dances.

The Festa di San Calogero in Naro is a dynamic celebration that highlights the town's strong religious beliefs and diverse cultural customs, offering an unforgettable experience to both locals and tourists.

Special Festival Treat
Pane di San Calogero (Bread of St. Calogero)

In Naro, Sicily, the Festa di San Calogero is not only a religious celebration but also a culinary event that showcases the region's rich gastronomic heritage. Central to this tradition is the Pane di San Calogero, special bread that holds both symbolic and spiritual significance.

The Pane di San Calogero is a unique bread crafted specifically for the festival. What makes this bread special is its connection to the saint's miracles and the community's faith. Bakers shape the bread into various forms, each representing different parts of the human body that San Calogero is believed to have healed. Common shapes include hands, feet, eyes, and ears, symbolizing the saint's healing powers.

The bread is made using traditional Sicilian wheat and is often flavored with local ingredients such as fennel seeds or olive oil, giving it a distinctive taste that reflects the region's culinary traditions. Before the festival, local families and bakeries prepare large quantities of this bread, viewing the act of baking as a form of devotion and participation in the celebration.

During the festa, the bread is brought to the Sanctuary of San Calogero where it is blessed in a special ceremony. This blessing is believed to imbue the bread with healing properties. After the blessing, some of the bread is distributed to the faithful, while the rest is kept by the owners to share with family and friends.

The tradition of the Pane di San Calogero goes beyond mere sustenance; it's a tangible representation of the community's faith, a symbol of the saint's miracles, and a way for the people of Naro to connect with their cultural and religious heritage. The sharing of this blessed bread among community members also serves to strengthen social bonds and reinforce the collective nature of the celebration.

Walking Tour of Naro

#1. Start at Piazza Garibaldi

Begin your day in the heart of Naro at Piazza Garibaldi, the central square. This bustling piazza is lined with charming cafes and historic buildings. Take a moment to soak in the lively atmosphere, watch locals go about their day, and perhaps enjoy a morning espresso at one of the outdoor cafes. The square is often adorned with colorful flower arrangements, adding to its picturesque charm.

#2. Chiesa Madre (Mother Church)

Just off the main square, you'll find the imposing Chiesa Madre.. Its magnificent baroque façade is a masterpiece of intricate stonework, featuring ornate columns, statues, and a grand central rose window. Step inside to marvel at the opulent interior, adorned with frescoes, marble altars, and beautiful stained glass windows that cast a colorful glow throughout the nave.

#3. Castello Chiaramontano (Chiaramonte Castle)

From the Chiesa Madre, take a brief uphill stroll through narrow, winding streets to reach the Castello Chiaramontano. This medieval fortress, perched on the highest point of Naro, offers breathtaking panoramic views of the town's terracotta rooftops and the rolling Sicilian countryside beyond.

Constructed in the 14th century by the powerful Chiaramonte family, the castle's golden-hued tuff stone walls contrast beautifully against the blue sky. Explore the castle's non-uniform layout, a result of additions over the centuries. Don't miss the square tower commissioned by Frederick II of Aragon in 1330, now integrated into the defensive walls. Walk along the ancient patrol path, imagining the guards of centuries past keeping watch over the town.

#4. Santuario di San Calogero (San Calogero Shrine)

Descend from the castle and make your way to the Shrine of San Calogero. This sacred site, dedicated to Naro's beloved patron saint, exudes an air of tranquility. The shrine's simple yet elegant architecture stands in contrast to the more ornate Chiesa Madre. Inside, you'll find a serene atmosphere perfect for quiet contemplation. Note the various ex-votos and offerings left by pilgrims, a testament to the deep faith and gratitude of the local community.

#5. Palazzo Malfitano

Make your way to the Palazzo Malfitano, a grand palace that exhibits the aristocratic history of Naro. The civic museum may have tours available to explore the interior and experience the lifestyle of Sicilian nobility.

Naro is a town that is filled with other churches to visit! So during your walk, if other churches have their doors open, peek inside.

Naro Festivals Throughout the Year

Festa della Madonna Addolorata (Feast of our Lady of Sorrows)

Good Friday (during Easter week)

The Feast of the Madonna Addolorata is a solemn and deeply moving celebration that takes place on Good Friday as part of Naro's Holy Week observances. This festival centers on a procession featuring the statue of the Madonna Addolorata (Our Lady of Sorrows), which is carried through the streets of Naro.

The procession typically begins at sundown, with participants dressed in traditional mourning attire carrying candles, creating a somber and reflective atmosphere. The statue of the Madonna, dressed in black to symbolize her grief, is accompanied by the haunting sounds of funeral marches played by local bands.

Festa di San Giovanni Battista (St. John the Baptist)

June 24

The Festa di San Giovanni Battista (Feast of St. John the Baptist) is a joyous celebration held annually on June 24th in Naro. This festival honors St. John the Baptist, who holds a special place in Sicilian tradition. The day begins with a solemn Mass, followed by a lively procession through the town's streets, featuring a statue of the saint. As the day progresses, the atmosphere becomes more festive. The town square comes alive with music, featuring both traditional Sicilian folk tunes and contemporary performances. Local dance groups often perform traditional dances, adding color and energy to the celebrations.

Food plays a central role in the festival, with street vendors and local restaurants offering a wide array of Sicilian delicacies. Traditional dishes associated with the feast, such as "pasta con le sarde" (pasta with sardines) and "cuccia" (a sweet wheat berry pudding), are particularly popular.

The evening typically culminates in a spectacular fireworks display, illuminating Naro's night sky and marking the climax of the festivities. This festival not only celebrates the saint but also serves as a time for the community to come together, strengthening social bonds and preserving local traditions.

Day Trip Options: Nearby Sites, Cities and Towns

Ravanusa: 15 kilometers (9 miles) north of Naro. This small inland town boasts a history dating back to the 17th century. Ravanusa is known for its production of high-quality olive oil and almonds, as well as its well-preserved historical center that offers a glimpse into traditional Sicilian life.

- Chiesa Madre: Dedicated to San Giacomo, featuring impressive baroque architecture
- Palazzo Bonaventura: A noble residence now housing the town's library and cultural center
- Parco Archeologico di Ravanusa: Showcasing finds from the nearby ancient Greek city of Kaukana
- Monte Saraceno: Offers panoramic views and houses the remains of an ancient fortification

Licata: 40 kilometers (25 miles) southeast of Naro. This coastal town boasts a rich history dating back to ancient Greek times. Licata is known for its beautiful beaches, historic port, and impressive archaeological finds. The town's economy is based on agriculture, fishing, and, increasingly, tourism.

- Castel Sant'Angelo: A 17th-century Spanish fortress overlooking the harbor
- Chiesa di Sant'Angelo: Houses the famous black statue of the town's patron saint
- Museo Archeologico: Displays important artifacts from the region, including the famous Aphrodite of Licata
- Spiaggia Marianello: A beautiful sandy beach perfect for relaxation

Palma di Montechiaro: 30 kilometers (19 miles) east of Naro. Founded in the 17th century by the Tomasi family, this town is famous as the setting for Giuseppe Tomasi di Lampedusa's novel "The Leopard." Palma di Montechiaro offers a mix of baroque architecture and natural beauty.

Sites to see:

- Palazzo Ducale, the grand residence of the Tomasi family
- Monastero del Rosario, a cloistered convent still active today
- Chiesa Madre dedicated to Maria Santissima del Rosario, with an impressive baroque façade
- Castello Chiaramonte, ruins of a 14th-century castle with panoramic views

Logistics

Train: Naro does not have its own train station. The nearest major station is Agrigento Centrale, located approximately 25 kilometers (15 miles) southwest of Naro. From Agrigento, you can connect to other parts of Sicily, including Palermo, Catania, and Syracuse. However, you'll need to arrange additional transportation from Agrigento to Naro.

Bus: Public bus services connect Naro with nearby towns and cities. The principal bus company serving the area is SAIS Trasporti. Buses run regularly to and from Agrigento, with less frequent services to other nearby towns. It's advisable to check the latest schedules as they may vary seasonally. The bus stop in Naro is located in the town center, near Piazza Garibaldi.

Car: Driving is often the most convenient way to reach and explore Naro. The town is accessible via the SS576 road from Agrigento. If you're coming from Palermo or Catania, you'll need to take the A19 autostrada and then connect to local roads. Renting a car gives you the flexibility to explore Naro and the surrounding areas at your own pace.

Parking: Parking in Naro can be challenging, especially in the historic center, where streets are narrow. There are several small parking areas around the town's periphery.

- Piazza Padre Favara: A small parking area near the town center.

- Via Vittorio Emanuele: Street parking available, but spaces are limited.

- Near Castello Chiaramontano there is a parking area which is convenient for sightseeing

Dining Recommendations

La Lanterna. Address: Via Armando Diaz, 7

This trattoria offers a genuine local dining experience with traditional flavors and a welcoming atmosphere. A perfect spot to enjoy time-honored meals using fresh, local ingredients.

Al Gallo D'Oro. Address: Piazza Cammilo Benso

A popular spot for both Sicilian and Italian cuisine, Al Gallo D'Oro serves delicious pizzas and local specialties, earning praise for its friendly service and authentic fare.

Accommodation

If visiting for the Festa di San Calogero, two nights is sufficient to see the events, sites, and even venture a bit out of town. I did not find hotels directly on the procession route in Naro.

Agriturismo Raffo. Address: Strada Provinciale 12

A 4-star agriturismo located 3 km from Naro, offering beautiful countryside views, a pool, free parking, and a wellness center. Guests can enjoy an authentic rural Sicilian experience while being close to key attractions like the Valley of the Temples in Agrigento.

Dimora Virone. Address: Contrada Paradiso, 13

A charming bed-and-breakfast offering cozy accommodations and a peaceful atmosphere, ideal for those seeking a quiet, personalized stay. Not directly in

Naro's city center.

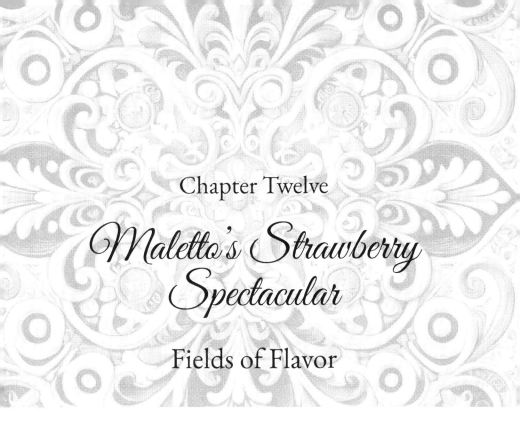

Chapter Twelve

Maletto's Strawberry Spectacular

Fields of Flavor

S agra della Fragola

Where: Maletto, province of Catania.

When: When the strawberries are ripe, late June / early July.

Event Website:

https://www.comune.maletto.ct.it/eventi/sagra_della_fragola.aspx

Average Festival Temperatures: High: 25°C - 30°C (77°F - 86°F). Low: 15°C - 20°C (59°F - 68°F).

Discovering Maletto: Sentinel of Mount Etna

Perched on the northwestern slopes of Mount Etna, Maletto stands as a silent sentinel overlooking the majestic volcano and the surrounding Sicilian landscape. This small, picturesque town, often overshadowed by its more famous neighbors, offers visitors a genuine glimpse into rural Sicilian life, set against the backdrop of Europe's largest active volcano.

The history of Maletto is intimately tied to the feudal period of Sicily. While the area has been inhabited since ancient times, the town as we know it today was founded in 1263 by Manfredi Maletta, the Count of Mineo and Grand Chancellor of the Kingdom of Sicily. The town's name is derived from its founder, serving as a lasting testament to its feudal origins. Throughout the centuries, Maletto changed hands among various noble families, each leaving their mark on the town's development.

Maletto enjoys a unique position at an elevation of approximately 960 meters above sea level, making it one of the highest towns in the province of Catania. This elevation provides Maletto with a cooler climate compared to coastal areas, influencing both its agriculture and its appeal as a summer retreat. The town is 60 kilometers northwest of Catania and is part of the Parco dell'Etna, the nature reserve surrounding Mount Etna. Maletto's landscape is characterized by lush forests, particularly rich in oak and chestnut trees, interspersed with agricultural lands.

Maletto has a population of around 3,500 residents.

The Strawberry Festival

Maletto may be a small town, but it hosts a strawberry festival that's larger than life. Nestled at the base of Mount Etna, Maletto's volcanic soil is rich in nutrients, creating ideal conditions for cultivating extraordinary strawberries, celebrated for their flavor, fragrance, and vibrant color. Every year since 1987, Maletto transforms into the "City of Strawberries," attracting hundreds of tourists and visitors eager to taste this iconic fruit at its best.

The festival spans three days, typically running from Friday to Sunday, and offers a sensory feast of strawberry-based experiences. It's not just a showcase for the town's prized strawberries but a full immersion into local traditions, food, and culture. One of the festival's highlights is the creation of a giant strawberry cake that weighs over a thousand kilos, made by local bakers and pastry chefs. This massive cake is proudly displayed and ceremoniously offered to all attendees, a symbol of Maletto's hospitality and the bounty of its lands.

Throughout the event, the streets of Maletto are lined with colorful stands and market stalls where local farmers proudly display their strawberries in various forms—from fresh fruit sold in plants and boxes to jams, syrups, and desserts. Among the sweet creations are strawberry gelato, delicate strawberry-filled cannoli, and traditional Sicilian cassata infused with strawberry flavors. Attendees can also enjoy unique strawberry granitas, rich strawberry tarts, and pastries drizzled with strawberry coulis. For a refreshing twist, try strawberry-infused drinks, including cocktails and freshly pressed juices. Complimentary samples invite visitors to savor these delights, highlighting different varieties of strawberries, such as the "reflowering" strawberry, which ripens from January to December, and the traditional strawberry, known for its sweeter taste and fragrant aroma.

Local chefs also take center stage, preparing strawberry-based dishes ranging from simple desserts to more creative, savory recipes like strawberry risottos and salads, showcasing the fruit's versatility.

The festival is not only about strawberries, but it also serves as a cultural celebration of Maletto and its surroundings. Visitors can enjoy traditional Sicilian music, folklore performances, and parades featuring locals dressed in colorful costumes. Children's activities, cooking demonstrations, and guided tours of nearby strawberry fields provide educational and fun opportunities for families. The event culminates with a grand finale on Sunday, often featuring fireworks or a concert that adds a festive touch to this beloved annual tradition.

By celebrating its famous strawberries, Maletto invites visitors to discover the charm of a Sicilian town that turns its agricultural riches into a sweet, shared experience.

Walking Tour of Maletto

#1. Castello di Maletto (Manfredi Maletta Castle)

This Swabian-Aragonese castle, constructed in 1263 by Count Manfredi Maletta, served as a fortified tower protecting a vital trade route between Messina and Palermo. The castle was built on the site of a previous Arab-Norman fortification, known as the Torre del Fano, which likely functioned as a lookout.

Visitors today can climb about 100 wooden steps to reach the ruins, which offer breathtaking panoramic views of the Nebrodi Mountains and Mount Etna. The site also gives insight into medieval military life, as it was once a key defensive stronghold for Sicily. The castle is one of Maletto's most iconic landmarks, embodying the town's rich history and connection to the surrounding landscape.

#2. Chiesa di San Michaele Archangelo (Church of San Michele Arcangelo)

The Mother Church of Maletto, built in the 19th century, is dedicated to the Sacred Hearts of Jesus and Mary. At the top of an impressive staircase, its façade is distinguished by a striking contrast between lava stone and white plaster. Inside, the church features three naves separated by intricately decorated stucco pillars, along with marble altars that are neoclassical in design. The 18th-century painting The Transit of Saint Joseph by Marcello Leopardi is of special note. This church is central to the town's spiritual life, and its elegant architecture adds to Maletto's cultural heritage.

#3. Chiesa di San Vicenzo Ferreri (Church of St. Vincent Ferreri)

Another important religious site in Maletto, the Church of San Vincenzo Ferreri, is dedicated to the town's patron saint. It plays a key role in local religious festivals, including processions held in honor of the saint. The church is an integral part of community life, acting as a focal point for religious and cultural gatherings throughout the year.

Maletto Festivals Throughout the Year

Estate Malettese (Maletto Summer Festival)

July and August

Various concerts, events in the piazza that accompany the Strawberry Festival.

Estate Malettese is a summer event in Maletto, Sicily, celebrated with a series of activities and festivities that reflect the town's cultural and social life. Typically held between July and August, it includes outdoor concerts, theatrical performances, art exhibitions, and sporting events, all of which aim to bring the local community together while entertaining visitors. A variety of food stalls often feature local Sicilian cuisine, allowing attendees to taste traditional dishes.

The festival promotes the town's agricultural heritage, sometimes featuring special markets or exhibitions related to Maletto's famous strawberries and other local products. Estate Malettese highlights both the vibrant cultural atmosphere and the scenic beauty of the area during the summer months.

Day Trip Options: Nearby Sites, Cities and Towns

Lago Gurrida: 8 kilometers (5 miles) east. A unique lake formed by lava flows from Mount Etna, damming the Alcantara River. This peaceful spot offers nature walks along the lakeshore, bird-watching opportunities (home to various waterfowl species), picnic areas with views of Mount Etna, and seasonal wildflower displays in spring.

Randazzo: 11 kilometers (7 miles) northeast. A captivating medieval town with a well-preserved historic center. Highlights include:

- Basilica of Santa Maria Assunta: A stunning 13th-century Norman-Gothic church with intricate architectural details and historic significance.

- Palazzo Clarentano: A 15th-century noble residence showcasing the grandeur of the era.

- San Martino Church: Known for its striking architecture crafted from black lava stone, reflecting the town's volcanic surroundings.

- Local Wine-Tasting Experiences: Randazzo is renowned for its production of Etna DOC wines, offering visitors an opportunity to savor unique flavors from the volcanic terroir.

Biancavilla: 31 kilometers (19 miles) southwest. A town known for its baroque architecture and as a gateway to the Simeto River Valley. Points of interest:

- Church of the Annunciation: A stunning baroque masterpiece with intricate design and a significant cultural heritage.

- Piazza Roma: The vibrant main square, lined with charming cafes and a lively atmosphere, perfect for soaking in local life.

- Villa Comunale: Beautiful public gardens offering panoramic views of the surrounding valley and a tranquil spot to relax.

- Local Pastry Shops: Known for their delectable offerings. Try the traditional "ossa di morto" cookies, a must for visitors.

Maniace: 15 kilometers (9 miles) northwest. A small town with a fascinating Norman history. Attractions include: Abbey of Santa Maria di Maniace, a 12th-century Norman monastery, Castello di Maniace (medieval castle ruins), hiking trails in the Nebrodi Mountains, local cheese producers who are famous for Provola dei Nebrodi.

Logistics

Train: The narrow-gauge Circumetnea Railway (Ferrovia Circumetnea) runs around the base of Mount Etna, connecting several towns. It provides a charming and leisurely way to venture around the region. The Circumetnea train stops at the Maletto station, offering connections to localities such as Randazzo and Catania. For broader regional and national connections, the nearest mainline train stations are in larger towns like Bronte or Catania.

Bus: The AST (Azienda Siciliana Trasporti) operates bus services that link Maletto with larger areas such as Bronte, Randazzo, and Catania. Schedules can vary, so it's a good idea to check the current timetable.

Car: To reach Maletto by car, the main highway from the nearest large city, Catania, is the A18/E45. From Catania, take the A18 toward Messina, 30 minute drive.

Parking: As Maletto is a small town with a ZTL (limited traffic zone) in its historic center, you should look for parking outside the restricted area. There are public parking spaces available along Via Umberto, which is just outside the ZTL but still within walking distance of the town center.

Dining Recommendations

Pizzeria Il Canale. Address: Via Professore Putrino, 1

Pizzeria Il Canale offers a variety of freshly baked pizzas with a crispy crust and flavorful toppings. It's a popular spot among locals for casual dining and takeaway, perfect for those looking for authentic Sicilian pizza.

Caffè e Pizzeria del Corso di Portale Vincenzo. Address: Via Umberto, 82/84

This café and pizzeria provides both coffee and pizza offerings, making it a brilliant spot for both a light snack and a hearty meal. They serve pizza made with fresh ingredients and have a cozy atmosphere for dine-in, with extended late hours for evening visitors.

Ristorante Fontana Murata. Address: SS 284 Km 8

Ristorante Fontana Murata is known for its wide range of Italian and Sicilian dishes, offering both traditional meals and modern takes on local cuisine. It's perfect for a more formal dining experience with a menu featuring fresh local produce and seafood options.

Accommodation

Maletto is a small village and does not have hotels. Staying in town for a sagra is not as important as staying over for a festival. If needed, here are a few options nearby.

Hotel Villa Dorata. Address: Contrada Serra La Nave Versante Etna Sud, 95030 Nicolosi

This 3-star hotel is located near the main crater of Mount Etna, offering a charming and scenic retreat. Set in a renovated princely residence, the hotel features elegant rooms with period furnishings. It provides free Wi-Fi, free parking, and breakfast available.

La Fucina di Vulcano. Address: SS. 284 C.da Piano Palo-Difesa, 95034 Bronte

This 3-star hotel restaurant offers a refined dining experience with local Sicilian flavors, complemented by a breathtaking view of Mount Etna. The restaurant specializes in both Italian and Mediterranean dishes, making it a popular choice for travelers.

Chapter Thirteen

FestaFusion Palermo

Melodies and Miracles

FestaFusion Palermo

#1: The Sicilia Jazz Festival: The Sicilia Jazz Festival takes place in Palermo from late June to early July, with performances at the Teatro di Verdura and throughout the historic center.

#2: Festa di Santa Rosalia: The Festival of Santa Rosalia, Palermo's largest festival, is celebrated from July 10th to 15th, featuring processions, concerts, fireworks, and traditional street food in honor of the city's patron saint.

#FestaFusion means two or more festivals happen at around the same time in the same town, so visitors can enjoy multiple events during their visit.

When: Jazz Fest Starts late June and runs for two weeks. Santa Rosalia is celebrated July 10-15th.

Where: Palermo

Event Website: https://siciliajazzfestival.com/

https://ilfestinodisantarosalia.it/

Average Festival Temperatures: High: 30-31°C (86-88°F). Low: 22-23°C

(72-73°F).

Discovering Palermo: Crossroads of Civilizations

Palermo, the vibrant capital of Sicily, stands as a living testament to the island's complex history and cultural diversity. Nestled in the heart of the Conca d'Oro (Golden Shell), a fertile plain framed by mountains and the Tyrrhenian Sea, this ancient city has been a coveted prize for many civilizations throughout its nearly 3,000-year history. Today, Palermo captivates visitors with its unique blend of architectural styles, bustling markets, rich culinary traditions, and the palpable energy of a metropolis that has witnessed the rise and fall of empires.

The history of Palermo is a tapestry woven from the threads of many cultures. Founded by the Phoenicians in the 8th century BCE as Ziz, meaning "flower," the city quickly became an important Mediterranean port. Its strategic location made it a prime target for conquest, and over the centuries, Palermo fell under the control of Carthaginians, Romans, Byzantines, Arabs, Normans, and Spanish rulers, each leaving an indelible mark on the city's character. Roger I of Sicily led the Normans in the conquest of Palermo in 1072, ushering in a period of cultural fusion between Norman, Arab, and Byzantine influences.

Under the Normans, led by rulers such as Roger II, Palermo flourished as the capital of the Kingdom of Sicily. This period was followed by Swabian rule under the Germanic emperor Frederick II and later Angevin rule under the French House of Anjou. Palermo experienced a golden age during this time, marked by thriving trade, religious diversity, and impressive architectural achievements such as the Palatine Chapel.

The Arab-Norman period (9th to 12th centuries) was influential, transforming Palermo into one of the most splendid cities in Europe. This era bequeathed to the city a legacy of architectural marvels that earned UNESCO World Heritage status in 2015, including the Norman Palace, the Palatine Chapel, and the Cathedral.

Palermo's Mediterranean climate, with hot summers and mild winters, has shaped its agriculture, architecture, and way of life. The surrounding countryside, rich in citrus groves and olive orchards, provides a stark contrast to the bustling urban center and offers a glimpse into Sicily's agrarian traditions.

Palermo is home to approximately 650,000 residents, making it the fifth-largest city in Italy.

#1: Sicilia Jazz Festival

The Sicilia Jazz Festival, held annually in Palermo, is a significant cultural event that takes place from the end of June to early July, with the primary venue being the Teatro di Verdura. Launched in 2021 by the Brass Group, an organization founded in 1974 by Ignazio Garsia to promote jazz in Sicily, the festival has grown into a prestigious event. The Brass Group has a deep connection to jazz culture in Palermo, having hosted legendary artists like Dizzy Gillespie and Miles Davis in past concerts. The group is also known for its Orchestra Jazz Siciliana, which plays a central role in the festival.

The festival's aim is to revive Sicily's jazz scene, which traces its roots back to figures like Nick La Rocca, and to provide a platform for jazz performances in iconic locations. The festival features over 100 concerts, with performances from world-renowned artists such as Gregory Porter, Marcus Miller, and Veronica Swift, alongside young talent from local music conservatories. In addition to concerts, the event includes book presentations and video screenings on the history and significance of jazz.

The Sicilia Jazz Festival offers a unique blend of music and culture, creating a magical experience for both jazz enthusiasts and those exploring Palermo's rich history and architecture

The festival takes place in some of Palermo's most prestigious and historic venues, enhancing the cultural and musical experience:

- **Teatro di Verdura**: This outdoor theater, set in the gardens of Palermo, is the festival's central stage. It offers a stunning backdrop for the performances, blending natural beauty with artistic excellence.
- **Santa Maria dello Spasimo:** A fascinating architectural landmark, this 16th-century church, which remains incomplete and roofless, provides an evocative atmosphere for jazz performances. Its open-air setting has been a favorite for blending music with the night sky.
- **Real Teatro Santa Cecilia:** One of Palermo's oldest theaters, dating

back to the 17th century, this intimate venue is perfect for jazz enthusiasts. The theater is the home of the Brass Group, adding historical resonance to the performances.

- **Sant'Anna Monumental Complex:** A baroque structure that now serves as a museum and cultural venue, this complex hosts several festival concerts, providing an elegant setting for jazz to be enjoyed in the heart of Palermo.

These venues not only showcase the best of jazz but also immerse visitors in the historical and cultural richness of Palermo. Together with performances from renowned international jazz musicians like Gregory Porter and Marcus Miller, the festival offers a unique, immersive experience that celebrates both music and Sicilian heritage.

#2: Festival of Santa Rosalia (Il Festino di Santa Rosalia)

For the past 400 years, Palermo has celebrated its patron saint, Santa Rosalia, with a festival from July 10th to July 15th. This is Palermo's biggest festival. The event features sacred processions, firework shows, concerts, and various street delicacies such as cassatelle di ricotta (deep-fried pastries filled with sweet ricotta cheese), pane con la milza (a sandwich of veal spleen sautéed in lard, sometimes with lung, served with or without cheese), and arancini (crispy fried rice balls filled with ragù, peas, and cheese).

Who is Santa Rosalia?

Rosalia Sinibaldi, born in 1130, likely in Palermo, was a noblewoman with an illustrious lineage. Her parents were direct descendants of Emperor Charlemagne, and her mother, Maria Guiscardi, was the niece of King Roger II of Sicily.

Legend has it that in 1128, King Roger II of Sicily was watching the sunset from the Royal Palace with his wife, Elvira of Castile. He saw a figure appear and say, "Roger, by the will of God, a rose without thorns will be born in the house of Sinibaldo, your relative." When Rosalia was born, she was given her name in honor of this prophecy.

As a young woman, Rosalia lived in luxury at her father's villa in Olivella and was educated at court. In 1149, she served as an attendant to Queen Sibylla of Burgundy. According to legend, on the eve of her arranged marriage, Rosalia saw the image of Jesus in a mirror. The next day, she cut off her blonde braids, rejected the marriage, and dedicated herself entirely to her faith—a vow she had made in childhood.

At the age of 15, Rosalia left the Royal Palace, her role at court, and her family's home. She sought refuge at the Church of the Santissimo Salvatore, then a monastery in Palermo. However, frequent visits from her parents and fiancé made it difficult for her to focus on her spiritual path.

She eventually left Palermo, leaving a letter in Greek and a wooden cross for the nuns. Rosalia then took refuge in a cave on her father's estate in Santo Stefano Quisquina, where she lived for 12 years. She marked the entrance to the cave with a Latin inscription documenting her way of life. Later, Queen Sibylla allowed her to return to Palermo, where she lived in a cave on Mount Pellegrino.

Rosalia passed away peacefully on September 4, 1170, at 40.

The History of the Procession of Santa Rosalia

On July 15, 1624, Rosalia's relics were discovered in a cave that now houses the Sanctuary of Santa Rosalia. Earlier that year, on May 7, a ship from Tunis had brought a devastating plague to Palermo. Less than a year later, on February 13, 1625, Saint Rosalia appeared to Vincenzo Bonello, a soap maker mourning the loss of his young wife to the plague. In his despair, Vincenzo considered ending his life, but the saint intervened, saving him. She told him that parading her relics through the city while chanting the "Te Deum Laudamus" would stop the plague.

When her remains were carried through the streets, accompanied by the sacred hymn, the plague miraculously stopped, with no new cases recorded, and the sick were healed. Even today, Saint Rosalia is believed to protect Palermo from disasters like earthquakes, storms, and thunderstorms. Today, the Sanctuary of Santa Rosalia, on Via Bonanno near Palermo, is a church and pilgrimage site built into the stone cliff of Mount Pellegrino, where her relics were found. As Palermo's fourth female patron saint, Saint Rosalia holds a special place in the city's heart.

The Procession

During the Festa di Santa Rosalia, one of the most captivating aspects of the celebration is the grand religious procession through the streets of Palermo. Central to this event are the confraternite (religious brotherhoods), which have been deeply embedded in Sicilian Catholic traditions for centuries. These brotherhoods, made up of laypeople, are tasked with organizing and participating in the procession, displaying deep devotion to Santa Rosalia, who saved Palermo from the plague in 1624.

The confraternite are easily recognized by their traditional garments, which typically comprise long tunics, often white or black, and capes that signify the specific group they belong to. Some brotherhoods also wear distinctive hoods or caps, known as "capi", which are sometimes pointed, and they often carry banners representing their confraternity. These garments not only symbolize their religious commitment, but also visually enhance the solemn and reverent atmosphere of the procession.

As they accompany the vara—the grand float carrying the statue of Santa Rosalia—through the city, the confraternities chant prayers and hymns, encouraging the onlookers to join in reflection and devotion. Their organized movements, combined with the sacred attire, make for a stunning visual display of faith. The procession culminates at the Cattedrale di Palermo, where final blessings and prayers are offered.

The involvement of the confraternite, along with their traditional attire, adds to the spiritual depth and historic continuity of the festival, linking centuries-old religious customs with Palermo's modern-day cultural identity. Their presence underscores the Festa di Santa Rosalia as not just a festive celebration but a deeply spiritual and community-centered event.

The Vara (Parade Float)

In 1686, a significant change occurred in the Saint Rosalia festival processions in Palermo. The four small carts initially used were replaced by a single large triumphal parade float. This float quickly became the centerpiece of the celebration, symbolizing the saint's triumph over adversity.

The float has evolved, becoming larger and more complex. Its boat-like base is key, symbolizing historical plague ships from North Africa in 1624. These Turkish vessels brought the plague to Palermo. This link ties the float to Saint Rosalia's story and her role as the city's protector. As the float became more intricate, it turned into the celebration's principal attraction. Its design, showcasing artistic talent, also tells Palermo's history and highlights Saint Rosalia's significance.

Paolo Amato, the architect, transformed it into a boat shape in 1701, which was later replicated in modern times. Throughout the Bourbon period, which ended in 1860, the lavish eighteenth-century float remained intact, displaying the court's wealth and luxury. Artisans made a grand basin float embellished with cherubs to celebrate the Unification of Italy.

In 1896, they created a parade float inspired by Giuseppe Petre. Its size prevented it from fitting through the city center streets, forcing it to detour through the outer streets. In 1924, they built a fixed carriage to honor the third centenary of the relic's discovery, which featured a central tower reaching a height of 25 meters.

U Fistinu - The Modern Festival

The Festival of Santa Rosalia in Palermo, also known as U Fistinu, takes place from July 10th to 15th each year. The first few days of the festival, from July 10th to 13th, are mainly dedicated to preparing for the grand procession on the 14th and are filled with local celebrations, street performances, and religious services. Here's what typically happens:

July 10-12

These days include various street events, art performances, and traditional Sicilian music. The city is vibrant with festive decorations, food stalls, and cultural exhibitions, all building up to the grand procession.

July 13

Events intensify with more activities and special masses held throughout the city. Local neighborhoods host their own small processions in honor of the saint, and there are concerts and other festive gatherings.

July 14

The artistic and popular celebrations culminate in a vibrant "popular procession" that traces a path from the Cathedral to the sea, representing a transition from darkness (the plague) to light (fireworks on the seashore).

Amidst music, songs, and various choreographies, the annual procession features a large triumphal float in the shape of a boat. Each year, the float showcases a new statue of the saint. The "various choreographies" include symbolic dance and theatrical performances, such as the Danze della Peste ("Dance of the Plague"), which depicts Palermo's suffering during the plague and its salvation through Santa Rosalia. These choreographed performances, alongside the music and singing, dramatize the procession, blending faith with folklore and cultural expression.

A key moment in the procession happens at the Quattro Canti, where the mayor lays flowers on the statue of the saint and shouts, "Viva Palermo e Santa Rosalia!" Later, fireworks light up the Marina (Forum area), marking the culmination of this dynamic and spiritually rich eve.

July 15

This day marks the peak of summer festivities, honoring both the discovery of Saint Rosalia's remains on July 15, 1624, and their first procession through the city on June 9, 1625. The celebration commemorates the miracle that stopped the plague, with the faithful singing the "Te Deum Laudamus" to celebrate the end of the epidemic and the healing of its victims.

Throughout the day, solemn masses are held in the cathedral.

At 6:00 p.m., the main event begins with a grand procession, featuring the Sacred Relics of Santa Rosalia carried in a magnificent silver Ark. The procession winds through the ancient streets of Palermo, pausing in Piazza Marina for the bishop's address to the city, and then continues to the Cathedral, where the day culminates with a final blessing and a fireworks display.

Walking Tours of Palermo

Palermo is like Rome or Venice; it is a city so full of treasure and history that you need a minimum of three days here. I've split the walking tour into two days. If you have limited time, I recommend either following the initial day tour mentioned here or selecting specific places of interest. Remember, Palermo is a sprawling capital city with a substantial historic center.

Walking Tour Day 1: Cathedral and Palazzo dei Normanni

#1. The Cattedrale di Palermo

Our first stops include the Cathedral of Palermo and a visit to the treasury, crypt, and rooftop for breathtaking views. You can start your day on a high note by entering the building as early as 7am, making the most of your time. We started early, not exactly at 7am, but early enough to visit all the sights and scale the roof before noon. If you have limited time in Palermo, prioritize this above everything else. It is a time capsule of art and architecture from the 9th century Arab mosque to recent updates and additions. Get ready to be amazed by its magnificence.

On a side note, the Piazza of the Cathedral has several coffee shops and breakfast options if you need food before you start or halfway through your visit.

Admission to the cathedral is free, but it's advisable to purchase tickets online in advance for the crypts, royal tombs, treasury, roof, and museum. Allocate three hours for this visit.

https://www.ticket-shop-cattedraledipalermo.it/amc/categoria-prodotto/biglieteria/

To avoid waiting in Piazza del Duomo, it's advisable to secure your tickets beforehand, especially for the timed entry attractions. This ticket on the website is called Diocesan Museum + Monumental Complex of the Cathedral + Roofs and costs 15euro.

Naturally, the statue at the Piazza's center is Santa Rosalia, the festival's patron saint.

People officially recognize the Cathedral as the Primatial Metropolitan Cathedral Basilica of the Holy Virgin Mary of the Assumption. The largest church in Italy south of Rome, it was constructed in 1184 on top of a 9th century mosque.

The chapel on the southern side is dedicated to Saint Rosalia, and hosts the monumental silver urn that holds the saint's body. The reliquary ark of the patron saint, created between 1631 and 1637, is an exceptional example of decorative arts representing the pinnacle of Sicilian Baroque. It is a magnificent and intricate creation by silversmiths from Palermo, serving as an unmatched processional monument.

The Building of the Cathedral of Palermo

Count Roger and Robert Guiscard played a crucial role in restoring Christian and Catholic control during the Norman era. In order to commemorate their territorial conquest of the island, they encouraged the construction of magnificent cathedrals in all the locations where the bloodiest battles took place. They set aside the most lavish construction for the cathedral in Palermo.

They promptly converted the mosque at this location for Christian worship. When transitioning to a Christian church, the building's exterior probably underwent only minor changes, such as converting the minarets into a bell tower.

King Roger II established a new kingdom with Palermo as its capital after being crowned in the cathedral. This sparked a period of extensive building in the city. However, on February 4, 1169, an earthquake caused severe damage to the recently converted cathedral, toppling the bell tower and part of the façade. The new Palermo cathedral was completed on April 6, 1185.

During the Norman and Swabian periods, Palermo thrived as a multicultural city where Christians, Muslims, and Jews peacefully coexisted, each practicing their faith. Under Frederick II, the city became the capital of the Holy Roman Empire, and its art and architecture were influenced by a blend of Middle Eastern, Nordic, and Germanic styles for nearly two centuries.

When arriving, be sure to explore the front entrance, walk around the building, and climb to the rooftop. The cathedral is a showcase of architectural influences, from its Arab origins to Norman, Gothic, Renaissance, Baroque, and Neoclassical styles—a true testament to Palermo's rich history.

Interior of the Cathedral

Enter through the 15th-century Aragonese Portico.

The Cathedral's design follows a Latin cross pattern, incorporating three naves divided by pillars. These pillars showcase statues of saints.

Giuseppe Piazzi, an astronomer, created a marble sundial with colored inlays representing constellations during modern renovations on the floor of the central nave. Created in the 17th century, the opulent altar of the Blessed Sacrament features bronze, lapis lazuli, and colored marble, following a design by Cosimo Fanzago.

Inside the presbytery, you'll find a magnificent wooden choir in Gothic-Catalan style from the late 15th century, along with an Episcopal throne that underwent partial restoration using fragments of ancient 12th-century mosaics.

The Royal Tombs

The first and second chapels of the right nave house the impressive imperial and royal tombs of the Normans. These tombs require a separate ticket for viewing.

King Roger II, who ascended to the throne in 1130, originally intended the cathedral he founded in Cefalù to be the mausoleum for his royal family. He had planned and arranged for two sarcophagi made of porphyry to be placed there. Porphyry, a dark red granite from Egypt, was extremely rare and valuable. The Romans reserved its use exclusively for imperial commissions due to its scarcity.

However, when Roger II died in 1154, his family interred him in the Cathedral of Palermo instead. They placed him in a porphyry tomb, though it's unclear how this tomb compared in elaborateness to those he had planned for Cefalù. Roger II's burial in Palermo established a new tradition of royal interments, leading to the creation of this extensive area filled with remarkably grand tombs.

These tombs are extraordinary works of art, unparalleled in their magnificence, and are certainly worth seeing during your visit to the cathedral.

Frederick II moved the two sarcophagi from Cefalù to Palermo's cathedral in 1215, intending them for himself and his father, Henry VI. Frederick II's sarcophagus is striking, with its urn supported by two pairs of exquisitely carved lions and topped by a canopy with porphyry columns.

The Royal Tombs area also houses several other notable burials. These include:

- Constance of Aragon (her crown is on display in the treasury)
- William, Duke of Athens (son of Frederick III of Sicily)
- Empress Constance of Hauteville (daughter of Roger II and mother of Frederick II)

- Albert of Bourbon of Naples and Sicily (son of Ferdinand IV of Naples and Maria Carolina of Austria)

The Crypt of Palermo Cathedral

Accessible through the right side of the cathedral, near the Chapel of Santa Rosalia, the crypt offers a peaceful retreat from the bustling main cathedral. Visitors can enter via either the Sacristy of the Canons or the New Sacristy. This underground chamber houses 23 sarcophagi, many dating back to the Roman period. The oldest tomb, from 1073, belongs to Archbishop Nicodemus of Palermo. In a recent archaeological discovery, researchers found the remains of Archbishop Giannettino Doria, dating to 1642, in one of the Roman crypts.

Among the notable sarcophagi is a Roman one depicting a couple with muses and a Norman sarcophagus adorned with intricate dragon engravings. The crypt's architecture is a fascinating blend of Norman, Gothic, and Baroque styles, reflecting the cathedral's long history. Some of the Roman sarcophagi were repurposed by later Christian occupants, showcasing the layered history of Palermo.

The crypt's cool, dim atmosphere provides ideal conditions for preserving ancient artifacts and remains. Periodic restoration work often leads to new discoveries about Palermo's past. The mixture of pagan and Christian imagery on some sarcophagi illustrates the cultural transition in Sicily during the early Christian era, making the crypt not just a burial place but a captivating historical record of Palermo's rich and diverse heritage.

The Cathedral Treasury

The Cathedral Treasury is one of the most captivating sites in Palermo. Similar to the Crown Jewels at the Tower of London, this treasury houses ancient treasures from various eras, some dating back 500, 700, or even 2,000 years. Palermo's cathedral boasts an impressive collection of gold, silver, jewels, precious silks, and crowns.

The treasures include sacred vestments from the 16th to 18th centuries, altar frontals, and chalices used during Mass. A notable item is the monstrance (an ornate vessel used for displaying the Blessed Host in Catholic ceremonies). One highlight is Constance of Aragon's golden tiara, an exquisite example of medieval craftsmanship adorned with intricate enamels, gems, and pearls. The treasury also holds beautifully decorated books and reliquaries.

This vast array of precious objects not only showcases the cathedral's wealth but also provides a tangible link to Palermo's rich history and the various cultures that have influenced the city over the centuries. Each piece tells a story of craftsmanship, devotion, and the changing artistic styles through the ages.

The Cathedral Roof

Ascending to the roof of Palermo Cathedral offers an unparalleled experience that rewards visitors with breathtaking panoramic views of the city and its surroundings. This vantage point provides a unique perspective on the cathedral's intricate architecture, allowing you to appreciate the ornate domes, towers, and rooflines up close.

From this elevated position, you can marvel at the sprawling cityscape of Palermo, with its blend of historical and modern buildings stretching out before you. The vista extends to the Conca d'Oro, or "Golden Shell," the fertile plain that cradles the city, and beyond to the shimmering waters of the Tyrrhenian Sea. On a clear day, the surrounding mountains frame the horizon, creating a stunning backdrop to the urban landscape.

The journey to the rooftop itself is part of the adventure, involving a series of ramps and spiral staircases that lead to external stairs. This climb not only offers glimpses of the cathedral's hidden structural elements but also builds anticipation for the spectacular view awaiting at the top.

Dome at the Roof Walkway

After descending from this bird's-eye view, take a moment to appreciate the cathedral's interior from a new perspective. The contrast between the soaring heights you've just experienced and the intricate details at ground level provides a comprehensive understanding of this architectural marvel.

To continue your exploration, exit the Cathedral and turn right to cross the alley, where you'll find the entrance to the Diocesan Museum and Bishops' Palace, further enriching your historical and cultural journey through Palermo.

#2. Stanze dell'Archivescovo (The Archbishops' Palace)

This used to serve as the house of the archbishop. The current archbishop may still use parts of the building for official purposes, but it is less common for modern bishops to live permanently in these grand historic residences.

The palace now houses the Diocesan Museum of Palermo (Museo Diocesano di Palermo), which features an extensive collection of religious art, artifacts, and treasures from the diocese, including works from the Norman, Renaissance, and Baroque periods. The museum occupies several rooms of the palace and is open to the public.

Enjoy yourself in the palace's 13 rooms, adorned with artwork from the 12th to 18th century, featuring sculptures, paintings, and exquisite decorations. Just like the cathedral's paid zones, the Archbishops' Palace was completely empty and tranquil when we visited. This peaceful atmosphere allows for an intimate exploration of the room's rich history and artistry.

Each room features unique decorations of Venetian glass, painted ceilings, and hand-painted floor tiles. The attention to detail in these spaces is truly remarkable, offering visitors a glimpse into the opulent lifestyle of Palermo's past archbishops.

Visiting the Archbishops' Rooms is a must for anyone interested in art, history, or architecture. Here, you can trace the evolution of Sicilian artistic styles over seven centuries, from Norman influences to Baroque extravagance. The rooms serve as a time capsule, each one telling a story of the changing tastes and power dynamics in Palermo's religious hierarchy.

The exquisite craftsmanship on display, from intricate frescoes to ornate furnishings, showcases the skill of local artisans and the wealth of the church during different periods. As you move from room to room, you'll notice how styles shift and blend, reflecting Sicily's unique position at the crossroads of various cultures.

#3. Palazzo dei Normanni (Norman Palace)

The Palazzo dei Normanni is a six-minute walk from the Cathedral, with a portion of the path leading through the park. Before visiting the palace, it's a good idea to have lunch. I recommend making a reservation at Ristorante Ai Normanni. The restaurant is conveniently on the route between the two places and has excellent food (see the Dining Recommendations section below).

History of the Palazzo dei Normanni, Europe's oldest royal residence

Originally intended as a fortress and home for the Norman kings of Sicily, construction of the Palazzo dei Normanni began in the 9th century on the site of former Arab fortifications. Under Roger II of Sicily, architects during the 12th century expanded and renovated the palace in a style that showcased the fusion of Norman-Arab architecture, which represented Sicilian art and culture.

Subsequent rulers, including the Swabians and Angevins, continued to use the palace as their royal residence and made additional modifications and additions.

Throughout the 16th to the 19th centuries, the Palazzo dei Normanni maintained its significance as both an administrative and ceremonial hub during the Spanish Habsburg and Bourbon epochs. Renovations during this time included Baroque-style additions and decorations.

Currently, the Sicilian Regional Assembly and the Office of the President of the Sicilian Region are in the Palazzo dei Normanni.

The palace, a fortress for centuries, is Europe's oldest royal residence and has housed the sovereigns of the Kingdom of Sicily, including Frederick II and Conrad IV, as well as the historic Sicilian Parliament. The Palatine Chapel, the primary goal for this visit, occupies the first floor of the palace.

The Magnificent Cappella Palatina (Palatine Chapel)

The Cappella Palatina was commissioned by Roger II, the Norman King of Sicily, in the twelfth century. Roger II's intention behind constructing this chapel was to showcase Sicily's multicultural identity and solidify his own royal authority. The construction of the chapel began in 1132, and it was finished the same year during the reign of Roger II.

Local Sicilian artists and artisans from the Byzantine Empire created these mosaics, which depict scenes from the Old and New Testaments, along with portraits of saints, angels, and biblical figures. You can still see the original Islamic architectural techniques in the chapel's arches, decorative motifs, and the use of muqarnas in the ceiling.

"Muqarnas ceilings" is the term commonly used to describe the wooden ceilings in Sicilian architecture that showcase Arab influence. Characterized by their intricate honeycomb-like design, these ceilings create a visually stunning effect frequently observed in mosques, palaces, and other significant architectural works. Sicily's muqarnas ceilings reflect the island's multicultural past and the architectural heritage influenced by Arabs.

A timed entry ticket is required to visit the Palace and the Cappella Palatina. I want to reiterate my recommendation to buy in advance. The Cappella has a limited capacity because it is a fairly small space, which is why they enforce timed entry.

I suggest using the excellent audio guide for the Capella Palatina. You'll find plenty to see in that small, beautifully decorated room.

Walking Tour Day 2: Centro Storico of Palermo

During the second day, we'll make our way to other important spots in the historic center. I have arranged the walking tour with the map in mind, but skip anything if it's overwhelming.

#1. Quattro Canti

The starting point will be the Quattro Canti, also known as the four corners. In medieval and Renaissance Palermo, the Quattro Canti was a significant meeting point and intersection that connected the city's principal streets and neighborhoods.

The Quattro Canti is a square that symbolizes the four cardinal directions. Between 1608 and 1620, when Sicily was under Spanish rule, the construction took place. The Baroque style exemplifies Sicilian architecture, as seen in the

Quattro Canti.

Elaborate Baroque decorations, such as statues, fountains, and niche shrines, embellish the facades of the buildings surrounding the square. A monumental facade with three levels adorns all four sides of the square, creating a harmonious and impressive architectural ensemble. On the lower level, each corner features a niche housing a statue that represents one of the four seasons, symbolizing the cyclical nature of time and life.

The middle tier showcases a statue representing either a Spanish king or a patron saint associated with the corresponding season below, linking the temporal and spiritual realms. Crowning the composition, the upper level proudly displays the coat of arms of the Spanish Habsburg monarchy, a testament to the powerful dynasty that ruled over Sicily during the Baroque period. This intricate decorative scheme not only beautifies the square but also serves as a visual narrative of the city's history, royal connections, and the interplay between nature and divine order.

#2. Fontana Pretoria

Next to the Quattro Canti, you'll find the Piazza Pretoria and its beautiful Fontana Pretoria.

The Fontana Pretoria earned the nickname "Fountain of Shame" (Fontana della Vergogna in Italian) shortly after its installation in Palermo in 1574. Originally designed for a private villa in Florence, the fountain was acquired by the Palermo Senate and placed in its current location in Piazza Pretoria. The nickname arose from the strong reaction of the local population to the perceived indecency of the statues' nudity.

This reaction was intense due to several factors. 16th-century Palermo was a deeply conservative and religious society, influenced by the Counter-Reformation movement within the Catholic Church. Unlike its original private setting, the fountain was now prominently displayed in a public square, directly facing the Church of Santa Catarina and near other religious buildings. The nude figures, common in Renaissance art, contrasted sharply with the more modest artistic traditions of Sicily at the time. Many locals misinterpreted the allegorical figures, seeing them as representations of corrupt politicians or courtesans rather than classical deities and virtues.

The nickname gained widespread use among the populace and has persisted for centuries, becoming an integral part of the fountain's identity and Palermo's cultural lore. Despite its controversial beginnings, the Fountain of Shame is now celebrated as one of Palermo's most significant artistic treasures.

In the Fountain's design, there are indeed allegorical elements that symbolize the four seasons, rivers, and deities associated with water and fertility. These include figures representing the rivers of Palermo, the twelve Olympian gods, and various nymphs and mythological creatures, all arranged in a complex hierarchical structure that reflects Renaissance ideals of harmony and proportion.

#3. Chiesa di San Giuseppe dei Padri Teatini (Church of St. Joseph of the Theatine Order)

For a panoramic view of Palermo's historic center, don't miss out on the Chiesa di San Giuseppe dei Teatini. Located to the right of the Quattro Canti (Four Corners) intersection, this church offers a unique vantage point. Visitors are welcome to explore the crypt, sacristy, and terrace, which afford. With its frescoes depicting scenes from the life of St. Joseph, the church's dome, one of the largest in Palermo, stands out. Notable for its frescoes depicting scenes from the life of St. Joseph, the church's dome, one of the largest in Palermo, stands out. Offering spectacular views of the Quattro Canti, Piazza Pretoria, and the surrounding area.

Constructed between 1612 and 1643, the church was built under the sponsorship of the Theatine Order, a group of Catholic priests founded in the 16th century as part of the Counter-Reformation movement. The Theatines, known for their commitment to clerical reform and spiritual renewal, left their mark on Palermo with this magnificent church.

San Giuseppe dei Teatini is a stunning example of Sicilian Baroque architecture. Lavishly decorated with stuccoes, frescoes, and marble embellishments, the interior is a sight to behold.he nave and chapels are adorned with ornate altarpieces, statues, and intricate decorative details, all showcasing the richness and devoutness of the Baroque era.

This church not only offers a spiritual experience but also serves as a testament to the artistic and architectural achievements of 17th-century Sicily. Its strategic location near the Quattro Canti makes it an essential stop for visitors exploring Palermo's historic center, providing both cultural insights and breathtaking views of the city.

#4. Chiesa e Monastero di Santa Caterina d'Alessandria (Church and Convent of St. Catherine of Alexandria)

The Chiesa di Santa Caterina d'Alessandria and the convent are in the same piazza. Built in the 16th and 17th centuries. Founded by the Confraternity of St. Catherine, the church in Palermo focused on promoting devotion to the saint and engaging in charitable works. Visitors can explore the convent, the nuns cells, and church for a small fee and discover the fascinating lives of the cloistered nuns throughout history. They also have a rooftop terrace.

I segreti del Chiostro (The secrets of the cloister bakery)

A secret spot within the Santa Caterina complex is the medieval bakery, "I segreti del Chiostro" (The secrets of the cloister). This bakery continues to employ the convent's age-old recipes to create their pastries, preserving and passing down Palermo's culinary heritage for future generations.

While Sicily's baking traditions have been influenced by various historical periods, including Greek colonization and Arab domination, it was during medieval times that the island's distinctive confectionery truly emerged, particularly within cloistered convents like Santa Caterina.

The monastery's bakery has specialized for centuries in making daily Sicilian biscuits, stuffed buns, cookies, jams, and sweets.

Throughout the Middle Ages and the Renaissance, the sale of breads and sweets was a significant income source for the monastery. This tradition continues today, offering visitors a taste of history. Whether you're looking for breakfast, a snack, or a delicious souvenir to take home, a visit to this bakery is highly recommended.

The staff at the bakery, while no longer nuns, are very pleasant and helpful. They take immense pride in their local traditions and creations, so don't hesitate to ask questions about the products.

The bakery operates daily from 9:30 to 1:30 and 3:00 to 6 p.m. For those who prefer not to go through the convent, there's an entrance on the side.

> **Did you know?**
> The tradition of convent bakeries in Sicily dates back to the Middle Ages, a time when nuns played a surprising role in the island's culinary history. Within the walls of Sicily's convents, nuns would create elaborate sweets and pastries as a way to sustain their communities financially. These heavenly confections were often inspired by religious symbolism, blending faith and flavor into treats that delighted both the devout and the aristocracy.
>
> Some of the most famous Sicilian pastries, such as cannoli, cassata, and frutta martorana (almond paste shaped into realistic fruits), owe their origins to the creativity of these skilled bakers. Many recipes remained closely guarded secrets, passed down through generations of sisters. These convent kitchens became renowned for their artistry, using ingredients like almonds, honey, citrus, and ricotta to craft masterpieces that reflected Sicily's rich agricultural bounty.

#5. Chiesa Santa Maria dell'Ammiraglio (Chiesa della Martorana) - The Matorana Church

La Martorana, also known as Chiesa della Martorana, is just a minute away from Santa Caterina bakery. Prepare to be amazed by yet another stunning church, complete with golden mosaics. Most people visit San Marco in Venice for its mosaics, unaware that the ones in Palermo are much older and more breathtaking! You can only visit this church between 10a.m. and 1p.m. every day. Paying 2 euro at the door helps keep the lights on and the church clean.

Established in the 1100s, the church dates back to Sicily's Norman period. Originally, the builders constructed it as a Greek Orthodox monastery in honor of Saint Mary of the Admiral.

Throughout centuries, the church has served as a place of worship for Greek Orthodox and Catholic communities. Presently, it still hosts Greek Orthodox masses. Commissioned by George of Antioch, the church was a project undertaken during his tenure as the admiral and prime minister of King Roger II of Sicily.

#6. Chiesa di San Giovanni degli Erimiti (Church of St. John of the Hermits)

Adjacent to La Martorana stands the Church of San Giovanni degli Ermiti. Its distinctive appearance, characterized by bright red domes atop a square body, gives the church the shape of a Greek cross. The main dome crowns the presbytery, which terminates in a niche. This central dome is echoed by similar ones on two quadrangular structures flanking the church, with the left one extending into a bell tower.

The interior of the church, while sparse in decoration, holds significant historical interest. Its bare walls and simple architecture provide a stark contrast too many of Palermo's more ornate churches, offering visitors a glimpse into the building's complex history. The church's design reflects a unique blend of Norman, Byzantine, and Islamic architectural influences, a testament to Sicily's rich multicultural past.

However, it's the cloister that truly captures the essence of the site's antiquity and tranquility. This part of the complex predates the current church structure and is one of the oldest and best-preserved sections of the original monastery. The cloister features a serene, lush garden that provides a peaceful retreat from the bustling city. An ancient Arab cistern, a remnant from the site's Islamic period, can also be found in this area, further emphasizing the layers of history present at San Giovanni degli Eremiti.

The combination of the church's striking exterior, its historically significant interior, and the ancient, tranquil cloister makes San Giovanni degli Eremiti a must-visit site for those interested in Palermo's rich architectural and cultural heritage.

#7. Chiesa del Gesù di Casa Professa

Just a 5-minute walk from Piazza Bellini lies the Chiesa del Gesù di Casa Professa, a hidden gem in Palermo's rich ecclesiastical landscape. While the exterior might seem understated, the interior is a breathtaking spectacle of color, art, and sculpture, making it one of the most popular spots for photography in Palermo.

The site's religious significance dates back to 844AD when a church dedicated to San Filippo d'Argirò was established here by Greek Orthodox monks, often referred to as Basilian monks after St. Basil the Great. This earlier church and its associated convent stood for centuries before the arrival of the Jesuits.

In the late 16th century, the Jesuit order began construction of the current Chiesa del Gesù, with work beginning around 1564. Initially, the church featured a typical Renaissance facade and architectural elements, reflecting the style of the time.

However, the church's most striking features came later. During the 17th century, several noble families and religious orders sponsored significant renovations and redesigns. These changes transformed the interior into the Baroque masterpiece we see today, while the exterior retained much of its Renaissance character.

The renovation process, which continued into the 18th century, saw the addition of elaborate stucco work, vibrant frescoes, polychrome marble decorations, and intricate altarpieces. This created a stunning contrast between the relatively simple exterior and the ornate, colorful interior that has made the church so popular with visitors and photographers.

#8. Teatro Massimo

The theater is one of the largest and most renowned opera houses in Europe, known for its grandeur and exceptional acoustics. An architectural masterpiece, the theater was completed in 1897. The richly decorated interior, fit or a king, showcases its opulence, making it an artistic landmark of Palermo.

Teatro Massimo

Palermo Festivals and Sagre Throughout the Year

Festa di Sant'Agata (Feast of Saint Agatha)

February 3rd to 5th

The Feast of Saint Agatha is one of Palermo's most important religious celebrations, honoring one of the city's patron saints. Saint Agatha, a Christian martyr from the 3rd century, is revered for her devotion and courage.

The festival includes:

- Sacred processions carrying Saint Agatha's relics through the city streets
- Fireworks displays that light up the night sky
- Traditional Sicilian dishes served at street stalls and restaurants
- Religious services and masses in churches throughout Palermo
- Cultural events and concerts celebrating Sicilian heritage

Palermo Pride

End of June

Celebration of the LGBTQ+ community, promoting diversity, inclusion, and equality. The event has grown significantly since its inception, becoming a major cultural highlight in the city's calendar.

The festival features:

- A colorful parade through the city center with floats and music
- Concerts and performances by local and international artists
- Street parties and social gatherings in Palermo's vibrant neighborhoods

Festival delle Marionette / Morgana (Puppet Festival) Festival

November (exact dates vary annually)

The Festival delle Marionette, also known as the Morgana Festival, is an international puppet theater festival celebrating Sicily's rich puppetry tradition, particularly the UNESCO-recognized Opera dei Pupi.

The festival includes:

- Performances by local and international puppet theater companies
- Workshops on puppet-making and manipulation techniques
- Exhibitions showcasing historic and contemporary puppets
- Lectures and discussions on the art and history of puppetry
- Special events highlighting Sicily's Opera dei Pupi tradition, which dates back to the 19th century and typically depicts chivalric stor- ies and local legends

Presepi di Palermo (Nativity Scenes of Palermo)

Throughout December

The Presepi di Palermo is a beloved Christmas tradition in Sicily's capital, featuring elaborate nativity scenes displayed throughout the city.

The event includes:

- Artistic nativity scenes set up in churches, public spaces, and private homes
- A mix of traditional and contemporary interpretations of the nativity story
- Guided tours of the most notable presepi displays
- Workshops on nativity scene creation techniques
- Special lighting and decorations throughout the city center
- Christmas markets selling local crafts and seasonal treats

This tradition, dating back to the 13th century, blends religious devotion with local artistic expression, showcasing Sicily's rich cultural heritage.

Day Trip Options: Nearby Sites, Cities and Towns

Segesta. Distance from Palermo: 70 kilometers (43 miles) An ancient Greek archaeological site nestled amidst rolling hills, renowned for its intact Doric temple and theater offering scenic views. Sites to see include a Doric temple, Ancient Greek theater, and scenic hillside views.

Bagheria. Distance from Palermo: 15 kilometers (9 miles) Famous for its historic villas and gardens, Bagheria is a draw for art and architecture enthusiasts. Sites to see include Villa Palagonia, with its whimsical statues, other historic villas, and ornate gardens.

Logistics

Train: Palermo Centrale serves as the primary train station in the heart of modern Palermo. It's about a 20-minute walk to the Cathedral of Palermo from here.

Bus: AMAT: The local public transportation company operates an extensive network of bus routes that cover Palermo and its suburbs. Buses provide an affordable way to connect different neighborhoods and important landmarks.

Tram: The Tram di Palermo tramline operates on a dedicated route and offers a convenient means of travel in the city center and nearby regions.

Metro:. Line A of the Palermo Metro, a rapid transit option, provides a connection from the city center to the northern suburbs, including the Central Railway Station (Stazione Centrale).

Car: It's recommended to avoid driving in the city due to heavy traffic, narrow streets, and the complex nature of navigating the historic center. Palermo has a well-established ZTL (limited traffic zone), where access is restricted for non-residents, and fines can be issued if entered without a permit.

Parking: Visitors are encouraged to park outside the ZTL in one of the larger parking garages or lots. Parking Italia or Piazzale Ungheria are good options.

Dining Recommendations

Ristorante Ai Normanni. Address: Piazza dei Vespri 6

Situated near the iconic Norman Palace, Ristorante Ai Normanni offers a sophisticated yet cozy dining experience. Specializing in traditional Sicilian dishes with a modern twist, the menu features fresh seafood, homemade pastas, and locally sourced ingredients. The charming outdoor seating area is perfect for soaking in the historic surroundings while enjoying beautifully crafted meals. I recommend making a reservation, especially during peak times, to ensure a spot at this popular restaurant.

Osteria dei Vespri. Address: Piazza Croce dei Vespri 6

Osteria dei Vespri is a renowned fine-dining restaurant located in the historic Kalsa district of Palermo. Set within Palazzo Gangi Valguarnera, famously known for its role in the film The Leopard, the restaurant offers a blend of Sicilian tradition with modern culinary techniques. The menu, led by chef Alberto Rizzo, is inspired by local ingredients with innovative twists, and the extensive wine cellar boasts over 600 labels from both Italy and around the world.

Antica Focacceria San Francesco. Address: Via Alessandro Paternostro 58

Founded in 1834, this historic restaurant is an institution in Palermo. Known for its traditional street food, including arancine (fried rice balls), pane con la milza (spleen sandwich), and other authentic Sicilian dishes, it's a great place to experience the flavors of Palermo's food heritage.

Accommodation

If you are able, I advise four nights in Palermo. The events of Santa Rosalia are significant, and if you want to do Jazz Fest events, plus walking tours four nights will be necessary.

**Palazzo Arone dei Baroni di Valentino. Address: Via Maqueda 91

This stunning historic residence is a short walk from the Quattro Canti. A private noble house with eight elegant rooms and suites, it offers beautifully preserved salons, antiques, and priceless cultural collections, making it an intimate yet grand boutique B&B experience.

*Hotel Quintocanto. Address: Corso Vittorio Emanuele 310

This 4-star hotel offers modern comforts and an excellent location right by the famous Quattro Canti. Its sleek design, a combination of classic and contemporary, is complemented by a spa, making it a perfect retreat after exploring the city.

*Eurostars Centrale Palace Hotel. Address: Via Vittorio Emanuele 327

A 4-star hotel in a historic building just minutes from the Cathedral. With elegant interiors, antique furnishings, and a rooftop restaurant offering views over Palermo, it combines luxury with convenience for those wanting to immerse themselves in the city's culture.

**Massimo Plaza Hotel. Address: Via Maqueda 437

Near the Teatro Massimo, this 4-star boutique hotel provides personalized service with spacious rooms. Its prime location allows easy access to Palermo's Cathedral and the historic heart of the city.

* These hotels are directly along Via Vittorio Emanuele, placing them on or near the procession route for Santa Rosalia. This would offer excellent access to the event.

** These are centrally located, though slightly off the primary route for the procession, but still within easy walking distance of key event points.

Chapter Fourteen

Sun, Sand and Splendor at Mondello

Immersion Experience

M ondello Beach: Palermo's Seaside Gem

Nestled between the imposing Monte Pellegrino and Monte Gallo, Mondello Beach offers a perfect escape from the bustling city of Palermo. This iconic Sicilian shoreline, with its powdery white sands and shallow turquoise waters, has long been a favorite among locals and tourists alike.

Why Mondello Beach Stands Out

Mondello Beach is renowned for its natural beauty, where soft, white sand meets crystal-clear waters, creating a paradise-like setting. The shallow waters make it ideal for swimming and wading, especially for families with young children. Surrounded by lush, mountainous landscapes, the beach has an almost secluded feel despite its popularity. Adding to its charm are the colorful wooden bathing huts lining the shore, echoing its 19th-century origins as a glamorous destination for European aristocrats. The beach boasts a vibrant atmosphere, especially during summer, with a lively mix of locals and tourists enjoying its offerings.

Visitors to Mondello Beach can indulge in a variety of activities. Beach relaxation is, of course, the primary draw, with ample opportunities for sunbathing, swimming, and enjoying the Mediterranean climate. Water sports such as windsurfing and sailing are popular for the more adventurous, thanks to the area's favorable winds. Beyond the beach, Mondello Village offers a chance to explore Liberty-style villas and stroll along the charming seaside promenade. Nature enthusiasts will appreciate the nearby Capo Gallo Nature Reserve, which features hiking trails with breathtaking coastal views. The crystal-clear waters also provide excellent conditions for snorkeling, allowing visitors to discover the vibrant marine life beneath the surface.

Culinary Delights

Mondello's culinary scene is a testament to Sicily's rich gastronomic heritage. Seafood specialties dominate the menus of local restaurants, with dishes like pasta con le sarde (pasta with sardines) and arancini (stuffed rice balls) being must-tries.

The beachfront is lined with charming restaurants and trattorias, offering the perfect setting for al fresco dining with views of the Mediterranean. For an authentic experience, visitors should check out the small fish market near the beach, where they can watch locals bargain for the catch of the day – a true slice of Sicilian life.

Getting There from Palermo

Located just 11 kilometers (7 miles) north of Palermo's city center, Mondello Beach is easily accessible. The journey takes about 20-30 minutes by car or taxi, depending on traffic.

For those preferring public transport, the 806 bus from Palermo runs frequently, especially during the summer months, offering a scenic ride to the beach. Alternatively, for a more active and immersive experience, visitors can rent a bike in Palermo and enjoy a picturesque coastal ride to Mondello.

Historical Significance

Mondello Beach has a rich history, having transformed from a swampy marshland into a coveted resort destination. The area is dotted with Art Nouveau architecture, each building telling its own story of the beach's glamorous past. A notable landmark is the famous Mondello pier, built in 1933, which was originally designed as a landing dock for seaplanes – a fascinating remnant of the area's luxurious heyday.

Nightlife

As day turns to night, Mondello takes on a different character. The beach becomes a gathering place for young locals, with a relaxed atmosphere featuring impromptu music sessions and bonfires. Unlike the more intense nightlife of Palermo, Mondello offers a laid-back evening scene, perfect for stargazing and socializing under the Sicilian sky.

Best Time to Visit

Mondello is beautiful all year, but the best time to visit depends on personal taste. July and August are the busiest and hottest months. For milder weather and fewer crowds, consider May-June or September-October. These months offer comfortable temperatures and a relaxed vibe. In May, you can catch the Windsurf World Festival, a highlight for water sports fans.

Practical Tips

When visiting Mondello Beach, it's advisable to bring or rent an umbrella, as the beach can get quite hot during peak summer months. Many beach clubs charge for loungers and umbrellas, so arriving early is recommended to secure a good spot.

While perfect for families and casual swimmers, the shallow waters extend quite far out, which may be less ideal for serious swimmers. Food lovers should try the local specialty "pane con le panelle" (chickpea fritter sandwich) available from beachside vendors. Lastly, visitors should remember that Mondello Beach is part of a protected marine area, so respecting the environment is crucial to preserving its natural beauty for future generations.

Whether seeking relaxation, adventure, or a deep dive into Sicilian culture, Mondello Beach delivers on all fronts. Its unique combination of natural beauty, rich history, and vibrant atmosphere makes it a true gem of the Sicilian coastline, inviting visitors to create lasting memories against the backdrop of the Mediterranean's sparkling waters.

Chapter Fifteen

The Magna Via Francigena

Immersion Experience: Palermo to Agrigento

The Great Way of the Francigena

A pilgrim route from France to Rome that connected other lands of the Norman French

A "cammino" (Italian for "walk" or "path") refers to a pilgrimage or long-distance trail, usually undertaken for spiritual, cultural, or personal reasons. In Italy, "cammini" are deeply rooted in both religious tradition and a desire to connect with nature and history. Here's an overview of what a cammino represents, why Italians have a tradition of doing these walks, and how this practice is developing.

I understand that embarking on a Cammino—those long pilgrimage walks that span great distances—is something you need to plan carefully for. It requires preparation, time, and physical endurance, and it's not for everyone. However, these routes are rich in history and tradition, making them popular pilgrimage options. Even if you're not sure if a long walk is right for you, I wanted to share the idea that these pilgrimages exist. For those who are curious, planning a trip to explore one of these ancient paths could offer a deeply rewarding experience, both physically and spiritually.

Magna Via Francigena

The Magna Via Francigena is one of the most significant pilgrimage routes in Sicily, part of the broader network of ancient Francigena routes that connected pilgrims across Europe. Around 1,000 to 2,000 people walk the Magna Via Francigena each year, one of Sicily's major pilgrimage routes stretching from Palermo to Agrigento. This number can vary based on the season, with the most popular times being spring and fall, as the summer heat can be intense along this 186-kilometer route.

Stretching from Palermo on the north coast to Agrigento on the south coast, this route spans approximately 180 kilometers (112 miles) and is typically divided into nine stages, with an average of 20 kilometers per day. The journey, suitable for hikers with some experience, offers a moderate level of difficulty as it covers diverse terrains, including hills, valleys, and rural roads. The route takes pilgrims through Sicily's varied landscapes, ascending and descending through mountainous regions, and generally takes 7-9 days to complete, depending on the pace and rest breaks. History

The Magna Via Francigena dates back to medieval times and earlier, when it served as a trade and pilgrimage route between the Mediterranean Sea and inland Sicily. The name "Magna Via" translates to "Great Way," emphasizing its historical importance. Pilgrims, traders, and armies once used this path as they journeyed between major Sicilian cities.

Stages

The traditional division of the Magna Via Francigena is

1. Palermo–Monreale: Start in the vibrant city of Palermo, known for its Norman architecture, and head towards the hilltop town of Monreale, home to the famous Monreale Cathedral with its magnificent mosaics. See FestaFusion: Melodies and Miracles chapter for more information.

2. Monreale–Santa Cristina Gela: Cross into rural landscapes, including olive groves and vineyards, while walking towards the small town of Santa Cristina Gela. For more information, see Guarded by Gold:

Moreal's Mosiacs and the Festival of San Castrense chapter.

3. Santa Cristina Gela–Corleone: This leg offers pastoral views, with trails leading to Corleone, a town known for its historical significance and connection to the Mafia, though it now emphasizes its cultural heritage.

4. Corleone–Prizzi: The route continues through more rugged terrain, leading to Prizzi, a village perched on a hill with stunning panoramic views.

5. Prizzi–Castronovo di Sicilia: One of the most scenic parts of the route, with views of mountains and valleys. Castronovo di Sicilia is an ancient town with Byzantine origins.

6. Castronovo di Sicilia–Sutera: This leg passes through the Sicanian mountains, bringing you to Sutera, one of Sicily's most beautiful villages, with its historic churches and caves.

7. Sutera–Racalmuto: Heading further south, the route traverses rural landscapes towards Racalmuto, known for its literary history.

8. Racalmuto–Joppolo Giancaxio: Passing through smaller towns and countryside, this stage takes you to Joppolo Giancaxio, a charming Sicilian town near Agrigento.

9. Joppolo Giancaxio–Agrigento: The last stretch of the journey ends in Agrigento, home to the famous Valley of the Temples, one of the most important archaeological sites in Sicily, featuring well-preserved Greek temples.

The Magna Via Francigena offers hikers a rich variety of landscapes, from rolling hills, vineyards, and olive groves to majestic mountains and coastal views, making it a rewarding experience for nature enthusiasts. Along the way, you'll encounter historical treasures such as medieval churches, Roman ruins, and ancient towns, each offering a glimpse into Sicily's deep cultural heritage.

The route also takes you through the heart of Sicily's culinary traditions, allowing you to savor authentic dishes like local cheeses, wines, olive oil, and pastries. Beyond the natural beauty and cultural experiences, walking the Magna Via Francigena with a group fosters deep connections, as the shared challenges, stories, and camaraderie often lead to life-long friendships formed over the course of the nine-day journey.

Accommodation

- Pilgrim Hostels (Ostello del Pellegrino): Several towns offer pilgrim accommodations at modest prices along the route. These hostels are designed for hikers and pilgrims, offering basic amenities.

- Hotels & Agriturismo: In many places, you can also stay in local hotels, B&Bs, or agriturismo (farm stays), where you can enjoy home-cooked Sicilian meals.

Map

A detailed map of the Magna Via Francigena can help you plan your route. You can find maps from various sources, like local pilgrimage associations or the official Magna Via Francigena website. I also recommend looking on Facebook as there are groups that organize walks there.

Why Do Italians Walk Cammini?

Religious Pilgrimage: Historically, cammini were a fundamental aspect of Christian pilgrimage. Italians (like many other Europeans) walked these paths as acts of faith, penance, or devotion. The idea of pilgrimage is central in Christianity, and Italy, with its many saints, shrines, and relics, offers many opportunities for such spiritual journeys. Walking to a sacred site was a way to purify the soul, seek miracles, or express gratitude to God or a particular saint.

1. Historical Tradition: Italy's history is rich with ancient roads, trade routes, and paths that connected cities, towns, and remote villages. Many of the modern hikes follow these ancient routes, preserving not only the physical paths but also the cultural traditions of the areas. Walking a cammino is, in a way, a journey back in time, offering an intimate experience of historical Italy. Italians have a deep sense of pride in their heritage, and walking these paths allows them to reconnect with their past.

2. Personal and Spiritual Growth: In recent decades, these hikes have become popular as a form of personal exploration. Many Italians

(and visitors) walk these routes not only for religious reasons but also to seek personal transformation, solitude, or mindfulness. Walking a long-distance route provides time for introspection, reflection, and a break from the fast pace of modern life.

3. Connection with Nature: Italy's walks often pass through some of the country's most beautiful natural landscapes, from the rolling hills of Tuscany to the rugged mountains of Sicily. For many Italians, walking a cammino is a way to immerse themselves in the natural beauty of their homeland. The routes often take hikers through national parks, protected areas, and remote villages that they would otherwise never experience.

4. Social and Community Bonding: While many walk cammini alone, there is a strong sense of community among pilgrims. Walks provide opportunities to meet other travelers, share stories, and form friendships. Italians, who value social connections and community life, often find the walking experience as much about the people they meet as the places they visit.

5. Health and Well-being: Walking has long been associated with good health, and Italians have embraced this aspect of walking to stay active and physically fit. Many walks provide a blend of physical challenge and relaxation, offering the benefits of exercise while allowing for moments of spiritual or cultural enrichment.

6. Eco-Tourism and Slow Travel: Cammini are aligned with the growing global trend of slow travel and eco-tourism, which emphasizes deeper, more sustainable connections with places visited. Italians are drawn to the idea of exploring their country on foot, engaging with local communities, and supporting small, rural economies along the way.

Chapter Sixteen

Trapani's Street Food Extravaganza

Stragusto's Feast of Flavors

S tragusto Food Festival

Where: Trapani, Sicily

When: Usually last weekend in July.

Event Website: https://www.stragusto.it/en/

Average Festival Temperatures: High: 31°C (88°F). Low: 21°C (72°F).

Discovering Trapani: Sicily's Gateway to the West

Trapani, a city of myths and salt, stands as a sentinel on Sicily's western coast, its curved harbor reaching out into the Mediterranean like a sickle. This ancient port city, known to the Romans as Drepanum, has been shaped by centuries of maritime trade, diverse cultural influences, and the enduring presence of the sea. Today, Trapani captivates visitors with its blend of history, natural beauty, and strategic importance as a gateway between Sicily and North Africa.

The history of Trapani stretches back to ancient times, with legends attributing its founding to Saturn, who supposedly dropped his sickle here, giving the city its crescent shape and ancient name. In reality, Trapani was likely established by the Elymians and later developed as a port by the Phoenicians. Over the centuries, the city passed through the hands of Carthaginians, Romans, Vandals, Byzantines, Arabs, and Normans, each leaving their mark on its culture and architecture. The medieval period saw Trapani flourish as a major trading port, particularly under Aragonese rule. The city's importance in salt production and coral craftsmanship contributed significantly to its prosperity, a legacy that continues to influence its economy and cultural identity.

Trapani occupies a unique position on a promontory extending into the Mediterranean Sea. The city is flanked by the Tyrrhenian Sea to the north and the Mediterranean to the south, with the rugged Monte Erice rising dramatically to the east. This strategic location has been crucial to Trapani's historical development and continues to shape its character today. The coastline is dotted with salt pans, creating a striking landscape of white pyramids and windmills that have become iconic symbols of the region. Offshore, the Egadi Islands beckon with their pristine waters and unspoiled nature, offering a stark contrast to the urban landscape of Trapani.

Trapani has a population of approximately 67,000 residents, making it a medium-sized Sicilian city. However, its influence extends far beyond its size, serving as the capital of its province and a crucial economic and cultural hub for western Sicily.

Mediterranean Street Food Festival

Stragusto is one of Sicily's most celebrated Mediterranean food festivals, held annually at the end of July in Trapani's historic center. Set in the vibrant Piazza Mercato del Pesce, this five-day event recreates the lively ambiance of ancient markets, offering visitors a rich blend of tastes, aromas, and traditions from Sicily and across the Mediterranean. The festival celebrates street food with a diverse selection of dishes from regions like Palermo, Trapani, Puglia, Tuscany, Tunisia, and even as far as Madagascar and Romania.

In addition to enjoying local and international specialties, visitors can indulge in top-tier Sicilian wines at a dedicated Wine Tasting area, which is perfectly situated along the scenic Tramontana walls terrace, offering breathtaking sunset views. The event transforms Trapani into the "capital of Mediterranean flavors" with culinary tours, food trucks, and interactive events for food enthusiasts.

The Stragusto Mediterranean Street Food Festival began in 2009 and has grown into one of Sicily's most beloved events. The festival also features wine tastings, cooking workshops, and live entertainment, making it a lively celebration of food and culture.

Stragusto features both traditional street food and inventive flavors. Street food artisans, who have preserved their regional culinary heritage for generations, take center stage. The festival is not only about the food but also about celebrating the diversity and charm of Mediterranean culture.

Featured Festival Foods

Panelle: These crispy chickpea fritters, seasoned with herbs, are a Palermo favorite, often served in sandwiches with a squeeze of lemon.

Arancini: Sicilian rice balls filled with ragù, mozzarella, or vegetables, coated in breadcrumbs and fried to perfection.

Sfincione: A thick, spongy pizza from Palermo topped with tomato sauce, onions, anchovies, breadcrumbs, and regional cheeses.

Pane ca Meusa: A sandwich filled with slow-cooked beef spleen, sometimes with lung, typically topped with caciocavallo cheese and lemon, a unique dish from Palermo.

Sweet Treats: Don't miss traditional Sicilian sweets like cassata and cannoli.

The festival also highlights typical Sicilian dishes from Trapani and the surrounding islands, accompanied by remarkable wine tastings, making Stragusto an unmissable experience for both food lovers and cultural explorers alike.

Trapani Walking Tour Day 1: Historical and Cultural Landmarks

#1. Porta Ossuna and Via Garibaldi

Porta Ossuna marks the entrance to Trapani's historic center. This ancient gate serves as a symbolic threshold between the modern city and its rich historical core. As you pass through, you're transported back in time, ready to explore the wonders of old Trapani.

Via Garibaldi, stretching from Porta Ossuna, is a picturesque street that encapsulates the essence of Trapani's charm. Lined with historic buildings, quaint shops, and inviting cafes, this thoroughfare offers a perfect introduction to the city's atmosphere. As you stroll along, you'll get a sense of daily life in Trapani, both past and present.

#2. Mura di Tramontana

The Tramontana Walls, or Mura di Tramontana, are the ancient northern city walls of Trapani. These impressive fortifications were originally built to protect the city from invasions, highlighting Trapani's historical strategic importance.

Today, the walls offer stunning vistas of the city and coastline. Walking along the scenic promenade atop the walls, visitors can appreciate breathtaking views of Trapani and the Mediterranean Sea. This vantage point provides a unique perspective on the city's layout and its relationship with the surrounding landscape.

The Mura di Tramontana stands as a testament to Trapani's rich architectural heritage and its centuries-old role as a key Mediterranean port. A visit here allows you to connect with the city's past while enjoying some of the most picturesque views in Trapani.

#3. Torrino Conca

Also known as the "Conca Tower," Torrino Conca is a fascinating relic of Trapani's renowned fortifications. Located near the Mura di Tramontana on the northern edge of the historic center, this tower is a prime example of medieval and early modern defensive architecture.

The Torrino Conca offers visitors a tangible link to Trapani's past, illustrating how cities once fortified themselves against potential invasions. Its strategic position provides another excellent viewpoint, complementing the panoramas from the Tramontana Walls.

#4. Cathedral of San Lorenzo

The Cathedral of San Lorenzo is a magnificent Baroque church that stands as one of Trapani's most important religious and architectural landmarks. Originally built in 1421 as the Church of San Lorenzo, it was elevated to cathedral status in 1844.

The cathedral underwent significant renovations in 1635, transforming it into a triple-aisled basilica. In 1740, renowned architect Giovan Biagio Amico oversaw further redesigns and expansions, including the addition of side chapels, a choir, a portico, a dome, and four towers. The interior features impressive Neoclassical stucco work and frescoes completed by Vincenzo Manno during this period.

Art lovers will appreciate the cathedral's remarkable collection, including Giacomo Tartaglia's local stone sculpture of The Dead Christ, Domenico La Bruna's depiction of the Eternal Father, and Andrea Carreca's San Giorgio. The most highly esteemed piece is a painting of the crucifixion attributed to Van Dyke.

Located at Via Generale Giglio Domenico, the Cathedral of San Lorenzo is not just a place of worship but a treasure trove of art and history. Its imposing presence and rich interior make it an essential stop on any Trapani walking tour.

#5. Lunch at a Local Trattoria

After a morning of sightseeing, it's time to experience Trapani's culinary delights. Look for a local trattoria where you can sample authentic Sicilian dishes. Some specialties to try include pasta with sardines (pasta con le sarde) or couscous di pesce, a nod to the North African influences in Sicilian cuisine.

#6. Torre di Ligny and Museo Civico Torre di Ligny

The Torre di Ligny is a historic watchtower that now houses the Museo Civico (Civic Museum). This unique site offers a blend of historical architecture and cultural exhibits, making it a must-visit location in Trapani.

The tower itself is a testament to Trapani's maritime history, while the museum houses a collection of artifacts that tell the story of the city and its surroundings. From the top of the tower, visitors can enjoy panoramic views of the city and the sea, offering a different perspective from earlier viewpoints.

As a bonus, the Spiaggia Torre del Ligny, the closest beach to town, is located here. If time and weather permit, you might want to take a quick stroll along the shore.

#7. Lungomare Dante Alighieri

As the day winds down, take a leisurely stroll along the Lungomare Dante Alighieri. This scenic promenade offers a perfect opportunity to reflect on your day while enjoying the beauty of the Mediterranean.

The walk is particularly enchanting during sunset when the sky and sea are painted in vibrant hues. It's a favorite spot for locals and tourists alike, offering a peaceful end to a day of exploration.

Top Sights for Day 2: Natural Beauty and Salt Pans

#1. Saline di Trapani e Paceco (Salt Pans and Windmills of Trapani)

Located between Trapani and Marsala, this area is famous for its traditional salt production, dating back over 2,000 years. Visitors can learn about the salt-making process, which relies on evaporating seawater in shallow basins, and explore the iconic windmills that have been vital to salt production since the 16th century. The Salt Pans are also part of a nature reserve, home to flamingos and other migratory birds, offering stunning views, especially at sunset. Guided Tours: https://wwfsalineditrapani.it/visite-guidate/?lang=en

You can tour the area, visit salt museums, and purchase high-quality local sea salt.

To get from Trapani to the Trapani salt pans, you have a few options:

- By Car: The salt pans, known as the "Saline di Trapani e Paceco," are about a 15-minute drive from Trapani. You can follow signs to Paceco, and there are specific roads leading to the saline flats. It's straightforward with a GPS or a map.

- By Bus: There are local buses that can take you from Trapani to the salt pans. Check local schedules and routes for the most current information. Consider taking a bus to Paceco, followed by a short walk or taxi ride to the salt flats.

- Bike: Biking is a pleasant way to get there if you're up for exercise. The area around Trapani and the salt pans is relatively flat and bike-friendly.

- By Tour: Many local tour operators offer trips to the salt pans. This

#2. Giardino Pubblico Villa Margherita (Public Garden)

Relax in the Public Garden: A peaceful green space in the city's heart, perfect for a leisurely stroll or rest.

3. Piazza Mercato del Pesce (Fish Market)

The Piazza Mercato del Pesce, or Fish Market Square, is a vibrant and essential part of Trapani's daily life and culinary culture. Located in the heart of the historic center, this lively square has been the site of Trapani's fish market for centuries.

The square is surrounded by beautiful historic buildings, including the Church of Sant'Agostino, which provides a picturesque backdrop to the market activities. In the mornings, especially, the square comes alive with local fishermen and vendors selling their fresh catch of the day.

Trapani Festivals Throughout the Year

Processione dei Misteri (Procession of the Mysteries)

Good Friday This is Trapani's most famous and significant religious festival.

During the 24-hour procession, life-size statues depicting the Passion of Christ are carried through the streets. The event dates back to the 17th century and is deeply rooted in local tradition. Visitors can witness the solemn procession, admire the intricate statues, and experience the profound spiritual atmosphere that envelops the city.

Trapani Comix and Games Festival

Third weekend in May

This event is dedicated to comics, games, storytelling, and contemporary mythologies. It takes place at Villa Margherita park in Trapani's historical center. Visitors can enjoy exhibits, meet artists, take part in gaming tournaments, and attend panels on various pop culture topics. The festival attracts both enthusiasts and curious onlookers, offering a unique blend of entertainment and cultural exploration.

Feast of Sant'Alberto (Feast of St. Albert)

August 7

This festival honors Sant'Alberto degli Abati, the patron saint of Trapani. The celebrations include religious processions and fireworks. Visitors can observe the devotion of local residents, enjoy traditional Sicilian music and dance performances, and participate in the festive atmosphere that fills the streets of Trapani.

Festa della Madonna di Trapani (St. Mary's Festival)

August 16

This feast day celebrates the Madonna of Trapani, one of the city's most revered religious icons. The festival features a grand procession with the Madonna statue carried through the streets, along with other festivities.

Opera Festival

July and August

Trapani's Summer Opera Festival is held in various historic venues across the city, including the ancient Greek Theater of Segesta. It features performances of classical and contemporary operas. Music lovers can enjoy world-class performances in stunning historical settings, combining cultural enrichment with the beauty of Trapani's architectural heritage.

Trapani Medievale (Medieval Trapani)

Fall (specific dates may vary)

The Trapani Medievale Festival celebrates the town's medieval history. Visitors can experience a variety of activities that transport them back to the Middle Ages, including reenactments, parades, traditional music, dance performances, markets, and demonstrations of ancient crafts and skills. Many participants dress in period costumes, creating an immersive historical atmosphere. This festival offers a unique opportunity to step back in time and experience the rich medieval heritage of Trapani.

Day Trip Options: Nearby Sites, Cities and Towns

Marsala. 32 km (20 miles) from Trapani. Marsala is a historic coastal city famous for its fortified wine and rich cultural heritage.

Marsala wine, named after the city where it's produced, is a fortified wine that has been a Sicilian specialty for over two centuries. Created in 1773 by English merchant John Woodhouse, this iconic wine is made primarily from white grape varieties such as Grillo, Inzolia, and Catarratto. The production process involves fortification with brandy or neutral spirits to increase alcohol content, followed by aging in wooden casks, sometimes for decades.

Marsala wines range from dry to sweet, with different aging classifications, and are enjoyed as an aperitif, dessert wine, or used in cooking. Visiting Marsala offers a unique opportunity to explore the wine's rich history and production process through cellar tours and tastings, allowing visitors to fully appreciate this important part of Sicily's cultural and culinary heritage. You will find:

- Historic center with baroque architecture. Stroll along the elegant streets lined with palazzi, churches, and piazzas that reflect the city's rich past. Key highlights include the Duomo di San Tommaso di Canterbury, with its grand façade and impressive interior, and the Porta Garibaldi, a historic gate marking the entrance to the old town. The piazzas, such as Piazza della Repubblica, are perfect for enjoying a coffee and soaking in the vibrant Sicilian atmosphere.

- Wine cellars offering Marsala wine tastings. Marsala is world-famous for its fortified wine, and no visit would be complete without exploring its renowned wine cellars. Visit historic wineries such as Cantine Florio or Pellegrino, where you can learn about the production process, the wine's history, and its international significance.

- Stagnone Nature Reserve with its salt pans. The Stagnone Nature Reserve is a breathtaking natural area just outside Marsala. Famous for its ancient salt pans and iconic windmills, the reserve offers stunning views, especially at sunset. The salt pans, still in operation today, showcase a traditional salt production method that has been preserved for centuries.

- Archaeological Park of Lilybaeum. This site, once a key Carthaginian and later Roman settlement, features impressive ruins, including sections of the city walls, mosaics, and remnants of ancient buildings. Highlights include the well-preserved Roman insula (urban block) and the House of the Mosaics, showcasing intricate floor designs.

- Museo Archeologico Baglio Anselmi. Located within a restored 19th-century wine warehouse, the Museo Archeologico Baglio Anselmi is home to an extraordinary collection of artifacts from Marsala's ancient history. The museum's centerpiece is the Punic Warship, a remarkably well-preserved Phoenician vessel from the 3rd century BCE, offering a glimpse into Sicily's maritime history.

Castellammare del Golfo. 40 km (25 miles). This picturesque coastal town is known for its beautiful beaches, historic harbor, and proximity to natural attractions.

- Medieval Castle Overlooking the Sea: This historic fortress offers breathtaking views of the sea and provides a glimpse into the town's rich past, housing a small museum showcasing local history.

- Charming Fishing Port: The picturesque port buzzes with activity, lined with colorful boats and waterfront cafes, making it a perfect spot for a leisurely stroll.

- Piazza Petrolo, the Main Square: This lively square is the heart of Castellammare, where locals and visitors gather to enjoy its charming atmosphere, surrounded by shops and restaurants.

- Nearby Scopello Village and Its Famous Tonnara: The quaint village of Scopello is renowned for its ancient tuna fishery, stunning rock formations, and crystal-clear waters, ideal for exploring and snorkeling.

Mozia (Mothia). 27 km (17 miles). An ancient Phoenician city on a small island in the Stagnone Lagoon, accessible by boat from Marsala.

- Archaeological Ruins of the Phoenician Settlement: Explore the remnants of this ancient city, including temples, residential structures, and artifacts that reveal the rich history of Phoenician civilization.

- Whitaker Museum: Located on Mozia, this museum displays an impressive collection of Phoenician artifacts, including the celebrated marble statue of the "Giovanetto di Mozia" (Young Man of Mozia).

- Ancient City Walls and Gates: The well-preserved fortifications and gates highlight the strategic importance and defensive ingenuity of the Phoenician settlers.

- Cothon (Artificial Inner Harbor): This unique harbor, carved into the island, showcases the advanced engineering skills of the Phoenicians and their maritime expertise.

- Salt Pans and Windmills on the Mainland: The salt flats and iconic windmills near the Stagnone Lagoon offer stunning views and in- sights into traditional salt production methods still practiced today.

Logistics

Train: Trapani has a train station in town.

Bus: Connects Trapani to major Sicilian cities and towns. Local buses available for getting around Trapani and nearby areas

Car: To reach Trapani from Palermo by car, take the A29 motorway heading west. It takes on average 1.5 hours.

Parking: In Trapani, parking can be challenging due to limited spaces in the historical center, especially during peak tourist seasons.

Here are some parking options:

- Porta Ossuna Parking: This is a convenient open-air parking lot close to the old town. It's a short walk from here to key attractions such as the port and the historical center.

- Piazzale Ilio: Located slightly outside the main center, this parking area offers ample space and is often recommended for long-term parking. It's a 10-15 minute walk to the center, or you can catch a shuttle.

Dining Recommendations

Osteria La Bettolaccia. Address: Via Gen. Enrico Fardella 25

A popular family-run osteria offering traditional Sicilian dishes with a focus on fresh, local ingredients. Known for its welcoming atmosphere, Osteria La Bettolaccia serves classic seafood pasta dishes and delicious desserts like cannoli. Reservations are recommended due to its popularity.

Hostaria San Pietro. Address: Via San Pietro 18

A charming restaurant located near the port, Hostaria San Pietro specializes in Trapani's famous seafood cuisine. The menu features an array of fish dishes, including couscous with fish and fresh pasta with sea urchins, offering an authentic taste of the Mediterranean.

Trattoria Cantina Siciliana. Address: Via Giudecca 32

Nestled in the historic Jewish quarter, this trattoria is renowned for its rustic Sicilian cooking. The ambiance is warm and traditional, and the menu highlights regional favorites, including pasta alla trapanese, fresh seafood, and a fine selection of local wines.

Museo del Sale (Salt Museum). When at the salt pans consider lunch at the museum's restaurant, Trattoria Del Sale: Serving authentic Sicilian dishes flavored with local salt.

Accommodation

Stragusto is a type of sagra, a food festival. It is not necessary to stay over, but there are significant sites to see here. If staying, I recommend two nights, and if wanting to tour the Egadi Islands four nights.

Hotel San Michele. Address: Via San Michele 16

A 3-star boutique hotel nestled in the historic center of Trapani, just a short walk from the port. With its elegant design, spacious rooms, and a blend of traditional and modern decor, it provides a comfortable stay with easy access to nearby attractions.

Central Gallery Rooms. Address: Via Garibaldi 58

Located on one of the main streets in Trapani's historic center, this 3-star property offers spacious, modern rooms in a beautifully restored building. The hotel is within walking distance of popular attractions, restaurants, and shops, making it a convenient choice for travelers.

Room of Andrea Hotel. Address: 31 Viale Regina Margherita

A 4-star hotel offering modern comforts combined with historic charm. Located in the heart of the city, the hotel features elegant rooms and suites equipped with amenities such as free Wi-Fi, flat-screen TVs, and air conditioning. Guests can enjoy a rooftop pool with panoramic views, complimentary breakfast, and dining options at its on-site restaurant.

Chapter Seventeen

FestaFusion Erice

Medieval Melodies and Sacred Splendor

FestaFusion Erice

#1. Erice Estate / Summer Festival: A vibrant summer-long festival in Erice featuring concerts, theater performances, and cultural events, celebrating the town's artistic and historical heritage.

#2. Festa di Maria Santissima di Custonaci: An annual religious celebration in honor of the Madonna of Custonaci, highlighted by a solemn procession through the streets of Erice, with locals carrying the revered statue of the Virgin Mary.

#FestaFusion means two or more festivals happen at around the same time in the same town, so visitors can enjoy multiple events during their visit.

Where: Erice

When: Summer Festival July through August. Festa di Maria Santissima di Custonaci last week in August.

Average Festival Temperatures: High: 24°C - 28°C (75°F - 82°F). Low: 16°C - 20°C (61°F - 68°F).

Exploring Erice's Hilltop Secrets

Erice is a historic town nestled in the province of Trapani, Sicily, Italy. Renowned for its breathtaking views, well-preserved medieval architecture, and rich cultural heritage, Erice stands as a testament to Sicily's diverse history. This picturesque town has become a magnet for tourists seeking to immerse themselves in the island's past while enjoying its present-day charm.

Phoenicians, Carthaginians, Romans, and Arabs have all called Erice home at various points in history. The medieval period was particularly significant for Erice, as it underwent substantial development under Norman rule. In ancient times, the town held great religious importance as a center for the cult of Venus Erycina, adding layers of mystique to its already rich history.

Perched atop Mount Erice, approximately 750 meters (2,460 ft) above sea level, Erice commands stunning views of the surrounding landscape. From its lofty position, visitors can gaze out over the city of Trapani and the shimmering waters of the Tyrrhenian Sea. The town's unique triangular shape is defined by steep slopes on all sides, creating a natural fortress that has helped preserve its ancient character through the centuries. Erice is famous for its frequent fog, which has earned it the poetic nickname "City in the Clouds." This meteorological phenomenon adds an air of mystery and romance to the town, especially during the cooler months.

According to recent estimates, Erice is home to a modest population of around 30,000 inhabitants. However, this number is far from static. The town experiences significant fluctuations in its population throughout the year, largely due to the ebb and flow of tourism. During peak seasons, Erice's narrow streets and historic squares bustle with visitors from around the world, temporarily swelling the population and infusing the town with a vibrant, cosmopolitan atmosphere.

#1 Erice Estate (Erice Summer Festival)

The Ericè Estate (Erice Summer Festival) is a highlight of the cultural calendar in Erice, transforming the medieval town into a lively hub of artistic and cultural expression from July through August. Set against the ancient cobbled streets and historic buildings, the festival offers a rich program of concerts, theater performances, art exhibitions, and outdoor events. What makes this festival particularly special is its variety: you could be listening to classical music one evening and enjoying contemporary theater or local folk performances the next.

The performances take place in various locations around Erice, including open-air venues like the picturesque Piazza San Giuliano, as well as within historical buildings like the Church of San Giovanni Battista, which provides a dramatic backdrop for evening concerts. The town's cultural and artistic energy is heightened by the medieval setting, allowing visitors to step back in time while enjoying modern performances.

Highlights of Ericè Estate include:

Classical and Contemporary Concerts: International and local musicians perform in stunning settings, blending the timeless beauty of Erice with captivating music.

Outdoor Theater: Theater performances under the stars bring to life both historical and contemporary themes, offering a unique experience for audiences.

Art Exhibitions: Throughout the festival, art exhibitions are hosted in historical buildings, showcasing works by both Sicilian and international artists.

As the festival runs for two months, it's easy to plan a visit that coincides with the religious Festa di Maria Santissima di Custonaci, allowing you to experience both cultural and religious events in one trip.

#2 Festa di Maria Santissima di Custonaci

The Festa di Maria Santissima di Custonaci, held during the last week of August, is one of the most important religious festivals in the region. The festival honors the Madonna of Custonaci, the patroness of Erice, and the surrounding area. Legend has it that the Madonna's miraculous intervention saved sailors from a terrible storm at sea, and her image has been venerated in the town ever since.

The festival brings together not just the people of Erice, but also visitors and pilgrims from nearby towns, all gathering to pay homage to the Madonna through processions, prayers, and cultural celebrations.

Day-by-Day Events:

Day 1 – Last Sunday of August: Opening Mass and Procession of the Banner

8:00 a.m. The festival opens with a solemn mass in the Church of Maria Santissima di Custonaci. Local dignitaries, clergy, and faithful gather for this important service.

10:00 a.m. Following the mass, the Procession of the Banner takes place. This symbolic procession moves through the streets of Erice, marking the official start of the festival.

6:00 p.m. The evening brings performances of sacred music in Piazza San Giuliano, with local choirs honoring the Madonna.

Day 2 – Monday: Cultural Events and Pilgrimages

9:00 a.m. Pilgrims from nearby towns start arriving in Erice, many of them on foot, to pay their respects to the Madonna.

12:00 p.m. Exhibitions related to the history of the Madonna and the Custonaci cult are held in the town's museums and cultural centers.

8:00 p.m. A theatrical performance takes place in the town center, portraying key moments in the legend of the Madonna's miraculous interventions.

Day 3 – Tuesday: Solemn Procession of the Madonna

8:00 a.m. Another morning mass is held at the Church of Maria Santissima di Custonaci.

6:00 p.m. The most anticipated event of the festival – the Solemn Procession of the Madonna through the streets of Erice. The statue of the Madonna, beautifully adorned with flowers and jewels, is carried by local men, accompanied by prayers, hymns, and a brass band.

9:00 p.m. As the procession winds through Erice, it makes stops at important points in the town for blessings and prayers. Crowds line the streets, holding candles, creating an atmosphere of reverence and devotion.

11:00 p.m. The day ends with a spectacular fireworks display visible from across the valley, lighting up the night sky over Erice.

Day 4 – Wednesday: Feast Day Celebrations and Farewell

10:00 a.m. A final mass is held in honor of the Madonna, where offerings are made by the local community.

4:00 p.m. Cultural performances continue in the main square, including folk music and traditional Sicilian dancing.

8:00 p.m. The festival concludes with a closing concert in the Piazza, celebrating both the religious and cultural significance of the event.

Walking Tour of Erice

#1. Porta Trapani

The tour of Erice begins at Porta Trapani, the ancient stone gateway that welcomes you into the heart of the town. This entry point sets the tone for what's to come as you step through the same archway that countless travelers and pilgrims have passed through over the centuries. Built in the medieval period, Porta Trapani is an ideal starting point for understanding Erice's history of defense and its strategic position atop Mount Erice. As you step through the gate, pause to appreciate the remarkable view of the countryside and coastline stretching below. This first glimpse of Erice's elevated vantage point is just a taste of the panoramic vistas that await you as you explore.

#2. Chiesa Madre and the Bell Tower

A short walk from Porta Trapani will bring you to the Chiesa Madre, or Mother Church, an imposing Gothic structure built in the 14th century. Originally commissioned by King Frederick III of Aragon, the Chiesa Madre was both a place of worship and a defensive outpost, as evidenced by its fortified bell tower.

Before you enter, take a moment to admire the exterior, which features crenellated battlements and a stunning rose window above the main portal. Step inside the church to experience its serene beauty, with vaulted ceilings, arches, and quiet chapels that provide a peaceful respite from the outside world. For an even more breathtaking experience, climb the church's bell tower, where you'll be rewarded with sweeping views over the town's red-tiled rooftops, the sparkling Tyrrhenian Sea, and the distant Aegadian (Egadi) Islands.

Bell tower and Chiesa Madre

#3. Via Vittorio Emanuele: A Stroll Through Erice's Heart

From the Chiesa Madre, follow the cobbled streets of Via Vittorio Emanuele, one of Erice's main thoroughfares. This street is the beating heart of the town, lined with charming shops, cafes, and artisanal boutiques selling everything from local ceramics to handwoven textiles.

#4. Castello di Venere: The Crown Jewel of Erice

Continue your journey uphill toward Erice's most iconic landmark, the Castello di Venere (Venus Castle). Perched on the edge of a cliff, this 12th-century Norman castle was built on the ruins of a temple dedicated to Venus Erycina, the goddess of love and fertility. The temple was a major pilgrimage site in ancient times, attracting sailors and travelers seeking the goddess's favor.

Walk through the castle's impressive stone archways, and as you explore the ruins, imagine the pilgrims who once made their offerings here. While much of the temple is gone, the aura of mystery and legend lingers. The castle offers one of the most awe-inspiring panoramic views in all of Sicily—on a clear day, you can see as far as the salt flats of Trapani, the Egadi Islands, and the distant coast of Tunisia.

#5. The Balio Towers

Just beyond the castle, you'll encounter the Torri del Balio (Balio Towers), two ancient watchtowers that were part of Erice's defensive fortifications. Standing sentinel over the town, these towers offer another vantage point for breathtaking views. Climb to the top and imagine the medieval guards who once stood watch here, keeping an eye on the surrounding seas for approaching enemies. From this height, it's easy to understand why Erice was considered an impregnable fortress town throughout much of its history.

#6. Piazza Umberto I: The Town's Social Hub

Next, make your way back toward Piazza Umberto I, the main square in the heart of Erice. This piazza has been the town's social and cultural hub for centuries, where locals gather to catch up on the latest news, and visitors mingle with residents over coffee or a glass of wine.

Here, you'll find a few of Erice's notable landmarks, including the Chiesa di San Giuliano, an elegant 17th-century church with a striking baroque façade. The church is another testament to Erice's deep religious roots, and its interior is equally captivating, featuring intricate stucco work and a beautifully adorned altar.

#7. Erice's Hidden Corners and Churches

As you continue to explore, venture off the main streets to discover Erice's hidden gems. The town is home to over 60 churches, many of which are tucked away in quiet corners. Among them is the Chiesa di San Martino, a small but beautiful church with intricate baroque details and a peaceful atmosphere. Another must-see is the Chiesa di San Giovanni Battista, which offers a more intimate, spiritual experience.

#8. Via Guarnotti

Wander into Via Guarnotti, one of Erice's quieter streets, where the medieval stone houses seem frozen in time. The silence here is palpable, and you'll feel as if you've stepped back into a distant century. As you explore these hidden alleys, you may stumble upon an ancient stone courtyard or a small, family-run shop selling handmade goods.

#9. Pepoli Museum

End your walking tour at the Museo Cordici (Pepoli Museum), housed in a historic palazzo in the town center. The museum is dedicated to Erice's archaeological history and cultural heritage, with exhibits featuring artifacts from the ancient temple of Venus, medieval relics, and Renaissance art. The museum offers deeper insight into the layers of history that define Erice, from its ancient roots to its medieval rise as a fortified town.

Erice Festivals Throughout the Year

Settimana Santa (Holy Week)

The week leading up to Easter (March/April, depending on the calendar).

Erice's Holy Week is marked by deeply religious and somber celebrations, particularly with the

Processione dei Misteri, a procession featuring wooden statues that depict scenes from the Passion of Christ. These statues are carried through the medieval streets of Erice, accompanied by mournful music, creating a reflective and reverent atmosphere. The tradition dates back centuries and continues to be a significant religious and cultural event in the town, attracting both locals and tourists.

Festa di San Giuliano (Festival of Saint Julian)

September 2nd

This festival honors Saint Julian, the patron saint of Erice. The celebration includes a religious procession where the statue of San Giuliano is carried through the streets of Erice, followed by a solemn Mass. The festivities extend throughout the town, featuring local food, music, and other traditional celebrations. The festival has deep historical roots in the town, with Saint Julian believed to have protected Erice from various dangers throughout its history.

Ericè Natale (Christmas in Erice)

Throughout December

During the Christmas season, Erice becomes a winter wonderland. The town is adorned with lights and festive decorations, with the cobbled medieval streets providing the perfect backdrop for holiday festivities. Christmas markets are set up, selling local crafts, food, and holiday treats.

Nativity scenes are displayed across the town, often incorporating traditional Sicilian elements. In addition to the markets, there are concerts and religious services held in the town's historic churches, creating a warm, festive atmosphere. Erice's transformation during the Christmas period is a magical experience for both residents and visitors.

Day Trip Options: Nearby Sites, Cities, and Towns

Custonaci. 13 kilometers (8 miles) southwest of Erice. A charming town known for its marble quarries and religious traditions. Highlights include: Sanctuary of Maria Santissima di Custonaci, a beautiful 15th-century church housing a revered Byzantine icon of the Madonna. The Grotta Mangiapane, a prehistoric cave dwelling that was inhabited until the mid-20th century, offering a unique glimpse into traditional Sicilian life. And Monte Cofano Nature Reserve which is a stunning coastal area with hiking trails, offering panoramic views of the Tyrrhenian Sea and unique flora and fauna.

Valderice. 7 kilometers (4 miles) east of Erice. A picturesque town nestled between the mountains and the sea. Visitors can enjoy: Molini Excelsior, a restored 19th-century windmill complex, now serving as a cultural center and museum, Chiesa Madre, the town's main church, dedicated to Christ the King, featuring modern architecture and beautiful stained glass windows, and Torre di Bonagia, a 16th-century watchtower offering panoramic views of the coastline and the Egadi Islands.

Buseto Palizzolo. 18 kilometers (11 miles) southeast of Erice. A small inland town surrounded by rolling hills and olive groves. Highlights include: Sanctuary of Maria SS. di Cropani, beautiful church housing a venerated statue of the Madonna, Castello Feudal, ruins of a medieval castle offering panoramic views of the countryside, and Bosco Scorace, a protected natural area ideal for hiking and picnicking, home to diverse flora and fauna.

Logistics

Train: The nearest railway station is located in Trapani. There is no direct train line to Erice itself, but the Trapani train station serves as the closest stop. From Trapani, you can continue to Erice by taking a cable car (funivia) or a bus, both of which offer scenic routes to the hilltop town.

Bus: AST Bus Service operates regular buses between Trapani and Erice.

Cable Car (Funivia) from Trapani: The cable car (Funivia) is a scenic and practical way to reach Erice from Trapani, avoiding the winding drive.

Car: Erice is about a 30-minute drive from Trapani via the SP31 and SP3 roads. The winding roads up the mountain offer stunning views, but they can be narrow and steep.

Parking: There is parking just outside the town center as cars are generally restricted from entering the narrow, cobbled streets of the historical center. The main parking area is Porta Trapani, which is near the gateway to the old town. It is a paid parking lot and within walking distance of the main attractions.

Dining Recommendations

La Pentolaccia. Address: Via Guarnotti, 17.

A traditional restaurant offering classic Sicilian cuisine with a focus on fresh, local ingredients. Their specialty is couscous (often seafood-based), but they also serve hearty pasta dishes and meat options. The atmosphere is cozy and intimate, reflecting the town's medieval charm. Located in the heart of the historic center.

Osteria Gli Archi di San Carlo. Address: Via Apollinis, 3.

Known for its beautiful garden seating and local Sicilian dishes, this restaurant offers a range of meat and fish options, including their signature swordfish rolls. The ambiance is rustic and romantic, making it perfect for a relaxing meal after exploring Erice. About a 5-minute walk from the main square.

Bakery Recommendation: **Pasticceria Maria Grammatico**. Address: Via Vittorio Emanuele, 14.

A must-visit for anyone with a sweet tooth. This famous pasticceria offers a wide variety of traditional Sicilian pastries, including cannoli, almond biscuits, and Genovesi (a local specialty). Perfect for a quick stop or takeaway. Distance from the center: Centrally located within the historic center.

Accommodation

If visiting for FestaFusion Erice, I recommend three nights in town. That will allow for visiting the sites and attending events. There is a lot to do nearby.

*Hotel Elimo. Address: Via Vittorio Emanuele, 75.

A 3-star hotel located in the heart of Erice's historic center. The hotel features simple yet comfortable rooms with traditional decor, many of which offer panoramic views of the surrounding area. It has an on-site restaurant and bar, and guests can enjoy the quaint garden. Right in the heart of the town.

*Hotel Moderno. Address: Via Vittorio Emanuele, 63.

This is a 3-star hotel known for its warm hospitality and prime location. Rooms are simple but cozy, offering free Wi-Fi, a TV, and air conditioning. The hotel's restaurant serves local Sicilian cuisine. Guests appreciate the proximity to the main sites. Located near the main square, within walking distance of key attractions.

Il Carmine. Address: Piazza del Carmine.

Set in a former Carmelite convent, this hotel offers a unique and peaceful stay in Erice. Rooms are simple yet comfortable, with a focus on preserving the historic charm of the building. The hotel includes a beautiful courtyard, perfect for relaxing after a day of sightseeing. Located within a 5-minute walk from the heart of the historic center.

*For the procession during the Festa di Maria Santissima di Custonaci, these hotels are on the procession route.

Chapter Eighteen

Dive Into the Egadi Islands

Immersion Experience: Trapani & Egadi Islands

The Egadi Islands (Aegadian Islands) are renowned for their breathtaking scenery, crystal-clear waters, and charming villages. Spread across three days, you'll have ample time to immerse yourself in the natural beauty of Favignana, Levanzo, and Marettimo, the three main islands, while exploring hidden gems, local culture, and indulging in Sicilian delicacies.

Day 1: Arrival in Favignana and Island Exploration

Begin your trip early in Trapani, catching a ferry or hydrofoil to Favignana, the largest of the Egadi Islands. The journey takes about 30 minutes by hydrofoil or an hour by ferry.

Book your tickets in advance, especially during summer, to avoid long lines.

Arrival in Favignana: Once on the island, you can rent a bike, scooter, or e-bike to get around. Favignana is known for its bike-friendly paths and easygoing atmosphere.

Cala Rossa – Favignana's Jewel in the Egadi Islands

Cala Rossa is often regarded as one of the most breathtaking beaches in Italy. Its captivating blend of striking red cliffs and translucent waters that shift from turquoise to deep blue create an otherworldly landscape. Whether you arrive by foot or by boat, Cala Rossa offers an unforgettable immersion into the natural beauty of Sicily's less-traveled gems.

Why Cala Rossa is Famous: Cala Rossa is more than just a beach—it's an ethereal landscape sculpted by nature. The name "Cala Rossa" (Red Cove) originates from a historical legend tied to the First Punic War, where the waters were said to have turned red from a bloody naval battle between the Romans and the Carthaginians. Today, the cliffs appear in various shades of red, especially during sunset, when the vibrant colors reflect off the rocky coastline.

But it's the water that truly steals the show—crystal-clear, shifting from deep blue to vivid turquoise depending on the time of day and sunlight. The clarity of the Mediterranean makes it a paradise for snorkeling and swimming, offering unparalleled visibility into the underwater world, where you can see fish darting among rocks and seagrass.

Getting There

You can either take a bike or scooter (both popular and eco-friendly options) or rent a boat to reach Cala Rossa. By bike or scooter: The journey to Cala Rossa from the port takes around 15-20 minutes and is a scenic route along winding coastal paths. While the terrain is rugged near the beach, it's part of what makes Cala Rossa so secluded and peaceful.

By boat: You can charter small boats from Favignana's port, offering the opportunity to visit Cala Rossa from the sea. This option provides stunning views of the cliffs and allows for easy access to the deeper waters perfect for snorkeling.

Other Interesting Information

Historical Quarry Sites: Cala Rossa's cliffs were once home to ancient tuff quarries, and you can still see remnants of the stone extraction that shaped much of the architecture of the Egadi Islands and surrounding areas. The quarries create unique natural pools carved into the rock, adding to the surreal landscape.

Best Time to Visit: The ideal time to visit Cala Rossa is during the shoulder seasons, in late spring (May-June) or early autumn (September-October), when the weather is warm, and the crowds are smaller.

Marine Life: The waters surrounding Cala Rossa are rich with marine life, making it a haven for divers and snorkelers. You can spot schools of fish, octopuses, and vibrant sea sponges just below the surface.

Cala Rossa is an unforgettable destination that offers both peace and adventure. Whether you're floating in its crystal-clear waters, admiring its dramatic red cliffs, or exploring its rich history, the cove captures the essence of Sicily's wild beauty. It's the perfect destination for anyone seeking to immerse themselves in the natural wonders of the Egadi Islands.

Dining Recommendations

Ristorante SottoSale. Address: Via Cristoforo Colombo, 55

Known for its refined Sicilian cuisine and focus on fresh seafood, this stylish restaurant offers dishes like tuna tartare, busiate with pesto trapanese, and grilled fresh fish. The cozy ambiance with outdoor seating creates a relaxed island vibe.

Trattoria da Papù. Address: Via Vittorio Emanuele, 16

A charming trattoria offering traditional Sicilian dishes in a casual setting. Specialties include couscous di pesce, pasta alla norma, and swordfish dishes. It's loved for its family atmosphere and home-style cooking.

Quello Che C'è. Address: Via Florio, 17

A hidden gem offering some of the best local seafood, including spaghetti with sea urchins. The focus is on quality and flavor, with a small but curated menu. Casual ambiance and friendly service make it ideal for an intimate meal.

Ristorante Camarillo Brillo. Address: Piazza Europa, 9

A vibrant spot known for its creative takes on traditional dishes using fresh local seafood and organic ingredients. Try the pasta con tonno fresco or grilled octopus for a delightful dining experience. The lively ambiance with indoor and outdoor seating is perfect for a casual yet memorable meal.

These options provide a variety of authentic flavors, whether you're in the mood for traditional Sicilian dishes or more creative culinary experiences.

Accommodation

1 Baglio sull'Acqua

Address: Contrada Madonna, 9, 91023 Favignana, Sicily

This 4-star boutique hotel is housed in a beautifully restored 19th-century Baglio, offering a peaceful retreat just a short distance from Favignana's beaches. Guests can enjoy elegant rooms with views of the surrounding countryside, a serene courtyard, and an Arab-inspired garden. The hotel also features an outdoor pool and an on-site restaurant, perfect for a relaxing and luxurious stay.

Hotel Il Portico

Address: Via Meucci, 3

This charming 3-star family-run hotel is located just steps from the port of Favignana and the town's main square, Piazza Matrice. Guests can enjoy modern rooms with private balconies, a rooftop terrace with sea views, and a renowned buffet breakfast. The hotel is perfect for travelers seeking comfort in the heart of the island.

Day 2: Levanzo–A Peaceful Escape

Your second day on Favignana offers the perfect opportunity to explore the nearby island of Levanzo, a tranquil gem in the Egadi archipelago. Begin your day with a quick ferry or hydrofoil ride from Favignana to Levanzo. The journey takes just 10-15 minutes, but it transports you to a world of serenity and unspoiled natural beauty.

As you step off the boat onto Levanzo, the smallest of the Egadi Islands, you'll immediately sense its peaceful atmosphere. Take some time to wander through the charming village, where whitewashed houses line cobblestone streets, and the pace of life seems to slow down. Stop at a local café for a morning coffee and perhaps a traditional Sicilian pastry, savoring the quiet ambiance and friendly local hospitality.

Grotta del Genovese

One of the highlights of Levanzo is the fascinating Grotta del Genovese. This prehistoric cave boasts remarkable Neolithic and Paleolithic cave paintings, offering a glimpse into the island's ancient past. It's advisable to arrange a guided tour in advance, as the cave can only be accessed by boat or through a guided walking tour. The experience of seeing these ancient artworks in their original setting is truly awe-inspiring and provides a unique perspective on the long history of human habitation in the region.

Beach Adventure: Cala Minnola

Cala Minnola stands out as a jewel among Levanzo's beaches, and for good reason. Located on the eastern coast of the island, this small cove is renowned for its pristine beauty and tranquil atmosphere. The beach is approximately a 30-minute walk from the main port and village of Levanzo, making it accessible yet secluded enough to avoid large crowds.

As you approach Cala Minnola, you'll be struck by the vivid contrast of colors. The beach is composed of smooth, white pebbles that give way to turquoise waters so clear you can often see straight to the bottom. This clarity makes it an exceptional spot for snorkeling, with vibrant marine life visible just offshore. The cove is embraced by rugged, rocky cliffs covered in Mediterranean scrub, adding to its picturesque charm and providing some natural shade during parts of the day.

What sets Cala Minnola apart is its unspoiled nature and lack of extensive services, which contributes to its serene ambiance. Unlike more developed beaches, you won't find rows of sun loungers or bustling beach bars here. This absence of commercial amenities preserves the cove's natural beauty and peaceful atmosphere. However, this also means you should come prepared with your own supplies - water, snacks, and any beach gear you might need for the day.

For history enthusiasts, Cala Minnola offers an additional point of interest. The waters off the beach are home to an ancient Roman shipwreck. While the wreck itself is not visible from the surface, knowing you're swimming above such a significant historical site adds an element of intrigue to your beach experience.

The walk to Cala Minnola from the port is an experience in itself, taking you along a scenic path with breathtaking views of the coastline. If the walk seems daunting, especially in the heat of summer, small boats occasionally offer transportation to the beach from the main port during peak season.

Choosing Cala Minnola allows you to experience one of Levanzo's most beautiful natural settings in its most authentic form. It's a place where you can truly disconnect, surrounded by the raw beauty of the Sicilian landscape and the mesmerizing Mediterranean Sea. The effort to reach this secluded spot is rewarded with an unforgettable beach experience that encapsulates the unspoiled charm of the Egadi Islands.

Beaches closer to the Ferry Port: The most accessible beach from the ferry port on Levanzo is Cala Dogana, which is located right next to the port. This small, picturesque beach offers crystal-clear waters and is perfect for a quick swim after arriving on the island.

Another option nearby is Cala Fredda, which is a short walk south along the coast from the port. It's a small pebble beach with calm, clear waters, great for swimming and relaxing. The path to Cala Fredda is easy to follow, and the walk takes around 10-15 minutes from the ferry port, making it a convenient option for visitors looking for a peaceful beach experience right after disembarking.

These two beaches offer the easiest access from the ferry, and both provide a serene and beautiful spot to enjoy the Mediterranean waters of Levanzo.

Dining Recommendations

Ristorante Paradiso. Address: Via Calvario, 19

This cozy, family-run restaurant is known for its fresh seafood dishes, including spaghetti ai ricci di mare (sea urchin pasta) and grilled fish, sourced directly from local fishermen. The outdoor seating offers stunning views of the sea, making it a perfect spot for a relaxed meal while soaking in the island atmosphere.

Panetteria La Chicca. Address: Via Calvario 23

Panetteria La Chicca is a beloved bakery in the picturesque village of Levanzo. Known for its authentic Sicilian fare, this charming establishment offers a variety of freshly prepared items, including:

- Kabbuci: Traditional Sicilian sandwiches made with pizza dough and generously filled with local ingredients.

- Arancini: Classic rice balls, crispy on the outside and savory within.

- Pizzette: Small, flavorful pizzas perfect for a quick bite.

We love the bakery for its warm hospitality and reasonable prices, making it a popular spot for both locals and tourists seeking genuine Sicilian flavors. Whether you're grabbing a quick snack before exploring the island or enjoying a leisurely meal, Panetteria La Chicca provides a delightful culinary experience that captures the essence of Sicilian cuisine.

Bar Romano. Address: Piazza del Porto, 7

A popular spot near the port, perfect for a quick bite or drink. Known for its light snacks, sandwiches, and granita (Sicilian shaved ice), it's a great place to grab a coffee or refreshing treat while enjoying views of the harbor.

Accommodation on Levanzo

Albergo (Hotel) Paradiso

Address: Via Calvario, 19

A small, family-run hotel offering comfortable rooms with stunning views of the sea. Known for its peaceful atmosphere and friendly service, it's a great choice for travelers looking to relax and enjoy Levanzo's quiet charm. The hotel also has a restaurant serving fresh seafood and traditional Sicilian dishes.

Dolcevita Egadi Eco Resort by KlabHouse

Address: Via Capo Grosso

Dolcevita Egadi Eco Resort by KlabHouse is a 4-star eco-friendly retreat located on the picturesque island of Levanzo, the smallest of the Aegadian Islands off the western coast of Sicily. The resort offers a serene escape, harmoniously blending modern comfort with the island's natural beauty.Return to Favignana: If not staying over, take the ferry back to Favignana to enjoy another peaceful evening on the island.

Day 3: Marettimo—A Nature Lover's Paradise

Ferry to Marettimo: On your final day, take a ferry to Marettimo, the furthest and most rugged of the Egadi Islands, known for its wild landscapes, hiking trails, and crystal-clear waters. The ferry from Favignana takes about an hour.

Exploring Marettimo's Coastline by Boat: Upon arrival, consider booking a boat tour around the island. Marettimo's dramatic coastline is best appreciated from the water, where you can visit hidden sea caves like Grotta del Cammello and Grotta della Bombarda. Many tours offer stops for snorkeling in remote, unspoiled coves.

Hiking and Nature Exploration: Marettimo is a hiker's paradise. After your boat tour, explore one of the island's many scenic trails, such as the trek to the Punta Troia Castle, a 12th-century fortress offering panoramic views of the island and surrounding sea. Alternatively, enjoy a hike through the Riserva Naturale Orientata, where you can immerse yourself in Marettimo's rugged beauty.

Relaxing by the Sea: Spend your final afternoon unwinding by the sea, swimming, and enjoying Marettimo's peaceful beaches. The island's untouched nature makes it the perfect place to soak in the tranquility of the Egadi Islands.

Dining Recommendations

Il Veliero. Address: Via Campi, 1

A charming restaurant offering a variety of fresh seafood dishes with a focus on traditional Sicilian cuisine. Highlights include spaghetti alle vongole (clam pasta) and grilled swordfish. The cozy ambiance and waterfront views make it a perfect place for a leisurely meal.

La Scaletta. Address: Via Umberto, 3

Renouned for its simple, authentic dishes made from fresh, local ingredients. The menu offers delicious seafood specialties like fritto misto (mixed fried seafood) and pasta with bottarga (cured fish roe). It's a popular spot for both locals and visitors, thanks to its relaxed vibe and excellent food.

Accommodation on Marettimo

Hotel Marettimo Residence

Address: Via Telegrafo, 3

A beautiful 4-star hotel residence offering modern, comfortable apartments with private balconies overlooking the sea. The property is set in a peaceful area, surrounded by lush gardens, and includes a pool. It's a great option for families or couples looking for a relaxing stay.

Evening Return to Trapani:

In the evening, return to Trapani by ferry. The ride back offers a peaceful conclusion to your three-day adventure among the crystal waters, hidden gems, and breathtaking scenery of the Egadi Islands.

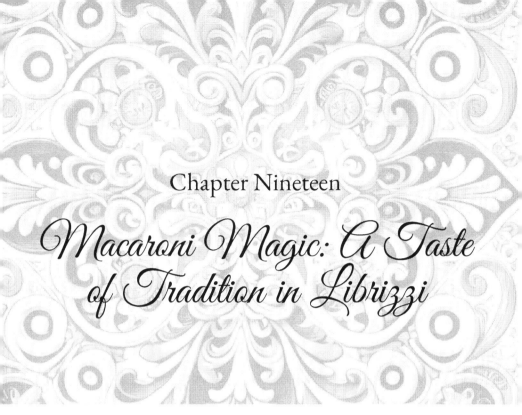

Chapter Nineteen

Macaroni Magic: A Taste of Tradition in Librizzi

Sagra dei Maccheroni

Where: Librizzi

When: First Saturday in August

Average Festival Temperatures: High: 30°C - 33°C (86°F - 91°F). Low: 18°C - 21°C (64°F - 70°F).

Discovering Librizzi: Hilltop Haven of the Nebrodi

Nestled in the verdant hills of northeastern Sicily, Librizzi stands as a picturesque testament to the island's rural charm and enduring traditions. This small town, perched high in the Nebrodi Mountains, offers visitors a glimpse into an authentic Sicilian way of life that has remained largely unchanged for centuries. With its panoramic views, medieval architecture, and strong agricultural heritage, Librizzi embodies the quiet beauty and rich cultural tapestry of Sicily's mountainous interior.

The history of Librizzi, like many small Sicilian towns, is shrouded in the mists of time. While the exact date of its founding is uncertain, the area has been inhabited since ancient times, with evidence of Greek and Roman settlements in the vicinity. The town's name is believed to derive from the Greek word "Eribreches," meaning "abundant in water," a nod to the natural springs that have long sustained the community. Librizzi's recorded history begins in the medieval period, when it was part of the Val Demone, one of Sicily's administrative districts under Arab and Norman rule. Over the centuries, the town developed as an agricultural center, its fortunes tied closely to the fertile land surrounding it.

Librizzi occupies a commanding position at an elevation of approximately 501 meters above sea level, in the heart of the Nebrodi Mountains. This location provides the town with a cooler climate compared to coastal areas, influencing both its agriculture and its appeal as a summer retreat. Librizzi is situated about 70 kilometers west of Messina and 150 kilometers east of Palermo, making it a hidden gem off the typical tourist path. The town's territory extends from the mountainous interior down towards the Tyrrhenian coast, encompassing a diverse landscape of forests, olive groves, and pastures.

Librizzi has a population of around 1,600 residents, reflecting the gradual decline common to many small Italian mountain towns. Despite its small size, Librizzi maintains a strong sense of community and cultural identity. The town is known for its production of high-quality olive oil, hazelnuts, and dairy products, particularly a local cheese called Maiorchino.

The Macaroni Festival

The Macaroni Festival, or Sagra dei Maccheroni, is a beloved culinary event held in the small village of Librizzi, located in the province of Messina, Sicily. Since its inception in 2002, the festival has become a staple for locals and visitors alike, celebrating the simplicity and richness of Sicilian culinary traditions, particularly the iconic macaroni pasta.

Each year, the festival takes place on an evening in early August, typically starting around 8:30 p.m. The streets of Librizzi's historic center, especially Piazza Catena and Via Roma, come alive with the vibrant sights, sounds, and smells of Sicily's finest street food. The heart of the celebration is the preparation of macaroni, handmade by skilled cooks and served with a savory sauce made from local tomatoes, fresh ricotta, and basil. This dish, while simple, embodies the flavors of the region, with all ingredients sourced locally to ensure authenticity and freshness.

The festival began in 2002 as an initiative to honor and promote the traditional foods of the region, particularly macaroni, which holds a special place in Sicilian cuisine. Over the years, it has grown in popularity and become a major event in the summer calendar for both the village and the surrounding areas. The event not only highlights the culinary delights of Librizzi but also offers visitors a glimpse into the village's agricultural heritage, with many families still making macaroni by hand as part of their everyday traditions.

During the festival, visitors can watch the lively spectacle of cooks juggling pots and pans, stirring vast quantities of pasta while singing and shouting, adding to the festive atmosphere. In addition to the famous macaroni, the event showcases a wide range of traditional Sicilian foods, including:

- Maccheroni al Sugo con Ricotta: The festival's star dish, featuring handmade macaroni pasta with a rich tomato sauce, fresh ricotta, and basil.

- Sfincione: A soft, thick pizza topped with tomatoes, onions, anchovies, and breadcrumbs.

- Cannoli and Cassata: Popular Sicilian desserts that offer a sweet conclusion to the meal.

- Local Wines: Wines from nearby vineyards, offering a perfect complement to the festival's dishes.

In addition to the food, the festival offers a variety of cultural experiences. Visitors can enjoy traditional Sicilian folk music, dancing, and guided tours of Librizzi's medieval streets. The village's agricultural history is also showcased with visits to old oil mills, millstones, and water-powered mills. For those interested in history, the Emigration Memory Museum tells the story of local emigrants to Australia and the United States, adding a layer of cultural depth to the festival.

Walking Tour of Librizzi

This walking tour will guide you through the most significant attractions, combining historical sites, panoramic views, and local experiences. The tour takes approximately 2-3 hours, depending on your pace and time spent at each location.

#1. Piazza Catena

Begin your tour at Piazza Catena, the heart of Librizzi. This central square is the town's main gathering place, surrounded by stone buildings that showcase the local architecture. Look for the ornate fountain in the center, a popular meeting spot for locals. If you're visiting in August, you might catch the lively Macaroni Festival held here, a celebration of local culture and cuisine.

#2. Church of San Michele Arcangelo

A 3-minute walk north from Piazza Catena brings you to the Church of San Michele Arcangelo. This church is a testament to Sicilian ecclesiastical architecture, blending various styles throughout its history. Inside, you'll find an intricately carved wooden altar and 18th-century frescoes depicting scenes from the life of St. Michael.

#3. Historical Center and Medieval Streets

Continue east from the church to explore Librizzi's historical center. Wander through narrow, winding alleys that have remained largely unchanged for centuries. As you stroll, keep an eye out for the 15th-century stone archway on Via Roma, a testament to the town's medieval past.

On Via Garibaldi, you'll find a small artisan workshop where you can see local craftsmen at work, keeping traditional skills alive. Early morning is the best time for this walk when locals are opening their shops and going about their daily routines.

#4. Belvedere di San Nicolò

A 10-minute uphill walk to the northeast of the town center brings you to the Belvedere di San Nicolò. This viewpoint offers one of the best panoramas in Librizzi. From here, you'll enjoy sweeping views of the Tyrrhenian Sea, and on clear days, you can spot the Aeolian Islands on the horizon. The surrounding countryside stretches out before you, a patchwork of olive groves and vineyards. For a truly spectacular experience, time your visit for sunset when the landscape is bathed in warm, golden light.

#5. The Emigration Memory Museum

Located in the renovated Palazzo Comunale, just a 5-minute walk from Belvedere di San Nicolò, you'll find the Emigration Memory Museum. This small but poignant museum showcases the history of emigration from Librizzi. Personal letters from emigrants and a reconstructed early 20th-century Librizzi kitchen bring to life the stories of those who left their homeland in search of new opportunities.

#6. Ancient Oil Mill at Frantoio Carcione

A 15-minute walk southwest from the museum takes you to Frantoio Carcione, a well-preserved example of a traditional Sicilian oil mill. Here, you can see original millstones and pressing equipment, offering insight into the age-old process of olive oil production. Guided tours are available, explaining each step of the process from harvest to bottling. For a true taste of Librizzi, call ahead (+39 123 456 7890) to arrange a tasting of local olive oils.

#7. Nature Walk to Madonna del Tindari Trail

Conclude your tour with a nature walk on the Madonna del Tindari Trail, which begins at the southern edge of town. This pleasant 2 km trail winds through olive groves and Mediterranean scrubland, offering a chance to experience the natural beauty of the region. As you walk, you'll be treated to panoramic views of the coast and, in spring, you might spot wild orchids among the diverse local flora.

This tour covers the main attractions of Librizzi while providing a mix of historical, cultural, and natural experiences. Remember to respect local customs and private property as you explore this charming Sicilian town.

Librizzi Festivals Throughout the Year

Festa della Madonna della Catena (Feast of Our Lady of the Chain)

The Sunday following August 15th (Assumption Day)

The Festa della Madonna della Catena in Librizzi embodies a deep connection to one of Sicily's most evocative Marian traditions. The title "Madonna della Catena" (Our Lady of the Chain) stems from a medieval Sicilian legend where the Virgin Mary miraculously freed prisoners who had been unjustly condemned.

When the feast arrives in the days following August 15th, the streets of Librizzi come alive with devotional fervor.

Festa di San Michele Arcangelo (Feast of St. Michael Archangel)

September 29th

The Festa di San Michele Arcangelo, celebrated on September 29th, holds even greater local significance as it honors Librizzi's patron saint. The celebration centers around the Chiesa Madre, from which the statue of St. Michael emerges for its annual procession through the town. The saint is portrayed in his traditional aspect as a warrior angel, complete with sword and scales of justice. Traditional sword dances are performed, linking the festival to ancient Sicilian cultural expressions.

Sagra della Mostarda di Uva

Late September

Sagra della Mostarda di Uva is held in Colla Maffone, a hamlet within the municipality of Librizzi in the province of Messina, Sicily. This festival celebrates the traditional preparation of grape mustard, a local delicacy, and typically takes place in late September. Organized by the Associazione Culturale "U Schiticchiu", the festival features tastings of the grape mustard alongside other regional specialties, accompanied by exhibitions of local crafts and live entertainment. The event aims to immerse visitors in the authentic flavors and traditions of the area.

Day Trip Options: Nearby Sites, Cities and Towns

Montalbano Elicona. 25 kilometers (15 miles) from Librizzi. Voted as one of Italy's most beautiful villages (Borghi più belli d'Italia), Montalbano Elicona is a centuries-old hilltop town with a well-preserved castle, the Castello di Montalbano.

Gioiosa Marea. 20 kilometers (12 miles) from Librizzi. Gioiosa Marea is a picturesque seaside town, recognized for its stunning beaches, such as Capo Calavà and the nearby reserve of Capo Milazzo. The town also offers beautiful coastal views and opportunities for water sports and hiking.

Logistics

Train: The closest train station is located in Patti, about 15 kilometers away. The Patti-San Piero Patti station is on the main rail line connecting Messina and Palermo, making it the most convenient station for accessing Librizzi.

Regional Bus Services: There are regional bus services, but buses are infrequent, so it is important to check schedules in advance. Services typically connect Librizzi with larger towns, such as Patti, where you can transfer to other routes.

Car: To reach Librizzi from Messina, you would take the A20 motorway towards Palermo

Parking: As for parking in Librizzi, the town has limited parking spaces, especially near the historic center, where narrow streets and limited access can make parking challenging. It's advisable to park just outside the center in designated public parking areas.

Dining Recommendations

Il Rosmarino Ristotipico. Address: Via Generale Carlo Alberto Dalla Chiesa, 222. Not in the historic center.

Il Rosmarino is a highly regarded restaurant offering traditional Sicilian cuisine with a focus on local ingredients. .

Accommodation

Librizzi is a very small town. I don't have recommendations in town for accommodation. This sagra would be a good day trip from Messina.

Chapter Twenty

FestaFusion Piazza Armerina

Medieval Knights and Our Lady of Victory

FestaFusion Piazza Armerina

#1 Palio dei Normanni. The festival commemorates the Normans, led by Count Roger I, who liberated Sicily from Arab control in the 11th century. In the heart of Sicily, Piazza Armerina became a symbol of Norman victory and Christian reclamation of the island.

#2 Festa di Maria Santissima delle Vittorie. This festival honors Maria Santissima delle Vittorie, the protector of Piazza Armerina.

#FestaFusion means two or more festivals happen at around the same time in the same town, so visitors can enjoy multiple events during their visit. These are **#Back2Back Festivals**, one followed by another.

Where: Piazza Armerina

When: Palio is August 12 to 14. Festa di Maria Santissima delle Vittorie August 15.

Festival Website: https://www.piazza-armerina.it/palio-dei-normanni/

Average Festival Temperatures: High: 26 - 30°C (79 - 86°F). Low: 20 - 23°C (68 - 73°F).

Discovering Piazza Armerina: A Timeless Mosaic of History and Art

Nestled in the heart of Sicily, Piazza Armerina is a captivating town known for its remarkable blend of history, art, and culture. Situated in the Enna province, this hilltop town stands at an elevation of approximately 721 meters, offering panoramic views of the surrounding countryside. With its ancient roots and well-preserved medieval and baroque architecture, Piazza Armerina provides a window into Sicily's rich past, while also showcasing its vibrant traditions.

Piazza Armerina's history dates back to ancient Roman and Byzantine times. Its highlight is the Villa Romana del Casale, a UNESCO World Heritage Site famous for its Roman mosaics. Built in the 3rd to 4th centuries AD, it reflects the luxury of the Roman elite and late Roman Empire culture. The town later thrived in the medieval era, especially under Norman and Swabian rule. Its strategic location made it vital for governance and defense. With a population of around 20,000 residents, Piazza Armerina is a vibrant community that flourishes on a combination of agriculture, tourism, and craftsmanship.

#1 Palio dei Normanni

The Palio dei Normanni is a major historical festival held in Piazza Armerina. It commemorates the Norman conquest of Sicily and the island's liberation from Arab rule. As one of the regions oldest and most renowned medieval reenactments, its origins can be traced back to the 12th century.

This three-day event takes place annually from August 12 to 14, blending historical and religious traditions. While the term "palio" can sometimes refer to a horse race or other competitive event, it specifically denotes a series of medieval historical reenactments in this context.

Day 1–August 12: The Delivery of the Banner

The festival begins with a religious and ceremonial reenactment in the historic center of Piazza Armerina. This day's event is known as the Consegna delle Chiavi (Delivery of the Keys), symbolizing the handover of the city's keys to Count Roger.

Historical Parade: The four districts (known as Contrade) of the city—Canali, Casalotto, Castellina, and Monte—take part in a parade with participants dressed in elaborate medieval costumes representing Norman soldiers, noblemen, and townspeople.

Blessing of the Banner: The highlight of the day is the presentation and blessing of the banner of the Madonna delle Vittorie in the Cathedral of Piazza Armerina, followed by a large procession where the banner is carried through the streets.

Day 2–August 13: The Corteo Storico (Historical Parade)

On this day, the streets of Piazza Armerina come alive with medieval pageantry.

Procession of Count Roger I: A grand procession featuring knights, foot soldiers, nobles, and commoners marches through the city, reenacting the entry of Count Roger and his Norman forces into the city. A large procession of foot soldiers, the Norman cavalry, and Count Roger carrying the papal banner of "Maria Santissima delle Vittorie" solemnly enters the city through Porta Castellina. The procession travels along the principal streets, eventually reaching Cathedral Square. There, accompanied by the sound of trumpets and drums, Count Roger is greeted by the city's representatives, including the Prior, the District Magistrate, the Notables, the Ladies, the Grand Magistrate with the Grand Lady, and the jousting knights from the four Contrade, historic districts.

Tournament Trials: The four Contrade prepare for the Palio by participating in trials that test the skill and precision of their horsemen. These trials are important for determining the order of the final competition on the following day.

In the Cathedral Basilica, the Grand Magistrate, accompanied by his pages, the Master of Ceremonies, and the Auctioneer symbolically hands over the keys. After the ceremony, the entire procession reforms and crosses the principal streets of the historic center, finally arriving at the lodges of the San Pietro district.

Day 3–August 14: The Palio and Jousting Tournament

The third and final day is the highlight of the Palio dei Normanni.

The Quintana Tournament: The centerpiece of the day is the Quintana jousting tournament, where knights representing the four Contrade compete in a series of events designed to test their strength, speed, and agility on horseback. The event takes place in the Field of Saint Hippolytus (Campo Sant'Ippolito), a large outdoor arena. Knights must charge at targets (representing Saracens) with a lance and try to hit a series of rings or shields while galloping at full speed.

Awarding of the Palio: The Palio, a richly decorated banner, is awarded to the knight and Contrada that show the most skill in the competition. This symbolic victory represents the Norman triumph over the Saracens.

#2 Feast of Our Lady of Victories

The Festa di Maria Santissima delle Vittorie, celebrated on August 15, coincides with the Feast of the Assumption of the Virgin Mary, and holds deep historical and religious significance for the people of Piazza Armerina.

The festival commemorates the Virgin Mary's role in the victory of the Normans, led by Count Roger I, over the Saracens in the 11th century. According to tradition, Count Roger I dedicated his military success to the Virgin Mary, as he believed her intercession was pivotal in securing the victory. As a result, the Madonna delle Vittorie (Our Lady of Victories) became a revered symbol of divine protection and intervention for the local population. This devotion is embodied in the statue of the Madonna, which is housed in the Cattedrale di Maria Santissima delle Vittorie.

The Festa di Maria Santissima delle Vittorie has been celebrated for over 900 years, dating back to the time of Count Roger I's conquest of Sicily in the late 11th century. It remains a key annual event, intertwining both religious devotion and local pride. The tradition has been passed down through the centuries, with each generation honoring the Virgin's role in their history, continuing to this day with a strong sense of community involvement. The event is not just a religious observance but also a celebration of Piazza Armerina's cultural heritage.

Events and Processions of the Festa di Maria Santissima delle Vittorie

Solemn Religious Mass: The festival begins with a solemn mass held in the

Cathedral of Piazza Armerina (Cattedrale di Maria Santissima delle Vittorie). During this service, the community gathers to honor the Madonna and give thanks for her protection. The mass is an important spiritual moment for locals and pilgrims alike, with prayers dedicated to the Virgin Mary and the Assumption. The cathedral is beautifully decorated for the occasion, with flowers and candles.

The Grand Procession of the Madonna delle Vittorie.

Carried through the streets of Piazza Armerina, the procession of the statue of the Madonna is the most significant part of the celebration. The statue of Maria Santissima delle Vittorie, adorned with gold, jewels, and intricate decorations, is carried on a platform by a group of strong devotees known as portatori.

Starting at the cathedral, the procession makes its way through the historic streets of the town, accompanied by clergy, religious orders, and thousands of followers. Along the way, bands play solemn music, and the streets are lined with people who offer prayers, sing hymns, and throw flower petals in honor of the Madonna. The procession usually lasts several hours as it winds its way through the historic center.

Along the procession route, many residents and pilgrims place offerings, such as flowers and candles, in front of the statue of the Madonna. These offerings symbolize gratitude for favors granted by the Virgin Mary and requests for future protection and blessings.

In certain areas, families may erect small shrines or altars to honor the Madonna as she passes. These shrines often include religious icons, candles, and other symbolic items.

Fireworks and Evening Festivities

After the religious events and processions, the festival takes on a more celebratory tone with fireworks displays in the evening. The fireworks, usually held in the main squares or near the cathedral, light up the night sky and can be seen from various parts of the town. The vibrant pyrotechnic displays are a mark of celebration and joy, adding a festive atmosphere to the solemnity of the religious processions.

Music and festive activities, including local bands and traditional Sicilian folk music, follow the fireworks. People gather in the town squares, enjoying food, music, and the sense of community that the festival fosters.

Cultural and Traditional Activities

In addition to the religious aspects, the festival often includes various cultural events, such as concerts, theatrical performances, and exhibitions. These events take place in public squares and cultural venues throughout Piazza Armerina.

Vendors selling traditional street food, like arancini, cannoli, and pane cunzatu, add to the festive atmosphere. Food stalls, local crafts, and artisanal products give visitors a chance to experience Sicilian flavors and traditions.

Connection to the Palio dei Normanni

The Festa di Maria Santissima delle Vittorie coincides with the ultimate day of the Palio dei Normanni, a three-day medieval reenactment that celebrates the Norman victory over the Saracens. The Palio ends with the presentation of the banner of the Madonna delle Vittorie, symbolizing the town's gratitude for the Virgin Mary's protection during the conquest.

On August 14, the knights who take part in the Palio pay tribute to the Virgin Mary by presenting the Palio banner at the cathedral, and on August 15, the religious aspects of the festival dominate with the grand procession and mass.

Walking Tour of Piazza Armerina

#1. Piazza Garibaldi

Begin the tour at Piazza Garibaldi, the central square of Piazza Armerina. You'll find cafés and shops surrounding the square, making it a perfect place to start your exploration. Here, you can visit the Chiesa di San Rocco (Church of St. Roch) and admire the Fontana Garibaldi, an 18th-century fountain.

#2. Cattedrale di Maria Santissima Delle Vittorie (Cathedral of Piazza Armerina)

Head uphill to the Cattedrale di Piazza Armerina, a stunning Baroque cathedral from the 17th century. The cathedral stands out with its beautiful dome and ornate façade. Inside, you'll find the statue of the Madonna delle Vittorie, the patron saint of the city; Count Roger I gifted the Madonna delle Vittorie statue after his victory over the Arabs in 1061.

#3. Castello Aragonese (Aragonese Castle)

Walk a short distance from the cathedral to reach the Castello Aragonese, a fortress from the 14th century. The castle offers sweeping views of the surrounding countryside and once played a key role in protecting the city.

The Aragonese rulers fortified the castle to defend Piazza Armerina, and it stood strong during numerous battles and sieges.

#4. Chiesa di San Pietro (Church of St. Peter)

Wander through the historic center's narrow streets to reach the Church of San Pietro, a small but striking Baroque church from the 17th century. Step inside to admire its intricate decorations and serene atmosphere.

#5. Palazzo Trigona

Visit Palazzo Trigona, located near the cathedral. This 18th-century noble palace now houses a museum. The Trigona family built the palazzo as a grand residence, showcasing Baroque architecture. The Trigona family held significant power in Sicily, and their palazzo reflects their wealth and influence. The museum's exhibits offer a deep dive into Piazza Armerina's rich history.

#6. Villa Romana del Casale

After exploring the city center, take a short drive to the Villa Romana del Casale, a UNESCO World Heritage Site, just outside the city. Built in the 4th century AD, this Roman villa houses some of the best-preserved mosaics in the world, depicting scenes from Roman mythology, daily life, and sports.

The villa likely belonged to a wealthy Roman aristocrat. Its mosaics, such as the famous "Bikini Girls" and the "Great Hunt", reveal the opulent lifestyle of Roman elites in Sicily during the late empire. A mudslide covered the villa for thousands of years, protecting the mosaics.

Mosaics of the Villa Romana

#7. Via Umberto I

After visiting the villa, return to the historic center and take a stroll along Via Umberto I, the city's main street. Lined with cafés, shops, and historic buildings, this street provides a glimpse of local life and offers plenty of opportunities to enjoy Sicilian hospitality.

#8. Chiesa di San Giovanni Evangelista

End the tour with a visit to the Church of St. John the Evangelist, another example of beautiful Baroque architecture. This church, built in the 17th century, features intricate stucco work, lavish altars, and fine frescoes that illustrate the craftsmanship of the era.

Piazza Armerina Festivals and Sagre Throughout the Year

Infiorata di Piazza Armerina (Flower Festival)

June

Celebrated on Corpus Christi Sunday, which falls on the second Sunday after Pentecost (typically in June)

The Infiorata is a flower festival with roots in 13th-century Rome, though it became popular in many Italian towns during the 17th and 18th centuries. In Piazza Armerina, this tradition has been embraced as a way to combine religious devotion with artistic expression.

Local artists and volunteers create intricate "carpets" made entirely of flower petals, seeds, and other natural materials along the town's streets. These floral masterpieces often depict religious scenes, local historical events, or geometric patterns. The designs are carefully planned and executed over several days leading up to the festival.

Festa di Sant'Anna (Feast of St. Ann)

July 26

The Festa di Sant'Anna celebrates St. Anne, the mother of the Virgin Mary and the grandmother of Jesus Christ. Veneration of St. Anne dates back to the early Christian church, with her feast day officially added to the Roman Catholic calendar in the 16th century. The festival serves as a time for families to come together, honoring the concept of motherhood and the important role of grandparents in family life. It also provides an opportunity for the community to reflect on their faith and cultural heritage.

Festa di San Lorenzo (St. Lawrence Feast Day)

August 10

The Festa di San Lorenzo honors St. Lawrence, one of Piazza Armerina's patron saints. St. Lawrence was a 3rd-century Christian martyr who served as a deacon in Rome. According to tradition, he was roasted alive on a gridiron, which is why he is often depicted holding this instrument. The festival combines religious devotion with community celebration. It begins with a solemn Mass in the Cathedral, followed by a procession carrying the statue of San Lorenzo through the streets. Throughout the day, the town is alive with various activities, including historical reenactments of the life of St. Lawrence, street fairs, and traditional music performances.

As night falls, the celebration culminates in a spectacular fireworks display.

Day Trip Options: Nearby Sites, Cities and Towns

Enna: About 30 kilometers (18 miles) north of Piazza Armerina. Known as the "Belvedere of Sicily," Enna offers breathtaking panoramic views from its lofty position and is steeped in history and mythology.

- Castello di Lombardia: One of the largest and most important medieval castles in Sicily, this fortress dates back to the Norman period. The castle features multiple courtyards, towers, and stunning vistas from the Torre Pisana, the tallest remaining tower. Exploring its ancient walls offers a glimpse into Sicily's medieval past and unmatched views of the surrounding countryside.

- Duomo di Enna (Cathedral of Enna): This grand Baroque cathedral is dedicated to Our Lady of the Assumption. Built on the foundations of an earlier church, the cathedral boasts a magnificent wooden coffered ceiling, detailed frescoes, and a beautiful facade.

- Lake Pergusa: Located a short drive from Enna, this tranquil lake is steeped in Greek mythology as the site where Hades abducted Persephone, daughter of Demeter. The lake is now part of a nature reserve, offering walking trails and opportunities to enjoy the serene landscape.

- Rocca di Cerere: This ancient site is associated with the goddess Demeter, and remnants of a sacred altar can still be seen. The Rocca offers a spiritual and historical perspective on Enna's ties to ancient Greek religion.

Morgantina and the Archaeological Park of Aidone: 22 kilometers (13 miles) northeast of Piazza Armerina. Once a flourishing Greek city, Morgantina offers a glimpse into ancient life with its well-preserved remains. Highlights include the Agora, where public gatherings took place, the Ekklesiasterion (assembly building), various temples, and the Greek theater, which is still used for performances today. The intricate mosaics found on-site showcase the artistry of the period.

Museo Archeologico di Aidone: Located in the nearby town of Aidone, this museum houses significant artifacts excavated from Morgantina, including the Venus of Morgantina, a stunning 5th-century BC statue. Other treasures include exquisite silverware, pottery, and a collection of terracotta figurines. The museum provides context and depth to a visit to Morgantina, bringing its ancient ruins to life.

These day trips from Piazza Armerina combine history, mythology, and scenic beauty, offering a rich exploration of Sicily's central region.

Logistics

Train: The nearest train station is in Enna, which is 30 kilometers (19 miles) away.

Local Buses: Piazza Armerina has a local bus service that connects different parts of the town, as well as nearby villages. Local buses are a good option for moving around town without a car, though schedules can be limited.

Regional Buses: The AST (Azienda Siciliana Trasporti) bus service offers connections between Piazza Armerina and larger Sicilian cities like Catania, Enna, and Palermo.

Car: The main road into Piazza Armerina is the SS117bis, which connects to the A19 autostrada (highway) between Catania and Palermo. As you approach the town, you'll likely enter via Viale Generale Muscarà, which leads into the historical center.

Parking: There are several options for parking:

- Piazza Falcone e Borsellino: A large parking area near the town center.

- Piazza Garibaldi: Another central parking option, though it may be busier.

- For visits to Villa Romana del Casale, there's a dedicated parking area near the archaeological site, about 5 kilometers southwest of the town center.

Dining Recommendations

Ristorante Trattoria Da Gianna. Address: Piazza Umberto I, 9

This family-run restaurant is beloved for its cozy and welcoming atmosphere. Trattoria Da Gianna serves traditional Sicilian dishes prepared with fresh, seasonal ingredients. Signature dishes include homemade pasta, Sicilian caponata, fettuccine with lemon, and their famous eggplant parmigiana. The warm hospitality of the owners, Gianna, and her husband, creates a homely dining experience, making it a favorite among both locals and tourists.

Trattoria Del Goloso. Address: Via Monte 32

Located in the historic center, Trattoria Del Goloso offers a rustic and authentic Sicilian dining experience. Known for its traditional recipes passed down through generations, this trattoria prides itself on hearty, home-cooked meals. The charming atmosphere, combined with excellent local dishes, makes it a must-visit for anyone looking to experience the true flavors of Sicily.

Osteria del Conte. Address: Via Garibaldi 77

This charming osteria is located near the Church of San Giovanni Evangelista and is celebrated for its cozy ambiance and traditional Sicilian cuisine. Signature dishes include rich eggplant parmigiana, fresh seafood, and hearty meat sauces, all served with an excellent selection of local wines. The homemade desserts, particularly the ice cream, are a highlight. With generous portions and attentive service, Osteria del Conte is a favorite for both locals and visitors looking for an authentic dining experience.

Amici Miei Ristorante. Address: Via Monte, 6

A hidden gem in Piazza Armerina, Amici Miei Ristorante offers a warm and inviting setting for savoring Sicilian flavors. Known for its attention to detail and beautifully presented dishes, this restaurant features a menu that includes specialties like pistachio-crusted lamb, homemade pasta, and exquisite cannoli. The friendly staff and cozy decor make it a perfect spot for an intimate meal or special occasion.

Accommodation

For festival travel, I recommend three nights at Piazza Armerina. There are sites to see in town, the Villa Romana and the FestaFusion events.

*Hotel Villa Romana. Address: Piazza Alcide De Gasperi, 18

Established in the 1980s, Hotel Villa Romana combines modern amenities with a long history of welcoming guests. Its central location provides easy access to Piazza Armerina's main attractions, including the historic center and Villa Romana del Casale. Guests appreciate the comfortable rooms and the hotel's dedication to hospitality, making it a reliable choice for visitors exploring the area.

*B&B Villa Romana. Address: Via Benedetto Croce

This delightful bed-and-breakfast offers a warm and personalized experience for travelers. Located near the renowned Villa Romana del Casale, it is a perfect base for those visiting the famous mosaics. Known for its friendly service and attention to detail, B&B Villa Romana provides a cozy atmosphere and excellent hospitality, ensuring a memorable stay.

GH Hotel. Address: Via Roma, 19

GH Hotel is conveniently located in the heart of Piazza Armerina, close to historical landmarks and the central square. Its strategic position makes it an ideal base for exploring the town's rich history and participating in FestaFusion events. Guests enjoy the comfortable accommodations and easy access to the cultural highlights of the area.

*Most centralized location for the events of the festival.

Chapter Twenty-One

Crafted in Clay, The Art of Caltagirone

Immersion Experience Caltagirone

In the province of Catania, Caltagirone is one of Sicily's most important centers for ceramics. Its rich history dates back to ancient times, influenced by Arab, Norman, and Spanish cultures. The town's fame for ceramics dates back to the Arab period in the 9th and 10th centuries, when the island was under Islamic rule. The Arabs introduced advanced pottery techniques, such as glazing and decorative tile work, which the locals adopted and expanded.

Over the centuries, Caltagirone's artisans became masters of this craft, blending the influences of the various cultures that ruled Sicily into their ceramic production. The town's architectural and artistic beauty is highlighted by its famous "Scala di Santa Maria del Monte," a monumental staircase with 142 ceramic steps, each featuring unique and colorful tiles.

Part of the UNESCO World Heritage Site Val di Noto, Caltagirone is renowned for its stunning Baroque architecture. Visitors come to admire its historical churches, palazzi, and, of course, its local ceramic craftsmanship, which has been a cornerstone of the town's identity for centuries.

Caltagirone's ceramics are known not only for their beauty but also for their functional use, with a tradition of producing items like vases, tiles, and plates that are both artistic and practical. Festivals such as the "Festa di San Giacomo" and Christmas nativity displays further showcase Caltagirone's vibrant cultural heritage.

Immerse Yourself with a Ceramics Class

Caltagirone offers several opportunities for visitors to take ceramics classes. Many local ceramic workshops (botteghe) provide hands-on experiences where participants can learn about traditional techniques, including shaping, glazing, and painting ceramics.

Popular options include:

- **Ceramiche Sofia**: A well-known workshop where participants can create their own ceramic pieces under the guidance of skilled artisans.

- **Bottega del Tornio:** Visitors can engage in pottery-making sessions, learn about the craft's history, and take home their finished creations (or have them shipped).

For ceramic enthusiasts and curious visitors, Caltagirone also offers the chance to explore a ceramic laboratory where you can participate in a ceramic course. There are options for individual courses or the "Didactic Laboratory," a special project designed for school groups or anyone interested in learning about ceramics.

These hands-on experiences provide an excellent opportunity to engage with Caltagirone's renowned ceramic traditions. For more information, contact Sicily in Travel at +39 333 9458579

Chapter Twenty-Two

FestaFusion Messina: Giants, Grace and Ferragosto

FestaFusion Messina

#1. Parade of Giants in Messina: This vibrant procession features towering figures of Mata and Grifone, legendary founders of Messina, parading through the streets with music and fanfare.

#2. Ferragosto: Celebrated on August 15, Ferragosto is a national holiday in Italy, marking the peak of summer with festivities, feasts, and religious observances.

#3. Feast of the Assumption of Mary: A deeply religious celebration on August 15, honoring the belief in the Virgin Mary's assumption into heaven, highlighted by special Masses and processions in Messina.

#FestaFusion means two or more festivals happen at the same time in the same town, so visitors can enjoy multiple events during their visit.

Where: Messina. Ferragosto and the Feast of the Assumption of Mary are celebrated throughout Italy, not just in Messina.

When: Parade of Giants August 10-14. Ferragosto and Feast of the Assumption of Mary are August 15.

Average Festival Temperatures: High: 26 - 30°C (79 - 86°F). Low: 20 - 23°C (68 - 73°F).

Discovering Messina: Guardian of the Strait

Messina, the third-largest city in Sicily, stands as a resilient sentinel at the northeastern tip of the island, guarding the narrow strait that bears its name. Known in ancient times as Zancle for its sickle-shaped harbor, Messina has played a pivotal role in Mediterranean history for over two and a half millennia. Despite facing numerous natural disasters and historical upheavals, the city has repeatedly risen from the ashes, embodying the indomitable spirit of Sicily and its people.

Messina's history dates back to ancient times, founded by Greek colonists in the 8th century BCE. Its prime location between Sicily and the Italian mainland made it a target for various powers, including the Carthaginians, Romans, Byzantines, Arabs, and Normans. The Normans turned it into a key trade hub and a vital part of the Crusades. The Renaissance marked its peak, making it one of the top Mediterranean ports. However, tragedy struck in 1908 with a devastating earthquake and tsunami, killing about half of its population. World War II added to the destruction. Yet, Messina always rebuilt, though much of its historical architecture has been lost.

Messina occupies a unique position at the northeastern tip of Sicily, separated from the Italian mainland by the Strait of Messina, which is only 3 kilometers wide at its narrowest point. This location has been both a blessing and a curse – providing the city with a natural harbor and strategic importance, but also exposing it to seismic activity. The city stretches along the coast and climbs the surrounding hills, offering stunning views of the Strait and the mainland beyond. The nearby Peloritani Mountains provide a dramatic backdrop and influence the local climate, which is typically Mediterranean but slightly milder than other parts of Sicily due to the moderating influence of the sea.

Messina has a population of approximately 220,000 in the city proper, with over 600,000 in its metropolitan area. Despite the destruction of many historical buildings with earthquakes and lava flows, Messina still boasts impressive architectural and cultural landmarks.

1 Parade of Giants in Messina

The Parade of Giants in Messina, or I Giganti di Messina, is one of the city's most iconic and culturally significant traditions, celebrated every August. The event features two massive statues, Mata and Grifone, towering representations of Messina's complex history of myth and conquest. These larger-than-life figures are deeply rooted in both legend and history, symbolizing the fusion of cultures that has shaped Messina over the centuries.

The tradition of the Giants dates back to the 16th century when the Senate of Messina commissioned the creation of the original wooden and canvas statues. The figures of Mata, a local woman of legendary beauty, and Grifone, a Moorish warrior, embody the myth of the founding of Messina. According to legend, Grifone, representing the Moorish invaders, falls in love with Mata, who initially resists his advances but eventually converts him to Christianity, symbolizing the triumph of good over evil and the reconciliation between different cultures.

Mata (riding a white horse) and Grifone (on a black horse) are seen as representations of opposites: good versus evil, earth versus heaven, and Christian versus Moor. Their story reflects not just the historical tensions between the Christian and Muslim populations during Sicily's medieval period, but also a broader allegory for human reconciliation and unity. Scholars debate the precise origins of the figures, though many agree they derive from a blend of Sicilian myth, medieval history, and possibly ancient traditions like those found in Hesiod's cosmogony.

By the 17th century, the use of these statues in religious ceremonies was restricted, but they continued to play a major role in secular festivals, especially around Ferragosto (the Feast of the Assumption). During World War II, the original statues were destroyed, but they were later reconstructed using plaster and placed on wheeled iron platforms to continue the parade tradition.

The Parade

The Parade of Giants usually takes place in mid-August as part of the larger Ferragosto celebrations in Messina. Mata and Grifone are colossal statues, each standing over 8 meters (about 26 feet) tall, comparable to a three-story building. These aren't static sculptures, but mobile figures that are paraded through the streets on platforms, creating a truly impressive spectacle.

Grifone, who leads the procession, is depicted wearing dark, imposing armor that gives him a formidable appearance. His armor likely features intricate designs and patterns typical of Moorish art, with elaborate engravings and metalwork that catch the light as he moves through the streets. Grifone's facial features might reflect a blend of European and North African characteristics, embodying the cultural fusion that shaped Messina's history.

Following behind Grifone is Mata, equally impressive in stature. In stark contrast to Grifone's dark armor, Mata is dressed in resplendent white, possibly resembling a wedding dress or a noble lady's attire from a bygone era. She might wear a crown or other regal accessories to emphasize her importance and symbolic role. Mata's facial features likely represent idealized Sicilian beauty, with a serene expression that contrasts with Grifone's more martial appearance.

Both figures are marvels of construction, designed to be mobile despite their enormous size. They're likely made of lightweight materials such as papier-mâché over a wooden or metal frame, allowing them to be maneuvered through the streets without compromising their impressive stature. Painted in vivid colors, these giants come to life as they move, possibly with mechanisms that allow for subtle movements of their heads or arms, adding to the sense of awe they inspire.

As Mata and Grifone parade through Messina, they tower over the crowds, creating a truly magnificent spectacle. Their massive size, combined with lively music, enthusiastic dancing, and the resonant ringing of church bells, creates an immersive experience that engages all the senses. The stark visual contrast between the two figures serves as a powerful representation of Messina's historical narrative of conquest and conversion.

Crowds gather to watch this dramatic procession, which weaves through the city's historic streets and is punctuated by various cultural performances. The parade culminates in a spectacular fireworks display over the city, symbolizing the triumph of light over darkness and the renewal of Messina's cultural spirit.

#2 Ferragosto

Ferragosto

Following the grand Parade of Giants, Messina's Ferragosto celebrations continue with a series of events that blend ancient traditions with modern festivities. This mid-August holiday, deeply rooted in Italian culture, takes on a unique character in the Sicilian city of Messina.

History of Ferragosto

August 15th marks the celebration of Ferragosto, which has its origins in ancient Roman history and has developed into an important public holiday in Italy, with religious and cultural significance.

The name "Ferragosto" is derived from the Latin term Feriae Augusti, which means "Holidays of Augustus." Emperor Augustus established it in 18 BC as a period of rest and celebration after the hard labor of the harvest. Festivities during the holiday, which encompassed both religious and secular customs, included horse races, games, and feasts. Masters traditionally gave bonuses to servants on this day of rest for workers and animals.

August holidays blended with older Roman traditions, including the Vinalia Rustica and the Consualia, which recognized the agricultural cycle and harvest. During the Middle Ages and Renaissance, Ferragosto continued to hold significance as a holiday. It was a time when people came together for community events, religious practices, and local fairs.

In Christian tradition, August 15th is also the feast of the Assumption of Mary, adding a religious dimension to the holiday. This combination of ancient Roman traditions, Christian significance, and modern-day festivities during the midsummer holiday makes Ferragosto a distinctive and long-lasting celebration in Italian culture.

Ferragosto Celebrations in Messina

In Messina, Ferragosto is marked by a vibrant array of events that showcase the city's rich cultural heritage and festive spirit:

1. **Religious Processions:** The day often begins with solemn religious processions honoring the Assumption of Mary. The Madonna Vara, a monumental votive float, is carried through the streets, accompanied by prayers and hymns.

2. **Beach Festivities:** As a coastal city, Messina's beaches come alive during Ferragosto. Locals and tourists alike flock to the shores for picnics, swimming, and sunbathing. Many restaurants and beach clubs organize special events and parties.

3. **Cultural Events:** The city hosts various cultural events, including open-air concerts, art exhibitions, and theatrical performances. These often take place in historic venues, blending Messina's rich past with contemporary celebrations.

4. **Culinary Traditions:** Food plays a central role in Messina's Ferragosto celebrations. Local specialties like arancini (rice balls), pasta alla Norma, and granita are enjoyed in abundance. Many families gather for large feasts, often featuring traditional Sicilian dishes.

5. **Fireworks Display:** The highlight of Messina's Ferragosto celebration is the spectacular fireworks show. As night falls, the sky over the Strait of Messina is illuminated with a dazzling pyrotechnic display, often lasting for over an hour. The fireworks are usually launched from barges in the strait, creating stunning reflections on the water and providing a perfect vantage point from the city's waterfront.

6. ***Boat Procession:** Unique to Messina is the traditional boat procession in the Strait. Decorated vessels, from small fishing boats to larger yachts, parade along the coast, often carrying effigies of saints or the Virgin Mary.

7. **Street Markets and Fairs:** The city's squares and main streets host lively markets and fairs, where local artisans sell traditional crafts, food products, and souvenirs.

8. **Sports Competitions:** Various sports events are organized, including swimming races in the Strait of Messina and friendly football matches between local teams.

The Ferragosto celebrations in Messina typically extend beyond August 15th, often lasting for several days. This extended festival period allows both residents and visitors to fully immerse themselves in the joyous atmosphere that envelops the city during this special time of year.

*Additional Detail for the Ferragosto Boat Procession

One of the most distinctive and captivating elements of Messina's Ferragosto celebration is the traditional boat procession in the Strait of Messina. This aquatic parade, known locally as "La Processione a Mare," is a vibrant display of faith, tradition, and maritime culture.

The boat procession typically takes place on the afternoon of August 15th, starting around 5:00 P.M. when the heat of the day begins to subside, but there's still plenty of daylight. The event is timed to conclude just before sunset, creating a spectacular view as the golden light reflects off the water and illuminates the decorated vessels.

The procession begins at the Port of Messina, near the statue of the Madonna della Lettera, the patroness of the city. From there, it proceeds along the coast, passing by notable landmarks such as the University of Messina, the Fountain of Neptune, and the Church of Christ the King.

The procession features a wide array of vessels, from small fishing boats and leisure crafts to larger yachts and even some historical replicas of traditional Sicilian boats. Many participants spend days or even weeks preparing their boats for the event, adorning them with colorful flags and banners, flower arrangements, religious symbols, and lights.

The centerpiece of the procession is usually a larger boat carrying a statue or effigy of the Virgin Mary, often the Madonna della Lettera. This boat is typically the most elaborately decorated and occupies a place of honor in the parade.

The procession follows a route that hugs the coastline of Messina, allowing spectators on land to follow its progress. The boats travel at a leisurely pace, often making a loop that extends from the port area to the Capo Peloro lighthouse at the northernmost tip of Sicily, before returning to the starting point.

The entire event usually lasts about two to three hours, depending on the number of participating vessels and weather conditions. As the procession nears its conclusion, it's not uncommon for the boats to sound their horns in unison, creating a cacophonous but jubilant tribute to the Virgin Mary and the spirit of Ferragosto.

Thousands of spectators line the shores of Messina to watch the procession.

Popular viewing spots include:

- The waterfront promenade (Lungomare Vittorio Emanuele III)
- The steps of the Shrine of Christ the King
- The area around the Fountain of Neptune
- Various beaches along the coast, such as Spisone and Sant'Agata

Many people bring picnics or purchase food from the numerous vendors that set up along the route. The atmosphere is festive, with music playing from both the shore and the boats, creating a lively soundtrack for the event.

The boat procession is more than just a spectacle; it's a profound expression of Messina's maritime heritage and religious devotion. It symbolizes the deep connection between the people of Messina and the sea that has shaped their history and livelihoods for centuries.

As the boats make their way back to the port in the growing twilight, they set the stage for the grand finale of Messina's Ferragosto celebrations: the breathtaking fireworks display that will soon light up the night sky over the Strait of Messina.

#3 The Feast of the Assumption of Mary

The Feast of the Assumption of Mary, celebrated on August 15th, is a cornerstone of Messina's Ferragosto celebrations, blending religious devotion with cultural traditions. This feast day holds particular significance in Messina, a city with a long history of Marian devotion.

The Feast of the Assumption traces its origins back to early Christian tradition. By the 5th and 6th centuries, the belief in Mary's Assumption—that the Virgin Mary was taken body and soul into Heaven—was already widespread in both the Eastern and Western churches.

The feast was officially established in the Eastern Christian Church around the 6th century, initially known as the "Dormition" (meaning "falling asleep") of Mary. The Eastern Church celebrated the feast to commemorate the end of Mary's earthly life and her bodily ascendance into heaven.

In Italy, the Church aligned the pagan Ferragosto with the Feast of the Assumption. This adaptation enabled the ancient holiday to persist, now honoring Mary's assumption into heaven within a Christian context.

In Messina, the Feast of the Assumption takes on special significance, intertwining with local traditions and the city's maritime heritage:

1. **The Madonna della Lettera:** Messina's celebration centers around their patroness, the Madonna della Lettera (Our Lady of the Letter). According to local tradition, the Virgin Mary sent a letter blessing the city of Messina. This unique aspect of Marian devotion adds an extra layer of importance to the Assumption celebrations in the city.

2. **Religious Processions:** The day begins with solemn processions through the city streets. The focal point is often a statue of the Madonna della Lettera, carried on the shoulders of the faithful. These processions typically start from the Cathedral of Messina and wind through the historic center.

3. ***The Vara:** A highlight of Messina's Assumption Day is the procession of the Vara, a massive, pyramid-shaped float over 13 meters tall. The Vara represents the Assumption of the Virgin and is adorned with clouds, angels, and at the top, figures representing the Holy Trinity crowning the Virgin Mary. The transportation of this enormous structure through the streets is a feat of coordination and devotion, often taking several hours.

4. **Mass Celebrations:** Special masses are held throughout the day, with the most important one typically celebrated at the Cathedral of Messina. The cathedral, dedicated to the Assumption of the Virgin, becomes the spiritual center of the city on this day.

5. **The Boat Procession:** As detailed earlier, the afternoon boat procession in the Strait of Messina is closely tied to the Assumption celebrations. Many boats carry images or statues of the Virgin Mary, creating a floating tribute to the Assumption.

6. **Traditional Offerings**: In keeping with ancient traditions, many Messinese make offerings to the Virgin on this day. These can range from flowers and candles to more elaborate votive gifts.

7. **Cultural Events:** The religious celebrations are often accompanied by cultural events such as concerts of sacred music, art exhibitions focusing on Marian themes, and historical reenactments.

*Additional Information - The Vara Procession in Messina

The Vara procession is one of the most spectacular and significant events of Messina's Feast of the Assumption celebrations. This ancient tradition, dating back to the 16th century, is a powerful display of faith, community, and Messinese cultural heritage. The procession begins at the Church of San Lorenzo and moves along Via Garibaldi towards Piazza Duomo, with the massive Vara structure pulled by hundreds of participants using thick ropes. The procession is slow, taking several hours with stops for prayers and hymns, creating a mix of solemnity and celebration. It culminates at the Cathedral of Messina, where a special Mass often marks the conclusion.

The Vara: A Description

The Vara is a colossal votive chariot, standing approximately 13.5 meters (about 44 feet) tall. It's an intricate, pyramid-shaped structure that narrows as it rises, creating a dramatic vertical spectacle. The Vara is not just large; it's a complex, artistic representation of Catholic theology and Marian devotion.

Key features of the Vara include a large, sturdy base platform on wheels, adorned with religious symbols and decorative elements. The structure consists of several tiers, each smaller than the one below, creating the pyramid effect. Throughout these tiers are numerous figures, including larger-than-life statues of the Apostles and other biblical figures at the base, angels in various poses (some appearing to be in flight) in the middle tiers, and representations of the sun, moon, and stars near the top. At the very summit is a representation of the Holy Trinity (Father, Son, and Holy Spirit) crowning the Virgin Mary.

The entire structure is lavishly decorated with gold leaf, vibrant paints, flowers, and lights. Interspersed throughout are stylized cloud formations made of papier-mâché or lightweight materials, giving the impression that the scenes are taking place in the heavens. The overall effect is a stunning, three-dimensional representation of the Assumption of Mary, with earthly figures at the bottom transitioning to heavenly scenes at the top.

The movement of the Vara through the streets is a remarkable feat of coordination and strength. The structure's size and weight, combined with Messina's narrow streets and warm August weather, make the procession a true test of devotion for those involved.

For visitors, the Vara procession offers a unique spectacle that combines religious fervor, historical tradition, and community spirit. The sight of this enormous, ornate structure slowly making its way through the city, surrounded by crowds of devoted participants and onlookers, provides a vivid and unforgettable image of Messina's rich cultural heritage.

The Feast of the Assumption in Messina seamlessly blends with the broader Ferragosto celebrations:

- The religious processions and masses provide a spiritual foundation for the day's festivities.

- The Vara procession often marks the official start of the Ferragosto celebrations in the city.

- The afternoon boat procession serves as a bridge between the religious observances and the more secular aspects of Ferragosto.

- The fireworks display at night, while part of the Ferragosto celebrations, is also seen by many as a tribute to the Assumption.

This integration of the Assumption feast into Ferragosto showcases Messina's ability to harmonize its deep religious traditions with its cultural heritage and love for festivity. It creates a unique celebration that honors both the spiritual significance of the Assumption and the joyous spirit of Ferragosto, making August 15th a truly special day in the Messinese calendar. This event draws crowds of about 100,000 each year.

Travel Trends during Ferragosto

Booking early is necessary if traveling to Messina for this FestaFusion. Many hotels and B&Bs in Messina may quickly fill up, and some visitors might need to seek accommodations in nearby areas or resort to vacation rentals. While a significant number of attendees are locals or Sicilians, a portion of the crowd comes from mainland Italy and other international destinations

High Travel Volume: Typically, around 30-35% of Italians take vacations during Ferragosto (the week of August 15). Roughly 18-21 million individuals are estimated to be traveling during this timeframe, taking into consideration Italy's population of around 60 million.

Walking Tour of Messina

#1. Cattedrale di Messina and Piazza Duomo

Begin the tour at Piazza del Duomo, the heart of Messina, and home to the stunning Cattedrale di Messina (Messina Cathedral). Originally built in the 12th century under Norman rule, the cathedral has been reconstructed several times due to the devastating 1908 earthquake and World War II bombings.

You'll find beautiful Byzantine-style mosaics and impressive Gothic and Romanesque architectural elements inside the cathedral. The cathedral also houses the tomb of Conrad IV of Germany, son of Frederick II, adding to its historical significance.

The Astronomical Clock of the Cathedral

A highlight of the cathedral is the Astronomical Clock, in the bell tower. Installed in 1933, it's considered the largest and most complex mechanical-astronomical clock in the world. At noon each day, it puts on an intricate display that lasts about 12 minutes. The spectacle begins with bronze mechanical figures coming to life. A golden lion, the symbol of Messina, raises the flag and roars three times, followed by a crowing cock that flaps its wings.

As the display continues, figures representing the days of the week rotate, and a scene from Christian iconography unfolds. Jesus emerges from a tomb, passing allegorical figures of the Church, Death, the Synagogue, and the four Evangelists. The Virgin Mary then appears and enters the scene. The show concludes with the chiming of Ave Maria bells. This daily performance attracts many visitors and offers a unique glimpse into Messina's artistic and technological heritage.

#2. Fontana di Orione (Fountain of Orion)

Next to the cathedral in Piazza del Duomo, you'll find the Fontana di Orione. This Renaissance fountain is both beautiful and a nod to Messina's mythological roots. Giovanni Angelo Montorsoli, a student of Michelangelo, built it in 1553. Many consider it one of Italy's finest.

The fountain celebrates Orion, Messina's mythical founder. Its design features three tiers, each packed with symbolism and carvings. The bottom basin displays eight masks, representing rivers from Sicily and Calabria. Above them, four river gods embody the Tiber, Nile, Ebro, and Camaro.

At the top, a statue of Orion stands tall, with his dog by his side. This highlights Orion's key role in Messina's founding myth and his protective symbolism.

The Fontana di Orione is not just a beautiful monument but also a masterpiece of hydraulic engineering for its time. Its complex system of pipes and spouts creates a mesmerizing display of flowing water, adding movement and life to the intricate stone carvings.

#3. Chiesa della Santissima Annunziata dei Catalani (Church of the Catalan saints)

A short walk along Via Garibaldi will bring you to the Chiesa della Santissima Annunziata dei Catalani, a small but historically significant church that stands as a testament to Messina's resilience and rich cultural heritage. Built between the 11th and 12th centuries, this church is one of the few medieval structures in Messina to have survived both the devastating 1908 earthquake and the bombings of World War II.

The church's name, "dei Catalani" (of the Catalans), comes from its later use by Catalan merchants who settled in Messina during the 14th century. This adds another layer to the building's rich history, tying it to the city's importance as a Mediterranean trading hub.

The church's architecture is a fascinating blend of Norman, Byzantine, and Arab influences, reflecting Sicily's diverse cultural history. Its exterior is particularly striking, featuring a distinctive red dome and intricate stone carvings. The façade is adorned with alternating bands of light and dark stone, creating a visually appealing striped effect characteristic of Norman-Arab architecture.

One of the most notable features of the church is its three apses at the eastern end, each decorated with blind arches and intricate stonework. The central apse is slightly larger and more elaborately decorated than the two flanking it, drawing the eye and emphasizing the building's symmetry.

Inside, the church's interior is more austere but no less impressive. The space is divided into three naves by columns with elaborate capitals. Look up to admire the wooden ceiling, a later addition that replaced the original Byzantine-style dome. The walls, once covered in frescoes, now reveal the church's architectural bones, allowing visitors to appreciate the skill of its medieval builders.

As you explore this architectural gem, take a moment to appreciate how it encapsulates Sicily's complex history. The Chiesa della Santissima Annunziata dei Catalani stands as a physical representation of the various cultures and civilizations that have left their mark on Messina over the centuries.

#4. Palazzo Zanca (Messina's City Hall)

Continue to Piazza Unione Europea to see Palazzo Zanca, Messina's City Hall. Rebuilt after the 1908 earthquake, this neo-classical building is home to the city's government. Take in the impressive façade, and explore the surrounding square, which features a statue of Giuseppe Mazzini, an important figure in Italian unification.

#5. Chiesa di San Francesco d'Assisi (Church of St. Francis)

Make your way to Viale Boccetta to visit the San Francesco d'Assisi Church, one of Sicily's oldest and most significant Franciscan churches. Built in the 13th century, this church holds a special place in Messina's religious and architectural history.

The church's exterior presents a blend of architectural styles, reflecting its long history and various restorations. While much of the original 13th-century structure was damaged in the 1908 earthquake, careful restoration work has preserved its medieval character. The façade, rebuilt in the 20th century, incorporates elements from different periods, creating a harmonious whole that tells the story of the church's resilience.

As you enter, you'll be struck by the spacious interior, typical of Franciscan churches designed to accommodate large congregations. The church houses several important medieval sculptures that survived the earthquake, offering a glimpse into Messina's artistic heritage. These sculptures, some dating back to the church's earliest days, showcase the skill of medieval craftsmen and the religious devotion of the era.

The Tomb of Fredrick of Aragon, King of Sicily

One of the most significant features of the church is the tomb of Federico d'Aragona. Federico, also known as Frederick III of Sicily, was King of Sicily from 1296 to 1337. He was a member of the House of Barcelona and played a crucial role in Sicilian history during the turbulent period following the Sicilian Vespers. His reign was marked by conflicts with the Angevin dynasty and the Papacy, as well as efforts to strengthen Sicily's independence.

Federico's tomb, located within the church, is not only a resting place for a powerful medieval ruler but also a fine example of 14th-century funerary art. The tomb's presence in this Franciscan church underscores the close relationship between the Aragonese dynasty and the Franciscan order in medieval Sicily.

As you explore the San Francesco d'Assisi Church, take time to appreciate both its architectural features and its historical significance. This church stands as a testament to Messina's rich past, its resilience in the face of natural disasters, and its importance as a center of power in medieval Sicily.

#6. Santuario della Madonna di Montalto (Sanctuary of Mary di Montalto)

Your next stop takes you to higher ground as you make your way up to the Sanctuary of the Madonna di Montalto, located on Viale Principe Umberto. This sanctuary, perched atop one of Messina's hills, offers not only spiritual significance but also breathtaking panoramic views of the city and the Strait of Messina.

According to local legend, the sanctuary's history dates back to the 13th century when the Virgin Mary appeared to a shepherd on this hill. This apparition led to the construction of the original church. However, like many of Messina's buildings, the sanctuary you see today is a reconstruction following the devastating earthquake of 1908.

The rebuilt sanctuary, completed in 1921, is a beautiful example of early 20th-century ecclesiastical architecture. Its design incorporates elements of the Romanesque and Gothic styles, creating a harmonious blend that pays homage to Messina's rich architectural heritage. The façade features a large rose window and is flanked by two bell towers, giving the sanctuary a commanding presence on the hillside.

As you approach the sanctuary, take note of the grand staircase leading up to the entrance. This ascent not only serves a practical purpose but also symbolizes the spiritual journey of pilgrims rising towards the divine.

Inside, the sanctuary is adorned with beautiful frescoes and mosaics, many of which depict scenes from the life of the Virgin Mary and the history of the sanctuary itself. The main altar houses a venerated statue of the Madonna di Montalto, which is the focus of local devotion and annual celebrations.

The Panoramic Terrace

One of the highlights of visiting this sanctuary is the panoramic terrace. From here, you can enjoy sweeping views of Messina, the bustling port, and the narrow Strait of Messina separating Sicily from mainland Italy. On clear days, you might even catch a glimpse of the Calabrian coast across the water. This vantage point offers a unique perspective on Messina's geography and its strategic importance as a maritime city throughout history.

The Sanctuary of the Madonna di Montalto remains an important religious site for the people of Messina, as well as a popular destination for both pilgrims and tourists. Its combination of spiritual significance, architectural beauty, and stunning views makes it a must-visit location on your tour of Messina.

#7. Museo Regionale (Regional Museum of Messina)

Walk to Viale della Libertà and visit the Regional Museum of Messina. The museum houses some of Messina's most treasured artworks, including works by Caravaggio and Antonello da Messina. It's a great place to dive into the city's artistic history. Be sure to see Caravaggio's "Resurrection of Lazarus" and Antonello da Messina's "Polittico di San Gregorio."

#8. Chiesa di Santissima Annunziata (Church of the Most Holy Annunciation)

Next, make your way to Piazza Annunziata to visit the Church of the Santissima Annunziata. This Baroque church, originally built in the 15th century, has a fascinating history of destruction and rebirth, mirroring Messina's own resilience.

The church's stunning façade is a masterpiece of Baroque architecture, featuring intricate stonework and sculptures. As you enter, you'll be struck by the beautiful interior, richly decorated with frescoes, marbles, and stucco work. The church houses several important artworks, including paintings by local artists and ornate altar pieces.

One of the church's most notable features is its ceiling, adorned with frescoes depicting scenes from the life of the Virgin Mary. Take time to admire the skilled craftsmanship and the play of light on the various textures and surfaces throughout the church.

The Church of the Santissima Annunziata also plays an important role in local religious traditions, hosting several festivals and processions throughout the year. If possible, try to time your visit to coincide with one of these events for a truly immersive cultural experience.

#9. Forte del Santissimo Salvatore and Madonnina del Porto

For the final stop of your tour, head to the tip of the sickle-shaped peninsula that forms Messina's natural harbor. Here, you'll find the Forte del Santissimo Salvatore, a 16th-century fort that offers panoramic views of the Strait of Messina and the city.

Next to the fort stands the Madonnina del Porto, a 60-meter tall column topped with a statue of the Madonna. This monument, visible to all ships entering the harbor, has welcomed visitors to Messina since 1934.

From this vantage point, you can enjoy a stunning view of the Strait of Messina, watching ships navigate the narrow passage between Sicily and mainland Italy. On clear days, you might even catch a glimpse of the Calabrian coast.

As the day winds down, this spot offers a perfect place to reflect on your tour of Messina. The changing colors of the sky at sunset, reflected in the waters of the strait, provide a memorable end to your exploration of this historic city.

Messina Festivals and Sagre Throughout the Year

Festival of the Madonna della Lettera (Feast of St. Mary of the Letter)

June 3rd

The Festival of the Madonna della Lettera is one of the most important religious celebrations in Messina, honoring the city's patron saint. According to legend, in 42 AD, the apostle Paul visited Sicily and preached in Messina. The citizens were so moved that they sent a delegation to Jerusalem to meet the Virgin Mary. She gave them a letter of blessing, which became known as the "Letter of the Madonna."

The festival begins with a solemn Mass at the Cathedral of Messina. Following this, a grand procession winds through the city streets, featuring a silver vara (a large, ornate platform) carrying a statue of the Madonna. The vara, weighing over a ton, is pulled by hundreds of devoted citizens. As night falls, the celebrations culminate in a spectacular fireworks display over the Strait of Messina, illuminating the sky and reflecting off the water in a breathtaking show of lights and colors.

Festa di Sant'Antonio (Feast of Saint Anthony)

June 13th

The Festa di Sant'Antonio is a beloved religious celebration honoring Saint Anthony of Padua. While Saint Anthony is particularly associated with the city of Padua, he is also highly venerated in Messina and throughout Sicily.

The festival begins with a solemn Mass at the Church of Sant'Antonio. Following the Mass, a procession carries a statue of the saint through the streets of Messina. Devotees often distribute small loaves of bread, known as "pani di Sant'Antonio" (Saint Anthony's bread), a tradition that stems from the saint's reputation for helping the poor and hungry.

Festa del Mare (Sea Festival)

July (exact dates vary)

The Festa del Mare is a vibrant celebration of Messina's deep connection to the sea. The event features a variety of maritime-themed activities. Visitors can enjoy boat tours of the Strait of Messina, fishing competitions, and demonstrations of traditional fishing techniques. There are often exhibitions of historic photographs and artifacts related to Messina's maritime history.

A highlight of the festival is the "Palio Marinaro," a traditional boat race in the waters of the strait. Teams representing different neighborhoods of Messina compete in colorful, traditional boats, creating a spectacular sight for onlookers.

The festival also celebrates the local seafood cuisine. Food stalls and restaurants offer a wide array of fresh seafood dishes, from grilled swordfish to seafood pasta. Live music performances, often featuring songs of the sea, and artisanal markets selling maritime-themed crafts add to the festive atmosphere.

Sagra della Melanzana (Eggplant Festival)

Typically held in August (exact dates may vary from year to year)

The Sagra della Melanzana is a gastronomic celebration of one of Sicily's most beloved vegetables: the eggplant. This festival takes place in various locations around Messina, with each town putting its own spin on the event. The eggplant, known locally as "melanzana," has been a staple of Sicilian cuisine for centuries, introduced by the Arabs during their occupation of the island.

During the festival, local restaurants and food stalls offer a wide array of eggplant dishes. Visitors can savor classic preparations like parmigiana di melanzane (eggplant parmesan), pasta alla Norma (pasta with eggplant and ricotta salata), and caponata (a sweet and sour eggplant relish). There are also more innovative creations, such as eggplant gelato or eggplant-based cocktails. The sagra often features cooking demonstrations, allowing visitors to learn traditional recipes and techniques. Live music, folk dancing, and artisanal craft markets add to the festive atmosphere, making it a true celebration of local culture and cuisine.

Festa di San Nicola (Feast of Saint Nicholas)

December 6th

The Festa di San Nicola is an important winter celebration in Messina, particularly in the district of Ganzirri. Saint Nicholas, known for his generosity and gift-giving, is celebrated with both religious and secular traditions.

The day begins with a Mass at the Church of San Nicola in Ganzirri, followed by a procession carrying the saint's statue through the streets. In keeping with Saint Nicholas's reputation as a protector of children, there are often special events for young people, including gift distributions and storytelling sessions about the saint's life.

In the evening, the celebration often concludes with a fireworks display over the lake of Ganzirri, creating a magical atmosphere that combines religious tradition with the natural beauty of the area.

Day Trip Options: Nearby Sites, Cities and Towns

Castroreale. 45 km (28 miles). Castroreale is a small hilltop town known for its panoramic views and rich baroque architecture. It's often referred to as the "Balcony of the Tyrrhenian Sea." Sites to see include: Church of Santa Maria degli Angeli, Civic Museum, Torre di Federico II (Frederick II Tower) and Palazzo Peculio.

Gole dell'Alcantara. 65 km (40 miles) from Messina. The Gole dell'Alcantara is a stunning natural wonder featuring a river gorge with unique basalt rock formations. It offers visitors beautiful scenery and outdoor activities. Sites to visit include: Alcantara River Gorge, Botanical and Geological Path, Small Byzantine church, and the adventure park with river activities.

Fiumedinisi. 30 km (19 miles) from Messina. Fiumedinisi is a small, picturesque town nestled in the Peloritani Mountains. It's known for its natural beauty, historic sites, and outdoor activities. Sites to see: Ruins of the Norman Castle, Church of Maria SS. Annunziata, Fiumedinisi River, and its waterfalls and hiking trails in the surrounding mountains.

Savoca. 30 kilometers (18.6 miles). A charming hilltop town, Savoca is famous for being a filming location for The Godfather. It offers a peaceful atmosphere, beautiful churches, and stunning views of the Sicilian countryside, making it a perfect day trip for history and film lovers.

Logistics

Train: Messina's Centrale Train Station connects the city with the rest of Sicily and the mainland. Trains run regularly to Catania, Palermo, and other major Sicilian cities.

Bus: The local bus service is operated by ATM Messina. Buses cover the entire city and connect to nearby suburbs, including popular areas like Torre Faro and Ganzirri.

Ferry: Messina is a major ferry hub, with frequent ferries to mainland Italy (Villa San Giovanni and Reggio Calabria) as well as nearby islands. Ferry port is near Messina Centrale station.

Tram: Messina has a single tram line that runs through the city along the coast, from Gazzi in the south to Annunziata in the north.

Car: Messina is well-connected by roads, making it accessible by car. Here are some key points about driving in Messina. The A18 autostrada connects Messina to Catania in the south, while the A20 connects to Palermo in the west. Driving in the city center can be challenging due to narrow streets and heavy traffic, especially during peak hours.

Parking: Parking in Messina can be challenging, especially in the city center. Here's what you need to know. There are both free and paid parking areas in Messina. Paid parking is usually indicated by blue lines on the ground. Many paid parking areas use a "Pay and Display" system where you purchase a ticket from a nearby machine and display it on your dashboard.

Dining Recommendations

I Ruggeri. Address: Via Pozzo Leone, 21

This refined restaurant combines contemporary cuisine with traditional Sicilian flavors. Popular dishes include tuna meatballs in sweet and sour sauce and linguine with sea urchins. Known for its elegant atmosphere and excellent service, I Ruggeri offers a well-curated wine list and beautifully presented dishes. It's a great option for those seeking a higher-end dining experience.

Casa & Putia Ristorante. Address: Via S. Camillo, 14

Located just a short walk from the Cathedral, Casa & Putia is a cozy and inviting restaurant offering a mix of Mediterranean and Sicilian cuisine. The restaurant focuses on high-quality, seasonal ingredients, and its menu features local favorites like seafood risotto and grilled meats.

Trattoria Paradisiculo. Address: Via Giuseppe Garibaldi

Offering friendly service and authentic Sicilian dishes, this trattoria is a popular choice among locals and tourists alike. The menu highlights include fresh seafood, pasta with sardines, and traditional Sicilian desserts. The restaurant offers a welcoming and casual dining experience.

Accommodation

Festival visitors will want to stay in town for four nights. There are several days of events. Many sites to see and if needed easy day trips.

**Royal Palace Hotel. Address: Via Tommaso Cannizzaro, 3

A 4-star hotel located near the train station and ferry terminal, the Royal Palace Hotel offers spacious rooms and modern amenities. Its central location makes it ideal for visitors exploring Messina or catching ferries to the Aeolian Islands or the mainland.

*Garibaldi R&B. Address: Via Giuseppe Garibaldi, 108

A charming small hotel offering bed and breakfast services in a prime location near the Messina Cathedral. The Garibaldi R&B combines comfort and convenience with its cozy atmosphere and attentive staff.

Hotel Touring. Address: Via Nicola Fabrizi

This 4-star hotel offers comfortable accommodations and great access to public transport. Known for its friendly staff, Hotel Touring is a good choice for those wanting to explore the city center.

*Hotel Sant'Elia. Address: Via I Settembre, 67

A budget-friendly option in Messina, Hotel Sant'Elia provides basic but comfortable rooms near the Duomo. It's popular with travelers looking for affordability and convenience in the heart of the city.

**Hotel Messenion. Address: Via Faranda, 7

A small, cozy hotel offering personalized service and comfortable rooms. Its central location near the Duomo and Messina's main attractions makes it a good choice for tourists.

**Re Vittorio De Luxe. Address: Via Nicola Fabrizi, 48

A boutique bed and breakfast known for its luxurious, modern decor and attention to detail. Re Vittorio De Luxe is located near the Duomo, making it an excellent base for exploring the city.

*On the procession route making these an excellent option for watching the procession of the Giants and the Vara Procession.

**Close to the procession route but not directly on it.

Chapter Twenty-Three

Saints and Sea Breezes in Lipari

Celebrating San Bartolomeo

Festa di San Bartolomeo

Where: Lipari, Aeolian Islands

When: August 24

Average Festival Temperatures: High: 26 - 30°C (79 - 86°F). Low: 20 - 23°C (68 - 73°F).

Discovering Lipari: Volcanic Jewel of the Tyrrhenian Sea

Lipari, the largest and most populous of the Aeolian Islands, rises from the Tyrrhenian Sea like a rugged emerald, its volcanic silhouette etched against the azure Mediterranean sky. With its rich archaeological heritage, dramatic landscapes, and vibrant maritime culture, this enchanting island has been a crossroads of Mediterranean civilizations for millennia. Today, Lipari serves as the bustling heart of the Aeolian archipelago, a UNESCO World Heritage site, offering visitors a unique blend of natural beauty, historical depth, and the laid-back charm of island life.

The history of Lipari stretches back into the mists of prehistory, with evidence of human habitation dating to the Neolithic period. The island's strategic location and abundant obsidian deposits made it a center of trade from ancient times. Greek colonists arrived in the 6th century BCE, establishing a settlement that would flourish for centuries. Lipari subsequently fell under Roman, Byzantine, Arab, and Norman rule, each leaving its mark on the island's culture and landscape.

The Medieval Castle, atop the ancient acropolis, showcases Lipari's layered history. Its walls guard archaeological treasures. Despite facing pirate raids and volcanic eruptions, Lipari has always bounced back. The island's people adapt to their environment.

Lipari, the largest island in the Aeolian archipelago, lies 30 kilometers off Sicily's northern coast. It's entirely volcanic, shaped by eruptions and seismic activity. The coastline features cliffs, hidden coves, and beautiful beaches, some with unique volcanic sand. Monte Chirica and Monte Sant'Angelo, two extinct volcanoes, dominate the interior. They offer stunning views of nearby islands and the sea. The island enjoys a Mediterranean climate, with hot, dry summers and mild winters, thanks to the surrounding sea.

Lipari has a population of approximately 12,000 permanent residents, though this number swells significantly during the summer tourist season.

The Festival of Saint Bartholomew

The Festival of St. Bartholomew (Festa di San Bartolomeo) is one of the most significant religious and cultural celebrations in the Aeolian Islands, with its epicenter on the island of Lipari. This vibrant festival honors St. Bartholomew, the patron saint of Lipari, and has been a cornerstone of the island's spiritual and cultural identity for over nine centuries.

The festival's origins can be traced back to the medieval period, likely around the 11th century. It began shortly after the arrival of St. Bartholomew's relics in Lipari, which were brought from Armenia during the tumultuous period of Islamic invasions in southern Italy. The islanders, seeking divine protection, embraced St. Bartholomew as their patron, believing he would safeguard them from various threats, including pirate attacks and natural disasters.

The construction of the Cathedral of San Bartolomeo during this period marked a significant milestone, establishing a spiritual focal point for the island. The festival evolved organically from the islanders' deep veneration for their new patron saint.

By the 12th century, the cult of St. Bartholomew had firmly taken root in Lipari's cultural fabric. The feast day on August 24th grew in importance and complexity over the centuries, incorporating both solemn religious observances and joyous cultural celebrations.

Life of St. Bartholomew

St. Bartholomew, also known as Nathanael, was one of the Twelve Apostles of Jesus Christ. Born in Cana of Galilee, he was introduced to Jesus by the Apostle Philip. The Gospel of John portrays Bartholomew as a sincere and faithful follower of Christ, known for his unwavering belief.

After Christ's Ascension, Bartholomew embarked on extensive missionary journeys, spreading the Gospel across various lands. Early Christian tradition holds that he preached in India, Armenia, Mesopotamia, Persia, and possibly Ethiopia. His mission in Armenia led to his martyrdom, where he faced brutal execution—traditionally described as being flayed alive and beheaded—for his role in converting people to Christianity.

The Festival of St. Bartholomew reaches its pinnacle on August 24th, transforming Lipari into a vibrant tapestry of religious devotion, cultural expression, and community celebration. The day unfolds with a series of events that blend centuries-old traditions with contemporary festivities:

1. **Solemn Mass:** The day begins with a grand mass at the Cathedral of San Bartolomeo, drawing locals, visitors, and clergy together in a display of communal faith and reverence.

2. **Procession of St. Bartholomew:** The heart of the celebration is the procession of St. Bartholomew's statue through Lipari's winding streets. This centuries-old tradition sees devout locals carrying the ornate statue, accompanied by the resonant pealing of church bells, fervent hymns, and solemn music. The procession's route, culminating at the port, symbolizes the saint's historical role in protecting the island.

3. **Blessing of the Sea**: At the port, a special ceremony takes place where prayers are offered, and the sea is blessed. This ritual underscores St. Bartholomew's role as protector of sailors and fishermen, a crucial aspect of life in the maritime community of Lipari.

4. **Fireworks Display**: As night falls, a spectacular fireworks show illuminates the sky over the sea, marking the transition from religious observance to festive celebration. The display is visible across Lipari and neighboring islands, uniting the archipelago in a moment of shared joy.

5. **Music and Festivities:** The evening ushers in a lively atmosphere of music, dance, and street performances. Local bands fill the air with traditional Aeolian melodies, while food stalls offer a tempting array of local delicacies such as pane cunzatu, arancini, and granita. Aeolian melodies have evolved to reflect the distinct cultural and environmental characteristics of the archipelago, emphasizing local experiences, legends, and the daily life of islanders, particularly in relation to fishing and volcanic activity.

6. **Cultural and Artistic Events:** The festival also features cultural exhibitions, concerts, and theatrical performances, showcasing the rich artistic heritage of Lipari and the broader Aeolian culture.

7. **Maritime Traditions:** Honoring Lipari's deep connection to the sea, the festival often includes boat parades. Fishing vessels, festively decorated, sail along the coast in a colorful display of the island's maritime history and ongoing seafaring traditions.

The Festival of St. Bartholomew is more than just a religious observance; it's a testament to Lipari's enduring cultural identity and community spirit. For over 900 years, this celebration has served as a unifying force, bringing together generations of islanders and visitors in a shared expression of faith, tradition, and joy.

Walking Tour of Lipari – Day 1

#1. Start at Marina Corta

Marina Corta Marina Corta is Lipari's picturesque old harbor. Stroll along the waterfront, where you'll find cafés, small fishing boats, and a view of the sea. It's a great place to grab a morning coffee or a pastry while soaking in the island's atmosphere. Near the harbor, you can see the Church of Souls in Purgatory (Chiesa delle Anime del Purgatorio), a small but charming church with a distinctive clock tower.

#2. Castello di Lipari (Lipari Castle)

From Marina Corta, head uphill to the Lipari Castle, which sits atop a rocky promontory. The castle complex includes ancient fortifications and the archaeological park, with ruins dating back to Greek, Roman, and Norman times. You can explore Greek and Roman theater ruins within the complex and enjoy panoramic views of the island and sea from the castle walls.

#3. Museo Archeologico Eoliano (Aeolian Archeology Museum)

While at the castle, visit the Aeolian Archaeological Museum within the complex. The museum houses an impressive collection of artifacts from the prehistoric era, through the Greek and Roman periods, up to the Norman occupation. The exhibits offer insight into the island's long history and its role in Mediterranean trade and culture. Don't miss the volcanic rock and mineral collection, which showcases the geological history of the Aeolian Islands.

#4. Cattedrale di San Bartolomeo (Cathedral of St. Bartholomew)

As the island's most important religious site, the Cathedral of San Bartolomeo is a must-see. Dating back to the 11th century and later rebuilt, it features a beautiful Baroque façade. Inside, you can admire beautiful frescoes and see the relics of St. Bartholomew, which play a central role in the annual festival. Adjacent to the cathedral, you'll find Norman cloisters worth exploring.

#5. Piazza Mazzini

After exploring the castle, walk down to Piazza Mazzini, one of Lipari's main squares. Enjoy the lively atmosphere as you pass small shops, local restaurants, and artisans selling handmade goods. You can take a break here, relax on a bench, or stop for lunch at a restaurant that offers traditional Aeolian dishes like pasta alla norma or pane cunzatu. Near the square, you can visit the Church of Santa Maria delle Grazie.

#6. Corso Vittorio Emanuele

From Piazza Mazzini, head along Corso Vittorio Emanuele, the main street in Lipari town. This pedestrian-friendly street is filled with boutiques, gelaterias, and local craft shops. It's a great place to experience the local culture, pick up souvenirs, or enjoy some Sicilian granita or cannoli. You'll also have the opportunity to sample local Malvasia wine in the shops along this street.

#7. Via Garibaldi to Marina Lunga

Continue your walk down Via Garibaldi, which will lead you to Marina Lunga, the principal port of Lipari. Enjoy the views of the sea, and the boats docked in the harbor. The seaside promenade here is perfect for a leisurely stroll, with stunning vistas of the nearby islands and the coastline.

#8. Belvedere Quattrocchi (Scenic lookout)

After exploring the port area, take a short walk or taxi ride to Belvedere Quattrocchi, one of the most breathtaking viewpoints on the island. The panoramic views over the cliffs and sea, with Vulcano Island in the distance, are stunning.

#9. Spiaggia Bianca (White Beach)

If you have time and the weather is favorable, head to Spiaggia Bianca, one of Lipari's most famous beaches. Known for its white pumice stone sand and crystal-clear waters, it's a perfect place to relax, enjoy the Mediterranean sun, and have a refreshing swim.

Discover the Aoleian Islands – Day 2

The Aeolian Islands received their name from Aeolus, the god of winds in Greek mythology, reflecting their breezy, maritime setting. Lipari, Salina, Vulcano, Stromboli, Panarea, Filicudi, and Alicudi are the seven main islands that make up the archipelago, each island with its distinct personality.

#1. Lipari: An excellent starting point for exploring the archipelago.

#2. Salina

Salina is the greenest of the Aeolian Islands, famous for its lush landscapes, vineyards, and caper farms. A caper is the edible flower bud of the caper bush (Capparis spinosa), a plant native to the Mediterranean region. These small, round buds are harvested before they bloom and are typically preserved in salt or pickled in vinegar. Capers are known for their tangy, salty, and slightly bitter flavor, which adds a unique burst of taste to dishes.

Capers range in size from tiny nonpareils (the most prized variety) to larger, more mature buds, which tend to be stronger in flavor. In addition to the buds, the fruit of the caper bush, known as caperberries, is also pickled and consumed.

It's the ideal destination for those who enjoy hiking, with trails leading up to the twin peaks of Monte Fossa delle Felci and Monte dei Porr,. Don't miss tasting the local Malvasia, a sweet dessert wine that Salina is renowned for.

#3. Vulcano

True to its name, Vulcano is an island of dramatic volcanic landscapes. Here, you can hike up to the Gran Cratere, an active volcano with steaming fumaroles, or relax in the mud baths and hot springs that are believed to have therapeutic properties. The island's extraordinary and otherworldly atmosphere is heightened by its beaches adorned with black sand.

#4. Stromboli

Stromboli is famous for its constantly erupting volcano. A visit to Stromboli offers a thrilling opportunity to see volcanic activity up close. Many tours include an evening hike to a viewpoint where you can safely watch the spectacular eruptions as the sun sets, casting a dramatic glow over the island.

#5. Panarea

Panarea is renowned for its chic, laid-back atmosphere, attracts a mix of celebrities and travelers seeking a quieter, more upscale escape. The island's pristine beaches, crystal-clear waters, and charming whitewashed houses make it an ideal destination for a relaxing day by the sea. It's also an excellent spot for snorkeling and diving.

#6. Filicudi and Alicudi

These two islands are the most remote and least developed of the Aeolian Islands, offering a true escape from the hustle and bustle of modern life. Filicudi captivates with its coves and prehistoric village ruins, while Alicudi offers a glimpse into a simpler, quieter way of life without paved roads and limited electricity.

Lipari Sagre Throughout the Year

Sagra del Cappero (Caper Festival)

June

The Sagra del Cappero, or Caper Festival, is a vibrant summer celebration dedicated to the capers that are a staple in Aeolian cuisine. Capers, the edible flower buds of the Capparis spinosa bush, thrive in the rocky, sun-drenched terrain of the Aeolian Islands. These small, round, green buds are typically pickled in brine or salt, resulting in their distinctive tangy, briny flavor that has become synonymous with the local gastronomy.

The festival, which usually takes place in early June, offers a cornucopia of caper-related activities and experiences. Local producers eagerly showcase their creativity with an array of dishes featuring capers as the star ingredient. Visitors have the opportunity to indulge in local specialties, savoring everything from caper-flavored pasta to fish dishes enhanced with zesty caper sauces. The adventurous palate might encounter caper pesto or refreshing salads incorporating freshly harvested capers.

Throughout the festival, cooking demonstrations captivate audiences, highlighting both traditional uses and innovative applications of capers in modern cuisine. Educational displays offer insights into the cultivation and processing of capers, shedding light on the labor-intensive harvesting process that takes place from late spring through early fall. Guided tours to local caper farms may be available for those keen to delve deeper, providing a firsthand look at the growing process.

Sagra del Pane e Vino (Bread and Wine Festival)

August

In the picturesque village of Quattropani on the island of Lipari, the Sagra del Pane e Vino (Bread and Wine Festival) unfolds each August, paying homage to two fundamental elements of Aeolian culinary tradition. This lively event brings together locals and tourists alike in a celebration of the region's gastronomic heritage, centered around the simple yet profound pleasures of bread and wine.

The festival is a sensory journey through the flavors of Lipari. Attendees have the chance to sample an impressive variety of local wines, including the famed Malvasia delle Lipari, a sweet wine that has become emblematic of the region. Complementing the wines is an assortment of traditional breads, often baked in wood-fired ovens, that impart a distinctive flavor and aroma. The air is filled with the enticing scent of freshly baked loaves as artisanal bakers demonstrate time-honored bread-making techniques, preserving skills passed down through generations.

Wine enthusiasts will appreciate the wine-making exhibitions that offer a glimpse into the process from grape to bottle, highlighting the care and expertise that go into each vintage. As visitors sip and nibble, they're treated to the lively rhythms of folk music and the swirling colors of traditional dance performances, adding a cultural dimension to the gastronomic experience.

Beyond its role as a showcase for local products, the festival serves as an important social gathering. It strengthens community bonds, facilitates the passing of culinary knowledge to younger generations, and offers a platform for local producers to connect directly with consumers. For visitors, it's an unparalleled opportunity to experience the authentic tastes of Lipari and gain insight into the island's rich agricultural heritage, all while participating in a joyous celebration of food, wine, and community.

Logistics

To reach Lipari, you need to take a ferry or a hydrofoil, which depart from several ports on mainland Italy and Sicily. Hydrofoils are faster but usually more expensive than ferries. Ferries are slower, but they can accommodate cars. It's advisable to book in advance during the summer and festival seasons, as the ferries and hydrofoils can fill up quickly, especially on weekends and holidays.

Here are the main departure points from Sicily

#1. Milazzo (Main departure point)

Milazzo is the most common and convenient departure point for ferries and hydrofoils to Lipari. Travel time: Hydrofoil: Around 1 hour. Ferry: Around 1.5-2 hours.

- Ferry Operators: Liberty Lines (hydrofoil), Siremar (ferry).

#2. Messina

Messina offers ferry and hydrofoil connections to Lipari. Travel time: Hydrofoil: Around 1.5-2 hours.

- Ferry Operator: Liberty Lines.

#3. Palermo

You can take a direct ferry or hydrofoil to Lipari from Palermo, but this option is less frequent than Milazzo or Messina. Travel time: 4 hours

- Ferry Operator: Liberty Lines

Logistics on Lipari

Taxis: Taxis are readily available at the port and in the main areas of Lipari town. They can take you to various points around the island, including popular sites and beaches.

Rental Scooters and Bikes: Many visitors opt to rent scooters or bicycles, which provide a flexible and convenient way to navigate the island's narrow roads and reach scenic spots.

Buses: There is a local bus service that operates around the island, connecting Lipari town to some of the other key areas, like Canneto, Quattropani, and Acquacalda.

Private Drivers: Some visitors hire private drivers for island tours or personalized transportation.

Boat Rentals: For a different perspective, boat rentals are available for exploring Lipari by sea and even visiting nearby islands in the Aeolian archipelago.

Walking: The island is relatively small, and many areas are easily accessible on foot, particularly around Lipari town.

Dining Recommendations

Ristorante Chimera. Address: Via Paolo Borsellino e Giovanni Falcone, Lipari

This restaurant offers stunning views and a menu that blends traditional Sicilian and Aeolian flavors. Known for its fresh seafood, locally sourced ingredients like capers and tomatoes, and friendly service, Ristorante Chimera is a popular choice for visitors. Located a short walk up the hill from the historic center, it is the perfect spot to enjoy a memorable meal while soaking in the island's beauty.

Trattoria del Vicolo. Address: Via Vittorio Emanuele

Nestled in a small alley near the harbor, this charming trattoria serves traditional Aeolian and Sicilian dishes in a cozy, welcoming atmosphere. Popular for its seafood risotto, pasta with capers and tomatoes, and octopus salad, Trattoria del Vicolo is loved by both locals and visitors for its authentic flavors and use of fresh, local ingredients.

Ristorante Filippino. Address: Piazza Municipio

One of the most famous restaurants in Lipari, Ristorante Filippino has been serving traditional Aeolian cuisine since 1910. Known for its excellent seafood and dishes like Aeolian-style swordfish, Filippino is situated in Marina Corta and offers a beautiful view along with its delicious food.

Accommodation

Hotel Tritone Lipari. Address: Via Mendolita

This 4-star hotel offers upscale accommodations with stunning sea views, a full-service spa, and an outdoor pool. Known for its luxurious amenities and relaxing atmosphere, Hotel Tritone provides free parking and Wi-Fi, making it a top choice for those seeking comfort and convenience on Lipari.

Hotel Mea Lipari - Aeolian Charme. Address: Via Falcone e Borsellino

A 4-star hotel offering elegant accommodations with two outdoor pools, dining options, and beautiful garden views. Hotel Mea is an excellent option for travelers who want modern amenities and a peaceful setting close to Lipari's center.

Hotel Giardino sul Mare. Address: Via Maddalena, 65

This 3-star hotel is a lovely seaside retreat with direct access to the beach. Offering an outdoor pool and sea-view terraces, it's perfect for a relaxing stay. The hotel provides basic but comfortable amenities, ideal for enjoying the natural beauty of Lipari.

*Odysseus Hotel Lipari. Address: Via Giuseppe Garibaldi

A 3-star hotel offering modern and well-appointed rooms. Odysseus Hotel is located near Lipari's main attractions and provides free Wi-Fi, breakfast, and a welcoming atmosphere. Its central location makes it a convenient base for exploring the island.

*Closest to the Cathedral and procession route for the Festa di San Bartolomeo.

Fall Celebrations
September through November

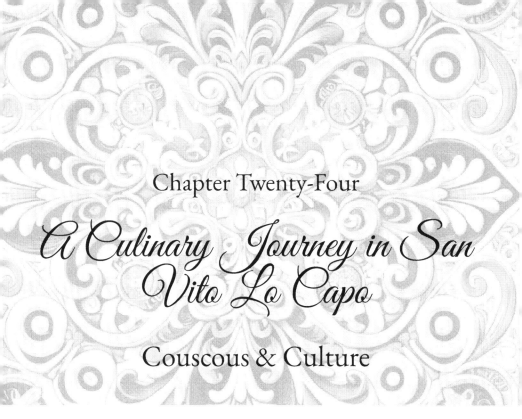

Chapter Twenty-Four

A Culinary Journey in San Vito Lo Capo

Couscous & Culture

C ous Cous Fest

Where: San Vito Lo Capo

When: Last week of September

Festival Website: https://couscousfest.it/

Temperatures: High: 25°C - 30°C (77°F - 86°F). Low: 17°C - 22°C (63°F).

Discovering San Vito Lo Capo: Sicily's Caribbean Paradise

Nestled between dramatic limestone cliffs and the crystal-clear waters of the Tyrrhenian Sea, San Vito Lo Capo stands as a beacon of natural beauty on Sicily's northwestern coast. This small coastal town, crowned by its iconic crescent-shaped beach of white sand, has transformed from a quiet fishing village into one of Sicily's most beloved seaside destinations. San Vito Lo Capo not only captivates visitors with its stunning landscapes but also enchants them with a unique blend of cultures, flavors, and traditions that reflect Sicily's rich and diverse heritage.

San Vito Lo Capo's history, though younger than other Sicilian towns, is captivating. Evidence of prehistoric settlement, like the Uzzo and Racchio caves in Zingaro Nature Reserve, exists. However, the town began to take shape in the Middle Ages. It's named after San Vito, a Christian martyr, and a 15th-century sanctuary built in his honor. This sanctuary, still standing today, once protected against pirates and guided sailors. Gradually, the town grew around it, relying on fishing and farming for centuries.

San Vito Lo Capo occupies a privileged position on a small peninsula that juts out into the Tyrrhenian Sea, about 40 kilometers northwest of Trapani. The town is flanked by two nature reserves: the Zingaro Reserve to the east and Mount Cofano to the west, creating a stunning natural amphitheater. Often compared to Caribbean shores for its beauty, the coastline features a 3-kilometer-long beach of fine, white sand.

The backdrop of Monte Monaco, rising dramatically behind the town, adds to the picturesque setting. This unique geography has shaped not only the town's development but also its climate, which is typically Mediterranean but moderated by sea breezes, making it a pleasant destination year-round.

San Vito Lo Capo has a permanent population of around 4,700 residents.

The Couscous Fest

Established in 1998 in San Vito Lo Capo, Sicily, the Couscous Fest, also known as Cous Cous Fest, was created. In collaboration with the municipality of San Vito Lo Capo, Massimo Bonelli, a local entrepreneur and food enthusiast, created the festival. Their goal was to celebrate the cultural and culinary connections between Sicily and North Africa, while also promoting tourism in the area. The festival's inception was inspired by the historical ties between Sicily and North Africa, particularly the Arab influence on Sicilian culture and cuisine during the Middle Ages. By focusing on couscous, a dish common to both regions, the organizers sought to highlight these shared culinary traditions and foster cultural exchange.

Couscous is a traditional North African dish made from tiny steamed balls of semolina flour. The word "couscous" refers both to the finished dish and to the pasta itself. It's a staple food throughout the Maghreb region (North Africa), including Morocco, Algeria, Tunisia, and Libya. Traditional couscous preparation involves steaming the semolina grains over a stew of meat and vegetables in a special pot called a couscoussier. The couscous is then fluffed to separate the grains and served with the stew spooned over the top, often accompanied by additional vegetables and sometimes dried fruit.

The presence of couscous in Sicily dates back to the Arab domination of the island, which lasted from the 9th to the 11th centuries. During this period, Arabs introduced various culinary traditions, ingredients, and techniques that significantly influenced Sicilian cuisine. Arabs brought couscous to Sicily during their rule over the island (827-1091 AD), and Sicilians adapted the dish to local tastes and available ingredients, particularly incorporating seafood instead of the traditional meat used in North African recipes. In western Sicily, especially in the Trapani area, couscous became a staple dish. The Sicilian version, known as "cuscusu" in the local dialect, is typically prepared with fish and seafood. Couscous in Sicily represents the historical connections and cultural exchanges between North Africa and the island, symbolizing the multicultural heritage of the region.

The Couscous Fest serves several important functions in promoting cultural exchange and culinary innovation. It brings together chefs and visitors from various Mediterranean countries, fostering understanding and appreciation of different cultures. The festival encourages chefs to create new variations of couscous, blending traditional methods with modern culinary techniques. It has become a significant event in Sicily's tourism calendar, attracting visitors from around the world and boosting the local economy of San Vito Lo Capo and surrounding areas. By celebrating couscous, the festival helps maintain awareness of this important culinary heritage. The Couscous Fest has grown from a local event to an international celebration, highlighting the power of food to connect cultures and preserve historical traditions while encouraging innovation and cross-cultural understanding.

Walking Tour of San Vito Lo Capo

Although the main draw of this bay is its picturesque beach, I have put together a walking tour of San Vito Lo Capo that focuses on the town's key attractions, natural beauty, and historical sites.

#1. San Vito Lo Capo Beach

Begin the tour with a stroll along the town's renowned sandy beach. Enjoy the beautiful turquoise waters and take in the stunning coastal views. It's a glorious spot to relax and take photos. The beach stretches for about 3 kilometers and is known for its white sand and crystal-clear water, often compared to Caribbean beaches.

#2. Santuario di San Vito (Sanctuary of San Vito)

Head towards the Sanctuary of San Vito, the historic center of the town. Originally a 14th-century chapel dedicated to Saint Vito, the sanctuary has developed over the centuries into a prominent religious site. Admire the fortress-like structure and the picturesque courtyard. The sanctuary's current appearance dates back to the 15th century, with its imposing square towers and thick walls reflecting its dual purpose as a place of worship and defense.

Sanctuary's Crypt

Visit the crypt of the Sanctuary, dating back to the 15th century. This space provides a glimpse into the sanctuary's history and architectural evolution. The crypt houses the remains of Saint Vito and his companions, Saints Modesto and Crescentia, and features beautiful frescoes depicting scenes from their lives.

#3. Torre di San Vito

Walk to the Torre di San Vito, a 16th-century watchtower built to protect the coast from pirate attacks. The tower offers panoramic views of the coastline and the surrounding area. Standing at 32 meters tall, it was part of a network of coastal towers used to spot approaching enemy ships and warn the population.

#4. **Stroll Through the Town Center** in Piazza Santuario and surrounding streets

Wander through the town center, where you'll find charming streets lined with shops, cafes, and restaurants. Enjoy the local atmosphere and perhaps stop for a coffee or gelato. Don't miss trying the local specialty, "cous cous alla trapanese," a dish that reflects the area's Arab influences.

#5. **Head to the Capo San Vito Promontory on the southern edge of the** town

Walk towards the Capo San Vito promontory for breathtaking views of the coastline and the Mediterranean Sea. The area offers excellent opportunities for photography and a peaceful retreat from the busier parts of town. On clear days, you might spot the outline of the Egadi Islands in the distance.

#6. Visit the Local Market in Piazza Santuario

Check out the local market where you can find fresh produce, local crafts, and regional specialties. It's a great place to pick up souvenirs and experience local life. Look for locally produced olive oil, sun-dried tomatoes, and "busiate," a type of pasta typical to the Trapani region.

San Vito Lo Capo Festivals and Sagre

Festa degli Aquilioni (International Kite Festival)

May

This colorful festival, which tours Sicily, concludes with a grand finale in San Vito Lo Capo. Internationally renowned kite flyers compete in acrobatic kite flying sessions set to music. The event attracts thousands of spectators who enjoy the spectacle of hundreds of kites filling the sky above the beautiful beaches of San Vito Lo Capo. Workshops, kite-making demonstrations, and family-friendly activities are also part of the festivities.

Festa di San Vito (Feast of Saint Vito)

June 15-17

This annual festival celebrates San Vito, the patron saint of the town, with religious processions, traditional music, and local festivities. The highlight is the grand procession of San Vito's statue, joined by residents and pilgrims. Included in the three-day event are special Masses, concerts of traditional Sicilian music, food stalls offering local specialties, and fireworks displays. The celebration culminates on June 17th, the feast day of San Vito.

Festa della Madonna della Salute (Our Lady of Health)

September 8

People show their reverence to the Madonna della Salute (Our Lady of Health) during this festival. The Madonna della Salute is significant as a symbol of divine protection and healing in Catholic tradition. The event includes a solemn religious procession through the town streets, with a statue of the Madonna carried by the faithful. Local celebrations feature traditional Sicilian food, music performances, and prayers for good health. The festival typically concludes with an evening Mass and a fireworks display.

San Vito Climbing Festival

October

This international festival for climbers takes place in the stunning natural surroundings of San Vito Lo Capo. The event comprises various climbing competitions on the area's limestone cliffs, catering to different skill levels from beginners to experts. Participants can enjoy bouldering, sport climbing, and deep-water soloing (climbing over water). The festival also includes climbing workshops, equipment demonstrations, film screenings about climbing, and evening social events where climbers from around the world can network and share experiences. Local guides offer tours of the best climbing spots in the region, showcasing the area's potential as a climbing destination.

Day Trip Options: Nearby Sites, Cities, and Towns of Interest

Monte Cofano Nature Reserve. 20 kilometers (12 miles) from San Vito Lo Capo. This stunning coastal reserve is characterized by its dramatic limestone mountain, Monte Cofano, which rises 659 meters above sea level.

The reserve offers:

- Scenic hiking trails with varying difficulty levels
- Breathtaking panoramic views of the Tyrrhenian Sea
- Rich Mediterranean flora and fauna, including rare plant species

- Ancient watchtowers and the 17th-century Tonnara del Cofano
- Beautiful, secluded pebble beaches ideal for swimming and snorkeling

Segesta. 60 kilometers (37 miles) from San Vito Lo Capo. This ancient city is one of Sicily's most important archaeological sites. . Visitors can explore:

- The remarkably well-preserved 5th-century BCE Doric temple
- An impressive Greek theater with panoramic views of the countryside
- The ruins of the ancient town, including fortifications and houses
- A small museum showcasing artifacts found at the site
- The nearby medieval village of Calatafimi-Segesta

Riserva Naturale dello Zingaro. 15 kilometers (9 miles) from San Vito Lo Capo. Sicily's first nature reserve, established in 1981, offers a pristine coastal landscape.

Highlights include:

- Seven kilometers of unspoiled coastline with pebble beaches and crystal-clear waters. Many hiking trails showcasing the diverse Mediterranean ecosystem
- Over 650 plant species, many of which are rare or endemic. Rich birdlife, including peregrine falcons and Bonelli's eagles
- Small museums dedicated to local traditions, such as weaving and rural life
- Spectacular cliffs and hidden coves perfect for swimming and snorkeling

Logistics

Train: The closest train station to San Vito Lo Capo is in Trapani, located about 38 kilometers away. From Trapani, you can take a bus or taxi to reach San Vito Lo Capo.

Bus: Several bus companies operate routes connecting San Vito Lo Capo with major cities in Sicily, such as Palermo and Trapani.

Car: By car from Trapani, the main road to take is the SP16. It takes about 45 minutes to arrive.

Parking: In San Vito Lo Capo, the historic center has a ZTL (Zona a Traffico Limitato), restricting access to cars, especially during peak tourist seasons. Here are a few options:

- Parking Savoia: Located at Via Savoia, this parking area is outside the ZTL and within walking distance to the beach and the town center.

- Parking Macari (Park and Ride): A park-and-ride option located just outside San Vito Lo Capo. During peak season, a shuttle service operates regularly to take visitors from the parking lot to the town center and beach area.

Dining Recommendations

Bottega Sugameli. Address: Via Duca degli Abruzzi, 88

This Sicilian restaurant offers a variety of local dishes, with specialties that reflect the rich culinary traditions of the area. It is known for its cozy ambiance and late closing hours, perfect for enjoying a meal late into the night.

Allantica Osteria. Address: Via Regina Margherita, 14

A traditional Italian restaurant offering a range of authentic dishes with a focus on regional flavors. Known for its warm and inviting atmosphere, this osteria is popular for its well-executed local cuisine.

La Battigia. Address: Via Savoia, 5

Offering a picturesque dining experience, this restaurant is popular for its fresh seafood and Italian dishes. The spacious outdoor seating adds to the appeal, providing a perfect spot for enjoying a meal by the water.

Accommodation

Hotel Capo San Vito. Address: Via San Vito, 1

A 4-star beachfront hotel offering luxurious accommodations with stunning sea views. Guests enjoy access to a gourmet restaurant, spa, and a private beach. Free Wi-Fi, breakfast, and beach access are included, making it an ideal destination for a relaxing seaside getaway.

Hotel Mira Spiaggia. Address: Via Litoranea Lungomare

This 3-star hotel is perfect for a casual, laid-back beach holiday, featuring dining options and a full-service spa. It provides free breakfast, Wi-Fi, and easy access to the beach, catering to both relaxation and adventure seekers.

Hotel Ristorante Tannure. Address: Via Regina Margherita, 91

A 3-star hotel known for its friendly service and on-site restaurant offering traditional Sicilian cuisine. Guests appreciate its simple yet comfortable accommodations with free Wi-Fi, air conditioning, and proximity to the beach.

Hotel Soffio D'Estate. Address: Via del Secco, 22

This highly-rated 3-star hotel offers peaceful sea views and a relaxed atmosphere. With free Wi-Fi, beach access, and breakfast included, it provides a quiet retreat for travelers looking to unwind by the coast.

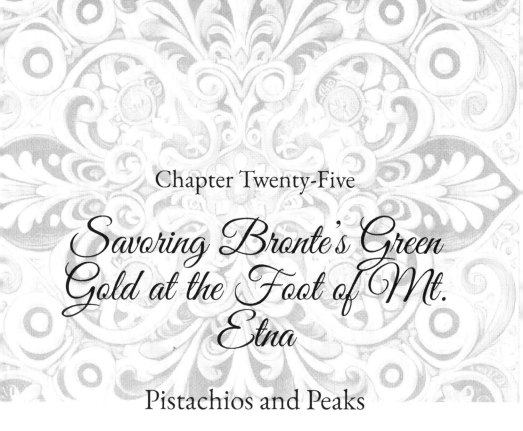

Chapter Twenty-Five

Savoring Bronte's Green Gold at the Foot of Mt. Etna

Pistachios and Peaks

Sagra del Pistachio

Where: Bronte

When: Last week of September, first week of October, aligned with pistachio harvest

Website: https://www.sagradelpistacchiodibronte.com/

Average Festival Temperatures: High: 22°C - 27°C (72°F - 81°F). Low: 13°C - 17°C (55°F - 63°F).

Discovering Bronte: The Emerald Town in Etna's Shadow

Nestled on the western slopes of Mount Etna, Bronte stands as a testament to Sicily's rich agricultural heritage and complex historical tapestry. Known worldwide as the "City of Pistachios," this small inland town offers visitors a unique blend of natural beauty, gastronomic delight, and surprising historical connections. Bronte's story is one of resilience and adaptation, shaped by the fertile volcanic soil of Etna and the diverse cultures that have left their mark on this corner of Sicily.

The history of Bronte stretches back to ancient times, with evidence of Greek and Roman settlements in the area. However, the town's modern identity took shape in the medieval period. The name "Bronte" is believed to derive from the Greek word "bronté," meaning thunder, perhaps a reference to the rumbling of nearby Mount Etna. The town's history took an unexpected turn in 1799 when King Ferdinand IV of Naples granted the estate of Bronte to British Admiral Horatio Nelson, in gratitude for his support against the French. This created the curious title of "Duke of Bronte," which was held by Nelson and his heirs until the 20th century. This British connection, while titular, added an intriguing layer to Bronte's cultural identity.

Bronte is 50 kilometers northwest of Catania, on the western slopes of Mount Etna. The town's territory spans a diverse landscape, from the volcanic foothills of Etna to the valley of the Simeto River. This unique position, with its volcanic soil enriched by centuries of Etna's eruptions, has created ideal conditions for agriculture, particularly for the cultivation of pistachios. The "Pistacchio Verde di Bronte DOP" is renowned worldwide for its intense flavor and vibrant green color. The looming presence of Etna, Europe's largest active volcano, not only shapes the landscape but also the daily lives and culture of Bronte's inhabitants.

Bronte has a population of approximately 19,000 residents. The town's economy is primarily based on agriculture, with pistachio cultivation and processing at its heart.

The Pistachio Festival

Bronte is a charming village nestled on the western slopes of Mount Etna, Europe's largest active volcano. While it's not the only town in this region - other notable communities on Etna's slopes include Zafferana Etnea, Nicolosi, and Randazzo - Bronte has gained particular fame for its pistachios and the festival that celebrates them.

Why Pistachios Thrive in Bronte

Bronte's pistachios are exceptionally high-quality because of the unique conditions in the area. The fertile, mineral-rich soil from Mount Etna's volcanic activity provides an ideal growing medium for pistachio trees. The nuts' distinctive flavor and vibrant green color are attributed to the soil's high levels of potassium, phosphorus, and magnesium.

Pistachio cultivation in Bronte benefits from the specific microclimate found on the western slopes of Etna. The area experiences hot, dry summers and mild winters, with significant temperature variations between day and night. This climate stress encourages the trees to produce more flavorful nuts. Bronte's pistachios are grown at elevations between 400 and 900 meters above sea level, which contributes to their slow growth and intense flavor development.

Local farmers still use many traditional, non-intensive cultivation techniques, which, combined with the unique environment, result in pistachios of exceptional quality.

The Festival Experience

The festival showcases an impressive array of pistachio-based foods. Visitors can sample traditional dishes like pasta with pistachio pesto and arancini with pistachio filling, as well as sweets such as pistachio gelato, cakes, cookies, and cannoli. More innovative creations like pistachio pizza and pistachio-flavored sausages are also available, alongside various pistachio-based products, including spreads, oils, and liqueurs.

Local chefs and home cooks give cooking demonstrations, highlighting traditional Sicilian recipes featuring pistachios. These shows often showcase both classic preparations and modern interpretations of dishes. The festival also includes demonstrations of traditional pistachio harvesting and processing methods. Visitors can observe hand-picking techniques used on the steep slopes of Etna, traditional roasting methods, and the process of removing pistachios from their shells.

Beyond food, the festival celebrates local culture with folk music and dance performances, craft demonstrations, and sales of local artisanal products. Historical exhibits about Bronte and its pistachio heritage provide context for visitors.

The educational component of the festival often includes conferences about sustainable agriculture and the importance of protecting traditional foods, guided tours of nearby pistachio groves, and workshops on the nutritional benefits of pistachios.

The festival highlights the importance of the DOP (Protected Designation of Origin) status of Bronte pistachios. Since 2009, the "Pistacchio Verde di Bronte DOP" label guarantees that only pistachios grown in the Bronte area using traditional methods can be recognized.

The Pistachio Festival not only celebrates a unique local product but also serves as a vibrant showcase of Sicilian culture, culinary tradition, and agricultural heritage. It has become a significant draw for both domestic and international tourists, helping to boost the local economy and preserve traditional farming practices in the region.

The Pistachio Delights to Find at the Sagra

- Pistachio Arancini: Traditional Sicilian rice balls filled with a savory pistachio mixture, offering a delightful twist on a classic favorite.

- Pistachio Gelato: Creamy and rich ice cream that captures the distinct taste of Bronte pistachios, providing a refreshing treat.

- Pistachio Pesto: A flavorful sauce made by blending pistachios with olive oil and herbs, commonly used to dress pasta dishes, adding a unique Sicilian flair.

- Pistachio Cannoli: Crisp pastry shells filled with sweetened ricotta cheese and studded with chopped pistachios, combining textures and flavors in a beloved dessert.

- Pistachio Granita: A semi-frozen dessert that offers a cool and nutty refreshment, perfect for warm festival days.

- Pistachio-Infused Sausages: Savory sausages enhanced with the subtle sweetness of pistachios, showcasing the nut's versatility in meat dishes.

- Pistachio-Studded Salami and Mortadella: Traditional cured meats embedded with pistachios, adding both visual appeal and a distinctive taste.

- Pistachio Pecorino Cheese: Aged sheep's milk cheese interspersed with pistachios, offering a harmonious blend of sharp and nutty flavors.

- Pistachio Pastries and Cakes: Various baked goods, including tarts and traditional Sicilian desserts, all featuring pistachios as a central ingredient.

Walking Tour of Bronte

#1. Piazza Spedalieri

Begin your tour at the central square of Bronte, Piazza Spedalieri. This vibrant hub of town life offers the perfect setting to start your journey. Take a moment to soak in the atmosphere at one of the local cafes, enjoying a coffee or gelato while observing the daily rhythms of Bronte's residents. The square serves as an excellent introduction to the town's character and provides a glimpse into local life.

#2. Church of San Vincenzo Ferreri

Dedicated to Bronte's patron saint, the Church of San Vincenzo Ferreri is a testament to the town's religious heritage. This 18th-century church showcases a stunning blend of Baroque and Neoclassical architectural styles. Its imposing facade features ornate decorations and columns, crowned by a bell tower with a distinctive clock. Step inside to admire the interior, where you'll find beautiful frescoes depicting scenes from Saint Vincent's life, a marble altar with intricate carvings, and a revered statue of Saint Vincent Ferrer. The church not only serves as a place of worship but also symbolizes Bronte's deep-rooted devotion.

#3. Santuario della Madonna Santissima Annunziata (Church of the Annunciation)

Dating back to the 16th century, the Church of Annunziata is renowned for its unique architectural features, particularly its window crafted from lava stone. This distinctive use of lava stone is a hallmark of Bronte's architecture, sourced from nearby Mount Etna and symbolizing the town's connection to the volcano. Inside, you'll find notable paintings including "The Annunciation" by an unknown 17th-century artist and a "Madonna and Child" attributed to the school of Antonello da Messina.

As you continue your walk through Bronte, keep an eye out for other examples of lava stone used in doorways, window frames, and decorative elements throughout the town, showcasing the material's durability and unique aesthetic appeal.

#4. Galleria Capizzi (Capizzi Gallery)

Housed in an 18th-century former Jesuit residence, the Capizzi Gallery offers a journey through art and history. The gallery features an extensive library with rare books and manuscripts, alongside an art collection showcasing local and regional artists.

Explore exhibits of historical documents related to Bronte's past, paintings depicting Sicilian landscapes and traditions, and rotating temporary exhibitions highlighting contemporary artists. This cultural treasure trove provides insight into the artistic and intellectual heritage of Bronte and the wider Sicilian region.

#5. Bronte's Historical Center

Immerse yourself in Bronte's rich history as you wander through the narrow, winding streets of its historical center. This area is characterized by traditional architecture and hidden gems waiting to be discovered. Look out for the 19th-century Palazzo Marziani with its ornate balconies, the Medieval Torre dell'Orologio (Clock Tower) offering panoramic views, and remnants of the ancient city walls. As you explore, you'll encounter traditional Sicilian balconies adorned with wrought-iron railings, tucked-away courtyards, small piazzas, and street shrines dedicated to various saints. Each corner of the historical center tells a story of Bronte's past.

#6. Bronte's Market Stalls

Along Via Etnea and the surrounding streets, you'll find Bronte's lively market stalls. This is your opportunity to explore and sample the local specialties, particularly the famed pistachio-based products. Browse through an array of pistachio pastries, spreads, pesto, and liqueurs.

The market also offers a selection of local crafts, including ceramics, lava stone jewelry, and textiles, as well as fresh seasonal produce. Engage with the friendly local vendors to learn about traditional products and recipes, gaining insight into the culinary and cultural heritage of Bronte.

#7. Pistachio Orchards

A short walk or drive from the town center will bring you to Bronte's renowned pistachio orchards. These groves are best visited between late August and early October during the harvest season. Here, you'll see rows of pistachio trees bearing their distinctive reddish-brown nuts, with farmers using traditional hand-picking and net collection methods.

The orchards offer stunning views of Mount Etna in the background, creating a picturesque setting. Learn about the unique volcanic soil that contributes to the pistachios' renowned flavor, Bronte's DOP (Protected Designation of Origin) status for its pistachios, and the fascinating biennial nature of pistachio harvests.

Depending on your pace and the time you spend at each site, the tour typically lasts between 2-3 hours.

Bronte Festivals Throughout the Year

Festa di San Biagio (Saint Blaise)

Held annually on February 3

San Biagio is a patron of Bronte, and his feast day is celebrated with processions and cultural events. The festival includes a solemn Mass at the Church of San Biagio, followed by a procession through the town streets. Local artisans set up stalls selling traditional crafts and foods, including pistachio-based treats.

Carnevale di Bronte

Held in February, leading up to Lent.

This carnival celebration features colorful parades, masquerade balls, and street performances. Local schools and community groups create elaborate floats and costumes, often incorporating themes related to Bronte's history and culture.

Festa di San Vincenzo Ferreri (St. Vincent Ferreri)

April 5-10

The Festa di San Vincenzo Ferreri in Bronte is a deeply rooted religious and cultural celebration. San Vincenzo Ferreri is venerated as the town's protector, and the festival commemorates his life and miracles. The tradition dates back centuries, with a significant religious procession featuring a statue of the saint carried through the town's streets. Community members, clergy, and musicians participate in this colorful event, which also includes a fair with rides, games, and concerts showcasing traditional Sicilian folk music.

Sagra della Ricotta e del Formaggio (Ricotta and Cheese Festival)

Usually held in spring.

Visitors can taste and purchase various types of locally produced cheeses, take part in cheese-making demonstrations, and enjoy traditional Sicilian dishes featuring ricotta and other cheeses.

Festa di Santa Maria dell'Odigitria (Feast of Mary Who Shows the Way)

Second Sunday of August

This festival in honor of the Madonna dell'Odigitria is a significant religious and cultural celebration in Sicily. The event includes religious ceremonies, processions, and various local festivities that bring the community together.

The highlight is the procession of the Madonna's statue through the streets, accompanied by fireworks and traditional Sicilian music. Townspeople celebrate with Sicilian customs, creating a vibrant atmosphere that blends faith and cultural pride, bonding the entire community. This festival also reflects a long-standing devotion to the Virgin Mary under the title "Odigitria" (Greek for "She who shows the way"). This title connects the festival to Byzantine origins, emphasizing the Madonna's role as a guiding figure.

Festa della Vendemmia (Grape Harvest Festival)

Held in late September or early October, coinciding with the grape harvest season.

This event celebrates the local wine-making tradition with grape stomping competitions, wine tastings, and folk music performances.

Festa di San Nicola (Feast of St. Nicholas)

December 6

This festival honors Saint Nicholas, another patron saint of Bronte. The celebration includes a special Mass, a procession with the saint's statue, and the distribution of small gifts to children, reflecting the saint's reputation for generosity.

Day Trip Options: Nearby Sites, Cities and Towns

Lago Gurrida. Approximately 15 kilometers (9.3 miles) from Bronte. A small lake formed by the damming of the Alcantara River by lava flows from Mount Etna. It's a tranquil spot where you can go for nature walks, observe birds, and take in the area's natural splendor.

Randazzo. 11 kilometers (7 miles) from Bronte. Known for its well-preserved historic center, beautiful churches such as the Basilica of Santa Maria, and its proximity to the Alcantara River and its gorges.

- **Castello Svevo** (remains of a 13th-century Norman castle) Activities:
  - Walking tour of the historic center
  - Visit to the local markets for traditional Sicilian products
  - Wine tasting at nearby Etna DOC wineries

Adrano. 29 kilometers (18 miles). Home to the Norman Castle, which hosts an archaeological museum, and the ancient Greek ruins of Adranon.

Logistics

Train: Circumetnea Railway (Ferrovia Circumetnea): This narrow-gauge railway runs around Mount Etna and includes a station in Bronte. It provides scenic travel options to and from Bronte, with connections to other towns on the Circumetnea line.

Mainline Trains: For broader regional connections, the nearest mainline train stations are in nearby towns such as Catania or Randazzo.

Local Buses: Buses operated by AST (Azienda Siciliana Trasporti) connect Bronte with other towns such as Catania, Randazzo, and Bronte.

Regional Buses: For longer journeys, intercity buses offer routes to major Sicilian cities and attractions.

Car: The closest major town to Bronte is Catania, about 50 kilometers away. If you are driving from Catania, you would take the SS121 (Strada Statale 121) heading west.

Parking: For parking in Bronte, it's advisable to park outside the ZTL (Zona a Traffico Limitato). You can find public parking areas near the outskirts of the historic center, such as: Parking Via Umberto: Located close to the town center but outside the ZTL, making it convenient for visitors. Parking near Piazza Spedalieri: Another option just outside the restricted zone, providing easy access to the main areas.

Dining Recommendations

Gennarino's Bistrò. Address: Corso Umberto

A cozy bistro offering a delightful mix of Sicilian and Mediterranean dishes, Gennarino's Bistrò is well-regarded for its charming ambiance and modern takes on traditional cuisine.

Protoosteria. Address: Via Luca Professor Placido, 22

This restaurant offers high-quality Mediterranean cuisine in a welcoming setting. It emphasizes fresh ingredients and local flavors, making it a favorite among both locals and visitors.

Bona Bonè. Address: Via Annunziata, 41, Bronte

A popular pizzeria in Bronte, Bona Bonè serves a wide variety of delicious pizzas made with fresh ingredients. It is known for its casual dining atmosphere and excellent value.

Accommodation

Staying overnight for sagre is optional. If you decide to stay in town, two nights would be enough to see the sights and enjoy the sagra. There are no hotels in the center of the village, but these are options in the vicinity.

I Cugi House. Address: Via Messina, 207, 95034 Bronte

A cozy bed-and-breakfast known for its friendly service, I Cugi House offers comfortable, air-conditioned rooms with free parking and breakfast. It's perfect for those seeking a homely atmosphere and personalized service during their stay in Maletto.

Hotel Villa Dorata. Address: Contrada Serra la Nave, 95030 Ragalna

This 3-star hotel is near the main crater of Mount Etna, offering a charming and scenic retreat. Set in a renovated princely residence, the hotel features elegant rooms with period furnishings. It provides free Wi-Fi, free parking, and breakfast, making it a superb choice for travelers who want to experience the natural beauty and history of Etna.

Rifugio Ariel. Address: C.da Serra la Nave, 95030 Ragalna

Rifugio Ariel is a 3-star hotel near the Etna region. It provides a rustic excellent base for exploring the surrounding landscapes and engaging in outdoor activities.

Chapter Twenty-Six

FestaFusion Militello

Madonna della Stella & Santissimo Salvatore

FestaFusion in Militello in Val di Catania

#1 Festa di Santissimo Salvatore: A vibrant religious celebration thSat honors the Santissimo Salvatore with processions, music, and fireworks, boasting a rich history that spans over 200 years.

#2 Festa della Madonna della Stella: This festival pays homage to the Madonna della Stella, featuring a grand procession through the town, cultural events, and a deep display of devotion from the local community.

#FestaFusion means two or more festivals happen around the same time in the same town, so visitors can enjoy multiple events during their visit.

Where: Militello in Val di Catania

When: August 18 and September 8

Average Festival Temperatures: High: 27°C - 30°C (81°F - 86°F). Low: 18°C - 21°C (64°F - 70°F).

Discovering Militello in Val di Catania: Baroque Marvel of Eastern Sicily

Nestled in the gentle hills of eastern Sicily, Militello in Val di Catania stands as a testament to the island's rich baroque heritage and enduring cultural significance. This small town, often overlooked by casual tourists, is a treasure trove of architectural splendor and historical depth. Recognized as part of the UNESCO World Heritage site "Late Baroque Towns of the Val di Noto," Militello offers visitors a glimpse into Sicily's golden age of baroque art and architecture, set against a backdrop of rural charm and timeless traditions.

The history of Militello stretches back to ancient times, with evidence of Greek and Roman settlements in the area. However, the town's defining moment came in the wake of the catastrophic earthquake of 1693, which devastated much of eastern Sicily. This disaster, while tragic, sparked a remarkable period of reconstruction that gave birth to the stunning baroque townscape we see today.

The Bonanno family, princes of Roccafiorita, played a crucial role in this rebirth, financing the construction of numerous churches and palaces that would come to define Militello's architectural character. This period of renewal not only reshaped the town physically but also reinvigorated its cultural and economic life, establishing Militello as a significant center of art and learning in 18th-century Sicily.

Militello is situated about 45 kilometers southwest of Catania, in the fertile valley that bears its name. The town is perched on a hill at an elevation of about 400 meters above sea level, offering panoramic views of the surrounding countryside. This inland location, away from the more touristed coastal areas, has helped Militello preserve its authentic character. The landscape around the town is a patchwork of citrus groves, olive orchards, and small farms, reflecting the agricultural traditions that have long been the backbone of the local economy.

Militello has a population of approximately 7,000 residents. While modest in size, the town punches well above its weight in terms of cultural significance.

#1 Festa di Santissimo Salvatore

Since 1788, Militello has celebrated the Most Holy Savior (Santissimo Salvatore in Italian), its patron saint, on August 18th. In Catholic tradition, the Most Holy Savior refers to Jesus Christ as the savior of humanity. While many towns have saints as patrons, Militello's choice of Christ himself as the patron is somewhat unique. The festivities begin a week earlier than the main celebration day.

Pre-Festival Events (August 8-17)

The celebration officially starts 10 days before with the "Cantata," featuring prayers, songs, the ringing of bells, and cannon fire. Each evening, a procession carries a canvas of Christ the Savior, an early 19th-century piece, through the town, signaling the approaching holiday.

During the nine days leading up to August 18th, known as the Novenario, there are daily religious ceremonies and processions, where a canvas depicting the face of Christ the Savior is carried through the streets. This period of novena is common in Catholic traditions, allowing the faithful to prepare spiritually for the upcoming feast day.

August 17 (Vigilia)

On August 17th, the Vigilia day, the local marching band traverses the streets in the morning, filling the air with festive music. In the evening, the Mayor, religious leaders, and authorities head to the Mother Church, accompanied by the festival committee. Each dignitary brings a silver key to unlock the bronze door of the sacellum, housing the statue of the Santissimo Salvatore. This ritual symbolizes the community's unified devotion and the special access granted on this holy occasion.

The day ends with the offering of candles and flowers at the Mother Church. After offering candles and flowers, they unveil the sacred canvas, likely revealing it for public veneration during the festival.

August 18 (Main Day of the Festival)

The day begins with 101 cannon shots and bells ringing throughout the town, a traditional way to mark the importance of the day and call the faithful to celebration.

A solemn pontifical mass is held in the morning, likely presided over by a bishop or high-ranking church official, emphasizing the significance of the feast. This is followed by the grand procession in the afternoon. The statue of Santissimo Salvatore is carried through the streets, allowing the entire community to participate in the veneration.

During the procession, families express their devotion by entrusting their newborns to the Patron, dressing them in red, a symbol of faith. This custom likely originated from the belief in divine protection and blessing for the youngest members of the community.

The celebration culminates in a colorful display of fireworks and a final ascent to Mount Calvary. While I don't have specific information about the terrain, the reference to Mount Calvary (or Golgotha in the Bible) suggests this may be a symbolic journey, possibly to an elevated area of the town or a nearby hill, representing Christ's path to crucifixion.

The event concludes with a Prayer Vigil on August 24th, followed by one last procession on August 25th, known as the "four songs". While I don't have specific information about these songs, they likely refer to traditional hymns or canticles sung during this final procession, possibly representing different aspects of Christ's life or the community's devotion.

Throughout the festival period, the town likely comes alive with not only religious observances but also cultural events, food stalls featuring local delicacies, and displays of traditional crafts, contributing to both the spiritual and economic life of Militello in Val di Catania.

#2 Festival of Our Lady of the Star

The Festival of Madonna della Stella, dedicated to the main patron saint of Militello in Val di Catania, is the most significant religious festival in the city. This celebration honors the Virgin Mary under the title "Our Lady of the Star," emphasizing her role as a guiding light and protector for the faithful.

The Virgin Mary is often associated with various titles and apparitions in Catholic tradition. The title "Madonna della Stella" or "Our Lady of the Star" likely refers to Mary's role as a celestial guide, much like the Star of Bethlehem guided the Wise Men to the infant Jesus. This symbolism of Mary as a guiding light for believers is deeply rooted in Catholic spirituality.

Santuario di Santa Maria della Stella, the main church in Militello, is dedicated to Santa Maria della Stella and serves as the focal point for the festival. It holds the precious statue of Maria Santissima della Stella, which is central to the festival celebrations.

The church and the devotion to Madonna della Stella have a rich history in Militello. The Santuario di Santa Maria della Stella was originally built in the 16th century but was severely damaged in the devastating 1693 Sicily earthquake. The church was subsequently rebuilt, incorporating elements of Sicilian Baroque architecture, which was characteristic of the post-earthquake reconstruction period in many parts of Sicily.

Celebrations in Honor of Madonna della Stella

August 29

The festivities begin on August 29th with the traditional procession known as the "Cantata," which winds through the principal streets of Militello in Val di Catania, accompanied by fireworks. This marks the start of a nine-day period of preparation leading up to the festival, known as a novena in Catholic tradition.

September 7

On September 7th, the day before the feast, the chapel doors are opened to reveal the precious simulacrum of Maria Santissima della Stella, a cherished statue crafted from golden wood and hemp in 1618. The statue, which was carefully restored after the 1693 earthquake by the sculptor Camillo Confalone, is then placed on an elaborate 18th-century wooden fercolo (processional cart). After the votive candle is presented by the Mayor, the statue is prepared for the grand procession on the following day.

September 8

On September 8th, the streets of Militello in Val di Catania are filled with emotion and devotion as the Madonna della Stella is carried through the town in a vibrant procession.

The celebration is accompanied by a range of events, including a parade of flag-wavers, performances by the town's band, fireworks, concerts, and other musical performances. This date, September 8th, is significant in the Catholic calendar as it marks the Feast of the Nativity of the Blessed Virgin Mary.

The Rivalry of Mariani and Nicolesi

A unique aspect of this festival is the historical rivalry between two groups in the town: the Mariani and the Nicolesi. This rivalry dates back to medieval times and intensified following the decrees of the Council of Trent in the late 16th century.

The Mariani are the devotees of the Madonna della Stella, whose main church is the Santuario di Santa Maria della Stella. They are named after their devotion to Mary (Maria in Italian).

The Nicolesi, on the other hand, are devoted to San Nicolò (Saint Nicholas), whose church is the Chiesa Madre di San Nicolò e del SS. Salvatore. They take their name from their patron saint.

While rooted in religious devotion, this rivalry has evolved into a friendly competition that adds a unique cultural dimension to the festival. During the celebrations, each group strives to outdo the other with more impressive fireworks displays and elaborate decorations throughout the city.

The competition between the Mariani and Nicolesi is most visible during their respective festivals. While the Mariani celebrate the Festival of Our Lady of the Star in September, the Nicolesi have their own festival honoring San Nicolò, typically celebrated in December.

This friendly rivalry not only adds excitement to the festivities but also serves to preserve and promote local traditions. It encourages community participation and fosters a sense of belonging and identity among the townspeople. The dynamic interplay between these two groups during the festivals highlights the deep-rooted traditions and passionate devotion that characterize Militello in Val di Catania's religious and cultural landscape.

Walking Tour of Militello

#1. Piazza Vittorio Emanuele III

Begin your tour at the heart of Militello, Piazza Vittorio Emanuele III. This bustling square is surrounded by stunning Baroque architecture. Take a moment to admire the ornate facades of the buildings that frame this historic center.

#2. Chiesa di San Benedetto e Santa Chiara (Church of St. Benedict and St. Claire)

A short walk from the piazza brings you to the Church of San Benedetto e Santa Chiara. Built-in the 17th century, this church is a prime example of Sicilian Baroque architecture. Marvel at its intricate façade before stepping inside to view the elegant frescoes and beautiful altarpieces.

#3. Museum of the Archdiocese

Continue to the Museum of the Archdiocese, housed in the former Convent of San Domenico. This museum boasts an impressive collection of sacred art spanning several centuries. Don't miss the exquisite wooden sculptures and intricately crafted silverware, showcasing the skill of local artisans throughout history.

#4. Chiesa di Santa Maria della Stella (Church of St. Mary of the Star)

Next, visit the town's main church, Santa Maria della Stella, also known as the Chiesa Madre. This landmark dates back to the medieval period but was rebuilt in the Baroque style after the devastating earthquake of 1693. As you approach, notice the church's imposing façade, a masterpiece of Sicilian Baroque architecture

Upon entering, you'll be struck by the grandeur of the interior. The church features a Latin cross plan with three naves separated by massive pillars. Look up to admire the ornate ceiling adorned with intricate stucco work and frescoes. The side chapels house numerous artistic treasures, including paintings and sculptures from various periods.

The church's crowning jewel is the statue of Maria Santissima della Stella, a revered 17th-century sculpture that holds a central place in local devotion. This wooden statue, adorned with precious jewels, is the focus of Militello's annual festival. Don't miss the elaborate silver monstrance, a masterpiece of Sicilian silversmithing, displayed in one of the side chapels.

Santa Maria della Stella

#5. Chiesa di San Nicolò (Church of St. Nicholas)

A short walk from the Chiesa Madre brings you to the Church of San Nicolò, another jewel in Militello's crown of religious architecture. This church, dedicated to St. Nicholas, has a long-standing historical rivalry with Santa Maria della Stella, reflecting the town's rich ecclesiastical heritage.

The church's façade, while more restrained than that of Santa Maria della Stella, is nonetheless impressive. Notice the elegant stonework and the central rose window. Inside, the church is a treasure trove of art and architecture. The interior is divided into three naves, with the central nave featuring a barrel vault adorned with frescoes depicting scenes from the life of St. Nicholas.

Pay special attention to the church's prized possessions: a 16th-century crucifix attributed to the school of Antonello Gagini, and a painting of the Madonna and Child by the Sicilian artist Filippo Paladini. The church also houses several reliquaries and liturgical objects of significant artistic and historical value.

#6. Santa Maria La Vetere (The Ancient Saint Mary's Church)

Continue your journey to Santa Maria La Vetere, a fascinating deconsecrated church that offers a unique window into Militello's past. This church was originally built by the Normans around 1090, shortly after they took the region from Saracen rule, it has witnessed centuries of history.

As you approach, notice the church's distinctive appearance - it's actually a partial remnant of the original structure. The left side of the church collapsed during the 1693 earthquake, leaving the crypt exposed. This unexpected architectural feature allows visitors to view the crypt from the walkway, offering a rare glimpse into the church's substructure.

The façade is particularly interesting. Look for the portal protected by a portico supported by two columns with lion bases, a symbol of the church's artistic significance. The portal's reliefs, dating back to 1506, still retain traces of their original polychrome paint, giving you an idea of how vibrant the church once looked.

Inside, or what remains of the interior, you can see evidence of the church's long and tumultuous history. The site was chosen near an older sacred area - a Christian cemetery from the late ancient or early medieval period. Over the centuries, the church was destroyed and rebuilt several times, including after a major fire in 1618.

Perhaps most intriguingly, Santa Maria La Vetere houses a crusader cemetery, a rare and historically significant feature. This cemetery provides a tangible link to the Crusades and the role that Sicily played in these historical events.

Despite its partial state, Santa Maria La Vetere remains a powerful testament to Militello's rich religious and cultural heritage, offering visitors a unique opportunity to literally see layers of history.

Romanesque Portal of Santa Maria La Vetere

#7. Via Porta della Terra

Take a leisurely stroll down Via Porta della Terra, a charming street that cuts through the historical center. Here, you'll encounter a delightful mix of Baroque palaces, ancient stone buildings, and small shops offering local crafts and delicacies.

#8. Palazzo Baldanza-Denaro

As you walk along Via Porta della Terra, make a stop at Palazzo Baldanza-Denaro. This palace showcases beautiful Baroque architecture and offers a glimpse into the opulent lifestyle of the local aristocracy. Admire its elaborate façade and, if possible, explore its grand interiors.

Tree Lined Street of Militello

#9. Castello Barresi-Branciforte (Castle)

Conclude your tour at the Castello Barresi-Branciforte, the ancient castle that once served as Militello's defensive stronghold. Although much of the original structure lies in ruins, the castle grounds provide a tangible link to the town's medieval origins. Enjoy panoramic views of Militello and the surrounding landscape from this elevated position.

Another Festival in Militello

Sagra della Mostarda e Ficodindia (Festival of the Ficodindia (cactus flower) and Mostarda (grape must))

First two weekends in October

The Sagra della Mostarda e Ficodindia is a beloved annual festival in Militello, Sicily, celebrating two local specialties: mostarda and ficodindia. This event has been a cherished tradition for over 32 years, showcasing the region's culinary heritage and agricultural bounty.

In this context, Mostarda likely refers to a sweet grape must reduction, not the mustard condiment. It's a traditional Sicilian product made from grape must, often used in desserts and pastries. This clarifies the confusion about mustard being classified as a fruit.

Ficodindia, known in English as prickly pear or Indian fig, is the fruit of the Opuntia ficus-indica cactus. While prickly pears are indeed associated with desert climates, they thrive in Sicily's Mediterranean climate. The island's warm, sunny conditions and well-draining soils are ideal for these cacti, which were introduced to Sicily centuries ago and have become an integral part of the landscape and cuisine.

Sicily, including the area around Militello, is not a true desert but has a semi-arid Mediterranean climate with hot, dry summers and mild, wet winters. This climate is perfect for cultivating both grapes (used for mostarda) and prickly pears.

During the festival, visitors can expect:

- Tastings of fresh ficodindia and various mostarda-based products
- Culinary demonstrations and workshops
- Local artisans selling traditional crafts
- Music and folkloric performances celebrating Sicilian culture
- Educational exhibits about the cultivation and history of these foods in the region

This festival not only celebrates these unique local products but also serves as a significant cultural and economic event for Militello, attracting tourists and food enthusiasts from across Sicily and beyond.

Day Trip Options: Nearby Sites, Cities and Towns

Vizzini. 18 kilometers (11 miles) from Militello. Vizzini, a town of rolling hills and stunning views, is steeped in literary history as the birthplace and muse of Giovanni Verga, a seminal figure in the Italian Verismo movement. Visitors can immerse themselves in Verga's legacy at the Casa-Museo di Giovanni Verga, where personal artifacts, manuscripts, and period furnishings bring the author's life and works to life. Strolling through the town's medieval streets reveals Baroque architectural gems like the Chiesa Madre di San Gregorio Magno, with its ornate facade and rich interior decor. The annual Cavalleria Rusticana Festival honors Verga's work with cultural events and performances, adding vibrancy to the town's historical charm.

Visitors can explore the Casa-Museo di Giovanni Verga, which preserves the author's memorabilia and offers insights into his life and works. The town's medieval streets and Baroque churches provide a charming backdrop for literary enthusiasts and history buffs alike.

Palagonia. 12 kilometers (7.5 miles) from Militello. Palagonia, often overlooked by travelers, offers an authentic Sicilian experience with its serene atmosphere and unpretentious beauty. The Church of San Giuseppe captivates visitors with its exquisite frescoes, while the Palazzo Gravina-Cruyllas stands as a testament to the town's noble past. Food lovers will delight in local specialties like sfincione, a thick Sicilian pizza, and pasta alla Norma, served in family-run trattorias that pride themselves on traditional recipes. For those visiting during festival times, Palagonia's lively streets come alive with processions and celebrations, reflecting the deep cultural roots of this charming town.

Grammichele. 32 kilometers (20 miles) from Militello. Grammichele is unique for its hexagonal street plan, a design element that sets it apart from other Sicilian towns. This layout, created during the town's post-earthquake reconstruction in 1693, converges at Piazza Carafa, a vibrant central square lined with cafes and shops. The Mother Church of San Michele Arcangelo, with its imposing Baroque architecture and intricate interior artwork, is a focal point of the town. History enthusiasts will enjoy the Archaeological Museum, which houses relics from ancient settlements, including pottery and tools. The town's innovative urban planning and historical depth make it a rewarding destination for curious travelers.

Mineo. 17 kilometers (10.5 miles) from Militello. Perched atop a hill, Mineo enchants visitors with its labyrinth of narrow alleys and centuries-old buildings. Literature buffs will appreciate its connection to Luigi Capuana, a major figure in the Verismo movement. The Casa Capuana, his birthplace, offers insights into the life and times of this influential writer. Mineo's ancient past is evident in the Castle of Mineo, a medieval stronghold with panoramic views, and the ruins of a Roman amphitheater, which hint at the town's prominence during antiquity.

The Church of San Pietro, with its grand bell tower and serene interior, is another highlight. Every spring, Mineo hosts festivals celebrating its rich heritage, including traditional Sicilian music and folklore.

Logistics

Train: Militello has a train station, part of the local railway network, connecting it to larger cities like Catania and Syracuse.

Bus: Buses provide another option for reaching Militello in Val di Catania, with services operated by local bus companies such as AST (Azienda Siciliana Trasporti).

Car: Arriving by car from Catania to Militello in Val di Catania is a straightforward journey of approximately 60 km southwest. The main route is via the SS385 (Strada Statale 385), which typically takes about 1 hour, depending on traffic conditions. As you drive, you'll pass through the picturesque Sicilian countryside, encountering other small towns and agricultural areas along the way.

Parking: Parking in Militello in Val di Catania is generally manageable due to its small-town nature. The town center and areas near major attractions offer several public parking options. While some streets may have free parking available, it's important to be vigilant about checking for any parking restriction signs. If you're planning a longer stay, it's advisable to consult with your accommodation about parking recommendations or inquire if they offer private parking facilities for guests.

For those traveling with larger vehicles or seeking designated parking areas, there is a spacious parking lot near the sports facilities on Viale Regina Margherita. This area includes two parking lots: a smaller one upon arrival and a much larger one in the opposite direction. The first is well-lit, while the second is slightly less illuminated, both located approximately 100 meters from the sports facilities.

As always, ensure your vehicle is parked in permitted areas to avoid fines, and consider reaching out to local authorities or your accommodation for the most current parking information.

Dining Recommendations

U Trappitu. Address: Via Principe Branciforte, 125

A popular restaurant offering Italian, Mediterranean, and seafood dishes with a warm and welcoming ambiance. Known for its high-quality service and delicious seafood, U Trappitu is a great spot for family dinners or special occasions.

U Pacha. Address: Via Donna Giovanna D'Austria, 43

Offering a variety of Italian and Mediterranean dishes, U Pacha is a cozy restaurant where you can enjoy a relaxed dining experience. The menu includes both seafood and pizza options, all served in a comfortable setting. This is our recommendation. The food was incredible.

Accommodation

Depending on how you organize for the festivals two nights in Militello should be sufficient to see the sites and partake in the events.

Militello Albergo Diffuso. Address: Corso XX Settembre, 82, Militello in Val di Catania

A charming 3-star hotel located in the heart of the town's historic center. An "albergo diffuso" in Italy offers rooms across several buildings with modern amenities, including Wi-Fi, air conditioning, and a flat-screen TV. So, not one palazzo with rooms but they buy up different spaces and convert them. The hotel is pet-friendly and features a shared kitchen, a garden, and terrace spaces, making it ideal for travelers looking to explore the local area on foot or by bike.

Because this hotel is an albergo diffuso I cannot say if some of their rooms may be on the procession routes. But you can certainly ask when you book.

Chapter Twenty-Seven
Cesarò's Taste of Tradition: Porcini & Black Pig Festival

Sagra del Suino Nero e del Fungo Porcino di Nebrodi

Where: Cesarò

When: October

Average Festival Temperatures: High: 22°C (72°F). Low: 13°C (55°F).

Discovering Cesarò: Mountain Haven of the Nebrodi

Perched high in the Nebrodi Mountains of northeastern Sicily, Cesarò stands as a testament to the island's rugged interior and enduring rural traditions. This small mountain town, often overlooked by tourists focused on Sicily's coastal attractions, offers visitors a glimpse into a way of life shaped by the rhythms of nature and centuries of pastoral culture. Surrounded by dense forests, rolling pastures, and pristine lakes, Cesarò serves as a gateway to the natural wonders of the Nebrodi Park and a custodian of Sicily's mountain heritage.

Cesarò's history, like many small Sicilian mountain towns, is ancient yet unclear. It has been inhabited since Greek and Roman times. However, the modern town began to form in the medieval period. The name "Cesarò" likely comes from the Latin "Caesarus," hinting at its Roman connections. Historically, Cesarò has focused on pastoral life. Raising sheep and cattle has been key to its economy and culture.

Cesarò is situated at an elevation of about 1,150 meters above sea level, making it one of the highest towns in Sicily. It lies within the heart of the Nebrodi Mountains, about 150 kilometers east of Palermo and 100 kilometers west of Messina. The town's territory encompasses a diverse landscape of mountains, forests, and high-altitude pastures known as "nebrodi." This unique environment is home to a rich variety of flora and fauna, including the rare Nebrodi black pig and numerous endemic plant species.

Cesarò has a population of approximately 2,300 residents.

The Festival of the Nebrodi Black Pig and Porcini Mushroom

For over 20 years, the Nebrodi Black Pig and Porcini Mushroom Festival in Cesarò has been a major gastronomic event. This multi-day festival usually lasts three days, drawing visitors from across Sicily and beyond. The festival celebrates two local delicacies: the Nebrodi black pig and porcini mushrooms.

The Nebrodi black pig, native to Sicily, is a medium-sized breed. Adult males typically weigh between 90 to 140 kg (198 to 308 lbs), while females weigh slightly less, around 80 to 120 kg (176 to 264 lbs). These pigs are known for their hardiness, being raised in semi-wild conditions in the Nebrodi mountains, which contribute to their lean meat and high-quality fat content, prized in Sicilian cuisine. Their dark, almost black coat is well-suited to the local environment, allowing them to thrive in the mountainous terrain.

Porcini mushrooms are highly prized in Sicily, especially in the Nebrodi Mountains, where they grow abundantly in the region's rich forests. The Nebrodi Mountains are known for their diverse ecosystems, and the cool, moist conditions in the high-altitude forests provide an ideal environment for porcini mushrooms (Boletus edulis), which thrive in these areas.

Sicily is known more for its Mediterranean climate, but the Nebrodi Mountains, with their unique conditions, produce high-quality porcini mushrooms that rival those found in northern Italy. These mushrooms have a robust, earthy flavor and are a popular ingredient in Sicilian cuisine, used in risottos, pasta dishes, and soups.

At the heart of the festival is the gastronomic village, where visitors can indulge in freshly prepared dishes featuring these local ingredients, cooked on-site to highlight their rich flavors. Activities range from cooking shows and tastings to guided tours of the surrounding area. The festival also includes cultural performances, exhibitions, and live music.

Porcini & Black Pig Festival Food

1. **Pasta with Porcini Mushrooms:** A simple yet flavorful pasta dish featuring fresh porcini mushrooms sautéed in olive oil with garlic and herbs, served over al dente pasta, often topped with local pecorino cheese.

2. **Porcini Risotto:** Creamy risotto made with fresh porcini mushrooms, slowly cooked to absorb their earthy flavor, with a touch of white wine and local Sicilian cheeses for richness.

3. **Grilled Nebrodi Black Pig Sausages:** Juicy sausages made from the Nebrodi black pig, seasoned with traditional herbs and spices, and grilled to perfection, offering a smoky and savory flavor.

4. **Nebrodi Black Pig Roasts:** Slow-cooked roasts from various cuts of the Nebrodi black pig, often prepared with local herbs and accompanied by a porcini mushroom sauce or served alongside roasted vegetables.

5. **Stewed Nebrodi Black Pig with Porcini Mushrooms:** A hearty dish featuring tender black pig meat slow-cooked with porcini mushrooms, tomatoes, and herbs, often served with rustic bread or polenta.

Walking Tour of Cesarò

#1. Piazza Umberto I

This is the main square and heart of Cesarò, perfect for starting your day. Enjoy an espresso and a traditional Sicilian pastry like cannoli or cassata at one of the local cafes. Take in the lively atmosphere as locals go about their day.

#2. Chiesa Madre di Santa Maria Assunta

This 16th-century church, just off the main square, is Cesarò's primary place of worship. Inside, admire the Baroque decorations and religious artworks, including paintings depicting the life of the Virgin Mary and intricate stucco work.

#3. Stroll through the Streets of the Historic Center

Wander through the narrow, cobblestone streets surrounding Piazza Umberto I. This area forms the historic center of Cesarò. While ceramics aren't a specific specialty of Cesarò, you might find some traditional Sicilian maiolica in local shops. Look out for artisanal wood carvings and textile products, which are more characteristic of the Nebrodi area.

#4. Explore the Nebrodi Regional Park Visitor Center

A short 10-minute walk from the town center, this center offers valuable insights into the Nebrodi Park's ecosystem. Learn about the famous Nebrodi black pig, local flora, and fauna. Pick up maps for hiking routes if you plan to explore further.

#5. Palazzo Zito

This 19th-century neoclassical building is about a 5-minute walk from the Visitor Center. While not always open to the public, its facade is worth admiring. Occasionally, it hosts temporary exhibitions on local history and culture, particularly during the summer months. Check with the tourist office in Piazza Umberto I for current exhibitions.

#6. End with a Taste of Local Dairy Products

Visit a local dairy shop like "Caseificio Cesarò" to sample renowned local cheeses. Try the Provola dei Nebrodi, a stretched-curd cheese, or the pecorino pepato, a sheep's milk cheese with peppercorns.

Cesarò Festivals and Markets

Fiera di San Calogero (Feast of Saint Calogero)

June 18-19

This annual festival honors San Calogero, the patron saint of Cesaro. The fair combines religious devotion with agricultural traditions. It features a solemn procession where a statue of San Calogero is carried through the town streets. Local artisans display their crafts, including woodwork, ceramics, and textiles. The agricultural aspect includes exhibitions of livestock, particularly sheep and cattle, which are important to the local economy.

Nebrodi Land Market

Every third Sunday of the month

This monthly market showcases the rich culinary and artisanal heritage of the Nebrodi area. Local producers offer a wide range of products typical of the Nebrodi mountains, including:

1. Cheeses: Such as Provola dei Nebrodi and Pecorino Siciliano

2. Cured meats: Including the famous Salame dei Nebrodi

3. Honey: Various types produced in the Nebrodi mountains

4. Mushrooms: Locally foraged varieties when in season

5. Hazelnuts: A specialty of the region

6. Olive oil: Extra virgin olive oil from local producers

7. Fruits and vegetables: Seasonal produce from nearby farms

8. Artisanal breads and pastries: Traditional Sicilian baked goods

The market also often features demonstrations of traditional crafts and occasional cultural events. It was established more recently, likely within the last few decades, as part of efforts to promote local products and support small-scale producers in the region.

Day Trip Options: Nearby Sites, Cities and Towns

San Teodoro. 15 kilometers (9 miles) from Cesaro. San Teodoro, nestled in the rolling hills of the Sicilian countryside, is not only known for its Wheat and Mutton Festival but also for its rural charm and unspoiled landscapes. Outside of festival time, you can explore the Church of San Teodoro Martire, a simple yet beautiful local church with historic significance. The town is surrounded by agricultural land, giving visitors a chance to see the authentic rhythms of rural life in Sicily. Hikers can take advantage of the trails that wind through the surrounding countryside, offering views of the Nebrodi mountains and opportunities to observe local wildlife.

Floresta. 20 kilometers (12 miles) from the town center. Known as the highest town in Sicily, Floresta stands at 1,275 meters above sea level and offers much more than the Ottobrando Festival. Beyond its famous October celebrations, the town's stunning panoramic views are a key attraction, with vistas of the Nebrodi Mountains and the Peloritani Range visible on clear days.

Logistics

Train: While there's no direct train service to Cesaro, the nearest train stations are in Capo d'Orlando or Sant'Agata di Militello. You would need to arrange additional transportation to reach Cesaro from these stations.

Bus: There may be limited bus services connecting Cesaro to nearby larger towns, but schedules can be infrequent and may not be reliable for tourists.

Car: The primary mode of transport to Cesaro is by car. This offers the most flexibility for exploring the town and surrounding areas. The closest big city to Cesarò is Catania, located approximately 80 km (50 miles) to the southeast.

Parking: As Cesaro is a small town, parking is likely available in the town center or nearby streets. Look for designated parking areas or follow local parking signs.

Dining Recommendations

Albergo Ristorante Mazzurco Di Mazzuco Masi Antonino E C. SNC.
Address: Strada Nazionale, Cesarò

A traditional restaurant and hotel with a family atmosphere, known for its Mediterranean cuisine and local specialties. The restaurant offers a variety of Sicilian dishes, including hearty portions of pasta, meats, and fresh local produce.

Birrificio Artigianale "Accussì". Address: Via Stradale Sant'Antonio, 110

This craft brewery is a favorite for its artisan beers and laid-back atmosphere. Visitors can enjoy a variety of beers on tap, along with snacks, in a cozy pub-style setting.

Accommodation

Overnight stays are not necessary for the sagre but if you choose to stay in town, I recommend one or two nights.

Albergo Ristorante Mazzurco Di Mazzuco Masi Antonino E C. SNC.
Address: Strada Nazionale

A traditional hotel with a cozy, family-run atmosphere. It is well-known for offering comfortable accommodations along with a restaurant that serves hearty Sicilian and Mediterranean cuisine. P

Hotel Ristorante Fratelli Mazzurco. Address: Via Conceria SS120, Cesarò

This 3-star hotel provides comfortable lodging and a highly-rated restaurant featuring traditional Sicilian dishes. Guests appreciate the laid-back ambiance, perfect for a peaceful retreat in the Nebrodi region.

Chapter Twenty-Eight
Wine & Warmth in Castelbuono

Festa di San Martino

Festa di San Martino

Where: Castelbuono near Cefalù

When: November 10-11

Average Festival Temperatures: High: 15°C (59°F). Low: 9°C (49°F).

Discovering Castelbuono: Medieval Charm in the Heart of the Madonie

Nestled in the lush Madonie mountains of northern Sicily, Castelbuono stands as a captivating blend of medieval architecture, rich culinary traditions, and natural beauty. This charming town, whose name literally means "good castle," is centered around its imposing 14th-century castle and offers visitors a journey through time, from ancient cobblestone streets to innovative gastronomic experiences. Castelbuono embodies the essence of Sicily's interior - a place where history is palpable, nature is awe-inspiring, and traditions are lovingly preserved.

The history of Castelbuono is inextricably linked to the powerful Ventimiglia family, one of the most influential noble houses of medieval Sicily. The town's defining moment came in 1316 when Francesco I Ventimiglia began construction of the castle that would give the settlement its name and character. Built over an earlier Arab fortress, the Castello dei Ventimiglia became the family's seat of power and the nucleus around which the town grew.

Over the centuries, Castelbuono flourished as a center of culture and commerce, with the Ventimiglias patronizing arts and attracting scholars and artisans. The town's importance in the region continued well into the modern era, leaving a legacy of architectural treasures and cultural traditions that continue to define Castelbuono today.

Castelbuono is situated about 100 kilometers southeast of Palermo, in the heart of the Madonie Regional Natural Park. The town sits at an elevation of approximately 423 meters above sea level, offering panoramic views of the surrounding mountains and valleys.

Castelbuono has a population of around 8,500 residents. In recent decades, Castelbuono has also emerged as a notable gastronomic destination, with innovative chefs and food artisans drawing inspiration from local ingredients and traditions to create acclaimed culinary experiences.

Festa di San Martino

The origins of the festival date back centuries, rooted in both religious reverence for Saint Martin and the agricultural traditions of Sicily. San Martino is the patron saint of soldiers, winemakers, and the poor. His feast day, November 11, marks the end of the agricultural year and the opening of the new wine season in Sicily. Traditionally, it was the time when farmers would taste their first batches of new wine, and families would gather to celebrate the harvest.

In Castelbuono, this tradition has evolved into a festival of food, wine, and community, mixing religious practices with joyous public gatherings. The town, known for its local agriculture and winemaking, has embraced this day as a celebration of new wine, chestnuts, and the spirit of giving. Chestnuts play a significant role in the festival due to their autumn harvest coinciding with the celebration, and their importance in local cuisine and economy.

Who is Saint Martin?

Saint Martin of Tours (316–397 AD) was a Roman soldier who converted to Christianity and became a monk. He is best known for a legend in which he encountered a poor man suffering in the cold. Saint Martin cut his military cloak in half and gave it to the man, symbolizing charity and compassion. He later became a bishop and was revered for his humility and kindness.

Saint Martin's feast day on November 11 is widely celebrated across Europe, but it has taken on a unique connection to winemaking and autumnal traditions in Sicily.

What Happens During the Festival?

In Castelbuono, the Festa di San Martino is celebrated over several days in mid-November, with wine tastings, food stalls, and performances happening before and after the actual feast day.

Religious Ceremonies and Processions

The festival begins with religious observances, including a special Mass dedicated to Saint Martin in Castelbuono's churches. This is followed by a traditional procession through the streets, where a statue of San Martino is carried in reverence by local residents. The procession usually takes place on November 11.

Wine Tastings and Chestnut Roasts

The days surrounding the feast are filled with tastings of the new wine (vino novello). Local wineries and producers offer samples of their latest batches, allowing visitors to enjoy the flavors of Sicily's autumn harvest. Chestnuts, which are also harvested in November, are roasted in the streets and paired with the wine. This combination of wine and chestnuts is a quintessential autumn experience in Sicily.

Music and Folk Performances

The streets of Castelbuono come alive with live music, especially Sicilian folk music, and performances by local musicians, as well as traditional dances. Street performers and local bands often perform in the town's squares, creating a lively and festive atmosphere.

Cultural Exhibits and Events

In addition to the food and wine, there are often cultural exhibits related to winemaking, local agriculture, and the history of Saint Martin. These may include art displays, photography exhibitions, and educational talks that focus on the region's traditions, helping to preserve and share local heritage.

> **Special Festival Food**
> **Biscotti di San Martino**
>
> These cookies are crunchy, round biscuits often flavored with anise, fennel seeds, or wine. They are typically enjoyed soaked in sweet wine or "Marsala" during the festival celebrations. These biscuits are an important part of the tradition and a symbol of the feast. Their significance lies in their connection to the harvest season and the opening of the new wine. The act of dipping these biscuits in wine is symbolic of the first tasting of the new vintage, a crucial moment in the winemaking calendar. Moreover, their round shape is said to represent the wheel of Saint Martin's chariot, tying them directly to the saint's legend and the festival's religious roots.

Walking Tour of Castelbuono

#1. Piazza Margherita and Church of Matrice Vecchia

Start the tour at Piazza Margherita, the heart of Castelbuono. This charming square is surrounded by cafes and shops. Here, you'll find the Church of Matrice Vecchia, which dates back to the 14th century. Built on the site of an earlier Norman chapel, it features a mix of Gothic, Norman, and Baroque styles. The interior is richly decorated, with beautiful frescoes and a remarkable 15th-century marble polyptych. Don't miss the ornate bell tower, added in the 17th century, which offers a striking contrast to the church's older elements.

#2. Castello dei Ventimiglia (Castle)

The Castello dei Ventimiglia is the town's iconic castle. Built in the 14th century by the powerful Ventimiglia family, the castle was a residence and a fortification. Today, it houses the Civic Museum and the Chapel of Saint Anne, the town's patron saint, where her relics are kept. The castle offers panoramic views of the town and surrounding countryside. Inside, you can explore the medieval architecture, including the grand hall and the dungeons, which provide insight into life during the Middle Ages.

#3. Chiesa di San Francesco (Church of St. Francis)

From the castle, it is a 5-minute walk to the Church of San Francesco, a Baroque-style church built in the 17th century. It stands out for its elegant façade and the peaceful cloister attached to it. Inside, you'll find a rich collection of artworks, including frescoes and a notable wooden crucifix. The church also offers a peaceful atmosphere for contemplation, a contrast to the lively streets outside. Pay attention to the intricately carved wooden choir stalls, a masterpiece of local craftsmanship.

#4. Museo Naturalistico Francesco Minà Palumbo (National History Museum)

A museum dedicated to the natural history of the Madonie Mountains and named after Francesco Minà Palumbo, a renowned 19th-century local naturalist and botanist. Minà Palumbo was known for his extensive research on the flora and fauna of the Madonie region. The museum showcases exhibits on local flora and fauna, geology, and the traditional lifestyles of the region's inhabitants. Highlights include a comprehensive herbarium collection and displays of endemic species unique to the Madonie Mountains.

#5. Fontana di Venere Ciprea (Fountain)

The Fontana di Venere Ciprea is one of Castelbuono's most famous fountains. Dating back to the 16th century, the fountain's name is linked to the mythological figure of Venus. Its artistic design is a beautiful example of Renaissance craftsmanship, and it has long served as an important source of water for the town. The fountain features intricate carvings and was once the center of local social life, where townspeople would gather to collect water and exchange news.

#6. Chiesa di Sant'Agostino (Church of St. Augustine)

The Church of Sant'Agostino is a smaller but charming church built in the 16th century. Its simple yet elegant exterior is contrasted by its beautifully decorated interior, which includes ornate altars and a collection of religious art. This church has played a key role in the town's religious life for centuries. Look for the unique blend of architectural styles, including Gothic and Renaissance elements, which reflect the church's long history and various renovations over time.

#7. Via Umberto I (Main Street)

Stroll along Via Umberto I, the main street in Castelbuono, which is lined with traditional Sicilian shops, cafes, and bakeries. This is the perfect place to stop and try some local delicacies, especially the famous manna and biscotti di San Martino. Manna is a natural sweetener extracted from ash trees grown in the surrounding Madonie mountains. It's used in various local sweets and is known for its health benefits. The street itself is a living piece of history, with its cobblestone paths and old buildings. Many of these structures date back to the 18th and 19th centuries, showcasing traditional Sicilian architecture.

#8. Chiesa della Madonna del Rosario (Church of Mary of the Rosary)

End the tour at the Chiesa della Madonna del Rosario (Church of St. Mary of the Rosary) a Baroque-style church that dates back to the 17th century. The church is known for its colorful frescoes and intricate stucco work inside. Pay special attention to the elaborate altar dedicated to the Virgin of the Rosary, which is adorned with precious marbles and intricate sculptures. The church also houses several important paintings by local artists, making it a treasure trove of Sicilian Baroque art.

This walking tour of Castelbuono covers approximately 2 kilometers and takes about 4-5 hours, including time to explore each site.

Castelbuono Festivals and Sagre Throughout the Year

Festa del SS. Crocifisso (Feast of the Holy Crucifix)

May 3

The Festa del SS. Crocifisso (Festival of the Holy Crucifix) is an important religious celebration in Castelbuono. This festival honors a 16th-century crucifix housed in the Castle Chapel. The celebration includes a solemn procession where the crucifix is carried through the town's streets, accompanied by prayers and hymns. The event draws many pilgrims and features religious ceremonies, traditional music, and local food specialties. It's a significant day for the community, blending religious devotion with cultural traditions.

Festa di San Pietro e Paolo (St. Peter and Paul)

June 29

The Festa di San Pietro e Paolo (Feast of Saints Peter and Paul) is a traditional religious festival celebrated in Castelbuono. While not as large as the Festa di Sant'Anna, it's an important day in the local calendar. The celebration typically includes a Mass in honor of the saints, followed by a procession through the town. Local families often prepare special meals, and there may be small gatherings or events in the town square. This festival reflects the deep-rooted Catholic traditions of the community and provides an opportunity for locals to come together in celebration.

Festa di Sant'Anna (St. Ann)

July 25-27.

The Festa di Sant'Anna is the most important religious festival in Castelbuono, dedicated to the town's patron saint, Saint Anne. The celebration includes processions, masses, and blessings. The highlight is the procession of the relic of Saint Anne, carried through the streets by locals. The festival also features concerts, fireworks, and traditional food stalls, drawing visitors from all over Sicily.

Ypsigrock Festival (Music Festival)

August

The Ypsigrock Festival is one of the most famous indie music festivals in Italy, held every August in Castelbuono. The event takes place in front of the Castello dei Ventimiglia and attracts a young, international crowd. Over the years, the festival has gained recognition for its eclectic lineup, which mixes emerging indie bands with established artists. The combination of music, history, and the stunning backdrop of the castle creates a unique festival atmosphere.

Castelbuono Jazz Festival

Mid-August to early September

The Castelbuono Jazz Festival is a renowned musical event that has been taking place annually since 1995. This festival brings together jazz musicians from around the world, offering a series of concerts in various locations throughout the town, including the picturesque Piazza Castello. The festival not only showcases established jazz artists but also provides a platform for emerging talents. It has become an important cultural event, attracting jazz enthusiasts from across Italy and beyond, and contributing significantly to Castelbuono's reputation as a center for arts and music.

Sagra dei Funghi (Mushroom Festival)

October

The Mushroom Festival is a key autumn event in Castelbuono, celebrating the region's rich variety of wild mushrooms, particularly those from the Madonie Mountains. The festival includes mushroom-themed food stalls, cooking demonstrations, and tastings. Visitors can sample dishes like mushroom pasta, grilled mushrooms, and mushroom-based specialties prepared by local chefs. There are also guided excursions into the surrounding mountains to learn about mushroom foraging.

Other Wine Festivals in Sicily Celebrated on Festa di San Martino

In Sicily, St. Martin's Day on November 11th is celebrated with various festivals that honor both the saint and the season's new wine. Across the island, towns and villages mark the occasion with lively festivals filled with local flavors, music, folklore, and unique traditions that reflect their identity. It's a time to honor both the saint and the Sicilian way of life, with festivities ranging from wine tastings to culinary competitions and even sporting events. Below is a list of some of the most notable St. Martin's Day festivals held across Sicily, each offering its own distinct charm and experiences. Here are some notable events across the island:

Agrigento Area

"Lu Sammartinu" in Ravanusa: This festival highlights autumnal products like ricotta, chestnuts, pork, and new wine. Attendees can enjoy craft markets, guided tours, and folkloristic performances.

San Martino in Cianciana: A celebration rich in flavors and traditions, featuring tastings of new wine alongside local delicacies such as "lu pani cunzatu" (seasoned bread), olives, cheese, and sfinci (a type of pastry).

Catania and Etna Area

Feast of San Martino in Acireale: This event offers a gastronomic journey with chestnut tastings, new wine, homemade macaroni, sausages, and typical desserts, showcasing local culinary specialties.

San Martino Festival in Misterbianco: Features roasted chestnuts, new wine, and local products, complemented by craft markets, exhibitions, and concerts.

Central Sicily

Feast of San Martino in San Cono: Attendees can savor local specialties like sausage, horse meat, and "ciciri ca cutini" soup, all accompanied by excellent local wines. The festival also includes a competition for the best local wine and various entertainment shows.

San Martino in San Michele di Ganzaria: Celebrates regional products with food stands offering pasta with wild boar ragù, tripe, chickpeas, "cunzato" bread, "cuccìa," cassatelle, cannoli, and more.

San Martino in Villarosa: Features an "Osteria in the square," parades of Sicilian carts, folklore performances, and tastings of typical Sicilian dishes.

Messina and Nebrodi Area

Palio of San Martino in Castell'Umberto: The highlight is the traditional "Corsa delle Botti," where teams from across Italy compete in a barrel race. The event also includes local craft stands and food stalls offering mushrooms, roasted chestnuts, hazelnut tagliatelle, homemade macaroni with sauce, "frittuli," and local wines.

These festivals provide a unique opportunity to experience Sicilian culture, cuisine, and community spirit during St. Martin's Day celebrations.

Day Trip Options: Nearby Sites, Cities and Towns

Petralia Soprana. 27 km (16.8 miles) from Castelbuono. Sitting at an altitude of 1,147 meters, Petralia Soprana is the highest town in the Madonie Mountains. Founded in the medieval period, it has a rich history influenced by various cultures, including Arab, Norman, and Spanish.

The town is renowned for its well-preserved historical center, featuring noble palaces and churches. Key attractions include the Chiesa Madre, dedicated to the Apostles Peter and Paul, with its impressive Baroque interior, and the Piazza del Popolo, the main square offering breathtaking views of the surrounding landscape. The town is also known for its traditional handicrafts, especially embroidery and woodworking.

Petralia Sottana. 24 km (14.9 miles). Located just below its sister town, Petralia Sottana has ancient origins, with settlements dating back to prehistoric times. The town played a significant role during the Norman conquest of Sicily in the 11th century.

Visitors should explore the Chiesa Madre, dedicated to Maria Santissima Assunta, which houses valuable works of art, including sculptures by the Renaissance artist Gagini. The Civic Museum "Antonio Collisani" offers insights into the area's geology, flora, and fauna. The town is also a gateway to the Madonie Geopark, making it an ideal base for nature enthusiasts and hikers.

Parco delle Madonie. Surrounding Castelbuono. Established in 1989, this natural park covers an area of about 40,000 hectares and is a paradise for nature lovers and outdoor enthusiasts. The park is home to more than half of Sicily's plant species, including rare and endemic plants like the Abies nebrodensis, a critically endangered fir tree.

Wildlife in the park includes the rare griffon vulture, golden eagles, and wild cats. Visitors can explore numerous hiking trails of varying difficulty, with popular routes leading to Monte Carbonara (the highest peak in the park at 1,979 meters) and Piano Battaglia, a small ski resort.

Logistics

Train: The nearest station is in Cefalù, 23 kilometers (14 miles).

Bus: AST (Azienda Siciliana Trasporti) operates regional bus services that connect Castelbuono to other towns in the Madonie Mountains and nearby cities such as Cefalù and Palermo. The bus service is reliable, though schedules may be limited on weekends or holidays. The main bus stop is located near the town center.

Car: Driving is a convenient way to reach Castelbuono, especially if you plan to explore the surrounding Madonie Mountains. Take the SS113 highway westward from Cefalù. The journey typically takes about 30-40 minutes, depending on traffic.

Parking: Piazza Margherita, Via Alduino Ventimiglia, and the Parcheggio Comunale are suitable choices for parking outside the ZTL (Zona a Traffico Limitato). Castelbuono enforces ZTL regulations, particularly in the historic center, so parking outside the restricted areas is essential to avoid fines.

Dining Recommendations

Ristorante Nangalarruni. Address: Via delle Confraternite, 10

Nangalarruni is one of the most well-known restaurants in Castelbuono, famous for its use of local ingredients, especially mushrooms from the nearby Madonie Mountains.

Antico Baglio. Address: Via Baglio, 12

Located in the historic center of Castelbuono, Antico Baglio offers a mix of traditional Sicilian cuisine with a modern twist. The restaurant emphasizes locally sourced products, including manna, cheeses, and meats, all served in a beautifully restored historic building, making it a favorite among visitors.

Accommodation

Hotel Paradiso delle Madonie. Address: Via Dante Alighieri, 82

A 4-star hotel located in the heart of the Madonie Regional Park. This modest hotel offers air-conditioned rooms, free Wi-Fi, and a bar with a terrace. It's close to local attractions like the Ventimiglia Castle and natural sites, making it an ideal base for exploring the town and surrounding countryside.

B&B Panorama. Address: Via Isnello, 34

This 3-star hotel offers a charming guesthouse experience with a terrace providing panoramic views of the surrounding area. Guests enjoy free parking, Wi-Fi, and air-conditioned rooms, making it a popular choice for those seeking a comfortable and scenic stay in Castelbuono.

Winter Celebrations

December through February

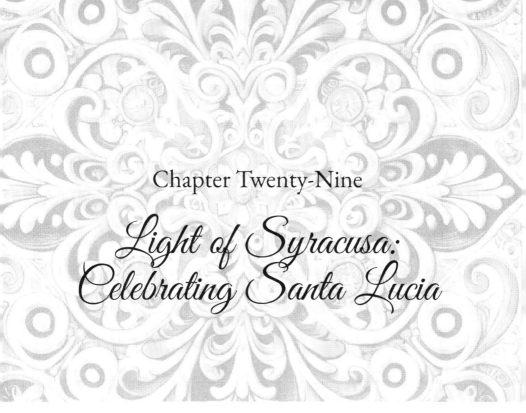

Chapter Twenty-Nine

Light of Syracusa: Celebrating Santa Lucia

Festa di Santa Lucia

Where: Syracusa (Siracuse)

When: November 30. Main Events December 9-13 and Final Event December 20

Average Festival Temperatures: High: 14°C - 18°C (57°F - 64°F). Low: 7°C - 10°C (45°F - 50°F).

Discover Syracuse and Ortygia: Crossroads of Ancient Civilizations

With its ancient heart of Ortygia, Syracuse stands as a living testament to the grand sweep of Mediterranean history. Once the most powerful city in the ancient Greek world, rivaling Athens in size and influence, Syracuse today offers visitors an unparalleled journey through time. From its stunning Greek theaters to its baroque piazzas, from its Doric temples to its medieval streets, Syracuse and Ortygia together form a palimpsest of civilizations, each layer revealing a new chapter in the story of Sicily and the wider Mediterranean world.

The history of Syracuse is nothing short of epic. Founded by Corinthian Greeks in 734 BC, the city rapidly grew to become one of the most important centers of the ancient world. Its power and wealth were such that it successfully resisted an Athenian invasion in 415 BC, a pivotal moment in the Peloponnesian War. The city reached its zenith under the rule of Dionysius the Elder in the 4th century BC, when its influence extended across much of Sicily and southern Italy. Syracuse later fell to the Romans in 212 BC, despite the ingenious defensive inventions of its native son, Archimedes. In subsequent centuries, the city passed through

Byzantine, Arab, Norman, and Spanish hands, each leaving its mark on the urban fabric. Throughout these changes, the island of Ortygia remained the heart of the city, a compact space where millennia of history coexist in a stunning architectural ensemble.

Syracuse is located on the southeastern coast of Sicily, about 250 kilometers southeast of Palermo. The modern city spreads across the coastal plain and nearby hills, but its historical core is concentrated on Ortygia, a small island connected to the mainland by two bridges. This unique geography has shaped Syracuse's destiny for nearly three millennia, providing natural defenses and a sheltered port that made it a coveted prize for successive empires. The surrounding landscape is one of remarkable beauty, with the Iblean Mountains rising to the north and west, and the azure waters of the Ionian Sea stretching to the east.

The commune of Syracuse has a population of approximately 120,000, making it the fourth largest city in Sicily. While the broader city has expanded inland, Ortygia remains the cultural and touristic heart of Syracuse, with a population of about 4,500 residents. The economy of Syracuse is diverse, with tourism playing a major role alongside agriculture, fishing, and services. The city's deep-water port continues to be significant for both commerce and tourism, with cruise ships bringing visitors from around the world.

The Festival of Santa Lucia

The Feast of Santa Lucia, celebrated on December 13th, began formally in the 11th century, although she had been venerated since the 4th century. Churches were built in her honor, and her devotion spread from Sicily to the rest of Italy and the wider Christian world.

The Catholic Church chose December 13th for her feast day because it was believed to be the winter solstice, the shortest day of the year. The choice symbolized bringing light to the darkest day, reflecting St. Lucy's association with light. After the introduction of the Gregorian calendar by Pope Gregory XIII in 1582, the solstice shifted to December 21st.

By the 13th century, Santa Lucia's celebrations in Sicily had become more organized, with processions and public festivities playing a key role in local traditions. Today, the feasts of Santa Lucia and Saint Agatha are among the most important events in Sicily's festival calendar.

Who is Santa Lucia?

According to legend, Santa Lucia was born around 283 AD in Syracuse. She was a young Christian noblewoman renowned for her piety and devotion. Despite being promised for marriage at the tender age of 5, Lucia pledged herself to Christ, setting the stage for a life of faith and sacrifice.

A pivotal moment in Lucia's story occurred when she and her mother visited St. Agatha's tomb to pray for her mother's healing. Through a vision and unwavering faith, her mother was miraculously cured. This event strengthened Lucia's resolve, leading her to ask for freedom from her marriage arrangement and permission to donate her dowry to the poor.

Lucia's decision to reject marriage, especially to a wealthy pagan suitor, brought her into conflict with the authorities during Emperor Diocletian's reign, a time of intense Christian persecution. Her arrest marked the beginning of her trials and the miraculous events that would define her legacy.

As the authorities attempted to execute Lucia, a series of supernatural occurrences unfolded. They found themselves unable to move her, even with the strength of a thousand men and oxen. She survived being set on fire and having boiling oil poured over her. When stabbed in the throat, Lucia continued to speak, prophesying Diocletian's fall and the coming peace for Christian believers.

Lucia's martyrdom came in 310 AD, but not before she received the sacrament, affirming her faith until the very end. Her death, however, was not the end of her story. Lucia became venerated as a saint, particularly beloved in Sicily. She gained renown as a protector of the blind and those with eye disorders.

In art and iconography, Santa Lucia is often depicted holding her eyes on a plate or carrying a lamp, symbolizing her role as a bearer of light and spiritual vision. These symbols became crucial in the Middle Ages when most people were illiterate and relied on such imagery to recognize and remember their saints.

Santa Lucia's story, a testament to unwavering faith and the power of belief in the face of persecution, continues to inspire and captivate people centuries after her death. Her feast day remains a significant occasion on the Christian calendar, keeping her memory and the values she embodied alive in the hearts of the faithful.

Festival Events

In Syracuse, the Santa Lucia celebrations begin on November 30th in the afternoon, featuring a vibrant parade in the streets of the historic center.

December 9

Dating back to 1599, statue of Saint Lucia is a rare silver simulacrum showing the saint with a palm and lily, representing purity, and a dagger embellished with gems. She holds a plate adorned with eyes, embodying the legend of losing her sight and becoming the Guardian of Vision. Lucia's name has its roots in the Latin word lux, which translates to light.

On December 9, the hidden silver statue of Santa Lucia is revealed in her chapel at the Cathedral of Syracuse, marking the start of the main events. For the rest of the year, she's locked in a cabinet, unseen by visitors.

December 12

During a religious ceremony in the Cathedral on the evening of December 12th, the silver figure of Lucia is moved from its chapel to the high altar.

December 13

On December 13, the primary celebration begins with a morning Pontifical Mass in the Cathedral. Starting at 3:30 p.m., the grand procession embarks on a route through the historic city center, culminating at the Basilica of Santa Lucia al Sepolcro. Relics and silver statue proceed solemnly to the Basilica, built on her martyrdom site. The Arab domination in Sicily resulted in the destruction of the original church, which was subsequently replaced in 1100AD.

During the several-hour procession, devoted participants fervently chant "Siracusana jè!" (She is a Syracusan) as part of their pilgrimage. Many pilgrims walk barefoot, holding lit candles, either to express gratitude or seek divine grace. Following Santa Lucia, twelve floral-adorned wooden candelabras lead the Senate Carriage and the Line, all dressed in 18th-century fashion. Upon arrival at Piazza Santa Lucia, the chimes of bells welcome the believers.

The Basilica attracts worshippers over eight days, who come to see the tomb of the saint and martyr and the exhibited relics.

Santa Lucia on Procession

The 60 men carrying the statue wear green hats as they represent the Confraternity of Santa Lucia, a lay brotherhood.

December 20

On December 20, Santa Lucia makes her way back to the Cathedral in a lengthy procession, pausing at the Basilica Santuario della Madonna delle Lacrime and the Umberto I Hospital for prayer. At Ponte Umbertino, fireworks light up the sky to celebrate the arrival of the group before the Saint moves on to the Cathedral and her chapel. Being part of this connected community during such a meaningful moment is incredibly moving.

In the oldest part of the city, devotees carry the statue on their shoulders through the historic streets of Ortygia, accompanied by flowers and flickering candles. The atmosphere is electric as crowds from the region, Sicily, and the world show immense emotion for their saint.

If you want to fully embrace the rich traditions and celebrations of Santa Lucia, it's advisable to arrive in Syracuse ahead of time. On December 9th, there will be lively celebrations, including a musical band parade, religious masses, and the blessing of relics.

Special Festival Treat
Cuccia

Cuccìa, a traditional Sicilian dish, is prepared by boiling wheat berries. Typically, people sweeten cuccìa and add ingredients such as ricotta, honey, sugar, cinnamon, and chocolate.

The recipe commemorates a miraculous event that occurred during a famine in Sicily. Legend has it that a grain-filled ship arrived in Syracuse on Santa Lucia's feast day, rescuing the starving population. As an expression of gratitude, the people abstained from baking bread and boiled the grain instead. Even now, on December 13th, Sicilians maintain their tradition of abstaining from bread and pasta as a type of fast.

Walking Tours of Syracuse

Some 50 years ago, the town had the reputation of being a slum that even Sicilians avoided. During the 1980s, investments led to a complete revitalization of the island of Ortygia. It is an absolute treasure and one of our favorite places in Italy. When we last visited Syracuse in May, the center was alive and vibrant. Polite Italian school groups on field trips, mostly under 18, made up over half of the visitors we encountered. Students also packed the ancient theater, where we attended a performance.

Walking Tour Day 1: Exploring Ortygia Island

Start the tour in Ortygia's vibrant center, the historic part of Syracuse, in Piazza Duomo.

#1. Duomo di Syracusa (Syracuse Cathedral)

The Cathedral of Syracuse has a long rich history. The structure on this site has been around since prehistoric times. Built in the 6th century BC, the Greek Temple of Athena was an impressive Doric structure with 6 columns on the short sides and 14 on the long sides. Plato and Athenaeus mention the shrine, and Cicero cites the looting of its ornament as a crime committed by Verres in 70 BC.

Cathedral of Syracusa

Between 1907 and 1910, Paolo Orsi's archaeological excavations revealed that the Greek temple had been built on even older foundations, unearthing numerous archaic and pre-Hellenic artifacts. Many of these historical finds are now housed in the Museo Archeologico Regionale Paolo Orsi in Syracuse.

In the 7th century, Saint Bishop Zosimo of Syracuse constructed the current cathedral, incorporating the original Doric columns from the ancient temple into its walls. These columns are still visible today, both inside and outside the building. The structure was converted into a mosque in 878 but was restored to a cathedral when Norman ruler Roger I recaptured the city in 1085. The nave roof and apse mosaics date back to the Norman period.

After the devastating earthquake of 1693, architect Andrea Palma was responsible for redesigning and overseeing the cathedral's reconstruction between

1725 and 1753. The facade is considered a relatively late example of High Sicilian Baroque, featuring intricately carved acanthus leaves in the capitals of the double order of Corinthian columns. Sculptor Ignazio Marabitti created the full-length statues that adorn the facade.

The cathedral's interior, a blend of rustic walls and Baroque details, consists of a nave and two aisles. Notable features include a 12th or 13th-century marble basin, a ciborium designed by architect Luigi Vanvitelli, and a statue of the Madonna della Neve by Antonello Gagini.

Greek Column visible inside of the Cathedral

St. Lucy and the Cathedral

The cathedral contains various relics of St. Lucy, the city's patroness, including bone fragments, a robe, a veil, and a pair of shoes, as of 2015. Her remaining artifacts live in Venice. Within the chest of the silver statue, you'll find three fragments of her ribs.

#2. Chiesa di Santa Lucia alla Badia (Church of St. Lucy at the Abbey)

The Chiesa di Santa Lucia alla Badia, located in Piazza Duomo, stands just a short walk south of the cathedral. This historic church is an important site in Syracuse, dedicated to the city's patron saint, St. Lucy. Its history dates back to the mid-15th century when a church and monastery were established at the site, possibly sponsored by Queen Isabella of Spain. However, both structures were destroyed in the devastating Sicily Earthquake of 1693. The church underwent extensive restoration in the 20th century due to damage sustained during World War II, with the tile flooring being replaced in 1970.

The church's facade is adorned with several notable features. Visitors should look for symbols of St. Lucy above the main entrance, as well as the Spanish monarchy's 1705 coat of arms. The entrance is framed by distinctive spiral columns, adding to the architectural intrigue. Inside, the main altar features a striking painting depicting St. Lucy's martyrdom. Interestingly, a second-floor balcony once allowed cloistered nuns to observe processions in the piazza, though this was removed during World War II for safety reasons.

The Chiesa di Santa Lucia alla Badia holds great significance in local tradition and religious life. It commemorates a miraculous event from 1646 when a dove reportedly signaled the arrival of famine relief. This miracle is celebrated annually in May during the Festa delle Quaglie di Santa Lucia (Quails of Santa Lucia festival), where nuns traditionally released doves and quails. The church plays a central role in the Festa di Santa Lucia, a major celebration held in December in Piazza del Duomo.

Visitors to the church will find themselves immersed in a rich tapestry of history, art, and local tradition. The building's architecture, with its blend of styles reflecting its long history and various restorations, offers a visual journey through time. Inside, the serene atmosphere invites quiet contemplation and appreciation of the religious artworks on display. The church's location in the heart of Syracuse's historic center makes it an easy addition to any walking tour.

#3. Fonte Aretusa (Fountain of Arethusa)

In the heart of Syracuse, the Fountain of Arethusa harbors a botanical marvel - thriving stands of papyrus, a plant rarely seen growing naturally in Europe. This unusual presence traces its roots to the Arab rule of Sicily between the 9th and 11th centuries AD. The Arabs, familiar with papyrus from Egypt, likely introduced it to the island, where it found an ideal home in the fountain's unique ecosystem.

The Fountain of Arethusa, steeped in Greek mythology as the resurfacing point of the nymph Arethusa, offers a perfect environment for papyrus. Its brackish waters, a blend of fresh spring water and sea spray, mimic the plant's native Nile Delta conditions. This ecological niche has allowed papyrus to persist here for centuries, creating a living link to Syracuse's ancient Mediterranean connections.

Today, the papyrus in the Fountain of Arethusa stands as a protected natural and historical treasure. It serves as a tangible reminder of Syracuse's rich past, bridging eras from ancient Greek legends to Arab influences and modern conservation efforts. This rare botanical feature adds another layer to the fountain's significance, enhancing its status as a symbol of Syracuse alongside Saint Lucy in the city's motto: "City of Water and Light."

#4. Temple of Apollo

Just a quick 5-minute walk from the waterfront, we'll reach the Temple of Apollo, one of Sicily's oldest Doric temples. The temple is a part of the most important ancient Greek monuments of Magna Graecia in the area, and it stands in front of the Piazza Pancali.

The Temple of Apollo in Syracuse is a remarkable ancient ruin dating back to the 6th century BC, making it one of the oldest Doric temples in Italy. Throughout its long history, this structure has undergone numerous transformations, reflecting the changing cultural and political landscape of Sicily. During the late Roman Empire, the temple was closed as part of the persecution of pagans.

Later, it was converted into a Byzantine church, though only remnants of a central door and the front steps remain from this period. The building's versatility continued during the Emirate of Sicily when it was repurposed as a mosque, serving the Islamic tradition. Following the Norman conquest, the structure was once again transformed, this time being rededicated as the Church of the Savior. Its final major alteration came in the 16th century when the Spanish incorporated it into their military barracks. This rich tapestry of architectural adaptations makes the Temple of Apollo a fascinating testament to Syracuse's diverse history.

#5. Daily Market in Piazza Pancali

The daily market in Piazza Pancali is a vibrant and essential part of life in Syracuse, Sicily. This bustling marketplace is a feast for the senses, offering a diverse array of products that cater to both locals and tourists alike. While food is a central focus, the market's offerings extend far beyond culinary delights.

At the heart of the market, visitors will find an impressive selection of fresh, local produce. Seasonal fruits and vegetables, many sourced from nearby farms, showcase the agricultural bounty of Sicily. The market is also renowned for its fish stalls, where the catch of the day is displayed on beds of ice, reflecting Syracuse's coastal location and rich maritime tradition. Food enthusiasts will appreciate the variety of local specialties available. Vendors offer an assortment of Sicilian cheeses, cured meats, olives, and sun-dried tomatoes. The aroma of freshly baked bread and pastries wafts through the air, tempting passersby with traditional Sicilian sweets like cannoli and cassata.

Fresh Produce in the Market

Beyond foodstuffs, the market is a treasure trove of local crafts and goods. Clothing stalls display a mix of trendy fashions and traditional Sicilian attire. Leather artisans showcase their handiwork in the form of bags, belts, and shoes, many of which are handcrafted using time-honored techniques. The market is also a hub for Sicilian ceramics, with colorful plates, vases, and decorative items adorned with intricate patterns and motifs typical of the region. Jewelry stalls glitter with both contemporary designs and pieces inspired by Sicily's rich history, often featuring motifs like the Trinacria, the symbol of Sicily.

The market typically operates in the morning hours, with vendors setting up their stalls at dawn and most businesses concluding by early afternoon. The lively atmosphere, with its chorus of vendor calls and the hum of negotiations, makes for an engaging and memorable experience. Visitors are encouraged to bring cash, as not all vendors may accept cards. Bargaining, while not as common as in some other Mediterranean markets, is not unheard of, especially for non-food items. For those looking to sample the market's fresh produce, many nearby cafes and restaurants incorporate these ingredients into their daily specials, offering another way to experience the flavors of the market.

> ### Caravaggio in Sicily
>
> Michelangelo Merisi da Caravaggio, one of the most renowned Baroque painters, fled to Syracuse in 1608 after escaping from prison in Malta, where he had been detained following a violent altercation. In Syracuse, he found refuge under the protection of local nobility, who recognized his extraordinary talent despite his troubled past.
>
> During his stay, Caravaggio painted several notable works, including the "Burial of Saint Lucy" for the Basilica of Santa Lucia. This masterpiece, characterized by his signature dramatic use of light and shadow (chiaroscuro), captures the martyrdom of Saint Lucy with poignant realism and emotional intensity.
>
> While originally housed in the basilica, the painting was later moved to the Church of Santa Lucia al Sepolcro, where it remains today (featured in the Day 2 tour).
>
> Caravaggio's time in Syracuse was a pivotal moment in his life and career. It was part of his larger flight across Sicily as he sought sanctuary from his legal troubles, which had escalated following his conviction for murder in Rome. This turbulent period saw the creation of some of his most profoundly spiritual and emotionally charged works, reflecting both his artistic brilliance and the desperation of a man on the run. His stay in Syracuse exemplifies how his personal struggles deeply influenced his art, infusing it with a raw power that continues to captivate audiences centuries later.

#6. Sunset Walk along the Lungomare

The Lungomare of Ortygia, Syracuse's historic island core, is a captivating seafront promenade that showcases the best of Sicily's coastal charm. This scenic walkway winds along the eastern and southern edges of the island, offering breathtaking views of the Ionian Sea. Beginning near the mythical Fonte Aretusa, the well-maintained path is perfect for leisurely strolls, jogging, or cycling.

As you traverse the Lungomare, you'll encounter a harmonious blend of natural beauty and rich history. Ancient defensive structures, now repurposed as viewpoints, dot the route, providing perfect spots for photography and sea-gazing.

The promenade reveals small beaches and rocky outcrops where you can pause for a swim or sunbathe. Towards the southern tip, the impressive 13th-century Castello Maniace comes into view, its silhouette striking against the azure backdrop. The Lungomare is particularly magical during sunrise and sunset, when the changing light paints the sky and sea in spectacular hues. Along the way, you'll find cafes and gelaterias for refreshments, as well as benches to sit and soak in the Mediterranean ambiance.

Walking Tour Day 2: Historical and Archaeological Syracuse

#1. Chiesa di Santa Maria al Sepolcro (St. Mary of the Sepulchre)

Located on Via Luigi Bignami in Syracuse, Santa Maria al Sepolcro is a hidden gem of Byzantine architecture. This small church, dating back to the 8th century, is one of the oldest in Syracuse and showcases a unique circular plan topped by a dome. The structure's design is reminiscent of early Christian martyria, which were built to commemorate saints or important religious events.

As you enter, you'll be struck by the intimate atmosphere and the play of light filtering through the small windows. The church's walls still bear traces of 12th-century frescoes, offering a glimpse into the artistic traditions of medieval Sicily. While much of the original decoration has been lost to time, the remaining fragments provide a tantalizing hint of the church's former glory. The simplicity of its current state only adds to its austere beauty and historical significance.

#2. Santa Maria delle Lacrime (Santuario della Madonna delle Lacrime, The Sanctuary of the crying Madonna)

A stark contrast to the ancient Santa Maria al Sepolcro, the Santuario della Madonna delle Lacrime is a monumental modern church that dominates the Syracuse skyline. On Via del Santuario, this impressive structure was completed in 1994 after decades of construction. The church was built to commemorate a miraculous event that occurred in 1953 when a plaster image of the Virgin Mary in a modest Sicilian home was said to have wept human tears for four days. This event, scientifically investigated and accepted by the Catholic Church, drew worldwide attention and led to the construction of this sanctuary.

The church's architecture is striking and controversial. Its modernist design features a massive conical structure soaring to a height of 102 meters (334 feet), meant to evoke the shape of a teardrop. The interior is equally impressive, with a vast central space that can accommodate up to 11,000 worshippers. Natural light floods the church through cleverly designed openings, creating a constantly changing interplay of light and shadow throughout the day.

At the heart of the sanctuary, you'll find the original weeping effigy of the Madonna, now enshrined above the main altar. The church also houses a museum that documents the 1953 miracle and the subsequent construction of the sanctuary. Regardless of one's religious beliefs, the Santuario della Madonna delle Lacrime is an architectural marvel and a powerful testament to modern faith and devotion.

Afternoon: Archaeological Sites

#3. Parco Archeologico della Neapolis (Archeological Park)

From Santa Maria delle Lacrime, it's about a 30-minute walk to the Parco Archeologico della Neapolis (or 5 minute taxi ride). This expansive archaeological park is a testament to Syracuse's rich history, spanning the Greek and Roman periods.

The Greek Theatre, one of the largest of its kind, was originally constructed in the 5th century BC and later rebuilt in the 3rd century BC. Carved into the hillside, it could once seat up to 16,000 spectators. The theater's excellent acoustics and picturesque setting have ensured its continued use for performances, particularly during the annual Greek theater festival held in May and June.

The Roman Amphitheatre, dating from the 3rd century AD, offers insight into the changing entertainment preferences under Roman rule. Though smaller than the Greek Theatre, it was designed for gladiatorial contests and wild animal hunts, reflecting the tastes of the time.

Perhaps the most intriguing feature of the park is the Ear of Dionysius, a limestone cave named by the painter Caravaggio in 1608 due to its resemblance to a human ear. Legend suggests it was used by the tyrant Dionysius to eavesdrop on prisoners, though it was more likely a water storage cistern. The cave's exceptional acoustics amplify even the slightest whisper, creating an otherworldly experience for visitors.

After exploring the park, enjoy a light lunch at a nearby café, savoring local Sicilian specialties like arancini or pasta alla Norma.

#4. Museo Archeologico Regionale Paolo Orsi (Regional Archeology Museum)

The Museo Archeologico Regionale Paolo Orsi in Syracuse, Sicily, stands as one of Europe's most significant archaeological museums. Named after Paolo Orsi, a renowned Italian archaeologist who made substantial contributions to the study of Sicilian prehistory and the Greek colonial period, the museum is housed in a modern building opened in 1988 within the Villa Landolina park.

The museum's collection is vast and diverse, spanning from prehistoric times through the Greek and Roman periods, and into the early Christian era. Visitors can explore an impressive array of artifacts, including the famous "Landolina Venus" statue, Greek vases and pottery, ancient coins, terracotta figurines, and stone and bronze sculptures. These items offer a comprehensive view of the region's rich cultural heritage. Organized chronologically and geographically, the museum helps visitors understand the historical context of each artifact. This layout enhances the educational value of the exhibits, providing insights into the daily life, art, religion, and technology of the ancient civilizations that once thrived in Sicily.

#5. San Giovanni Catacombs (Catacombs of St. John)

End your day at the San Giovanni Catacombs, a vast underground necropolis dating back to the 4th century AD. Among the largest outside of Rome, these catacombs offer a haunting glimpse into early Christian burial practices. nearby, you can also visit the Crypt of San Marciano, traditionally believed to be where Syracuse's first bishop was martyred. This tour covers approximately 5 km (3.1 miles) of walking. While this is manageable for most visitors, taxis are readily available if you prefer. Consider purchasing a combined ticket for the Archaeological Park and the Paolo Orsi Museum for a more cost-effective experience.

Syracuse from Above

Walking Tour Day 3: Art, Culture, and Relaxation

#1. Castello Maniace

At the tip of the island of Ortygia is Castello Maniace. It is among the most significant buildings associated with Frederick II in Sicily.

The name "Castello Maniace" comes from Giorgio Maniace, a Byzantine commander who likely built an early military structure there in the 11th century, though no remains exist today. The current castle, mainly built between 1232 and 1240 under Frederick II, has a Swabian core. Later centuries added more features. In the 1500s, modifications included cannon batteries and integrated the castle into Charles V's defenses. The 17th century saw the addition of the diamond-shaped Forte della Vignazza by Carlos de Grunembergh. In 1704, a lightning strike blew up a tower used as a powder magazine, destroying the castle's northeastern wing.

#2. Galleria Regionale di Palazzo Bellomo

This museum is housed in a stunning 13th-century palace and boasts an extensive collection of medieval and Renaissance Sicilian art. As you explore the gallery, you'll encounter notable works by Antonello da Messina, including his famous "Annunciation." The museum also showcases a variety of Byzantine icons and Gothic sculptures. Keep an eye out for temporary exhibitions featuring contemporary Sicilian artists, which offer a fascinating contrast to the historical pieces. To enhance your visit, consider renting an audio guide, available in multiple languages, which can provide deeper insights into the artworks and their historical context.

#3. Piazza Archimede

A short five-minute walk from Palazzo Bellomo will bring you to Piazza Archimede, the central square named after Syracuse's most famous citizen, the mathematician Archimedes. The focal point of this charming piazza is the Fountain of Diana, created in 1906 by sculptor Giulio Moschetti. This impressive fountain depicts the myth of the nymph Arethusa's transformation into a fountain, surrounded by intricate sculptures of sea monsters, nymphs, and tritons.

As you admire the fountain, note the diverse architecture surrounding the square. You'll see a captivating mix of Baroque and Liberty style buildings, including the notable Palazzo Gargallo and the ornate Post Office building. The square is lined with several cozy cafes and gelaterias, making it the perfect spot for a mid-morning break. Enjoy a coffee or gelato while people-watching and soaking in the lively atmosphere of this historic piazza.

#4. Jewish Bath (Mikveh)

In the afternoon, make your way to the Jewish Bath, or Mikveh, located at Via Alagona, 52. Note that a reservation is required to visit this remarkable site. The Syracuse Mikveh is one of the oldest and best-preserved ritual baths in Europe, dating back to the 6th century AD. This ancient bath is truly a marvel of construction, carved directly into the limestone bedrock and situated 18 meters underground. It's fed by a natural spring, which was crucial for its ritual purification purposes. As you descend into the bath, you'll be stepping back in time to an era when Syracuse had a thriving Jewish community.

The existence of this Mikveh is evidence of a Jewish presence in Sicily since Roman times, though sadly, the community was expelled in 1492 during the Spanish Inquisition. Guided tours, available in multiple languages, typically last 30-45 minutes and offer fascinating insights into Jewish purification rituals and the local history of Syracuse's Jewish community.

Syracuse Festivals and Sagre Throughout the Year

Festa di San Sebastiano (St. Sebastian)

January 20th

Saint Sebastian is an important patron saint of Syracuse. This festival has been celebrated for centuries, with its origins dating back to the early Christian era. The main events include: religious processions through the streets, masses at the Church of San Sebastiano, traditional music and hymns, food stalls, and markets.

Festa di San Corrado (St. Corrado)

February 19th

San Corrado Confalonieri is the patron saint of Noto, a city near Syracuse. While the main celebrations occur in Noto, Syracuse also honors this saint. The festival dates back to the 14th century when San Corrado lived as a hermit near Syracuse. Events include religious processions, masses, and small local celebrations.

Festa di Santa Lucia delle Quaglie (St. Lucy of the Quails)

First Sunday in May

This festival honors Santa Lucia, the patron saint of Syracuse, and is connected to a miracle attributed to her in 1646. During a severe famine, a ship full of quails unexpectedly arrived in the harbor, providing food for the starving population. The festival includes a procession of Santa Lucia's silver statue, the release of quails (now symbolic and not involving live birds), masses, religious ceremonies, music, and dance performances.

Sagra del Pesce (Fish Festival)

May to July

This modern festival celebrates Syracuse's rich fishing tradition and seafood cuisine. While not as old as the religious festivals, it has become an important part of the city's cultural calendar. Events typically include: cooking demonstrations by local chefs, music and entertainment, and boat tours of the harbor.

Ortigia Sound System Festival

July

A relatively new addition to Syracuse's festival calendar, this electronic music festival has been running since 2014. It takes place on the island of Ortigia and features performances by international and local electronic music artists, DJ sets in various locations around the island, art installations and multimedia projects, daytime beach parties, and nighttime concerts.

Ortigia Film Festival

July

This annual independent film festival, established in 2009, takes place in the historic center of Ortigia. It showcases: Italian and international independent films, short film competitions, and outdoor screenings in picturesque locations.

Festa della Madonna delle Lacrime (The Crying Madonna)

August 29th to September 1st

The Festa della Madonna delle Lacrime (Feast of the Crying Madonna) is held annually in Syracuse from August 29th to September 1st, commemorating a miraculous event in 1953 when a plaster image of the Virgin Mary was said to have wept tears. This event deeply moved the faithful and led to the construction of the Santuario della Madonna delle Lacrime, a large basilica that now houses the image.

The celebration includes masses, a candlelight procession through the streets, and fireworks, drawing pilgrims and visitors from around Sicily and beyond. The event is a poignant reflection of the local community's devotion to the Virgin Mary and the lasting impact of the miraculous event.

Day Trip Options: A Boat Ride plus Nearby Sites, Cities and Towns

Sailing Through Time - A Boat Ride Around Ortygia

A boat ride around Ortygia offers a unique blend of romance and history, providing an unparalleled perspective on Syracuse's layered past. As you drift along the coastline, the deep blue Mediterranean contrasts with ancient stone walls, creating a visual journey through time.

Departing from the harbor, you'll first encounter the imposing Castello Maniace, a 13th-century fortress built by Emperor Frederick II. Its robust architecture, standing sentinel at the island's tip, appears particularly dramatic from the water. As you continue, ancient sea walls come into view, some crumbling, others intact, all hinting at Ortygia's once-impenetrable defenses.

The legendary Fonte Aretusa, a freshwater spring steeped in Greek mythology, appears as a serene oasis along the shore. Its lush papyrus plants offer a moment of tranquility amid the excitement of the ride. Hidden sea caves, once shelters for ancient sailors, provide an exhilarating adventure. As your boat enters these natural grottos, ethereal light and echoing waves create a mystical atmosphere.

Circling back, you'll pass the Ponte Umbertino, gracefully arching over the sea and connecting Ortygia to the mainland. This sight beautifully blends the old with the new, symbolizing Syracuse's connection to its past and present. For the most enchanting experience, consider a sunset tour when golden light bathes the city, and a refreshing sea breeze offers respite from the Sicilian heat. While we booked with Ortygia Boat Tour in advance, many companies offer tours, each with its unique perspective. You can easily find friendly staff offering tours as you stroll along the marina near the bridges.

Avola. 30 kilometers (19 miles) away. Avola is a charming town known for its production of the famous Nero d'Avola wine and its beautiful beaches. Rebuilt after the 1693 earthquake, the town features a unique hexagonal layout. Visitors should explore the Tonnara di Avola, a former tuna processing plant that offers insights into the area's fishing history. The town's coastline boasts crystal-clear waters perfect for swimming and relaxation. Architecture enthusiasts will appreciate the Chiesa Madre (Mother Church) and the elegant Palazzo Modica. Avola offers a blend of historical interest, natural beauty, and culinary delights.

Pantalica. 45 kilometers (28 miles) from Syracuse. Pantalica is an extraordinary archaeological site and a UNESCO World Heritage site, featuring over 5,000 rock-cut tombs dating from the 13th to the 7th centuries BCE. This necropolis is set in a stunning natural landscape, making it an ideal destination for both history buffs and nature lovers.

Visitors can hike through the rugged terrain, exploring the ancient tombs carved into the limestone cliffs. A highlight of the site is the Anaktoron (Prince's Palace), believed to be the remains of a prehistoric leader's residence. The site offers breathtaking panoramic views of the Anapo valley, combining archaeological interest with natural beauty. Pantalica provides a unique glimpse into Sicily's prehistoric past and offers excellent opportunities for hiking and photography.

Logistics

Train: Syracuse has a train station with connections to major cities like Catania, Palermo, and Messina. However, many small towns may not have direct rail access. Check schedules for specific routes.

Bus: Intercity buses connect Syracuse with towns like Noto, Ragusa, and Modica. Companies like AST and Interbus offer regular services.

Car: Renting a car is the most flexible option, especially for exploring rural areas and nature reserves.

Parking: Syracuse has paid parking lots near the historic center and free parking on the outskirts. In small towns, street parking is common, but be sure to check for local regulations.

Dining Recommendations

Spizzica Al Vecchio Lavatoio. Address: Via Maniace, 8.

Our recommendation, although chaotic the food was excellent. This waterfront restaurant offers delightful seafood dishes and pizzas.

Ristorante Regina Lucia. Address: Piazza Duomo, 6

Located at the end of the piazza, this elegant restaurant offers upscale Sicilian cuisine with a focus on seafood. Perfect for a refined dining experience in Ortygia.

A Putia. Address: Via Roma, 8

A small, cozy restaurant offering delicious Sicilian pasta and grilled dishes. It's popular for both its casual ambiance and flavorful local cuisine.

Ristorante Don Camillo. Address: Via Maestranza, 96

This Michelin-rated restaurant offers a refined menu blending traditional and modern Sicilian flavors, making it a perfect spot for a splurge meal.

Pizzeria Schiticchio. Address: Via della Maestranza, 40

Known for its Neapolitan-style pizzas, this casual pizzeria offers great value and flavorful dishes, with outdoor seating on a lively street.

Accommodation

*Algilà Ortigia Charme Hotel. Address: Via Vittorio Veneto, 93

This 4-star hotel is located in a restored baroque building in the heart of Ortygia, offering elegant accommodations. With dining options, free Wi-Fi, and air conditioning, it's an excellent choice for exploring nearby historical landmarks.

*Grand Hotel Ortigia. Address: Viale Giuseppe Mazzini, 12

A 5-star hotel that combines historic charm with modern amenities. It offers a rooftop dining experience and is located within walking distance of the Cathedral. Popular for its beach access and stunning views of the sea.

*Antico Hotel Roma 1880. Address: Via Roma, 66

This 4-star hotel is just steps from the Cathedral of Syracuse, located on Via Roma, right on Ortygia. The hotel is an ideal choice if you're looking to stay along the St. Lucy procession route. It's known for its charming historical ambiance, and a restaurant offering local delicacies.

Ortea Palace Hotel, Sicily, Autograph Collection. Address: Via Riva Nazario Sauro, 1

A 5-star luxury hotel located in a historic post office building, this hotel offers high-end services like a spa, pool, and stunning views of the harbor. It's close to the Cathedral but also set on the water's edge.

Re Dionisio Boutique Hotel. Address: Via Eolo

This 3-star hotel offers modern comforts like a spa and beach access while maintaining proximity to Ortygia. Its stylish and boutique design makes it popular for visitors looking for a contemporary vibe.

*These hotels are directly along or very near the procession route for the Festa di Santa Lucia.

Chapter Thirty

Experience Ancient Stories in the Greek Theater

Immersion Experience Syracuse

Experience History Live: Attend a Show at the Greek Theater in Syracuse, Sicily

Imagine sitting under the stars, the cool Mediterranean breeze gently brushing against your face, as the age-old stone theater around you echoes with the powerful voices of actors performing a timeless Greek drama. Attending a show at the Greek Theater in Syracuse, Sicily, is more than watching a performance—it's immersing in a unique historical and cultural event that connects you to Western civilization's origins.

Today, the theatre is one of Sicily's most visited attractions, especially from mid-May to the end of June, when it is transformed into a buzzing hive of dramatic activity, just as it was 2,500 years.

The Greek Theater of Syracuse: A Historical Gem

Greek Theater of Syracuse, built in 5th century BC, is among world's most impressive ancient theaters. The theater in the Neapolis archaeological park was a focal point of culture and politics in the old city, where people came together for performances, debates, and public events. During its prime, it was able to accommodate up to 15,000 spectators, showcasing its grand design for large-scale productions.

Why Attend a Show at the Greek Theater?

1. Immerse Yourself in History

Watching a performance in the Greek Theater of Syracuse allows you to step back in time. The very stones beneath you have witnessed countless stories unfold, from the works of Aeschylus, Sophocles, and Euripides to modern interpretations of classic dramas. As the sun sets and the stage lights flicker on, the ancient ruins come alive, transporting you to a different era. It's not just a show—it's a chance to join living history.

2. Authentic Greek Drama

There is no better place to experience Greek drama than in a Greek theater. The acoustics, architecture, and ambiance of the theater are all designed to enhance the overall theatrical impact. Whether you are watching a tragedy, comedy, or a satirical play, the setting adds a layer of authenticity that you simply can't replicate in a modern theater. The performances here often stay true to the original scripts, providing a genuine representation of ancient Greek culture and art.

3. Diverse Performances to Enjoy

While the Greek Theater of Syracuse is famous for its classical Greek drama performances, it also hosts a variety of other events throughout the year. These can include modern plays, operas, concerts, and cultural festivals. No matter your taste, there's likely a performance that will captivate you and provide a deeper understanding of both traditional and contemporary Sicilian culture.

4. A Scenic and Memorable Location

Set against the stunning backdrop of the Sicilian landscape, the Greek Theater offers breathtaking views of the surrounding area. Before the performance, you can explore the archaeological park, marvel at the nearby ruins, and soak in the rich history that permeates. As the performance begins, the natural surroundings enhance the atmosphere, making the experience even more unforgettable.

When planning to attend a show at the Greek Theater, it's essential to check the schedule well in advance, especially for the popular summer performances when the weather is ideal for outdoor shows. Due to the theater's popularity and historical significance, productions often sell out quickly, so booking your tickets early is highly recommended. For more details and ticket information, visit the official Istituto Nazionale del Dramma Antico website.

On the day of the performance, arrive early to explore the archaeological park and find your seat at a leisurely pace. This also allows you to soak in the calm ambiance before the crowds arrive. Dress comfortably, as the seating is on stone steps, and consider bringing a light jacket for cooler evenings. For added comfort during the performance, either bring your own cushion or take advantage of the cushion rental service offered inside the theater. While sitting on the ancient stones is an interesting experience, it can become uncomfortable over time, making a cushion a worthwhile addition to your visit.

Chapter Thirty-One

A Taste of Sicily

Immersion Experience: Syracuse

Imagine returning from your vacation not just with photos and souvenirs, but with the ability to recreate the flavors of your journey in your own kitchen. This is the magic of taking a cooking class during your travels, and nowhere is this experience more rewarding than in Sicily.

Sicily, an island steeped in history, boasts a culinary tradition as rich and diverse as its cultural heritage. While dining out can offer a taste of this gastronomic wonderland, participating in a cooking class provides an immersive experience that will transform your vacation into a journey of flavors, skills, and unforgettable memories.

A Personal Slice of Sicily: Our Cooking Adventure

During our recent trip to Sicily, my husband and I embarked on a culinary adventure that became the highlight of our vacation. We booked a private cooking class with Gilda, a local culinary expert, through Cesarine. Gilda's home, just a short drive from the historic island of Ortygia in Syracuse, became our classroom for the day.

In Gilda's charming outdoor kitchen, we were initiated into the sacred art of preparing and cooking arancini - those delightful Sicilian rice balls that are a staple of the island's cuisine. The experience was hands-on, intimate, and absolutely delicious. As we shaped the arancini and watched them turn golden in the oil, we felt a connection to centuries of Sicilian tradition.

Why Would You Want to Cook During Vacation?

1. **Deeper Cultural Immersion**: Food is the heart of any culture. By learning to cook local dishes, you're not just tasting Sicily - you're understanding its history, its people, and their way of life.

2. **Unique, Hands-on Experience**: Instead of being a passive observer, you become an active participant in creating Sicilian cuisine.

3. **Lifetime Skills:** The techniques and recipes you learn will stay with you long after your tan fades, allowing you to relive your vacation every time you step into your kitchen.

4. **Memorable Stories:** "I ate at a great restaurant in Sicily" is nice, but "I learned to make arancini from a Sicilian nonna in her own kitchen" is a story you'll never tire of telling.

What to Expect in a Sicilian Cooking Class

1. **Hands-On Cooking:** You'll be involved in every step of the process. In our class, we assembled the arancini together while Gilda prepared the ragu and rice.

2. **Traditional Techniques:** Learn time-honored methods passed down through generations.

3. **Enjoy Your Creations:** The reward for your efforts? A delicious meal that tastes all the better because you made it yourself.

4. **Take-Home Knowledge:** Leave with recipes and skills that will allow you to bring a taste of Sicily to your home kitchen.

Ready to add this unforgettable experience to your Sicilian itinerary? You can book through Cesarine or if you're in Syracuse, contact Gilda Failla directly at gildafailla@yahoo.com.

Chapter Thirty-Two
Epiphany & La Befana in Cefalù
Gifts and Tradition

Epiphany & The Befana

Where: Cefalù and throughout Italy

When: January 6

Festival Average Temperatures: High: 12.2°C (54°F). Low 7.8°C (46°F).

Discovering Cefalù: Norman Splendor on the Tyrrhenian Coast

Nestled between a rocky promontory and the azure waters of the Tyrrhenian Sea, Cefalù stands as a harmonious blend of medieval charm and coastal allure. This picturesque town, with its imposing Norman cathedral rising above a maze of narrow streets, offers visitors a unique combination of historical richness, architectural splendor, and seaside relaxation. Cefalù embodies the diverse heritage of Sicily, where cultures and epochs intertwine to create a tapestry of experiences that captivate travelers from around the world.

The history of Cefalù stretches back to ancient times, with its name derived from the Greek word "Kephaloidion," meaning "head" or "cape," referring to the distinctive rocky promontory that dominates its skyline. While evidence of Greek and Roman settlements exists, it was under a Norman rule that Cefalù gained its most defining feature. In 1131, King Roger II began the construction of the magnificent cathedral, allegedly fulfilling a vow made after surviving a storm at sea. This event marked the beginning of Cefalù's golden age, transforming it into an important religious and cultural center. Throughout subsequent centuries, under Swabian, Angevin, and Spanish rule, the town continued to grow, each era leaving its mark on the urban landscape.

Cefalù is on the northern coast of Sicily, about 70 kilometers east of Palermo. The town is built on a promontory that juts out into the Tyrrhenian Sea, creating a natural harbor that has been crucial to its development. The dramatic backdrop of the Madonie Mountains, rising sharply behind the town, adds to its picturesque setting.

Cefalù has a population of approximately 14,000 residents, a number that swells significantly during the summer months.

The Epiphany and the Befana

Epiphany is a Christian feast celebrated on January 6th, marking the visit of the Three Wise Men (Magi)—Caspar, Melchior, and Balthazar—to the infant Jesus in Bethlehem. The Magi, guided by a star, brought gifts of gold, frankincense, and myrrh to honor him as a king. This event is seen as the first manifestation of Christ to the Gentiles, making it an important celebration in the Christian calendar.

In Italy, Epiphany is particularly known for the legend of La Befana, a friendly old witch who delivers gifts to children on the night of January 5th. According to tradition, La Befana was invited to accompany the Magi, but the invitation was declined. She later regretted it and has been searching for the Christ child ever since, giving gifts to obedient children and coal to the naughty ones.

Cefalu Celebrations

On January 6, 2024, Cefalù will celebrate the Solemnity of the Epiphany of the

Lord at its iconic Cattedrale di Cefalù. This celebration is an important event in the town's religious calendar, bringing together both locals and visitors in celebration.

The highlight of the day will be a Solemn Pontifical Mass at 6:00 p.m., presided over by the Bishop of Cefalù. During this mass, children will receive a special blessing, and there will be a symbolic arrival of the Three Wise Men organized by the city.

In addition to the religious events, visitors can explore the town's Via dei Presepi, a special exhibit of Nativity scenes scattered throughout the streets and shop windows. The church and city of Cefalù have curated a stunning display of traditional and creative presepi (Nativity scenes), offering a unique glimpse into local craftsmanship and culture. The exhibit includes locations such as:

- Vistita Boutique, Via G. Matteotti, 37
- Bar Duomo, Piazza Duomo, 24
- Basilica Cattedrale, Piazza Duomo

Nativity scenes can also be admired at several other sites across the town, including churches like Parrocchia SS. Salvatore alla Torre and the Chiesa della SS.ma Trinità, which will host the Diocesan Nativity Scene Exhibit at the Complesso Monumentale di S. Domenico.

Special Festival Treats
Epiphany

Buccellati: Short crust biscuits filled with dried figs, honey, almonds, and orange peel.

Almond Nougat: A sweet confection made from almonds and honey, often enjoyed during festive seasons.

Candied Fruits: Various fruits preserved in sugar, adding a sweet touch to the celebrations.

These delicacies are typically enjoyed during the Epiphany across Sicily, including Cefalù, adding a sweet note to the festive season.

Cefalù, with its UNESCO-listed Norman Cathedral, offers a spiritual and cultural immersion during the Epiphany. The charming town becomes even more vibrant with processions, events, and stunning nativity displays scattered throughout its picturesque streets, creating a perfect blend of faith, art, and tradition.

Visitors can also enjoy a stroll through the ancient streets of Cefalù, admire the festive lights, and explore the unique mix of sacred and secular traditions that make Epiphany in Sicily a memorable experience.

Whether you're attending mass or exploring the Via dei Presepi, the celebration of the Epiphany in Cefalù promises to be a deeply moving and culturally rich experience.

Walking Tour of Cefalù

Cathedral of Cefalù

#1. Piazza Duomo and Cefalù Cathedral

Start the tour at the heart of Cefalù, the Piazza Duomo. The Cefalù Cathedral, a UNESCO World Heritage Site, was built in 1131 by Norman King Roger II after he survived a storm and vowed to build the church in gratitude. This magnificent structure is renowned for its stunning Arab-Norman architecture and impressive Byzantine mosaics. The cathedral also reflects the political and cultural ambitions of Roger II, symbolizing his power and Sicily's role as a crossroads of civilizations during the Norman reign. Over the centuries, it became a cornerstone of religious life in Cefalù and an enduring emblem of the town's history.

Cathedral Interior

As you enter, you'll be struck by the grandeur of the nave, supported by recycled classical columns. The highlight is undoubtedly the Byzantine mosaic of Christ Pantocrator in the apse, created by twelfth-century artisans from Constantinople. This awe-inspiring image depicts Christ giving a blessing with his right hand while holding the Gospels in his left. The vibrant colors and intricate details of the mosaic are truly breathtaking.

Don't miss the side chapels, particularly the Chapel of St. John, which features beautiful 16th-century frescoes. The wooden choir stalls, dating from the 16th century, are also worth noting for their intricate carvings.

Climb to the Roof

For those seeking a more adventurous experience, the climb to the cathedral's roof is highly recommended. The ascent involves navigating narrow, winding staircases, but the effort is well rewarded with panoramic views of Cefalù and the Tyrrhenian Sea.

From this vantage point, you can appreciate the cathedral's architectural details up close, including the intricate stonework and the massive Norman towers. The vista stretches across the red-tiled roofs of the old town to the blue expanse of the sea, with the distinctive rock of Cefalù (La Rocca) dominating the skyline.

View of the Cloister from the Roof

The Cloister

Next to the cathedral is the charming cloister, a serene space that offers a stark contrast to the grandeur of the main building. Built in the late 12th century, the cloister features delicate double columns supporting pointed arches. Each column capital is uniquely carved with biblical scenes, mythological figures, and plant motifs.

The cloister's peaceful atmosphere invites contemplation, and its well-preserved state allows visitors to imagine the daily lives of the monks who once walked these paths. In the center, you'll find a lovely garden with a fountain, adding to the tranquil ambiance.

Renaissance Cloister of Cefalù

#2. Lavatoio Medievale (Medieval Washhouse)

From Piazza Duomo, head down to the Lavatoio Medievale, a well-preserved medieval washhouse fed by the Cefalino River. The structure dates back to at least the 16th century and shows the advanced water engineering used by the town. Its basins and stone channels were an essential part of daily life for centuries, offering a glimpse into Cefalù's past.

#3. Osterio Magno (Norman Palace)

Walk along Corso Ruggero to reach Osterio Magno, a Norman palace said to have belonged to King Roger II himself. This 11th-century structure was later expanded, becoming a symbol of the town's medieval power. It houses various exhibitions today, but its stone walls tell stories of Cefalù's Norman past.

#4. Museo Mandralisca

A short walk from Osterio Magno, you'll find the Museo Mandralisca. This small but rich museum features a fascinating collection of art and archaeology, including the famous "Portrait of an Unknown Man" by Antonello da Messina. Founded by the nobleman Enrico Pirajno di Mandralisca, the museum also showcases Greek ceramics and local treasures from Cefalù's history.

#5. Porta Pescara

Continue the tour to Porta Pescara, an ancient gate leading to Cefalù's beachfront. This medieval stone archway once served as a gateway to the town's fishing port. From here, you'll have a panoramic view of the Tyrrhenian Sea, an ideal spot to pause and soak in the coastal beauty before heading to your next stop.

#6. The Rocca di Cefalù

The most significant climb of the day, the Rocca di Cefalù, is a towering limestone hill that overlooks the town. It's about 45 minutes to the top, but well worth the hike for the history and views. At the top, you'll find the remains of the Temple of Diana, a 9th-century BC megalithic structure believed to have been dedicated to a water deity. You'll also explore remnants of Byzantine fortifications. The panoramic views of Cefalù and the surrounding coast are unforgettable. Or you can just admire the Rocca from the town.

#7. Bastione di Capo Marchiafava

After descending from the Rocca, make your way to the Bastione di Capo Marchiafava. The Bastione is a 17th-century fortification onBeautiful views of the Tyrrhenian Sea can be enjoyed on the scenic coastal drive. the northeastern edge of Cefalù's old town. This small but significant structure offers visitors a blend of historical intrigue and stunning coastal views.

Built in the early 1600s, the bastion was an integral part of Cefalù's coastal defense system. The Mediterranean was frequently troubled by pirate raids during this period, particularly from North African corsairs. The bastion, along with other fortifications along the coast, protected the town and its inhabitants from these maritime threats.

#8. Lungomare (Cefalù Beach)

End the tour at the beautiful sandy beach of Cefalù. The Lungomare is a perfect place to unwind after a day of exploring the town's historical sites. You can take a leisurely walk along the coastline, take a dip in the sea, or relax at one of the many cafes lining the beach. The beach has been a vital part of Cefalù's history, serving as a hub for fishermen and now as a major attraction for visitors.

This walking tour of Cefalù covers approximately 3.5 kilometers, taking about 4-6 hours, including time to explore each site. Overall, Cefalu is a pleasant place to visit and easy to enjoy.

Cefalù Festivals Throughout the Year

Cefalù Carnevale

February/March (dates vary, occurring before Lent)

Cefalù's Carnival is a vibrant pre-Lenten celebration. The streets come alive with colorful parades featuring elaborate masks and costumes, accompanied by live music and dancing. This festive period typically lasts several days, culminating in the symbolic "burning" of the Carnival king effigy. Traditional Sicilian sweets like cannoli and pignolata are enjoyed during this time.

Infiorata di Cefalù (Flower Festival)

June (usually coinciding with Corpus Christi)

The Infiorata is a breathtaking floral art festival where the streets of Cefalù are transformed into a canvas of intricate flower carpets. Local artists and volunteers work through the night to create these ephemeral masterpieces using petals, seeds, and natural materials. The festival celebrates the arrival of spring and often incorporates religious themes, particularly when it aligns with Corpus Christi.

Festa del Santissimo Salvatore (Christ Most Holy Savior)

August 2-6

This is Cefalù's most significant religious festival, honoring the town's patron and celebrating the Transfiguration of Christ. The five-day event begins with the raising of the festival banner and includes daily religious processions, traditional Sicilian music performances, and local games. The highlight is the grand religious service held in the Norman-Byzantine cathedral on August 6. To end the festival concludes there is a spectacular fireworks display over the sea. It is magnificent.

Festa della Madonna della Luce (Madonna of the Light)

September (specific dates may vary)

Dedicated to the Madonna of Light, this autumn festival holds deep significance for Cefalù's residents. It features solemn religious processions through the town's narrow streets, with participants carrying a statue of the Madonna. The event is enriched by performances of traditional Sicilian folk music and dances. While smaller in scale compared to the Festa del Santissimo Salvatore, it offers a more intimate glimpse into local religious traditions and community spirit.

Day Trip Options: Nearby Sites, Cities and Towns

Madonie Mountains. 50 km (31 miles) from Cefalù, The Madonie Regional Natural Park is a great destination for nature lovers. The park offers hiking trails with stunning views of the Sicilian countryside, picturesque villages, and diverse flora and fauna. Visitors can explore beech forests, climb mountain peaks, and potentially spot rare wildlife like the Sicilian fir tree and the European wildcat.

Santo Stefano di Camastra. 55 km (34 miles) from Cefalù Known for its colorful and intricately designed ceramics, Santo Stefano di Camastra is a paradise for art enthusiasts. The town is filled with artisan shops selling hand-painted pottery and ceramics, making it a great place for souvenir shopping. The ceramics here are renowned for their vibrant colors, often featuring intricate patterns inspired by Sicilian folklore, nature, and historical motifs. Bright yellows, deep blues, and rich greens are commonly used, creating eye-catching designs on plates, vases, and decorative tiles. You can also visit its ceramics museum to learn about the history of this craft in the region and watch local artisans at work.

Logistics

Train: Cefalù is well-connected by train to major cities in Sicily, such as Palermo and Messina.

Bus: There are several bus services connecting Cefalù to nearby towns and tourist destinations, including Palermo and the surrounding coastal areas.

Car: Driving from Palermo to Cefalù is a popular option for tourists and locals alike. The route primarily follows the A20 motorway, also known as Autostrada Messina-Palermo. The journey covers approximately 70 kilometers (43 miles) and typically takes about an hour, depending on traffic conditions. Beautiful views of the Tyrrhenian Sea can be enjoyed during the scenic coastal drive.

Parking In Cefalù can be challenging, especially during peak tourist seasons. The historic center is largely pedestrianized, with limited parking options. There are several paid parking areas on the outskirts of the old town, including a large parking lot near the train station. It's advisable to arrive early to secure a spot, particularly in the summer months. Some hotels in Cefalù offer private parking for guests, which can be a convenient option if you're staying overnight.

Dining Recommendations

La Botte. Address: Via Veterani

This restaurant offers traditional Sicilian cuisine with a focus on fresh seafood and pasta dishes. They are especially known for their swordfish and Sicilian-style sardines, offering an authentic taste of the region's culinary heritage.

Al Faro. Address: Via Presidiana

Known for its scenic views and fresh seafood, Al Faro is a favorite for diners looking to enjoy a meal with a sea view. Their grilled fish and seafood platters are particularly popular, making it a great spot for enjoying local maritime flavors.

Accommodation

Hotel Alberi del Paradiso. Address: Via dei Mulini, 18-20

A 4-star hotel set in lush gardens, this elegant establishment offers panoramic views of Cefalù and the sea. It features a pool, spa, restaurant, and beach shuttle service, making it ideal for guests seeking a peaceful retreat with easy access to the town and beach.

Hotel - Residence Calanica. Address: Contrada Vallone di Falco

A 4-star resort offering a serene atmosphere with stunning sea views, dining options, and access to various activities. Its relaxed setting is ideal for those looking for a tranquil vacation.

Hotel Le Calette. Address: Via Vincenzo Cavallaro, 12

A 5-star luxury hotel with upscale accommodations, a spa, and a pool. Le Calette is renowned for its breathtaking sea views and top-tier services, including private beach access and fine dining.

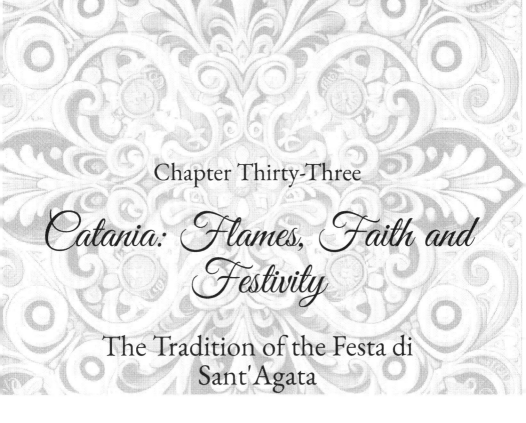

Chapter Thirty-Three
Catania: Flames, Faith and Festivity

The Tradition of the Festa di Sant'Agata

La Festa di Sant'Agata

Where: Catania

When: February 3 to 5

Event Website: https://santagatacatania.it/en/

Average Festival Temperatures: High: 16-17 °C (61-63 °F). Low: 8-9 °C (46-48 °F).

Discovering Resilient Catania: City in the Shadow of Etna

Rising from the ashes of devastating earthquakes and volcanic eruptions, Catania stands as a testament to human resilience and creativity. Sicily's second-largest city, with its striking baroque architecture carved from dark volcanic stone, presents a dramatic contrast against the backdrop of Mount Etna, Europe's most active volcano. This vibrant metropolis, where ancient ruins coexist with bustling markets and innovative industries, offers visitors a dynamic blend of historical grandeur, culinary delights, and the raw power of nature.

The history of Catania is one of repeated destruction and rebirth. Founded by Greek colonists in the 8th century BC, the city has been shaped by successive civilizations - Greek, Roman, Byzantine, Arab, Norman, and Spanish - each leaving its mark on the urban fabric. However, it was the catastrophic earthquake of 1693 that most profoundly transformed Catania.

In its aftermath, the city was rebuilt in the Baroque style, using the abundant local black lava stone, creating the unique architectural character that defines Catania today. This rebirth earned the city its nickname "la città nera" (the black city) for its distinctive lava stone buildings, and exemplified the resilient spirit that has come to characterize Catania throughout its tumultuous history.

Catania occupies a strategic position on Sicily's eastern coast, nestled between the Ionian Sea and the imposing mass of Mount Etna. This location has been both a blessing and a curse - the fertile volcanic soil has supported rich agriculture, while periodic eruptions and earthquakes have posed constant threats.

The city of Catania has a population of approximately 300,000, with over 750,000 in its metropolitan area, making it the center of Sicily's most populous conurbation. The economy of Catania is diverse and dynamic, blending traditional industries with high-tech sectors. The city has earned the "European Silicon Valley" moniker for its growing IT and tech industry, hosted in the Etna Valley technology park.

Traditional sectors such as agriculture, fishing, and food processing remain significant, while tourism, boosted by the city's rich cultural heritage and proximity to Mount Etna, plays an increasingly important role.

The Festival of Saint Agatha

Sicilians view the festival of Saint Agatha as a major celebration. She is additionally a patron saint for the Republic of San Marino and the island of Malta. People have celebrated her since her martyrdom on the 5th of February in 251 AD. As per Italian media, the St. Agatha festival is the world's third largest in attendance. It has been celebrated for centuries.

Who is St. Agatha?

Saint Agatha was a 3rd-century Christian martyr from Catania, Sicily. Historical records confirm her existence and veneration, though many details of her life are based on legend.

According to tradition, Agatha was a beautiful noblewoman who dedicated herself to Christianity. Quintianus, the Roman consul in Sicily, sought to marry her and force her to renounce her faith. When Agatha refused, Quintianus had her imprisoned and tortured. Despite severe physical abuse, including the mutilation of her breasts, Agatha remained steadfast in her beliefs.

Legend tells that during her imprisonment, St. Peter appeared to Agatha in a vision, miraculously healing her wounds. This event, while not historically verified, is a significant part of her hagiography.

After further torture, including being rolled over hot coals, Agatha died in prison in 251 AD. Her death was said to be accompanied by an earthquake, which some interpreted as divine judgment against her persecutors.

Following her death, Agatha's tomb became a site of pilgrimage. A story circulated that mysterious youths placed a marble tablet at her grave, inscribed with words honoring her faithfulness and patriotism.

Throughout history, many miracles have been attributed to Saint Agatha's intercession. She remains an important figure in Christian tradition, particularly venerated in Catania and other parts of Sicily.

The Festival of Saint Agatha

Taking place from the 3rd to the 5th of February every year, the event can incorporate upwards of one million people, comprising locals, devotees, and tourists. Years after the death of Saint Agatha, Mount Etna threatened Catania with a violent eruption. To stop the lava from advancing, the inhabitants used the white veil that was placed over Agatha's tomb. A miracle took place. On the 5th of February, the anniversary of her martyrdom, the veil turned red and halted the eruption. The citizens annually adorn it with lights in commemoration of this triumphant event.

February 3

The celebration starts with a ceremonial opening of the gate in the Cathedral, and removal of the statue and relics of Saint Agatha. The atmosphere as the saint is prepared for the festivities is electric. Government, schools, and businesses close from February 3rd through the 6th. The pinnacle of Catania's yearly events. The church overflows with locals who wave white fabric known as "cannamuni" or "cannemi," large white handkerchiefs or cloths, often embroidered with images related to Saint Agatha or religious motifs.

The waving of these handkerchiefs holds symbolic significance. The white color symbolizes purity and devotion to Saint Agatha. Waving these towels is believed to call upon Saint Agatha's protection and blessing in the city and its people. The waving of cannamuni is a crucial element of the rituals and ceremonies during the Feast of Saint Agatha, adding to the solemnity and fervor of the religious celebrations in Catania.

Procession of the Candelore

The festivities begin on February 3rd with the Procession of the Candelore—eleven large, gilded candles symbolizing the various trades of Catania. Each Candelora is a tall, beautifully decorated wooden structure, often adorned with flowers, ribbons, and lights, standing several meters high and weighing several hundred kilograms. These Candelore represent the different guilds or trades of the town, with each guild traditionally having its own Candelora.

The procession, accompanied by local leaders, civil and military authorities, as well as townspeople, moves through the streets to Piazza Duomo, where the Processione della Cera begins. This is the offering of candles to Saint Agatha, starting at Piazza Stesicoro and ending at the Cathedral of Sant'Agata. During the procession, powerful men known as "Candelori" carry the Candelore, performing coordinated movements to maneuver these heavy structures through the streets. Music, cheers, and prayers accompany them, adding to the excitement and fervor of the event. The day concludes with a grand fireworks display in Piazza Duomo, an integral and highly anticipated part of the celebration.

Candelora awaiting the Procession

February 4

The second day of the Festa di Sant'Agata begins with the Aurora Mass at dawn, held in the Cathedral of Catania. After the Mass, the dramatic exit of the statue of Saint Agatha takes place, a moment filled with anticipation and emotion. The statue is carried on the fercolo, a large, intricately decorated silver carriage adorned with beautiful metalwork and flowers, which holds the saint's relics.

The procession is led by hundreds of "devoti," followers dressed in traditional white tunics ('u saccu) and black caps. Carrying the fercolo is a physically demanding task due to its weight and the long duration of the march, as it continues through the streets of Catania from early morning until late at night. The devoti and other participants follow the statue with large candles, chanting and shouting, "All devout, all citizens, long live Sant'Agata!" as a sign of their devotion.

As the procession winds through the Baroque streets, it passes key sites related to Saint Agatha's life, including locations connected to her imprisonment, torture, and eventual martyrdom. These pauses are marked by special prayers and blessings, allowing moments of reflection amidst the celebratory atmosphere.

Key moments include a stop at Piazza Borgo, where a fireworks display lights up the sky, and the exhilarating cchianata de' Cappuccini at Via Sangiuliano, where the statue is pulled uphill in a symbolic display of strength and devotion. This rush, filled with cheers and the waving of handkerchiefs, leads to Piazza San Domenico before the procession continues into the night.

The event concludes late at night with the fercolo's return to the Cathedral, closing the second day of this deeply spiritual and grand celebration.

February 5th and 6th

On February 5th, the third day of the Festa di Sant'Agata, the grand celebration continues with one of the most exciting and highly anticipated events of the festival: the long procession through the heart of Catania, beginning in the morning. The statue of Saint Agatha, carried on the fercolo, travels along Via Etnea, passing significant landmarks in the city, including Piazza Università, Piazza Stesicoro, and Villa Bellini.

One of the emotional highlights of this day is the cchianata di San Giuliano, where devotees pull the heavy silver fercolo uphill at a run along the steep Via Sangiuliano, symbolizing their intense devotion and strength.

Thousands of onlookers line the streets, cheering and waving handkerchiefs in support of the participants. The procession continues late into the night, eventually reaching Piazza Cavour, where a sense of anticipation builds as the celebration approaches its final hours.

As the early morning of February 6th nears, the most awaited moment arrives: the return of the statue to the Cathedral. This moment is never precisely timed, adding to the excitement and anxious anticipation as thousands of followers await the statue's return.

Throughout the night, the façade of the Cathedral of Catania is beautifully illuminated with a stunning light projection, while fireworks fill the sky above Piazza Duomo, creating a spectacular grand finale to the third day of celebrations.

Special Festival Foods
The Minni, the Olivette, Le Crespelle, and the Polpette di Cavallo

The Festival of Sant'Agata in Catania is one of the oldest and most deeply rooted celebrations in Sicily, and its long history is reflected in the abundance of festival foods associated with it. Over centuries, these foods have become a way to honor the saint while showcasing Catania's rich culinary heritage.

1. Minni di Sant'Agata

The first food that is a tradition of this annual festival is called the Minni di Sant'Agata which means Saint Agatha's breasts. Don't blame the messenger! These are to remind us of the miracle in which St. Peter restored her breasts after her torturers had cut them off.

A traditional sweet and specialty in Catania, this shortbread pastry cup is filled with fresh sweetened ricotta cheese, and often seasoned with orange zest or candied orange, and covered with white icing. There is a pink version filled with pastry cream, always with a cherry on top.

2. Olivette di Sant'Agata

The Olivette di Sant'Agata: small almond pastries that pay tribute to the olive tree that miraculously sustained Saint Agatha. The bakers primarily use almond paste (marzipan) to make these pastries, shaping them into small olive-like forms and then coating them in green sugar. They are often prepared at home, sold in bakeries, and shared with family and friends during the celebration.

3. Le Crespelle

You'll find crespelle con la ricotta—dough balls fried golden brown and filled with creamy ricotta cheese – at street vendors along the parade route.

4. Polpette di Cavallo

Food vendors along the route sell polpette di cavallo: large meatballs that seem more like a small hamburgers and are made from horse meat. Americans may find it strange to eat horse meat, but it is more common, even as carpaccio (raw), in Italy. No, my husband and I have not built up the courage to try them.

Walking Tour of Catania

#1. Basilica Cattedrale di Sant'Agata

The Basilica Cattedrale di Sant'Agata, dedicated to Catania's beloved patron saint, stands as both a symbol of faith and a chronicle of the city's tumultuous history. Its resilience mirrors the spirit of Catania itself, a city repeatedly reborn from the ashes of disasters. Originally built between 1078 and 1093 by the Norman Order of Roger I following their conquest of Sicily, the cathedral was constructed on the ruins of an ancient Roman bath complex, becoming a focal point of devotion to Saint Agatha, a martyr revered for her bravery and piety.

Throughout its history, the cathedral has faced many devastations. The earthquake of 1169 caused extensive damage shortly after its initial construction. In 1669, Mount Etna's lava flows reached the city, altering its landscape and damaging parts of the cathedral. The catastrophic earthquake of 1693 proved to be the most devastating event, leading to an almost complete reconstruction during the Baroque period. The post-1693 rebuilding efforts, led by Giovanni Battista Vaccarini, transformed the cathedral into a masterpiece of Sicilian Baroque, adding intricate details and grandeur befitting the city's most sacred monument.

Cathedral of Sant'Agata with its Gray Lava Stone

The façade of the Basilica Cattedrale di Sant'Agata is an awe-inspiring blend of classical and Baroque elements, reflecting centuries of artistry and cultural heritage. Its most striking feature is the row of granite columns, repurposed from Catania's ancient Roman Theatre, tying the cathedral to its classical past. Designed by Vaccarini, the facade is adorned with statues, floral motifs, and intricate reliefs, hallmarks of Sicilian Baroque artistry. At its center, a niche holds a statue of Saint Agatha, symbolizing her enduring presence in the city's life.

The cathedral's exterior, built from gray lava stone sourced from the slopes of Mount Etna, gives the structure a dramatic and solemn appearance. This material serves as both a practical and symbolic choice, embodying the resilience of the city and its people. Rising above the facade, the bell towers add a striking silhouette to the Sicilian sky. Next to the cathedral is the Chapel of the Holy Sacrament, where Saint Agatha's relics are preserved and venerated, adding to the site's spiritual significance.

Interior of the Cathedral

Stepping inside, visitors are greeted by a vast, awe-inspiring interior. The Latin cross plan creates a sense of grand spirituality with its three naves and numerous chapels. Each chapel is a treasure trove of religious art, dedicated to various saints and adorned with masterful frescoes, sculptures, and intricate stucco work.

The heart of the cathedral lies behind an ornate iron gate, where the relics of Saint Agatha are reverently preserved. During the annual Feast of Saint Agatha, these relics become the focal point of passionate celebration, drawing pilgrims from far and wide. The artwork surrounding this sacred space vividly depicts the life and martyrdom of the beloved saint, serving as both a historical record and a source of spiritual inspiration.

From its soaring domes to its meticulously crafted altars, every corner of the Cathedral of Sant'Agata speaks to the incredible skill of the artisans who contributed to its creation. It stands not just as a place of worship, but as a living museum of Sicilian art, architecture, and faith, inviting visitors to marvel at its beauty and contemplate its profound historical and cultural significance.

#2. Chiesa della Badia di Sant'Agata (Church of the Convent of St. Agatha)

The Chiesa della Badia di Sant'Agata, an architectural gem nestled in the heart of Catania, stands as a testament to the city's rich religious and artistic heritage. This magnificent abbey church, dedicated to Saint Agatha, graces the northern side of the cathedral, adjacent to a serene park, creating a harmonious ensemble of sacred architecture.

Constructed between 1735 and 1767, during the height of the Sicilian Baroque period, the chiesa served as a Benedictine convent for women. Its creation was part of a broader movement in 18th-century Sicily that saw the flourishing of monastic institutions, particularly those catering to the spiritual needs of noblewomen.

The church's façade is a masterpiece of Baroque design, characterized by its dynamic interplay of convex and concave surfaces, ornate decorations, and elegant proportions. This frontage serves as a captivating prelude to the massive structure behind it, hinting at the grandeur within.

However, the true marvel of the Chiesa della Badia di Sant'Agata is its extraordinary dome. This colossal octagonal cupola dominates not only the church but also the Catania skyline. Its unique concave shape is a rare architectural feature, showcasing the innovative spirit of its designers and the skilled craftsmanship of local artisans. The dome's distinctive form creates fascinating plays of light and shadow both inside and outside the church, changing with the movement of the sun throughout the day.

One of the church's most remarkable features is its accessible rooftop. Visitors who ascend to this vantage point are rewarded with breathtaking panoramic views. From here, one can admire the intricate details of the nearby Cathedral, gaze upon the sprawling cityscape of Catania, marvel at the church's own impressive dome from a unique perspective, and take in the awe-inspiring sight of Mount Etna looming in the distance. On clear days, the glistening waters of the Ionian Sea complete this stunning vista.

Importantly, the church has been designed with accessibility in mind. For those unable to climb the stairs, an elevator is available, ensuring that all visitors can experience the magnificent views from the rooftop. This thoughtful addition underscores the church's commitment to inclusivity and its role as a shared cultural treasure.

The interior of the chiesa, while less frequently discussed than its exterior, is equally impressive. It features elaborate frescoes, intricate stuccowork, and valuable artworks that reflect the spiritual and artistic sensibilities of 18th-century

Sicily. The church's design and decorations were intended not only to inspire religious devotion but also to showcase the wealth and prestige of the Benedictine order and its noble patrons.

#3. The University of Catania

The University of Catania is typical of Italian universities. Instead of a campus typical of most U.S. cities, the University of Catania has buildings and spaces all over town that bear signs of the university, including the one on Piazza Duomo.

#4. Via Etnea

If you're looking for the most Instagram-worthy street in Catania, look no further than Via Etnea, with its vibrant umbrellas, an art installation. This iconic street is one of the principal thoroughfares in the city, running from the Piazza Duomo near the Cathedral of Sant'Agata, up towards the base of Mount Etna.

#5. Teatro Massimo Bellini

The Teatro Massimo Bellini, inaugurated in 1890, stands as a crowning jewel of Catania's cultural landscape. Named after the city's beloved native composer, Vincenzo Bellini, this magnificent opera house is a testament to Sicily's rich musical heritage and architectural prowess. Designed by Carlo Sada in the Sicilian Baroque style, the theater boasts a stunning horseshoe-shaped auditorium with four tiers of boxes, renowned for its exceptional acoustics. Its opulent interiors, adorned with intricate frescoes and lavish decorations, transport visitors to the golden age of Italian opera.

The theater has played host to world-class performances since its opening night, which fittingly featured Bellini's masterpiece "Norma." Today, it continues to be a vibrant center for opera, concerts, and ballet, drawing music enthusiasts from around the globe. Visitors can explore this architectural marvel through guided tours, offered Tuesday through Saturday mornings, which provide unique insights into the theater's history, backstage areas, and the life of its namesake composer.

Whether admiring the grand foyer, ascending the majestic staircase, or marveling at the ceiling fresco by Ernesto Bellandi, a visit to the Teatro Massimo Bellini offers an unforgettable journey into the heart of Catania's artistic soul. Open for guided tours only. Click the link teatromassimobellini.it to learn more.

#6. Teatro Romano di Catania

The Roman Theatre of Catania, nestled in the heart of the city, stands as a remarkable testament to the ancient Roman presence in Sicily. This archaeological treasure, a key component of the Parco Archeologico Greco-Romano, offers visitors a captivating glimpse into the entertainment and cultural life of Roman Catania. The site comprises two distinct structures: a larger, impressively preserved theater and a smaller, more intimate semicircular venue known as the Odeon. Both structures date back to the second century AD, showcasing the architectural prowess and urban planning of the Roman Empire at its height.

For centuries, these magnificent structures lay hidden beneath layers of urban development, their existence known but their full extent a mystery. It wasn't until the nineteenth century that extensive excavations began to reveal the true grandeur of the site. The painstaking work of archaeologists gradually unearthed the theater's impressive seating areas, stage, and intricate architectural details. Today, visitors can walk through the same corridors and sit on the same stone seats that once accommodated thousands of Roman citizens, connecting them directly to the daily life of ancient Catania.

#7. Castello Ursino

In a six-minute walk toward the sea, you will find Castello Ursino. Emperor Frederick II, King of Sicily, built Castello Ursino between 1239 and 1250 using lava stone, as one of his royal castles. Local lords had attempted to assert independence, and in 1220, Frederick II ordered the destruction of all non-royal castles in Sicily. The builders constructed Castello Ursino to emphasize royal power and provide defense for the capital, believing it to be an impregnable fortress. Currently, it is open to the public and houses the Civic Museum of Catania.

#8. Palazzo Biscari

This monumental private palace stands as a testament to Catania's resilience and artistic renaissance following the devastating earthquake of 1693. Built by the noble Paternò Castello family, the palace grew in grandeur over the years, becoming one of the most impressive examples of Sicilian Baroque architecture. The exterior facade, adorned with intricate stonework and playful cherubs, hints at the opulence within.

Once inside, you'll be mesmerized by the rococo interiors, where every surface seems to come alive with ornate decorations. The frescoed ceilings tell stories of mythology and local history, while the carefully preserved furnishings transport you to the lavish lifestyle of 18th-century Sicilian aristocracy. Of particular note is the grand ballroom, a masterpiece of design with its mirrored walls and stunning views over the city. While traditionally open for group tours, individual visitors can now also experience the palace's splendor through pre-arranged guided visits. As we walk through its halls, imagine the grand parties and political intrigues that once filled these rooms, shaping the history of Catania.

#9. Monastero dei Benedettini di San Nicolo l'Arena (Benedictine Monastry of St. Nicholas)

Our next stop takes us to one of Europe's largest monasteries, the Monastero dei Benedettini di San Nicolo l'Arena. This vast complex, a city within a city, offers a fascinating journey through centuries of Catanian history and culture. Founded in the 16th century and extensively rebuilt after the 1693 earthquake, the monastery showcases a blend of architectural styles from Gothic to Baroque. As we enter, you'll be struck by the sheer scale of the complex, which includes two magnificent cloisters, each telling its own story of monastic life.

The monastery's library, with over 160,000 books, attracts both book lovers and scholars. Our tour covers the church and monastery, showcasing the blend of spiritual and intellectual life in the Benedictine tradition. Tours are offered every hour detailing the monastery's history, architecture, and culture. Even outside tour hours, some areas remain open, inviting visitors to enjoy the tranquility and architecture. As you walk through, reflect on its journey from a religious hub to a part of the University of Catania, keeping its legacy of learning and contemplation alive.

#10. Chiesa di San Placido

Our final stop brings us to the Chiesa di San Placido, a hidden gem in Catania's rich tapestry of religious architecture. This church, open 24 hours a day, offers a unique opportunity for spiritual reflection or architectural appreciation at any time. Built in the 18th century, the church's facade is a beautiful example of Sicilian Baroque, with its curved lines and ornate decorations typical of the style. As we step inside, take a moment to admire the harmonious interior, where light plays off the polychrome marble decorations and illuminates the fine artworks adorning the walls and altars. But the church is just the beginning of our exploration here.

Behind it lies a vast convent complex, a testament to the once-thriving monastic community that called this place home. Of particular interest within the convent is a medieval candle workshop, offering a rare glimpse into the practical skills and industries that supported monastic life. This workshop, still preserved with its original tools and setup, provides a tangible link to the daily lives of the monks who once walked these halls. As we explore this sacred space, consider the continuity of tradition it represents, from the timeless rituals of worship to the ancient craft of candlemaking, all persisting in the heart of modern Catania.

Catania Festivals and Sagre Throughout the Year

One Day Music Festival

May 1, 2024

One Day Music Festival is one of Sicily's most popular music events, held annually on La Playa Beach in Catania. The festival is known for its mix of electronic, rap, and alternative music, drawing both local and international artists. The all-day event runs from morning until evening, providing festival-goers with a full day of music and beach fun. Since its founding in 2009, the festival has grown steadily, attracting more than 20,000 participants in recent years.

Beer Catania Spring

Late May

The Beer Catania Spring festival is a celebration of craft beer, held annually in late May. It brings together beer enthusiasts and features around 20 Sicilian and Italian craft beer producers. The festival is set in the scenic cloisters of Istituto Ardizzone Gioeni, near the top of Via Etnea. The event also includes street food stalls, live music performances, and workshops, making it a lively cultural gathering. It's a chance to taste locally brewed beers while enjoying Catania's vibrant atmosphere.

Etna Comics

June 6-9, 2024

Etna Comics is the largest comic and pop culture festival in southern Italy, attracting tens of thousands of visitors each year. Held at the Le Ciminiere Trade Fair Centre, this vibrant event offers something for fans of comics, games, TV series, cinema, music, and more. It's an immersive experience featuring special guests, workshops, concerts, and exhibitions, making it a must-attend for pop culture enthusiasts. The festival has grown exponentially since its inception in 2009, and it's now a major cultural event in Sicily. The schedule typically runs from morning until late evening, with a bustling atmosphere throughout the four-day event.

Catania Summer Festival

June to September

The Catania Summer Festival is a series of cultural events held throughout the summer in various historic locations across the city. From June to September, you can experience concerts, theater performances, and dance shows set against the backdrop of Catania's iconic landmarks, such as the Villa Bellini and Castello Ursino. The festival showcases both local and international talent, transforming the city into a hub of artistic activity and offering something for every cultural taste.

Marranzano World Fest (Folk Music Festival)

June

The Marranzano World Fest in Catania is a unique celebration of the harp, known locally as the marranzano. This annual festival, typically held in September, brings together musicians, artisans, and enthusiasts from around the world to honor this small yet versatile instrument. The marranzano, deeply rooted in Sicilian folk tradition, takes center stage in a series of concerts, workshops, and exhibitions. Visitors can experience performances ranging from traditional Sicilian folk music to contemporary experimental sounds, all featuring the distinctive twang of the jew's harp.

Day Trip Options: Nearby Sites, Cities and Towns

Acireale. 18 kilometers or 11 miles to the north. Acireale is a charming Sicilian town known for its stunning baroque architecture and beautiful churches. The town's historical center is a treasure trove of architectural wonders, with the Piazza del Duomo at its heart. Here, visitors can admire the magnificent Acireale Cathedral, dedicated to Maria Santissima Annunziata, with its impressive façade and ornate interior.

One of the main attractions of Acireale is its famous carnival, one of the most popular in Sicily. The Carnival of Acireale typically takes place in February, leading up to Lent. It's known for its elaborate floats adorned with flowers and allegorical figures, as well as its satirical papier-mâché masks. The carnival features parades, music, dancing, and various competitions, attracting visitors from all over Italy and beyond.

Aci Trezza and Aci Castello. About 10-15 kilometers or 9 miles north. Aci Trezza and Aci Castello are two picturesque coastal towns that offer a perfect blend of natural beauty and historical significance.

Aci Trezza is renowned for its striking lava rock formations known as the Cyclopean Isles or "Isole dei Ciclopi." These basalt islets jutting out of the sea are linked to the legend of Odysseus and the Cyclops Polyphemus from Homer's Odyssey. The town's waterfront is lined with colorful fishing boats, and visitors can enjoy fresh seafood at local restaurants while taking in the views of the islands.

Aci Castello, just a short distance from Aci Trezza, is dominated by its impressive Norman Castle. Built in 1076 on a lava rock overlooking the sea, the castle now houses a civic museum showcasing local archaeological finds and offering insights into the area's volcanic history. Climbing to the top of the castle provides breathtaking panoramic views of the coastline and the Ionian Sea.

Logistics

Train: The main train station is Catania Centrale.

Bus: AMTS (Azienda Metropolitana Trasporti e Sosta Catania) The city's public bus service operates many routes that cover Catania and its suburbs.

Regional Buses: There are also intercity buses, AST, that connect Catania with other cities and towns in Sicily.

Catania Metro: The metro system in Catania is relatively small, but efficient. It has one operational line that runs from the western suburb of Nesima to the port area, covering important stops like the central railway station (Stazione Centrale) and the city center.

Car: With public transportation options in Catania, it is advised to park outside the city and not try and navigate inside with a car.

Parking: Here are a few parking options to avoid the ZTL (limited traffic zone only for citizens and taxis):

- Parcheggio Europa: This large underground parking lot is located near the central Via Etnea. From here, you can walk or use public transport to reach key sites.

- Parcheggio Borsellino: Situated near the Porto di Catania, this parking facility provides good access to the historic center with a short walk.

- Parcheggio Sosta Catania Centro: Located outside the restricted zone but near central areas, this is a convenient choice for visitors wanting proximity to the main attractions without worrying about entering the center.

Dining Recommendations

Canusciuti Sicilian Café for Pastries and Arancini. Address: Via Santa Maria della Lettera, 13

To find a minni di Sant'Agata, even outside of the festival week, the Canusciuti Sicilian Café is perfect. It's a four-minute walk from the Cathedral and offers great coffee, Sicilian pastries, and a delicious local version of arancini with a mozzarella center and meat sauce ragu. This hearty treat is a must-try for anyone visiting.

Etnea Roof Bar & Restaurant. Address: Via Etnea

For lunch or dinner with a view, make a reservation at Etnea Roof Bar & Restaurant with "UNA cucina." This rooftop restaurant is located just a fifteen-minute walk from the Cathedral and offers breathtaking views and traditional Sicilian cuisine. The friendly staff and fantastic atmosphere make it an excellent choice for escaping Catania's bustling streets.

Munnu Arancinu. Address: Via Giuseppe Garibaldi, 22

A cozy spot specializing in arancini (rice balls), Munnu Arancinu offers a variety of flavors, from the classic ragu to inventive takes. It's an affordable and delicious way to experience one of Sicily's most famous street foods.

Accommodation

Hotel Centrale Europa. Address: Via Vittorio Emanuele II 167

Situated directly on Piazza Duomo, this hotel offers picturesque views of the Elephant Fountain and the Cathedral. Its central location provides easy access to Catania's main attractions, and the welcoming atmosphere ensures a comfortable stay.

Palazzo Marletta Luxury House Hotel. Address: Via Erasmo Merletta 7

Housed in an 18th-century building, this luxury hotel combines historical charm with modern amenities. Located just steps from the Cathedral, it features elegantly decorated rooms and personalized services, making it ideal for travelers seeking a refined experience.

Hotel Biscari. Address: Via Anzalone 7 (Via Vittorio Emanuele)

Set in a historic building, Hotel Biscari is only 200 meters from the Cathedral and close to the Bellini Opera Theater. Guests appreciate the spacious rooms, complimentary Wi-Fi, and the delightful breakfast served on the terrace with panoramic city views.

Palazzo Marletta. Address: Via Erasmo Merletta, 7

This elegant 3-star hotel is situated in a historic palace and offers refined accommodations with beautiful views. It's located near Piazza Duomo, making it an excellent spot for watching the St. Agatha procession as it passes through the heart of Catania.

Duomo Suites & SPA. Address: Via Garibaldi, 23

This 4-star hotel offers chic rooms and modern amenities like a rooftop terrace and spa. It is ideally positioned near Piazza Duomo, providing great access to view the procession.

Palace Catania | UNA Esperienze. Address: Via Etnea, 218

A luxurious 4-star hotel with a rooftop bar offering stunning views of Mount Etna and the city. Located along Via Etnea, a key route for the St. Agatha procession, this hotel is perfectly situated for experiencing the festivities.

Le Suites del Duomo Luxury. Address: Piazza Duomo, 32

A stylish bed and breakfast located right in Piazza Duomo, this spot offers modern rooms with exceptional views of the Cathedral and the procession as it passes directly in front.

*All of these hotels are along the procession route of St. Agatha for the festival.

Chapter Thirty-Four

Into the Lava, a 4x4 Ride on Mount Etna

Immersion Experience: Catania

Explore Mount Etna via 4x4 or Quad Bike

Mount Etna, Europe's largest and most active volcano, is one of Sicily's most awe-inspiring natural wonders. Etna, with its snow-capped peaks, smoking craters, and rugged terrain, stands at over 3,300 meters above sea level. While there are many ways to explore this iconic volcano, one of the most exhilarating options is to take a guided tour by 4x4 or quad bike.

What to Expect on a 4x4 or Quad Bike Tour of Mount Etna

1. An Exciting Journey Through Varied Terrain

The adventure always begins with a bit of safety information and a quick tutorial on how to operate the 4x4 vehicle or quad bike. Prepare yourself for driving on narrow trails that snake through verdant pine and birch forests, across jagged lava fields, and up steep mountain paths. The vehicles can navigate the challenging volcanic landscape, granting access to otherwise inaccessible regions.

2. Stunning Lava Flows and Volcanic Landscapes

As you make your way up Mount Etna, you'll witness stunning lava fields, with some still in the process of cooling following recent eruptions. These vast, barren expanses of black lava rock create an otherworldly landscape, where you can see the marks of the volcano's explosive history. Some tours take you to see the historic lava flows, like the famous 1992 flow that threatened the town of Zafferana Etnea, or more recent flows that showcase the ever-changing nature of the volcano. We witnessed hotels that were partially visible beneath previous lava flows.

3. Explore Etna's Craters and Volcanic Features

One highlight of a 4x4 or quad bike tour is the opportunity to explore some of Mount Etna's craters and unique volcanic features up close. Depending on the tour and the current volcanic activity, you might visit the Silvestri Craters, which are inactive and easily accessible. These craters, created by eruptions in the late 19th century, offer a safe and fascinating glimpse into the power of volcanic activity. You may also have the chance to see fumaroles, where steam and gas escape from the ground, giving you a firsthand look at Etna's geothermal energy.

4. Panoramic Views from High Altitudes

As you climb higher up the slopes of Mount Etna, the scenery becomes even more breathtaking. You'll reach altitudes where you can enjoy panoramic views of the surrounding landscape, including the shimmering coastline of eastern Sicily, the lush vineyards and orchards that thrive on Etna's fertile slopes, and, on clear days, views that stretch all the way to the Aeolian Islands.

5. Discover Etna's Unique Flora and Fauna

Mount Etna is not just about lava and craters; it is also a rich ecosystem with diverse flora and fauna. As you traverse the volcano's slopes, you'll notice the changing vegetation, from lush forests at lower altitudes to hardy plants that cling to life amidst the volcanic rock at higher elevations.

6. Optional Stops at Local Farms and Wineries

Many tours also include stops at local farms, wineries, or honey producers on Etna's lower slopes. Here, you can taste local products such as Etna DOC wines, olive oil, honey, and other delicacies that benefit from the rich volcanic soil.

Tour Operators

- Go-Etna offers both half-day and full-day 4x4 tours of Mount Etna, including off-road adventures through the volcanic landscape, old lava flows, and even a visit to the Gole dell'Alcantara. They provide both group and private tours, with pickup options from Catania, Taormina, and nearby areas.

- Etna Finder specializes in small group 4x4 tours on Mount Etna and the Alcantara Valley, offering scenic routes and educational insights into the history of the volcano. They also include optional wine tasting experiences.

Chapter Thirty-Five
Monreale: Guarded by Gold
Festa di San Castrense

Festa di San Castrense

Where: Monreale

When: February 11

Average Festival Temperatures: High: 15°C (59°F). Low: 7°C (45°F).

Monreale: A Jewel in Sicily's Crown

Nestled in the hills overlooking Palermo, Monreale stands as a testament to Sicily's rich and diverse history. This small but significant town, whose name translates to "Royal Mountain," has been shaped by centuries of cultural influences from Arab, Norman, Spanish, and Italian rulers.

Monreale is located in the Metropolitan City of Palermo, in the northwestern part of Sicily. Perched on the slope of Monte Caputo, about 8 kilometers (5 miles) southwest of Palermo, the town offers breathtaking views of the Conca d'Oro (Golden Shell), a fertile valley famed for its citrus groves. The town's elevation, ranging from 310 to 390 meters (1,020 to 1,280 feet) above sea level, provides a cooler climate compared to the coastal areas, making it a refreshing retreat during hot Sicilian summers.

While the town's magnificent cathedral would later become its defining feature, Monreale's strategic position and pleasant climate had already made it an attractive settlement location. The cathedral's construction in the late 12th century transformed Monreale into an important religious and cultural center, around which the medieval town grew and flourished.

In 2015, the cathedral, along with other Norman sites in Palermo, was inscribed on the UNESCO World Heritage List, recognizing its outstanding universal value. Today, Monreale has a population of approximately 39,000 inhabitants - a mix of long-time residents, whose families have lived in the area for generations, and newer arrivals drawn by the town's beauty and proximity to Palermo.

The Festival of Saint Castrense

The Festa di San Castrense is one of the most important religious festivals in Monreale, celebrated annually on February 11th in honor of Saint Castrense, the town's patron saint. Saint Castrense, a 5th-century bishop, holds a special place in the hearts of the people of Monreale, where he is revered as a protector against dangers and diseases. The festival is deeply rooted in the town's history and traditions, featuring solemn religious observances, a grand procession, and heartfelt participation from local religious organizations.

The origins of the festival date back to medieval times, when the people of Monreale chose San Castrense as their patron saint. San Castrense, originally from North Africa, fled to Italy during the Vandal persecution of Christians in the 5th century. After arriving in Campania, he became the bishop of Capua, where he was known for his miracles and spiritual leadership. His relics were brought to Monreale, and his veneration spread throughout the region over the centuries.

The festival has been celebrated for centuries as an expression of faith and gratitude for San Castrense's protection over the town, particularly during times of plague and pestilence. Monreale's connection with its patron saint remains strong, with generations of families participating in the festival and honoring his legacy.

Events and Highlights

The Festa di San Castrense spans several days of religious and communal activities, with February 11th as the main day of celebration. Below is a breakdown of the key events that take place during this special occasion.

February 8: Preparations and Opening Mass

6:00 P.M.

The festivities begin with a Mass of Preparation in the Monreale Cathedral, where the community gathers to prepare for the feast spiritually. This Mass often includes prayers for the town and blessings for the upcoming procession. Local clergy lead the service, emphasizing the importance of San Castrense's role in protecting Monreale.

February 9: Triduum of Prayers

5:00 P.M.

On this day, the Triduum of Prayers begins, which is a three-day period of prayer and reflection leading up to the feast day. Devotees gather in the cathedral for special services dedicated to San Castrense, reciting prayers and asking for his intercession for the town's well-being.

February 10: Eve of the Feast

7:00 P.M.

The eve of the feast is marked by a solemn Vigil Mass held in the Cathedral of Monreale. This evening Mass is particularly moving, as families and parishioners come together to reflect on San Castrense's legacy and offer thanks for his protection. The Mass typically features hymns dedicated to the saint and concludes with a short candlelight procession within the cathedral.

February 11: Feast Day of Saint Castrense

Morning: Solemn Mass and Procession of the Relics

The main day of celebration begins with a Solemn Mass in the Monreale Cathedral, officiated by the Archbishop of Monreale, accompanied by clergy from nearby towns. The Mass is dedicated to San Castrense, with prayers and readings that recount his life and miracles.

After the Mass, the Procession of the Relics takes place. The relics of San Castrense, usually a small piece of his bones or clothing, are carried through the streets in a richly decorated reliquary. The faithful follow behind, reciting prayers and singing hymns, with bands providing traditional music that echoes through the narrow streets of Monreale.

Afternoon: Civic Celebration. Following the procession, the town gathers for a civic celebration in Monreale's main square. Local officials and clergy give speeches reflecting on the significance of the day and the town's historical devotion to its patron saint. This part of the event is more relaxed, often including performances by local musicians and traditional folk dancers.

Evening: Final Blessing and Fireworks. The day ends with a Final Blessing in the cathedral, where the Archbishop offers blessings to the town and the participants of the festival. Following this religious conclusion

Walking Tour of Monreale

#1. Duomo di Monreale (Cathedral of Monreale)

The Monreale Cathedral is an exquisite example of architecture that combines Norman, Arab, and Byzantine elements. King William II of Sicily (William the Good) commissioned the development of the Cathedral in 1174.

The Legend

Legend has it that William dozed off beneath a carob tree near Monreale while hunting in the Palermo woods. In a dream, the Holy Virgin appeared to him and told him to build a church in this location.

Upon removing the carob tree, they discovered a treasure in its roots, and they used its golden coins to finance the construction. William's goal was to outshine the nearby Cappella Palatina in Palermo, which also showcases Sicily's fusion of Norman, Arab, and Byzantine influences. They started building Monreale in 1172, and Pope Alexander III gave permission only after the fact in 1174. In 1267, the building, which included an annexed abbey, was completed, and the church was consecrated in the presence of Pope Clement IV.

The Interior

With its renowned Byzantine mosaics, the Cathedral's interior encompasses about 6,340 square meters (68,200 square feet) of wall space. The mosaics depict biblical scenes, stories from the Old and New Testaments, daily life scenes, and portraits of saints, angels, and historical figures. The mosaics display intricate details, vibrant colors, and gold backgrounds that shimmer beautifully.

Old Testament Stories in Mosiac

Above the decorated arches is the story of Noah's Ark on the lower level. In the first panel, they built the ark. Next, you witness the placement of animals on the ark. A bird in the second panel alerts Noah that dry land is nearby. Third, they arrive; fourth, animals get off; and so on.

Above the Noah's Ark story is the story of creation from an 11th century perspective. God creates water in the first section between the windows, followed by land in the second section. In the third section, the sun and moon are placed in the sky of the Earth, as it was believed they revolved around it. Next, God brings forth the birds and animals. The 5th panel shows God creating Adam using his laser eyes. God took a break on the 7th day, sitting on Earth.

The muqarnas ceiling of the Cathedral of Monreale is an intricate architectural feature showcasing Islamic influence in a Christian setting. Muqarnas refers to a form of ornamental vaulted ceiling made up of geometric, honeycomb-like tiers of niche-like structures, creating a stunning, three-dimensional effect.

In the Cathedral of Monreale, this Islamic-inspired design is beautifully integrated into the Norman architecture, highlighting the blending of Arab, Byzantine, and Western styles that characterized Sicily during the medieval period. The result is a visually striking ceiling that plays with light and shadow, symbolizing the rich cultural fusion of the time.

The Roof

By ascending to the cathedral roof, we obtained a better look at the golden tesserae composing the mosaics. Along the way, there's a window positioned just below the roof. From above, the view is truly extraordinary. Climbing onto the roof isn't difficult. Ascend the narrow stone staircase inside to reach the top.

View of the Cloister of Monreale from the Roof

Cloister of Monreale

Adjacent to the cathedral, the Benedictine Cloister (Chiostro dei Benedettini) stands as a masterpiece of medieval architecture. Built in the late 12th century, this serene space showcases 228 intricately carved marble columns, each boasting a unique design. The cloister's architecture is a captivating blend of Norman, Gothic, and Islamic styles, reflecting Sicily's rich cultural tapestry.

As you wander through the square courtyard, measuring 47 meters on each side, you'll be surrounded by a beautiful garden centered around an ornate fountain. The cloister's walls are adorned with stunning mosaics depicting biblical scenes and vignettes of daily life in Norman Sicily. Don't miss the monks' washing area (lavabo), featuring an elaborate fountain that speaks to the monastery's former grandeur. As you explore, keep an eye out for the special column that depicts King William II offering the church to the Virgin Mary, a testament to the cloister's royal patronage.

#2. Diocesan Museum

Housed in the former dormitory of the Benedictine monks, the Diocesan Museum offers a fascinating glimpse into Monreale's religious history. The museum's collection spans centuries, featuring an impressive array of medieval liturgical vestments, including the opulent coronation robe of King Roger II. As you move through the exhibits, you'll encounter intricately crafted silver reliquaries and precious religious artifacts that speak to the wealth and devotion of past generations.

The museum also preserves a collection of ancient manuscripts and illuminated codices, providing insight into monastic life and medieval scholarship. Art enthusiasts will appreciate the paintings from the 16th to 18th centuries, while history buffs can examine archaeological findings from the surrounding area.

#3. Piazza Vittorio Emanuele

As you exit the cathedral complex, you'll find yourself in Piazza Vittorio Emanuele, the vibrant heart of Monreale. This square has been the center of town life since medieval times, hosting markets, festivals, and civic events through the centuries. The piazza is surrounded by a picturesque ensemble of baroque and liberty-style buildings, creating a charming architectural backdrop.

The impressive Town Hall (Palazzo di Città) stands as a reminder of Monreale's historical importance. In the center of the square, you'll notice a 19th-century bandstand, still used for summer concerts. The piazza is lined with inviting cafes and traditional Sicilian pastry shops, offering the perfect opportunity for a refreshment break. For a true taste of local flavor, stop by Pasticceria Enzo & Carlo, a beloved institution since 1965, and indulge in a crispy cannolo or a sweet, ricotta-filled cassata.

#4. Chiesa del Santissimo Crocifisso (Church of the Holy Crucifix)

A short stroll down Corso Pietro Novelli brings you to the Chiesa del Santissimo Crocifisso, an 18th-century church renowned for its ornate baroque façade. As you step inside, you'll be greeted by an interior rich with artworks. The church houses several important pieces, including exquisite sculptures by the renowned artist Ignazio Marabitti. Of particular note is a wooden crucifix dating back to the 16th century, its craftsmanship a testament to the skill of medieval artisans.

The walls are adorned with vivid frescoes depicting the Passion of Christ, their colors still vibrant after centuries. This church plays a significant role in local religious life, particularly during Easter celebrations when it becomes a focal point for processions and services. The blend of artistic beauty and spiritual significance makes the Chiesa del Santissimo Crocifisso a must-visit site on your Monreale tour.

#5. Belvedere of Monreale (Viewpoint)

Continuing down Corso Pietro Novelli, you'll reach the Belvedere of Monreale, a panoramic viewpoint that offers breathtaking vistas of the Conca d'Oro valley and the distant city of Palermo. This vantage point eloquently illustrates Monreale's strategic importance throughout history, providing a clear view of the surrounding landscape that once made it an ideal location for defense and agriculture. Informative panels at the belvedere explain the geography and history of the area, helping visitors understand the layout of the land and the significance of various landmarks visible from this height.

For photography enthusiasts, visiting during the golden hour just before sunset can yield stunning images as the fading light bathes the valley in warm hues. On clear days, you might want to bring binoculars to spot famous landmarks in Palermo, adding another layer of interest to your visit.

#6. Chiesa di San Castrense

Located on Via Roma, the Chiesa di San Castrense is a church steeped in local devotion, dedicated to Monreale's patron saint. Originally constructed in the

16th century and rebuilt in the 18th century, the church's architecture is a captivating mix of baroque and neoclassical styles. Inside, visitors can view the revered relics of San Castrense, including a beautifully crafted silver bust of the saint.

The church's interior is a showcase of religious art, featuring ornate marble altars and vibrant 18th-century frescoes that bring biblical stories to life. Every year on May 8th, the chiesa becomes the center of town celebrations during the festa of San Castrense, a lively event that combines religious devotion with traditional Sicilian festivities. Whether you're interested in religious history, art, or local culture, the Chiesa di San Castrenze offers a window into the spiritual heart of Monreale.

#7. Collegio di Maria

As you continue along Via Roma, you'll come across the Collegio di Maria, a historical building that exemplifies the elegance of Sicilian baroque architecture. Founded in 1719 as a school for girls and young women, this institution played a crucial role in the education and social development of Monreale for centuries. The building's façade showcases the ornate decorative elements typical of the baroque style, while inside, a beautiful courtyard centered around an old well speaks to daily life in centuries past.

Today, the Collegio serves as a vibrant cultural center, hosting exhibitions and events that celebrate both Monreale's history and its contemporary arts scene. Of particular interest is a small museum dedicated to traditional Sicilian textiles, offering insight into the island's rich craft heritage. The Collegio di Maria stands as a testament to Monreale's commitment to education and culture, bridging the town's past and present.

#8. Castello degli Uscibene

For the final stop on your tour, head uphill to the Castello degli Uscibene, a 12th-century Norman castle that offers a fitting conclusion to your exploration of Monreale's history. Built by William II as a royal hunting lodge, this castle, though now largely in ruins, provides a tangible link to Sicily's Norman past. The remaining structures showcase elements of Norman-Arab architecture, a unique style that flourished during this period of cultural fusion.

Surrounded by ancient olive groves and fragrant citrus orchards, the castle grounds offer a sensory journey into Sicily's agricultural heritage. The panoramic views from this elevated position are truly spectacular, encompassing Monreale, the Conca d'Oro valley, and the distant Mediterranean Sea. It's a view that has remained largely unchanged for centuries, allowing visitors to imagine the landscape as it appeared to Norman kings. The castle is typically open to visitors on weekends, though it's advisable to check local schedules. When planning your visit, wear sturdy shoes for the uphill walk and bring water, especially during the warm summer months.

This walking tour of Monreale covers approximately 3-4 kilometers and can be comfortably completed in 4-5 hours, allowing ample time for visits inside the sites and moments of reflection at each stop.

Monreale Festivals Throughout the Year

Festa del Santissimo Crocifisso (Festival of the Holy Crucifix)

May 1st to May 3rd.

The Festa del Santissimo Crocifisso, celebrated from May 1st to May 3rd, is the most significant festival in Monreale's cultural calendar. This centuries-old tradition dates back to 1625 when, according to local legend, a severe drought threatened the region's crops and livelihood. The people of Monreale, in their desperation, carried a crucifix through the streets in prayer. Miraculously, it began to rain, saving the harvest. Since then, the Holy Crucifix has been venerated for its perceived miraculous powers, and the annual festival was established to commemorate this event.

Monreale's three-day celebration blends religious devotion with festive spirit. Its highlight is the grand procession of the Holy Crucifix through the town. Thousands gather to see it. The crucifix, adorned with flowers, is carried by the faithful.

Traditional music fills the air. Local bands play solemn marches. The town buzzes with events. These include sacred concerts in the cathedral, art exhibitions, and plays about the miracle. Food stands offer Sicilian delicacies.

The festival ends with a fireworks display. It lights up the sky above Monreale's cathedral, symbolizing joy and renewal.

Estate Monrealese (Monreale Summer Festival)

July and August.

The Estate Monrealese, held throughout July and August, is a vibrant celebration of arts and culture that transforms Monreale into a hub of creativity during the warm summer months. This festival, which began in the 1980s as a way to attract tourists and showcase local talent, has grown into a significant event on Sicily's cultural calendar.

During these two months, the entire town becomes a stage for various artistic expressions. The picturesque Piazza Guglielmo II, with the stunning backdrop of the Norman cathedral, serves as the main venue for many events. Here, visitors can enjoy open-air cinema screenings, featuring both classic Italian films and contemporary works. The square also hosts concerts ranging from classical orchestras to popular music acts, often featuring both local Sicilian artists and internationally renowned performers.

Theater enthusiasts can attend performances that often draw inspiration from Sicily's rich mythological and historical heritage. Art exhibitions pop up throughout the town, showcasing works by local artists and artisans, often blending traditional Sicilian crafts with contemporary artistic expressions. Many of these exhibitions are housed in historical buildings, offering visitors a unique opportunity to explore Monreale's architectural gems.

The festival also includes gastronomic events celebrating Sicilian cuisine, with food tastings and cooking demonstrations highlighting local specialties. The Estate Monrealese not only provides entertainment but also serves as a platform for cultural exchange, bringing together locals and visitors in a celebration of Sicilian arts and traditions.

Festival Organistico di Monreale (Monreale Organ Festival)

September.

The Festival Organistico di Monreale, held each September, is a celebration of sacred music that showcases the magnificent organ of Monreale's cathedral. This festival, initiated in the late 20th century, has become a prestigious event in the world of classical and sacred music, attracting renowned organists from across the globe.

The festival's main attraction is the cathedral's organ, a masterpiece of craftsmanship installed in 1969 by the Danish firm Th. Frobenius & Sons. With its 4,186 pipes, it is considered one of the finest organs in Italy, capable of producing a wide range of tones and textures that perfectly complement the cathedral's exceptional acoustics. Throughout the festival, this remarkable instrument comes to life under the skilled hands of international organists. The program typically features a diverse repertoire, ranging from Baroque masterpieces by composers like Bach and Buxtehude to contemporary organ compositions.

Many performances also include collaborations with choirs, orchestras, or solo instrumentalists, creating a rich tapestry of sacred music. The concerts, held in the awe-inspiring setting of the Norman-Byzantine cathedral, offer attendees a transcendent experience where music, history, and spirituality converge. Beyond the performances, the festival often includes lectures and workshops on organ music and its history, attracting music students and enthusiasts. These educational components contribute to the preservation and promotion of organ music, ensuring that this traditional art form continues to resonate with new generations.

Natale a Monreale (Christmas in Monreale)

December, throughout the Christmas season.

Natale a Monreale transforms the town into a winter wonderland throughout the Christmas season, blending religious observance with festive cheer. This celebration, deeply rooted in Sicilian traditions, has evolved over centuries to become a beloved annual event that draws visitors from across the region.

As December arrives, Monreale's streets come alive with twinkling lights and elaborate decorations. The town's main square, Piazza Guglielmo II, becomes the focal point of celebrations with a towering Christmas tree and a life-sized nativity scene, or presepe, showcasing Sicily's rich tradition of craftsmanship. Local artisans set up festive markets where visitors can find unique handcrafted gifts, traditional Sicilian sweets, and seasonal decorations. These markets not only provide shopping opportunities but also serve as gathering places where locals and visitors alike can enjoy mulled wine and roasted chestnuts while soaking in the holiday atmosphere. Throughout the season, the cathedral hosts special services and concerts, including midnight Mass on Christmas Eve, which attracts worshippers from far and wide.

The cathedral's stunning golden mosaics provide a magnificent backdrop for these spiritual gatherings, creating an unforgettable experience for attendees. Children eagerly await the arrival of Babbo Natale (Santa Claus) and La Befana, a kind witch who brings gifts on Epiphany Eve. Parades featuring these beloved characters often wind through the town's streets, much to the delight of young and old alike. Local schools and community groups contribute to the festivities with performances of traditional Sicilian Christmas songs and living nativity scenes, keeping age-old customs alive.

As the year draws to a close, Monreale celebrates New Year's Eve with a grand party in the main square, featuring live music, dancing, and a spectacular midnight fireworks display over the cathedral, welcoming the new year with joy and anticipation.

Day Trip Options: Nearby Sites, Cities, and Towns

Caccamo. 45 kilometers (28 miles) southeast of Monreale. A medieval town perched on a hillside, Caccamo is renowned for its imposing Norman castle and picturesque old town.

Highlights include:

- Castello di Caccamo: One of Sicily's largest and best-preserved medieval castles, offering panoramic views of the surrounding countryside and featuring a museum with medieval artifacts.

- Chiesa Madre (Mother Church): A 17th-century Baroque church dedicated to San Giorgio, known for its ornate interior and beautiful frescoes.

- Piazza Duomo: The town's main square, home to several historic buildings and a great spot to experience local life and cuisine.

Scopello. 75 kilometers (47 miles) west of Monreale. Scopello is a charming coastal village celebrated for its crystal-clear waters, stunning scenery, and timeless Sicilian charm. Nestled along the coast, this idyllic spot is perfect for those seeking natural beauty, history, and authentic local experiences.

One of the main highlights is the Tonnara di Scopello, an ancient tuna fishery that is now a symbol of the village's historical ties to the sea. The picturesque stone buildings of the tonnara are set against a backdrop of dramatic sea stacks, known as faraglioni, rising from the turquoise waters. This area has become a favorite destination for swimmers, snorkelers, and photographers, offering both stunning visuals and a connection to Scopello's maritime heritage.

The Borgo di Scopello, the village's quaint center, enchants visitors with its cobblestone streets, stone houses, and a small piazza that exudes old-world charm. Traditional Sicilian restaurants and cafés line the square, inviting guests to savor local delicacies such as pane cunzato (seasoned bread), fresh seafood, and Sicilian pastries. The laid-back atmosphere makes it an ideal place to relax and take in the region's culture.

Scopello is also the gateway to the Zingaro Nature Reserve, a protected coastal area renowned for its hiking trails, secluded coves, and diverse flora and fauna. Visitors can explore pristine beaches, scenic viewpoints, and the unspoiled beauty of one of Sicily's most treasured natural parks.

Segesta. 65 kilometers (40 miles) southwest of Monreale. An important archaeological site showcasing ancient Greek architecture in a stunning natural setting.

Highlights include:

- Temple of Segesta: A remarkably well-preserved Doric temple from the 5th century BCE, standing majestically on a hilltop surrounded by rolling countryside.

- Ancient Theater: A horseshoe-shaped Greek theater with panoramic views of the surrounding valleys and the distant Mediterranean Sea.

- Archaeological Museum: Houses artifacts found at the site, providing context to the ancient city's history and culture.

Logistics

Train: Palermo Centrale is the closet station (10 kilometers / 6 miles away)

Bus: From Palermo: Monreale is well-connected by bus from Palermo. The most common and convenient bus service is operated by AMAT (Palermo's public transport company).Bus Line: 389P is the main bus line from Palermo to Monreale.

Car: Driving Directions: Monreale is a short 10–15-minute drive from Palermo. The main route is via the SS186 and SP69 roads, which are relatively straightforward and scenic.

Parking: Piazzale della Repubblica Parking: Located near the entrance to the town and about a 5-minute walk from the cathedral, this parking lot offers paid parking and is convenient for visitors.

Via Antonio Veneziano Parking: This street offers some parking spaces, and it's a short walk from the center. There is also a parking garage at Via Strada Ferrata, though it's slightly farther from the cathedral (about 10-15 minutes by foot).

Parking in Monreale can be limited, especially during busy times or festivals. It's advisable to arrive early if driving or to consider taking public transportation.

Dining Recommendations

Pizzeria Guglielmo di Milazzo Girolamo. Address: Piazza Guglielmo II, 5.

Located just steps from the cathedral, this restaurant specializes in Sicilian dishes and wood-fired pizzas. It has a relaxed, family-friendly atmosphere and offers both indoor and outdoor seating. The menu includes classic pasta dishes, fresh seafood, and traditional desserts like cannoli.

Bricco & Bacco. Address: Via Dante, 15

This restaurant offers a blend of traditional Sicilian cuisine and modern twists on classic dishes. Known for its fresh ingredients and stylish presentation, the menu includes antipasti, pasta, meat dishes, and a selection of local wines. The atmosphere is cozy yet elegant, making it ideal for a romantic dinner or special occasion.

Il Giardino Degli Aranci. Address: Via Santa Maria Nuova, 1.

This restaurant is known for its scenic outdoor seating, offering views over Palermo and the surrounding countryside. The menu focuses on Sicilian specialties, with an emphasis on fresh, seasonal ingredients. Dishes range from pasta and seafood to hearty meat options. It's popular for its ambiance and local wines. Distance from Cathedral: About a 5-minute walk.

Taverna del Pavone. Address: Via Antonio Veneziano, 50.

This cozy restaurant serves traditional Sicilian fare in a welcoming, family-run atmosphere. The menu offers a variety of pasta dishes, grilled meats, and local fish. The service is friendly, and the prices are reasonable for the quality and portion sizes. Distance from Cathedral: About a 4-minute walk.

Accommodation

*Opera Boutique Rooms. Address: Via Circonvallazione, 34, Monreale

A boutique 4-star hotel offering elegantly designed rooms with modern amenities. Located just steps from Piazza Duomo, it provides easy access to both the Duomo and the festival route.

*Carrubella Park Hotel. Address: Via Umberto I, 51

This 3-star hotel is located within walking distance of the Duomo and offers great views of Palermo. It's a convenient location for festival-goers looking to witness the St. Castrense procession.

**B&B Monreale Re Ruggero. Address: Via Arcivescovado, 9

This is a charming bed and breakfast located in the heart of Monreale, just a few steps from the cathedral. It offers comfortable rooms with modern amenities like free Wi-Fi, air conditioning, and private bathrooms. It's known for its warm hospitality and offers a cozy, intimate atmosphere. Distance from Cathedral: A 2-minute walk.

**Palazzo al Carmine. Address: Via Palermo, 64

This 3-star hotel offers a mix of modern comfort in a historical building. It features clean, spacious rooms with air conditioning and breakfast included. The location is highly convenient for visiting the Monreale Cathedral and the surrounding areas. Free Wi-Fi is available.

**B&B Elvira Al Duomo. Address: Via B. Civiletti, 11

This bed and breakfast offers a prime location in Monreale, just steps from the cathedral. Rooms are bright and comfortable, with modern amenities such as free Wi-Fi, air conditioning, and en-suite bathrooms. Breakfast is typically included in the stay.

*On the procession route for the Festival of St. Castrense.

**Near but not directly on the procession route.

Chapter Thirty-Six

Train Ride with Mt. Etna Vineyards & Views

Immersion Experience: Catania or Bronte

For travelers seeking a unique and immersive journey, the Circumetnea Railway provides an unforgettable way to explore the diverse regions surrounding the majestic Mount Etna.

What is the Circumetnea Railway?

The Circumetnea Railway (Ferrovia Circumetnea) is a historic narrow-gauge railway that circles the base of Mount Etna, the largest active volcano in Europe. Originally constructed in the late 19th century, this railway was built to connect the remote towns and villages around the volcano to Catania, providing a vital lifeline for trade, commerce, and everyday life. Its completion in 1898 marked a significant development for local commerce and travel, enabling the exchange of goods like wine, olive oil, and pistachios while fostering a stronger sense of community among the towns.

Today, the railway is not only a vital transport link but also a charming way to explore Sicily's countryside and experience authentic local culture. Covering a distance of about 110 kilometers, the Circumetnea runs from the bustling city of Catania to the coastal town of Riposto, offering passengers a leisurely journey through picturesque landscapes. The train cars retain a retro charm, with their quaint interiors and slower pace that harks back to a simpler era. Along the way, travelers are treated to panoramic views of vineyards, olive groves, lava fields, and traditional Sicilian villages, all set against the dramatic backdrop of Mount Etna's ever-present silhouette. For visitors seeking an off-the-beaten-path adventure, the Circumetnea Railway provides a unique and memorable glimpse into the heart of rural Sicily.

The Route: What to Expect

The Circumetnea Railway winds its way through a series of charming and lesser-known towns that showcase the authentic side of Sicilian life. Along the route, you'll pass vineyards, olive groves, and small hamlets, all set against the stunning backdrop of Etna's towering presence. Some of the most noteworthy stops include:

- ***Catania:** Starting from the bustling city of Catania, famous for its Baroque architecture and vibrant street markets, the railway takes you away from the city's energy and into the tranquil countryside.

- **Adrano:** Known for its Norman castle and its proximity to natural parks, Adrano is a great stop for those interested in history and nature. Explore the ancient Bridge of Saracens nearby, which spans the Simeto River, offering picturesque views of the landscape.

- ***Bronte:** Famous for its world-renowned pistachios, Bronte offers visitors the chance to explore its local delicacies and even visit nearby vineyards producing Etna wines, which are some of the most esteemed in Sicily. Don't miss the Pistachio Museum, where you can learn about the history and cultivation of this prized nut.

- **Randazzo**: ThThis medieval town, built from black lava stone, is surrounded by vineyards producing Etna DOC wines. A stop here offers the chance to visit local wineries and sample the region's unique volcanic wines. Stroll through the town's narrow streets and admire its ancient churches, including the striking Basilica of Santa Maria.

- **Linguaglossa**: A gateway for adventurers looking to explore Etna's northern slopes, Linguaglossa is not only a haven for outdoor enthusiasts but also home to several vineyards along the Etna Wine Route, where visitors can taste wines and tour the vineyards. The town also features charming artisan workshops where you can see local craftsmanship in action.

- **Riposto:** The final stop on the journey. Riposto is a coastal town where you can relax by the sea after your inland adventure. Its charming marina and seafood restaurants offer a lovely end to the railway trip. While here, visit the bustling fish market to get a sense of the town's maritime heritage.

*Cities with chapters in this book.

Vineyard and Olive Grove Experiences

The fertile soil of Mount Etna, enriched by volcanic ash, makes the surrounding area ideal for wine and olive oil production. Along the route, travelers have the unique opportunity to visit some of Sicily's most renowned vineyards and olive groves.

- **Vineyards:** Towns like Randazzo, Bronte, and Linguaglossa are part of the Etna DOC wine-producing region. Visitors can tour the vineyards, learn about the unique cultivation methods required for growing grapes in volcanic soil, and sample a range of red and white wines, including the famed Etna Rosso.

- **Olive Groves:** Olive oil production is also a staple of the region, with groves scattered around towns like Adrano and Bronte. Some olive farms offer guided tours where visitors can see the process from harvesting olives to pressing and bottling the oil (in the fall). These visits often conclude with a tasting of fresh olive oil, often accompanied by traditional Sicilian bread and cheese.

Why Travel by Circumetnea?

For tourists, the Circumetnea Railway offers a chance to experience Sicily in a way that few others do. Unlike the fast-paced modern trains, the Circumetnea invites travelers to slow down and appreciate the natural beauty, historical towns, and rural landscapes of the island.

- **Spectacular Views:** As the train meanders through the Sicilian countryside, you'll have front-row views of Mount Etna, passing through lava fields, fertile valleys, and charming towns. It's a photographer's dream, with constantly changing scenery that showcases the island's diverse geography.

- **An Adventure for All Seasons:** Whether you visit in the spring when the countryside is lush, or in winter when Etna's slopes are capped with snow, the railway provides a picturesque journey year-round. Winter travelers can even use the railway to access the ski slopes of Mount Etna.

- **Off the Beaten Path:** While cities like Catania and Taormina attract the majority of Sicily's tourists, the Circumetnea Railway takes you to towns that feel untouched by mass tourism. It's a perfect way to get off the beaten path and discover hidden gems that most visitors overlook.

Tips for Travelers

- **Plan Your Stops**: While the entire journey takes about 3.5 hours without stops, it's highly recommended to break up the trip by visiting towns along the way.

- **Bring Snacks:** While some stations may have small cafes or markets, it's a good idea to pack water and snacks, especially if you're planning to take a longer trip.

- **Check the Schedule:** The train doesn't run as frequently as other lines, so be sure to check the schedule in advance, particularly if you plan to get off and reboard at multiple stops.

- **Book Vineyard or Olive Grove Tours in Advance:** To make the most of your experience, consider booking wine-tasting or olive oil tours in advance, as some locations may require reservations.

The Circumetnea Railway generally does not require advance booking, especially for casual travelers looking to ride the train between towns. Tickets are typically purchased on the day of travel at the stations along the route, or via website and app.

The prices are quite affordable. However, if you're planning a larger group excursion or want to combine your trip with specific wine or vineyard tours, booking those experiences ahead of time is recommended.

For current schedules, fares, and updates, you can visit the official website of the Circumetnea Railway at Ferrovia Circumetnea. It's a good idea to check the timetable, as services can vary depending on the season, and trains don't run as frequently as other major lines.

Chapter Thirty-Seven

FestaFusion Agrigento

A Symphony of Blossoms and Faith

FestaFusion Agrigento

#1 Sagra del Mandorlo in Fiore (Almond Blossom Festival): this festival celebrates the almond blossom season with cultural events, music, and food.

#2 Festival of Saint Gerlando (Festa di San Gerlando): Saint Gerlando patron saint of Agrigento

#FestaFusion means two or more festivals happen at around the same time in the same town, so visitors can enjoy multiple events during their visit.

Where: Agrigento

When: San Gerlando is February 25th and Sagra del Mandorlo in Fiore takes place at the end of February beginning of March.

Event Websites:

https://www.visitsicily.info/en/evento-new/sagra-mandorlo-in-fiore-agrigento/ and https://www.sangerlando.it/

Average Festival Temperatures: High: 15-16°C (59-61°F). Low: 8-9°C (46-48°F).

Discovering Agrigento: Guardian of Ancient Splendor

Perched on a plateau overlooking Sicily's southern coast, Agrigento stands as a living testament to the grandeur of ancient Greek civilization. This city, once known as Akragas, is home to some of the most impressive and well-preserved Greek temples outside of Greece itself. The famous Valley of the Temples, a UNESCO World Heritage site, draws visitors from around the world to marvel at its ancient wonders, while the modern city above offers a glimpse into contemporary Sicilian life, creating a unique juxtaposition of past and present.

The history of Agrigento stretches back to the 6th century BCE when it was founded as Akragas by Greek colonists from Gela. The city quickly rose to prominence, becoming one of the richest and most powerful Greek colonies in the Mediterranean. Under the rule of tyrant Theron, Akragas reached its zenith, marked by the construction of magnificent temples and public buildings. The Roman conquest in 210 BCE marked the beginning of a long period of decline, though the city remained inhabited throughout the medieval and modern periods. The rediscovery of its ancient ruins in the 18th and 19th centuries brought renewed attention to Agrigento, establishing it as a key site for understanding the legacy of Magna Graecia.

Agrigento is situated on Sicily's southern coast, about 140 kilometers southeast of Palermo. The modern city sits atop a hill, while the ancient ruins spread across a lower ridge known as the Valley of the Temples. This unique topography, with its commanding views of the Mediterranean Sea, played a crucial role in the city's ancient defenses and continues to provide breathtaking vistas for visitors today. The surrounding countryside is characterized by rolling hills, olive groves, and almond orchards, creating a picturesque setting that has changed little since ancient times.

Agrigento has a population of approximately 60,000 residents.

#1: Festival of Almond Blossom (Sagra del Mandorlo in Fiore)

The modern version of the Mandorlo in Fiore festival in Agrigento began in 1934. Count Alfonso Gaetani initiated the event, inspired by the beauty of almond blossoms in the Valley of the Temples. The festival was designed to celebrate the arrival of spring and promote tourism in the region, building upon the ancient Sicilian custom of honoring blooming almond trees as a symbol of nature's rejuvenation.

The area around Agrigento provides ideal conditions for almond trees to thrive. The Mediterranean climate offers mild, wet winters and hot, dry summers, while the well-draining, rocky, limestone-rich soil suits the trees perfectly. Abundant sunlight throughout the year and natural protection from strong winds provided by the landscape further contribute to the successful cultivation of high-quality almonds in the region.

During the festival, a wide array of almond-based dishes and products are featured, showcasing the versatility of this local ingredient in Sicilian cuisine. Main courses might include pasta alla Trapanese, a pesto-like sauce made with almonds, tomatoes, and basil, or pasta with pesto di pistacchi e mandorle, combining pistachios and almonds. Side dishes often incorporate almonds, such as caponata siciliana con mandorle, a sweet and sour eggplant dish, or insalata di finocchi e arance con mandorle, a refreshing fennel and orange salad with toasted almonds.

Meat and fish dishes also benefit from the addition of almonds. Festival-goers might enjoy pesce spada alla siciliana con mandorle, a swordfish dish with an almond crust, or involtini di pollo alle mandorle, chicken rolls stuffed with almonds and herbs. Desserts are a particular highlight, with traditional treats like cassata siciliana featuring almond paste, pasta di mandorle (almond pastries), and the refreshing granita di mandorle, an almond-flavored iced dessert. These culinary delights are often showcased through cooking demonstrations, tastings, and special menus at local restaurants during the Mandorlo in Fiore, allowing visitors to fully appreciate the almonds in Sicilian gastronomy.

During the evenings, live music performances are a significant part of the festivities. Local and international bands often take to stages set up around the city, playing a mix of traditional Sicilian folk music and more contemporary styles. These concerts can range from intimate acoustic sets to larger, more energetic performances that get the crowd dancing.

In addition to musical performances, the festival features evening cultural events such as traditional dance showcases. These might include performances of Sicilian folk dances, often accompanied by live music, allowing visitors to experience the rich cultural heritage of the region.

The city's historic center and the Valley of the Temples are often illuminated with special lighting during the festival, creating a magical nocturnal ambiance. Some years, there might be light shows or projections on historic buildings, adding a modern touch to the ancient surroundings.

Food and wine tastings are another popular nighttime activity during the Mandorlo in Fiore. Local restaurants and vendors often stay open late, offering visitors the chance to sample Sicilian delicacies and wines under the stars.

Depending on the specific program for the year, there might also be nighttime parades, street performances, or outdoor theater productions. These events contribute to the festive atmosphere and provide entertainment for visitors of all ages throughout the evening hours.

It's worth noting that the exact nighttime program can vary from year to year, so visitors are encouraged to check the festival's official schedule for the most up-to-date information on evening events and performances.

#2: Festival of Saint Gerlando (Festa di San Gerlando)

The Festival of Saint Gerlando (Festa di San Gerlando) is a significant religious and cultural event in Agrigento, Sicily.

February 23rd

Morning: A solemn pontifical mass is celebrated, often presided over by the Archbishop of Agrigento. During this service, local authorities, including the police, pay homage to Saint Gerlando by offering prayers and providing oil for the lamp that burns continuously before the saint's reliquary urn, symbolizing enduring devotion.

Evening: The "Notte Medievale" (Medieval Night) begins around 6 PM. This event features a grand procession carrying the relics of San Gerlando from Piazza Municipio to the cathedral, passing through Via San Girolamo and Via Duomo. Participants dress in medieval costumes, recreating the atmosphere of the saint's era and commemorating his arrival in Agrigento. The evening continues with medieval-themed games, music, and dance performances, immersing attendees in the historical context of the time.

February 24th

Cultural Activities: The day is often dedicated to cultural events, including exhibitions, lectures, and presentations that delve into the history and significance of Saint Gerlando and the cathedral. For instance, in 2024, a day of studies was held to mark five years since the cathedral's structural reinforcement, featuring presentations on the work undertaken and ongoing monitoring efforts.

February 25th

Religious Services: As the eve of the saint's feast day, multiple masses are held throughout the day in the cathedral. These services are well-attended by the faithful, reflecting the community's deep reverence for their patron saint.

Evening Celebrations: The evening may feature additional religious ceremonies, including vespers and special prayers dedicated to Saint Gerlando. In some years, the festivities include musical performances or other cultural events that celebrate the city's heritage and the saint's legacy.

Who is San Gerlando?

Saint Gerlando's appointment as the bishop of Agrigento occurred in 1088 when the bishopric of Agrigento selected him for this honor. Gerlando, who had a Franco-Norman background, served as the Bishop of Agrigento until his death. The term "Episcopal figure" refers to his role as a bishop, overseeing the religious affairs of the diocese. The Catholic Church officially recognized San Gerlando as a saint in 1159, formalizing his veneration.

Gerlando's importance in Agrigento's history stems from his role in re-converting the area to Christianity after two centuries of Muslim rule. His charitable works were notable, but it was his preaching that truly set him apart. Gerlando was known for his eloquence, described as "sweet as honey," which allowed him to effectively communicate with and convert both Jews and Muslims through persuasion rather than force.

Today, Saint Gerlando's relics are preserved in a silver urn at the cathedral of Agrigento, serving as a tangible connection to the saint for the faithful. The people of Agrigento continue to invoke his name for protection against natural disasters, using the phrase "San Giullannu senza ddannu" (San Gerlando defend us from harm or damages). This tradition was particularly evident during the catastrophic landslide of July 19-20, 1966, when residents prayed daily to the saint. The absence of casualties in this disaster reinforced the local belief in Saint Gerlando's divine intervention, further cementing his importance in the religious and cultural fabric of Agrigento.

Walking Tour Valley of the Temples (Valle dei Templi) – Day 1

The Valley of the Temples (Valle dei Templi), a UNESCO World Heritage Site, is a must-visit destination near Agrigento, Sicily. This archaeological park offers a stunning glimpse into ancient Greek civilization. The site is easily accessible from Agrigento's historical center by car, taxi, or bus, making it an ideal first stop on your tour.

To fully appreciate the Valley's grandeur, plan to spend at least three to four hours exploring the site. The archaeological park spans a vast area, with its remains spread along a ridge. A walking path approximately 2.5 kilometers (1.55 miles) long connects the various temples and structures. The terrain can be challenging, with uneven, dusty surfaces and ancient cobbled streets, so comfortable, sturdy footwear is essential.

For a more in-depth experience, consider joining a guided tour. Options include private and group daytime tours, sunset tours, and illuminated night tours. The night tours, available from July to September, offer a magical experience with the temples dramatically lit against the night sky. These tours begin at 8:30 P.M., with the park closing at 11 P.M. Advance booking through the official website https://www.lavalledeitempli.it/visite-guidate/is recommended.

If you prefer a self-guided experience, audio guides are available at the ticket booth. However, be prepared to leave your driver's license or passport as a deposit. While informative, the audio guide can be cumbersome if you're planning a one-way route through the temples. To avoid long queues and stay comfortable in the Sicilian heat, purchasing tickets in advance is advisable.

The Valley of the Temples showcases the grandeur of ancient Akragas, once one of the most important Greek colonies in Sicily. The site boasts several well-preserved Doric temples, each with its own fascinating history:

The Temple of Zeus (Jupiter) stands out as the largest in the valley. Although mostly in ruins now, its sheer scale hints at the ambition and wealth of ancient Akragas. Nearby, the Temple of Concordia is one of the best-preserved ancient Greek temples in the world, rivaling even the Parthenon in Athens. Its near-perfect condition is due to its conversion into a Christian church in the 6th century AD, which helped protect it from destruction.

The Temple of Hera (Juno), perched on a hill, offers panoramic views of the valley and the sea beyond. Its location and design reflect the importance of Hera, queen of the Greek gods, in ancient worship. While less intact, the Temple of Heracles (Hercules) is one of the oldest structures in the valley, dating back to the 6th century BC.

Temple of Hera

The unfinished Temple of Olympian Zeus is a testament to the grand ambitions of Akragas. Had it been completed; it would have been one of the largest temples in the ancient world. Its incomplete state offers valuable insights into ancient construction techniques.

The Temple of Concordia, dedicated to the Roman goddess of harmony, stands as one of the best-preserved ancient Greek temples in the world, rivaling even the Parthenon in Athens with its stunning Doric architecture; its remarkable state of preservation is largely due to its conversion into a Christian church in the 6th century AD, which protected it from destruction and allowed modern visitors to marvel at its near-intact colonnade, pediments, and overall structural integrity that have endured for over two millennia.

The layout of Akragas and the Valley of the Temples reflects sophisticated Greek urban planning principles. Temples, public buildings, and residential areas were carefully arranged around sacred and civic spaces, creating a harmonious cityscape.

The city's golden age ended abruptly with the Carthaginian conquest in 406 BC. This marked the beginning of a long decline, culminating in the Roman conquest during the Punic Wars. As the population dwindled, many of the grand monuments fell into disrepair.

It wasn't until the 18th century that explorers rediscovered the Valley of the Temples. Extensive excavation and restoration work in the 19th and 20th centuries revealed the site's historical importance, leading to its recognition as a UNESCO World Heritage Site in 1997.

Today, the Valley of the Temples stands as a testament to the enduring legacy of ancient Greek civilization in Sicily, offering visitors a unique journey through time amidst its awe-inspiring ruins.

Walking Tour of the Historical Center of Agrigento – Day 2

#1. Duomo di San Gerlando (Cathedral of San Gerlando)

Perched atop the city, the Cathedral of San Gerlando is a majestic testament to Agrigento's rich history. Built in the 11th century under Norman rule, this architectural marvel showcases a unique fusion of Norman, Gothic, and Baroque styles. As you approach, you'll be greeted by a grand piazza and an impressive staircase comprising five sets of broad steps adorned with pillars and intricate iron railings.

The cathedral's facade, though relatively unassuming, speaks to its ancient origins. Inside, prepare to be awestruck by the elaborate Baroque stucco decorations, featuring festoons, garlands, floral designs, and cherubs crafted by an unknown 18th-century artist. The apse houses a magnificent pipe organ and wooden choir stalls by 17th-century carver Onofrio Vicari. Don't miss the large fresco depicting the Apotheosis of Mary on the vault, or the painting of Saint Gerlando spreading God's word in Agrigento. A remarkable acoustic phenomenon known as "the spokesperson" allows whispers from the presbytery to be heard 85 meters away, adding an air of mystery to this sacred space.

#2. Mudia - Museo Diocesano Agrigento in the Palazzo Vescovile

Adjacent to the cathedral, the Bishop's Palace now houses the Diocesan Museum (Mudia). This 11th-century building, originally constructed for Bishop Gerlando, has undergone numerous expansions and renovations over the centuries, particularly after the 1693 earthquake. The museum offers a treasure trove of religious artifacts, including valuable furnishings, sacred vestments, and paintings depicting religious episodes. Each piece tells a story of Agrigento's spiritual journey through the ages. The palace itself, with its blend of architectural styles reflecting various historical periods, serves as a physical timeline of the city's evolution.

#3. Lucchesiana Library

Founded in 1765 by Bishop Andrea Lucchesi Palli, the Lucchesiana Library stands as a beacon of Agrigento's intellectual heritage. This haven for bibliophiles houses an impressive collection of over 60,000 volumes, including rare manuscripts, illuminated codices, and incunabula. The library's interior is a sight to behold, with its original furnishings, including ornate reading tables and beautiful shelves. Despite facing periods of neglect and infestation, extensive restoration work beginning in 1977 has returned the library to its former glory. Beyond books, the collection includes valuable ancient artifacts such as gems, coins, and stones, offering a multifaceted glimpse into history.

The library held over sixty thousand volumes, manuscripts, illuminated codices, and incunabula in 2020.

#4. Chiesa di Sant'Alfonso Maria de' Liguori

This church holds the distinction of being the first in the world dedicated to Saint Alphonsus. Construction began in 1840 and was completed in 1855 by the Redemptorist Fathers, who had arrived in Agrigento in 1761 while Saint Alfonso di Liguori was still alive. The church's history is deeply intertwined with that of the nearby Lucchesiana Library, as the Redemptorist Fathers were entrusted with managing the library alongside their religious duties. The interior of the church is adorned with a series of paintings by Sicilian artist Giovanni Patricolo, created in the latter half of the 19th century, adding to its cultural and artistic significance.

#5. Belvedere Panoramico "Città Antica" (Scenic lookout)

As you continue down the street past the Chiesa di Sant'Alfonso Maria, you'll reach this charming viewpoint. The Belvedere offers breathtaking panoramic views of Agrigento's ancient and medieval architecture, as well as the surrounding Sicilian countryside and the distant Mediterranean Sea. This spot provides an excellent opportunity to appreciate the city's unique topography and the way its historical layers have unfolded over millennia. It's an ideal location for photography or simply taking a moment to absorb the beauty of Agrigento's landscape.

#6. Chiesa di Santa Maria dei Greci (Church of St. Mary of the Greeks)

This church, one of the oldest in Agrigento, is a fascinating blend of ancient Greek and medieval Christian architecture. Built in the 13th century, it stands on the foundations of an ancient Doric temple, believed by some scholars to be the temple of Athena Lindia and Zeus. This unique positioning reflects the city's long history of cultural amalgamation. The church's structure incorporates elements of the ancient temple, including some original columns, providing a tangible link to Agrigento's Greek past. Inside, visitors can admire Byzantine-style frescoes and the visible remains of the Greek temple beneath the floor, offering a literal view into the layers of Agrigento's history.

#7. Via Atenea

Conclude your tour with a stroll down Agrigento's primary artery, Via Atenea. This vibrant street serves as the pulsing heart of the city's historical center. Lined with an eclectic mix of shops, cafes, restaurants, and historic buildings, Via Atenea offers a perfect blend of past and present. As you walk, you'll pass by many palazzi (palaces) from various eras, their facades telling stories of Agrigento's evolving architectural styles. The street bustles with activity, filled with locals going about their daily lives and tourists exploring the city's charms. It's an excellent place to indulge in people-watching, do some shopping, or simply soak in the lively atmosphere of contemporary Agrigento while surrounded by echoes of its rich history.

In total, the walk in the center of Agrigento is 2.4 kilometers (1.5 miles).

Agrigento Festivals and Sagre throughout the Year

Festival of Saint Calogero (Festa di San Calogero)

June 18, 2024

This religious festival honors Saint Calogero, Agrigento's beloved saint known for his healing powers. The festival features solemn religious processions, fireworks, and communal celebrations. Devotees carry the statue of Saint Calogero through the streets, accompanied by music and prayers, while locals prepare traditional dishes to share. The focal point is the Sanctuary of Saint Calogero, just outside the city.

Soul's Food Nights

Date: July 2024

Soul's Food Nights combines the best of Sicilian cuisine with live performances of blues, soul, and gospel music. Held in the stunning backdrop of the Valle dei Templi, the event brings together food lovers and music enthusiasts for an evening of culinary delights and world-class performances. Set against the illuminated Temple of Concordia and Temple of Juno, it creates a unique atmosphere.

FestiValle (International Jazz Festival)

Date: August 8-11, 2024

FestiValle is an international jazz and digital arts festival held annually in the Valley of the Temples. This boutique festival features performances from renowned artists across genres, including jazz, world music, and electronic sounds. Attendees enjoy concerts in a stunning outdoor setting, surrounded by ancient temples. It's a cultural highlight of Agrigento's summer calendar, drawing both local and international visitors.

Day Trip Options: Nearby Sites, Cities and Towns

Eraclea Minoa. Located approximately 50 kilometers west of Agrigento, Eraclea Minoa offers a perfect blend of history and natural beauty. This ancient Greek settlement, perched dramatically on a white cliff overlooking the Mediterranean, was founded in the 6th century BC. The archaeological site features the remains of a Greek theater carved into the hillside, offering spectacular sea views.

Visitors can explore the ruins of ancient houses and admire sections of the original city walls. The on-site museum houses a collection of artifacts found during excavations, providing insight into daily life in ancient times. Beyond its historical significance, Eraclea Minoa boasts a stunning beach with fine golden sand and crystal-clear waters. The beach is flanked by a picturesque pine forest, offering shade and perfect spots for picnicking. Nature enthusiasts will appreciate the nearby Foce del Fiume Platani Nature Reserve, home to diverse flora and fauna, including migratory birds.

Porto Empedocle. Just 15 kilometers southwest of Agrigento, Porto Empedocle is a charming coastal town with a rich maritime heritage. Originally named Molo di Girgenti (Pier of Agrigento), it was renamed in 1863 after the Greek philosopher Empedocles. The town's heart is its bustling fishing port, where visitors can watch local fishermen bring in their daily catch. The seafront promenade, lined with colorful buildings, offers delightful views of the Mediterranean and is perfect for evening strolls.

Porto Empedocle gained international fame as the birthplace of Andrea Camilleri, creator of the beloved Inspector Montalbano series. Fans of the books and TV shows can visit Camilleri's childhood home and explore locations that inspired his writings. The town's seafood restaurants are a major draw, serving fresh catches prepared in traditional Sicilian styles. Don't miss the imposing 16th-century Torre di Carlo V, a watchtower built to defend against pirate attacks, which now houses a small museum. The nearby Lido Rossello offers golden sands and clear waters for beach lovers, perfect for a relaxing day by the sea.

Palma di Montechiaro. Situated 30 kilometers southeast of Agrigento, Palma di Montechiaro is a town steeped in history and literary significance. Founded in 1637 by Carlo Tomasi, ancestor of Giuseppe Tomasi di Lampedusa (author of "The Leopard"), the town boasts a wealth of baroque architecture.

The centerpiece is the magnificent Palazzo Ducale (Ducal Palace), also known as Palazzo Montechiaro. This 17th-century palace offers visitors a glimpse into the life of Sicilian nobility, with its ornate rooms and period furnishings. One can enjoy breathtaking panoramic views of the surrounding countryside and the

Mediterranean Sea from its terrace.

The nearby Chiesa Madre, dedicated to Maria Santissima del Rosario, is a stunning example of Sicilian baroque architecture, with its imposing facade and richly decorated interior. Literature enthusiasts will appreciate the town's connection to "The Leopard," as many believe Palma di Montechiaro inspired the fictional town of Donnafugata in the novel.

The Monastery of the Benedictine Sisters, founded by Isabella Tomasi (fictionalized as Blessed Corbera in the book), is another point of interest, known for its unique sweets made by the nuns. For those seeking natural beauty, the nearby Palma di Montechiaro beach offers a less crowded alternative to more touristy coastal areas, with its clear waters and rugged shoreline.

Logistics

Train: Agrigento Centrale. This main railway station in the center of the modern city serves of Agrigento and its surrounding areas. Part of the national railway network operated by Trenitalia, it offers connections to various destinations across Sicily and mainland Italy, including major cities like Palermo, Catania, Messina, and beyond.

Bus (ATV): A local bus service operated by Azienda Trasporti Villaggio del Mediterraneo (ATV) connects different neighborhoods within the city and nearby suburbs.

Regional Buses: Regional buses connect Agrigento with the other main cities of Italy. Autolinee SAIS Trasporti. SAIS operates services connecting Agrigento with Palermo, Catania, and other cities in Sicily, as well as providing local routes within the Agrigento area.

Car: If you're driving from Palermo, the closest large city to Agrigento, the journey is approximately 130 kilometers (80 miles) and takes around 2 hours by car.

Parking: Parking in Agrigento (Town Center). Agrigento's historic center has a ZTL (Zona a Traffico Limitato) to control traffic, especially during festivals. You should park outside the restricted areas to avoid fines and unnecessary hassles.

Parcheggio Pluripiano Agrigento (Via Gioeni), located a short distance from the town center, this is a large multi-story parking garage that provides safe and convenient parking outside the ZTL. From here, it's a simple walk into the heart of the city.

Dining Recommendations

A'Putia Bottega Siciliana. Address: Via Porcello, 18/20

This cozy eatery offers traditional Sicilian street food and sandwiches in a warm, inviting atmosphere.

Civicododici. Address: Via Vullo, 12

This charming restaurant offers a fusion of Sicilian and Mediterranean dishes. With a stylish, contemporary interior and a menu featuring fresh, locally sourced ingredients, Civicododici is known for its innovative take on traditional recipes.

Trattoria Concordia. Address: Via Porcello, 8

A traditional trattoria located close to the city center, Trattoria Concordia serves up classic Sicilian comfort food. Known for its home-cooked meals, welcoming atmosphere, and excellent service, it's a favorite for those seeking authentic Sicilian dining experiences.

Accommodation

Hotel Villa Athena. Address: Via Passeggiata Archeologica, 33

This 5-star hotel is a luxury property located within the Valley of the Temples. It features exclusive access to the archaeological park and stunning views of the Temple of Concordia. Amenities include a spa, outdoor pool, and fine dining at La Terrazza degli Dei. It's known for its elegant rooms and personalized service, perfect for those looking to explore Agrigento's rich history while staying in comfort.

Atenea Luxury Suites. Address: Via Atenea

A cozy 3-star hotel located in the heart of Agrigento's historic center, offering air-conditioned rooms, free parking, and proximity to the town's main attractions. It's an affordable choice for travelers looking for a comfortable stay near Via Atenea, Agrigento's main shopping street.

*B&B Terrazze di Montelusa. Address: Piazza Lena, 6

A refined 3-star B&B featuring a rooftop terrace with views of the Valley of the Temples. The hotel is well-known for its charming hospitality and proximity to key sites, making it a perfect spot for tourists looking to explore Agrigento while enjoying a relaxing environment.

*Le Terrazze di Pirandello. Address: Via Atenea, 273

This bed & breakfast offers free parking and cozy accommodations with modern amenities. It's well-situated along Agrigento's main street, providing easy access to restaurants, shopping, and local attractions.

Il Melograno. Address: Via Empedocle

A 5-star hotel offering top-notch luxury with modern amenities. Guests can enjoy a relaxed atmosphere with access to nearby historical sites such as the Valley of the Temples. Ideal for travelers seeking an elegant and comfortable stay in Agrigento.

*Closest to procession route for the Festa di San Gerlando.

Chapter Thirty-Eight

Scala dei Turchi

Immersion Experience: Agrigento

Scala dei Turchi, or "Staircase of the Turks," is a stunning rocky cliff on the coast of Realmonte, near Porto Empedocle in southern Sicily, Italy. This geological marvel has become a major tourist attraction, partly due to its breathtaking natural beauty and partly because of its mention in Andrea Camilleri's popular series of detective stories about Commissario Montalbano.

The name "Scala dei Turchi" has its roots in local history and legends. The "Turks" in the name refers to the frequent piracy raids by Saracens during the Middle Ages and later by Barbary pirates. These raiders were often called "Turks" because the Ottoman Empire, which lasted from 1299 to 1922, encompassed much of North Africa. The pirates found shelter in this area, which was less exposed to winds and provided a safer place for landing and boarding their ships.

Geologically, the Scala is a true wonder. It's formed by marl, a sedimentary rock with a characteristic white color, created from the remains of planktonic foraminifera. This formation belongs to the Trubi Formation, a marine sedimentary unit dating back to the Lower Pliocene (Zanclean) age. Fascinatingly, these rocks were deposited after the Zanclean flood, when the Mediterranean refilled following its near-complete desiccation during the Messinian salinity crisis. The cliff's distinctive staircase shape, which gives it its name, lies between two sandy beaches and has been sculpted over millennia by wind and waves.

Scala dei Turchi

As you approach Scala dei Turchi, the sea air hits you, mingled with the scent of wild Mediterranean herbs. The white limestone underfoot feels smooth and cool, shaped by centuries of wind and sea. The cliffs gleam in the sunlight, and as you climb the natural steps, you can hear the gentle waves lapping against the base. The contrast of the turquoise waters against the bright, almost blinding white rock dazzles the senses.

Visitors to Scala dei Turchi can engage in a variety of activities. The smooth, natural steps of the cliff offer an adventurous climbing experience and great photo opportunities. At the base of the cliffs, sandy beaches provide perfect spots for relaxation, sunbathing, or swimming in the typically calm and inviting waters. The clear waters around Scala dei Turchi are also ideal for snorkeling, offering underwater exploration for those who bring their gear.

For a truly magical experience, stay until dusk to witness a spectacular sunset. The changing colors of the sky reflected on the white cliffs create an unforgettable atmosphere. Nature enthusiasts can explore the surrounding area, which is rich in Mediterranean flora. Keep an eye out for native plants like rosemary, thyme, and prickly pears as you walk through the landscape.

The top of Scala dei Turchi rewards visitors with breathtaking views of the coastline and the sea. It's a popular spot for photography throughout the day, but especially during sunrise and sunset when the white cliffs glow in the changing light.

Conservation Efforts and Challenges

The unique beauty of Scala dei Turchi has led to growing concerns about its preservation. In August 2007, recognizing its exceptional value, the municipality of Realmonte applied for the inclusion of Scala dei Turchi, along with the nearby Roman Villa Aurea, in the UNESCO World Heritage List.

However, the site has faced significant challenges. Years of complaints about poor environmental protection, erosion, and vandalism by tourists came to a head in February 2020. Italian prosecutors took the drastic step of seizing control of the site and ordering its temporary closure for monitoring. They also announced an investigation into a man who claimed ownership of the site, which was in dispute with the Realmonte local authority.

The fragility of the site was further highlighted in January 2022 when vandals stained the white cliffs with red paint, causing outrage and emphasizing the need for stricter protection measures.

Visitors are strongly encouraged to admire the beauty of Scala dei Turchi while respecting its fragile nature. This means avoiding the removal of any rock or sand, staying on designated paths, and properly disposing of any waste. By practicing responsible tourism, we can help ensure that this natural wonder remains intact for future generations to enjoy.

Practical Information and Nearby Attractions

Since there is no train stop nearby, you'll need either a car or a driver from Agrigento to take you to Scala dei Turchi, which is about a 20-minute drive. If you're driving yourself, be aware that parking can be challenging, especially during peak tourist season.

There are two main options for parking near Scala dei Turchi:

1. Official Parking Area: There's a dedicated parking lot located about 500 meters from the beach access point. This lot is managed by the local authorities and charges a fee (typically around €3-5 for the day, but

prices may vary). While it's a bit of a walk to the beach, this is the most secure and legal option.

2. Roadside Parking: Some visitors choose to park along the road leading to Scala dei Turchi. However, this is not recommended for several reasons. It's often illegal, can be dangerous due to the narrow roads, and your car may be at risk of being towed or ticketed. Additionally, during busy periods, the police may block off road access, allowing only authorized vehicles.

It's strongly advised to use the official parking area, arrive early to secure a spot (especially in summer), and be prepared for a short walk to the site. If you have mobility issues, you might want to consider hiring a local driver or joining a tour that provides transportation.

Spring Celebrations

March through April

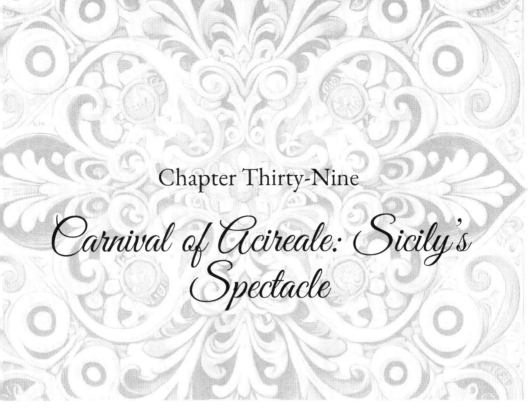

Chapter Thirty-Nine
Carnival of Acireale: Sicily's Spectacle

Carnivale Acireale

Where: Acireale

When: March (date varies by year calculated as 40+ days before Easter)

Event Website: https://www.carnevaleacireale.eu/en

Average Festival Temperatures: High: 14°C (57°F). Low: 7°C (44°F).

Discovering Acireale: Baroque Jewel of the Ionian Coast

Perched on a series of lava terraces overlooking the Ionian Sea, Acireale stands as a testament to Sicilian resilience and artistic splendor. This elegant town, renowned for its ornate baroque architecture and vibrant Carnival celebrations, offers visitors a captivating blend of natural beauty, historical richness, and lively Sicilian culture. Nestled between the azure waters of the Mediterranean and the looming presence of Mount Etna, Acireale invites exploration of its lavish churches, bustling piazzas, and the fascinating legends that have shaped its identity.

The history of Acireale is steeped in myth and marked by natural calamities that have repeatedly reshaped the town. According to legend, the area was originally settled by Xiphonia, a nymph who fled the cyclops Polyphemus. The town's name derives from Aci, a mythical shepherd turned river-god, whose tales are interwoven with the local landscape.

The modern town, however, began to take shape in the 14th century, growing around the Basilica of Saints Peter and Paul. Acireale's defining moment came in the aftermath of the catastrophic 1693 earthquake, which devastated much of eastern Sicily. In the rebuilding that followed, the town emerged as a showcase of Sicilian Baroque architecture, with grand churches and palazzi rising from the ruins, crafted from the dark volcanic stone that gives Acireale its distinctive appearance.

Acireale occupies a stunning position on Sicily's eastern coast, about 16 kilometers north of Catania. The town is built on a plateau of lava rock, formed by ancient flows from Mount Etna, which looms majestically to the west. This elevation, rising about 161 meters above sea level, provides Acireale with breathtaking views of the Ionian Sea and the rugged coastline known as the Riviera dei Ciclopi.

The surrounding area is characterized by citrus groves, benefiting from the fertile volcanic soil, and dramatic geological features such as the Timpa, a steep volcanic cliff that separates the town from the sea.

Acireale has a population of approximately 50,000 residents, making it one of the larger towns in the Province of Catania.

Carnivale of Acireale

The Carnival of Acireale, also known as Carnevale di Acireale, is one of Italy's most famous pre-Lenten celebrations, transforming the baroque town into a vibrant spectacle of art, culture, and festivities. Located near Catania on the eastern coast of Sicily, Acireale's carnival dates back to the 16th century. It began as a simple festivity with playful throwing of citrus fruits and eggs but has since evolved into one of the island's most important cultural events. The introduction of the Cassariata—parades of ornately decorated horse-drawn carriages in the 19th century—marked a pivotal moment in its history, laying the foundation for the elaborate floats seen today.

The Catholic Significance of Carnival

The name "Carnival" itself reveals its deep connection to the Catholic faith. The word comes from the Latin "carne" (meat) and "vale" (farewell), literally meaning "farewell to meat." Carnival marks the final indulgent days before Lent, the 40-day period of fasting and penitence leading up to Easter. During Lent, Catholics traditionally abstain from eating meat, reflecting a period of spiritual preparation, repentance, and simplicity. Carnival, therefore, represents a last chance for celebration and feasting before this solemn period begins.

The timing of Carnival is closely linked to the date of Easter, with festivities culminating on Martedì Grasso (Fat Tuesday), the day before Ash Wednesday, which marks the start of Lent. This celebratory period often begins as early as a month before, building in excitement and culminating in the vibrant parades and events leading up to Fat Tuesday.

Acireale's Carnival embraces this joyous tradition with its spectacular parades of allegorical and flower-covered floats, each a reflection of local artistry and satire. Carnival is not just about fun—it symbolizes the duality of life's pleasures and the reflection that follows during Lent. It blends historical religious significance with modern-day creativity, maintaining its role as both a cultural and spiritual event in Sicily.

The Festival Highlights

The festival runs for several weeks, culminating in the days before Martedì Grasso (Shrove Tuesday). Each day of the carnival brings a different set of spectacles, combining artistic expression, local culture, and community participation. Here's a breakdown of what visitors can expect throughout the festival:

Opening Weekend

The festivities begin with a grand opening parade, introducing the first set of Carri Allegorici Grotteschi, or allegorical floats. These monumental creations, crafted by local artisans from papier-mâché, showcase satirical depictions of political and cultural figures. As the parade commences, the streets fill with excited spectators eager to see this year's designs.

The floats, some reaching heights of several stories, slowly make their way through the city. Each one presents a unique caricature, exaggerating the features and actions of well-known personalities. Politicians might be seen in comical poses; their policies lampooned through clever visual metaphors. Cultural icons and celebrities are transformed into larger-than-life figures, their public personas playfully distorted.

Many floats incorporate simple animatronics, bringing an element of movement to the sculptures. Heads might turn, arms wave, or mouths open and close in sync with recorded speeches or sound effects. These mechanical elements add to the overall spectacle, drawing laughs and cheers from the crowd.

The artistry is evident in the detailed paintwork and the skillful molding of the papier-mâché. Vibrant colors and intricate designs catch the eye, while the sheer scale of the floats impresses onlookers. As each new creation passes by, it provokes discussion, amusement, and sometimes heated debate among the spectators.

This parade sets the tone for the Carnivale, showcasing the creativity, humor, and artistic skill of the local community. It's a celebration of satire and craftsmanship that brings the town together in a spirit of festivity and cultural expression.

Street performers, including jugglers, stilt-walkers, and musicians, flood the streets to entertain crowds, and food stalls offer delicious foods, as always!

Weekday Events

During the weekdays, smaller parades continue, and workshops for mask-making and float construction are available for visitors who wish to immerse themselves in the artistic process. Street musicians and theatrical performances are also common, creating an energetic and colorful atmosphere.

As evening falls, the atmosphere of the Carnivale transforms with the Sfilata dei Carri Infiorati—parades of flower-covered floats. These delicate floral masterpieces add a romantic and ethereal quality to the festivities as they wind through the lamp-lit streets of Acireale.

Each float is a stunning display of natural beauty, covered entirely in a vibrant tapestry of flowers. Local artisans and florists work tirelessly to create intricate designs using a variety of blooms, from fragrant roses and carnations to delicate daisies and orchids. The floats depict various scenes and themes, often drawing inspiration from Sicilian folklore, nature, or classical art.

As the parade begins, the sweet scent of thousands of flowers fills the air, mingling with the coolness of the evening breeze. The soft glow of street lamps illuminates the floats, creating a magical ambiance that captivates spectators. The petals seem to shimmer and dance in the gentle light, bringing the floral sculptures to life.

Music accompanies the procession, with traditional Sicilian melodies floating through the streets. The slow movement of the floats allows onlookers to appreciate the intricate details of each creation, from carefully arranged color gradients to three-dimensional figures formed entirely of blossoms.

Spectators line the route, their faces lit with wonder as they witness this unique blend of nature and artistry. Children point excitedly at their favorite designs, while adults marvel at the skill and patience required to create such ephemeral beauty.

The Sfilata dei Carri Infiorati offers a serene and poetic counterpoint to the earlier satirical parades, showcasing a different facet of Acireale's artistic heritage. It's a celebration of nature's beauty and human creativity, leaving a lasting impression on all who witness it and adding a touch of floral elegance to the vibrant tapestry of Carnivale festivities.

Final Weekend (Saturday to Martedì Grasso)

The festival reaches its crescendo during the final weekend, from Saturday to Martedì Grasso (Shrove Tuesday). This period showcases the most impressive Carri Allegorici—massive floats standing up to 12 meters tall, which represent the pinnacle of the carnival's artistic expression. Unlike the earlier floats, these behemoths are equipped with intricate mechanical parts that bring the satirical characters to life, moving and gesturing to the delight of onlookers. These masterpieces are the result of months of painstaking work by local artisans, who combine traditional papier-mâché techniques with modern engineering to create truly awe-inspiring spectacles.

The Carri Allegorici are the stars of a highly anticipated contest, judged on criteria such as artistic merit, technical complexity, and effectiveness of satire. This competition is a source of great pride and fierce rivalry among the city's different quarters, each vying for the prestigious title of best float. Alongside these grand displays, the streets come alive with masked balls and costume contests for both children and adults. Revelers don elaborate outfits ranging from traditional Sicilian characters to contemporary pop culture figures, adding to the carnival's vibrant tapestry of color and creativity.

Martedì Grasso marks the grand finale of the Carnivale. The day is filled with a whirlwind of activities, including the final parades of the competing floats and the much-awaited announcement of the contest winners. As night falls, all eyes turn to the Ionian Sea, where a spectacular fireworks display illuminates the sky. This dazzling show symbolizes both the joyous conclusion of the carnival and the solemn beginning of Lent, bridging the gap between celebration and reflection.

Throughout the festivities, the Carnivale of Acireale serves as a powerful platform for artistic expression and social commentary. Many of the floats and performances offer humorous and satirical takes on current events, cleverly addressing political issues or cultural trends. This tradition of satire allows the community to engage with and critique societal norms in a festive, accessible manner. Moreover, the carnival plays a crucial role in preserving traditional crafts. The intricate art of papier-mâché float construction is passed down through generations, ensuring that this unique form of artistic expression continues to thrive in the modern era.

Why Acireale?

Acireale's carnival is not just a local celebration; it is a cultural landmark that attracts over 100,000 visitors annually, swelling the town's population far beyond its usual 50,000 residents. The economic impact is substantial, generating millions of euros through tourism, local spending, and artisanal sales. This festival keeps Acireale's historic traditions alive while offering a fresh and creative take on Sicily's dynamic cultural identity.

Whether you visit for the colorful parades, the artistic floats, or simply to immerse yourself in the local culture, the Carnival of Acireale provides an unforgettable experience, a dazzling showcase of Sicilian artistry and festive spirit.

Food Recommendations During Carnival

While enjoying the carnival, don't miss traditional street foods like pasta alla norma (classic pasta dish with fried eggplant, tomato sauce, ricotta salata, and basil), panelle (Thin, crispy chickpea flour fritters, usually served in a sandwich with a squeeze of lemon), sfincione (thick, spongy pizza topped with tomato sauce, onions, anchovies, and breadcrumbs, more akin to focaccia than traditional pizza.), and of course, the island's famous sweets like cassata and granita.

Walking Tour of Acireale

#1. Piazza del Duomo

At the heart of Acireale lies the majestic Piazza del Duomo, the town's main square and the perfect starting point for our tour. This expansive baroque plaza is surrounded by some of Acireale's most important buildings. Take in the grandeur of the space, noting the intricate lava stone paving and the central fountain. This square has been the center of civic and religious life in Acireale for centuries, hosting everything from daily markets to festive celebrations.

#2. Basilica Cattedrale di Santa Maria Annunziata (Cathedral of the Most Holy Mary)

Dominating the eastern side of the Piazza del Duomo is the Cathedral of Maria Santissima Annunziata. This imposing baroque structure, rebuilt after the 1693 earthquake, features a magnificent façade adorned with columns and statues. Step inside to admire the frescoed ceilings, marble altars, and the chapel dedicated to Saint Venera, Acireale's patron saint. The cathedral is not just a religious center but a testament to the town's resilience and artistic achievements in the face of natural disasters.

#3. Basilica di San Pietro e Paolo (Basilica of Saints Peter and Paul)

A short walk from the cathedral brings you to the Basilica of Saints Peter and Paul, one of Acireale's oldest churches. Its origins date back to the 16th century, though it was significantly rebuilt after the 1693 earthquake. The church's baroque façade is a masterpiece of local craftsmanship, featuring intricate stonework and sculptures. Inside, admire the frescoes and the ornate chapels. This basilica is a prime example of Sicilian baroque architecture and artistry.

#4. Palazzo Modò

Continue your walk to Palazzo Modò, a stunning example of baroque civil architecture. This noble residence, built in the 18th century, is renowned for its elaborate balconies supported by grotesque figures – a characteristic feature of Acireale's unique interpretation of the baroque style. While the interior is not typically open to the public, the exterior alone is worth admiring for its exquisite craftsmanship and the insight it provides into the life of Acireale's aristocracy during the baroque period.

#5. Chiesa di San Sabastiano (Church of St. Sebastian)

Next, visit the Church of San Sebastiano, another jewel of Acireale's baroque heritage. This church, dedicated to Saint Sebastian, boasts a distinctive convex façade that sets it apart from other religious buildings in town. The interior is equally impressive, with elaborate stucco work and valuable paintings. Pay special attention to the ceiling frescoes and the marble altars. The church's unique architecture and rich decorations make it a must-see for art and history enthusiasts.

#6. Zelantea Library

A short distance away is the Zelantea Library, one of the oldest public libraries in Sicily. Founded in the 18th century, it houses a vast collection of books, manuscripts, and historical documents. While the library's primary function is research, visitors can admire the beautiful reading room and, if lucky, view some of the rare volumes on display. This site offers a glimpse into Acireale's intellectual history and its commitment to preserving knowledge.

#7. Villa Belvedere

As you continue your walk, you'll reach Villa Belvedere, a public garden offering breathtaking views of the Ionian Sea and the coastline. This 19th-century park is a perfect spot to rest and enjoy nature. The villa contains various species of plants, charming walkways, and several viewing points. It's particularly famous for its panoramic terrace, which provides stunning vistas of Mount Etna and the Riviera dei Ciclopi. This green oasis in the heart of Acireale is beloved by locals and visitors alike for its beauty and tranquility.

#8. Piazza Lionardo Vigo

Vigo Make your way to Piazza Lionardo Vigo, named after a famous local poet and scholar. This square is known for its beautiful Fountain of the Naiads, created in the early 20th century. The fountain depicts mythological water nymphs and is a popular meeting point for locals. The square offers a more relaxed atmosphere compared to the grand Piazza del Duomo and is an excellent place to observe daily life in Acireale.

#9. Timpa Nature Reserve

Conclude your tour with a visit to the Timpa Nature Reserve, accessible via a scenic path from the town center. This protected area showcases the dramatic volcanic landscape that characterizes this part of Sicily. The reserve features a series of lava terraces that descend steeply to the sea, covered in lush Mediterranean vegetation. Hiking trails offer spectacular views of the coastline and Mount Etna. The Timpa is not just a natural wonder but also an important archaeological site, with remains of ancient settlements visible along the paths.

This 4-5 hour walking tour covers the main historical, architectural, and natural attractions of Acireale, offering a comprehensive experience of the town's baroque splendor and coastal beauty. Each site provides unique insights into Acireale's rich cultural heritage and its harmonious blend of human artistry and natural wonders.

Acrireale Festivals and Sagre Throughout the Year

Festa dell'Epifania (Epiphany Festival)

January 6

This enchanting festival marks the ceremonial conclusion of the Christmas season in Acireale, blending religious devotion with folklore traditions. The city's historic center transforms into a living tableau, featuring an elaborate presepe vivente (living nativity scene) where local residents dress in period costumes to recreate scenes from Biblical times. The highlight of the celebration is the much-anticipated arrival of La Befana, a beloved character in Italian folklore depicted as a kindly witch who delivers gifts to children.

Festa di San Sebastiano (Saint Sebastian Festival)

January 20

One of the city's most significant religious celebrations, the Festa di San Sebastiano holds particular importance in Acireale's spiritual calendar. The festival honors Saint Sebastian, the third-century Christian martyr known as a protector against plague and illness. The celebration begins with a solemn Mass at the Church of San Sebastiano, followed by an elaborate procession through the city's baroque streets.

The procession features the ornate silver statue of the saint, carried on the shoulders of the faithful (called portatori), who consider this task a great honor passed down through generations. The statue's journey is accompanied by the city's historic brass band playing traditional marches and religious hymns. Local confraternities, dressed in their ceremonial robes, participate in the procession, carrying ancient banners and religious symbols.

Around the festival, the streets are lined with bancarelle (traditional stalls) selling local delicacies such as pasta alla Norma, arancini, and traditional almond pastries. The evening culminates in a spectacular fireworks display over the Baroque cityscape, with the best viewing spots along Via Galatea.

Settimana Santa (Holy Week)

The week leading up to Easter Sunday (dates vary each year)

Acireale's Holy Week observations represent some of Sicily's most evocative religious traditions. The week begins with Palm Sunday, when olive branches (traditionally used in place of palms in Sicily) are blessed and distributed to the faithful. Each day features distinct ceremonies and processions, with the most significant events occurring during the Triduum (Holy Thursday through Easter Sunday).

On Holy Thursday, the churches of Acireale prepare their "Sepolcri" – elaborate altars decorated with wheat sprouts grown in darkness (symbolic of Christ's death and resurrection), surrounded by flowers and candles. Local families traditionally visit seven churches on this evening, a practice known as "La Visita dei Sepolcri."

Good Friday witnesses the most somber procession, the "Processione dei Misteri," featuring life-sized sculptural groups depicting scenes from Christ's passion. These processional groups, some dating back to the 18th century, are carried through torch-lit streets while the "Lamentazioni" (traditional funeral dirges) are sung by local choirs.

Easter Sunday transforms the city's mood with joyous celebrations, including the "Madonna che Scappa" (Running Madonna) ceremony in Piazza Duomo, where a statue of the Virgin Mary is carried in a running motion to meet the risen Christ – a moment celebrated with doves released into the sky and church bells ringing throughout the city.

Festa del Limone (Lemon Festival)

Typically held in June

Celebrating Acireale's renowned citrus heritage, the Festa del Limone showcases the prized local lemons, particularly the IGP-protected Femminello variety, known for its intense fragrance and essential oil content. The festival transforms the city's main thoroughfares into a citrus-themed exposition, with elaborate displays featuring thousands of lemons arranged in artistic patterns.

Local producers present an array of lemon-based products, from traditional limoncello and marmalades to contemporary innovations in cosmetics and household products. Culinary highlights include chef demonstrations of classic Sicilian lemon-based dishes such as pasta al limone, granita al limone, and the famous lemon salad with red onions.

Festa di Santa Venera (Saint Venera Festival)

July 26

The Festa di Santa Venera stands as Acireale's preeminent religious and cultural celebration, honoring the city's patron saint with a grandeur that draws visitors from across Sicily. Saint Venera, a 2nd-century martyr, is deeply venerated in Acireale, with celebrations spanning several days around her feast day.

The festival begins with the opening of the silver urn containing the saint's relics, housed in the Cathedral. The main procession features the saint's massive silver vara (ceremonial carriage) carried by over a hundred faithful portatori, followed by religious confraternities, brass bands, and thousands of devotees carrying traditional candles called "torce."

The procession's route passes through elaborately decorated streets, with baroque buildings illuminated by artistic light installations known as luminarie. Traditional street foods like scacciate (stuffed focaccia) and iris (fried sweet pastries) are sold from stands throughout the historic center.

The celebration culminates in a renowned fireworks display over the Timpa coastline, considered one of Sicily's finest pyrotechnic shows, featuring unique effects that reflect off the Ionian Sea. Local pyrotechnic artists compete to create the most spectacular display, a tradition dating back centuries.

Festa dei Sapori e dei Saperi (Festival of Flavors and Knowledge)

Usually held in October

This autumn festival celebrates the rich gastronomic and cultural heritage of Acireale and the surrounding area. Set against the backdrop of harvest season, the festival transforms the city's historic center into an open-air museum of Sicilian culinary traditions.

Local producers set up themed areas dedicated to different aspects of regional cuisine: from street food specialists preparing arancini and scacciata to pastry artisans showcasing traditional sweets like pasta di mandorle (almond pastries) and granita with brioche. Master chefs conduct workshops on traditional recipes, with a particular focus on dishes that represent Acireale's unique position between Mount Etna and the Ionian Sea.

The "saperi" (knowledge) component includes demonstrations of traditional crafts such as puppet making, ceramic painting, and lace making. Cultural events feature performances of traditional music and dancing, storytelling sessions sharing local legends, and lectures on the area's culinary history.

Day Trip Options: Nearby Sites, Cities, and Towns

Aci Castello. 13 kilometers (8 miles). Aci Castello is a picturesque coastal town known for its Norman castle perched on a rocky cliff overlooking the sea. Visitors can explore the castle, which houses a small museum with local artifacts. The town also offers beautiful views of the Cyclops Islands and has several charming seafood restaurants. It's an excellent spot for a relaxing day by the sea and to soak in some local history.

Cavagrande del Cassibile Nature Reserve. 115 kilometers (71 miles). This nature reserve features a spectacular canyon carved by the Cassibile River. The highlight is a series of small lakes known as "laghetti," where visitors can swim in crystal-clear waters. Hiking trails offer breathtaking views of the canyon and surrounding landscape. It's an ideal spot for nature enthusiasts, hikers, and those looking to escape the summer heat.

Logistics

Train: Acireale has a train station (Stazione di Acireale) located about 2 km from the city center. It's on the Messina-Catania line, with regular connections to major cities like Catania (20-30 minutes) and Taormina (40-50 minutes). From the station, you can take a local bus or taxi to reach the historic center.

Bus: AST (Azienda Siciliana Trasporti) operates local bus services within Acireale and to nearby towns.

Regional Buses: SAIS Trasporti and Interbus connect Acireale with other Sicilian cities. The main bus station is located near Piazza Duomo in the city center.

Car: Driving to Acireale is convenient via the A18 motorway (Messina-Catania).

Parking: Several parking options are available:

- Parcheggio Capomulini: A large parking area near the coast.

- Parcheggio Note that some areas in the historic center have limited traffic zones (ZTL).

Dining Recommendations

Ristorante Pizzeria La Vela. Address: Strada Provinciale 2, 55

Located along the scenic coastline, Ristorante Pizzeria La Vela offers a relaxing dining experience with spectacular seaside views. The restaurant is known for its authentic Italian cuisine and a wide variety of pizzas made with fresh, local ingredients. Popular with both locals and visitors, it's the perfect spot to enjoy traditional dishes, while soaking in the beauty of the Mediterranean. The warm, casual atmosphere and friendly service make it ideal for families and groups.

Trattoria Lo Scalo. Address: Viale Jonio, 25

A gem for seafood lovers, Trattoria Lo Scalo specializes in traditional Sicilian seafood dishes. With a focus on freshness, the restaurant serves a variety of locally caught fish and shellfish, prepared using time-honored recipes that celebrate the island's culinary heritage. Located near the water, the trattoria offers an intimate, relaxed setting where guests can savor rich Sicilian flavors. Signature dishes include grilled fish, pasta with seafood, and hearty antipasti, all served with warm Sicilian hospitality.

Accommodation

*****Grand Hotel Maugeri.** Address: Piazza Garibaldi, 27

A 4-star hotel located in the historic center of Acireale, just a 5-minute walk from the cathedral. This hotel offers modern comforts, including spacious rooms, free parking, and a restaurant that serves Sicilian cuisine.

*****Best Western Hotel Santa Caterina.** Address: Via Santa Caterina, 42/b

This highly-rated hotel offers stunning views over the sea and is a short walk from the carnival route. With comfortable rooms, a rooftop terrace, and a restaurant serving local Sicilian cuisine, it's a perfect spot for enjoying the vibrant carnival atmosphere while also relaxing in a serene environment.

*****ibis Styles Catania Acireale.** Address: Via Madonna delle Grazie, 98/A/B

This eco-friendly hotel is just a short distance from the parade route, offering modern and spacious rooms, free Wi-Fi, and parking. It's a great option for those wanting easy access to both the carnival festivities and nearby attractions like the Catania coast.

*These hotels are near the parade route for Carnivale.

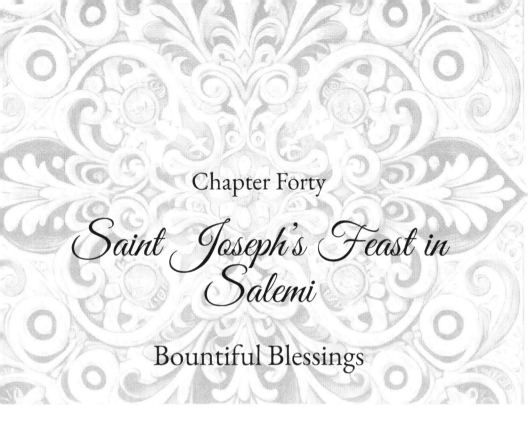

Chapter Forty

Saint Joseph's Feast in Salemi

Bountiful Blessings

La Festa di San Giuseppe

Where: Salemi

When: March 19

Average Festival Temperatures: High: 15°C (60°F). Low: 9°C (48°F).

Discover Salemi: Echoes of the Past Amid Olive Groves

Salemi is an ancient town located in the province of Trapani in western Sicily, Italy. Perched on a hill at an elevation of about 450 meters above sea level, it offers panoramic views of the surrounding countryside. The town's history dates back to ancient times, with settlements in the area traced to the Elymian, Greek, and Roman periods.

Salemi gained prominence during the Middle Ages under Arab and Norman rule. Its name likely derives from the Arabic "Salem" meaning peace. The town played a significant role in the Risorgimento, briefly serving as the first capital of a united

Italy when Giuseppe Garibaldi arrived there in 1860 and declared himself dictator of Sicily.

Salemi is a small town with a population of approximately 10,000 inhabitants. Its economy is primarily based on agriculture, with olive oil and wine production being notable local industries. The town is known for its well-preserved medieval core, featuring narrow winding streets, churches, and a Norman-Swabian castle.

Salemi's architectural heritage reflects its long history, with Arab, Norman, and Baroque influences visible in its buildings and urban layout. In recent years, the town has attracted attention for its innovative "1 Euro House" scheme, aimed at revitalizing its historic center by selling abandoned properties for a symbolic price to those willing to renovate them.

Festival of St. Joseph

The Festa di San Giuseppe in Salemi is one of the most heartfelt and symbolic celebrations in Sicily, occurring annually on March 19th. This day honors Saint Joseph, the patron saint of workers and the protector of the family. Deeply rooted in both religious devotion and agricultural tradition, the festival celebrates not only Saint Joseph's role in Christian teachings but also the season's bounty, as spring begins to bring renewal to the land.

Salemi's celebration is famous for its Tavole di San Giuseppe (Saint Joseph's Tables), lavishly decorated altars filled with food, bread, and religious symbols, which play a central role in the festival. These altars are crafted in homes and churches, honoring the saint's protection and giving thanks for the harvest and the health of families. The festival also serves as a moment for the community to come together, with many people opening their homes to share the feast with visitors, neighbors, and pilgrims.

The Origins of the Tradition

The origins of the Tavole di San Giuseppe date back centuries, arising from a time of famine when, according to legend, the people of Sicily prayed to Saint Joseph for relief. After their prayers were answered, the people created elaborate altars in thanksgiving, offering food to the poor as a symbol of their gratitude. This tradition continues today, and the tavole, with their intricate displays of bread, fruit, vegetables, and symbolic religious decorations, have become one of the most recognizable aspects of the festival.

March 18: Preparation and Blessing of the Tavole

In the days leading up to the festival, families and churches begin preparing the altars. These altars are adorned with elaborate bread sculptures, shaped to represent symbols such as the Holy Family, doves, angels, and flowers. The bread is hand-formed and baked by the community, reflecting the devotion of the participants. In addition to bread, the tables are covered with an abundance of vegetables, fruit, and dishes made with local ingredients. On the eve of the feast day, a solemn blessing of the altars takes place. Local priests and townspeople gather in homes and churches where the tables have been set up. Prayers are offered, and the altars are blessed to ensure the festival begins in a spirit of devotion and thankfulness.

March 19: Feast Day of San Giuseppe

The day begins with a mass in the Church of San Giuseppe. The faithful gather to honor Saint Joseph, with prayers focused on protection, work, and family. After the mass, the Procession of the Holy Family begins. Participants representing the Holy Family, dressed as Joseph, Mary, and the child Jesus, walk through the streets of Salemi. They visit the altars that have been set up in homes and churches, reenacting the tradition of the Holy Family seeking shelter. After the meal, the food on the altars is distributed to the less fortunate in the community, following the tradition of giving back to those in need. This charitable act is a core component of the festival, ensuring that the feast is not only about celebration but also about service.

March 20: Cultural Events and Farewell

On the day after the feast, Salemi hosts a series of cultural events, including folk music performances, traditional dances, and exhibitions showcasing the region's artisanal crafts. The atmosphere is festive, with the streets filled with music and laughter as the community celebrates the successful conclusion of the festival. The festival officially concludes with a farewell mass in the Church of San Giuseppe, where prayers are offered for the protection of the town and its people in the coming year.

Symbolism of the Bread and Food

One of the most unique aspects of the Festa di San Giuseppe in Salemi is the symbolism behind the bread and food offered on the altars. The bread, often shaped like religious symbols, represents abundance and gratitude. The bread sculptures are not just sustenance but also works of art, meticulously crafted by the women of the town in the weeks leading up to the festival.

Key elements of the altar include:

Bread: Shaped into religious symbols, such as the Sacred Heart or the tools of Saint Joseph (hammers, nails, saws), the bread is central to the altar's message of devotion and gratitude.

Fish and Vegetables: As Saint Joseph's Day falls during Lent, the food on the altars is typically vegetarian or pescatarian, with dishes like pasta con le sarde, frittata, and grilled vegetables being staples.

Fava Beans: These beans are a symbol of luck and prosperity, as they were a life-saving crop during times of famine in Sicily.

The Festa di San Giuseppe in Salemi offers a beautiful mix of faith, community, and Sicilian tradition. Whether you're there to admire the intricately designed altars, participate in communal meals, or simply enjoy the atmosphere of devotion, this festival is an unforgettable experience that celebrates the values of sharing and gratitude.

Salemi Festivals and Sagre Throughout the Year

Welcome Back Tony Scott Festival

July

This unique festival celebrates the life and music of Tony Scott, the world-renowned jazz musician of Salemi origins. The two-day event features jazz concerts with performances by local and international musicians, bringing together jazz enthusiasts and honoring Scott's legacy in his ancestral home.

Sagra della Busiata (Pasta)

August

This popular food festival celebrates the traditional Sicilian pasta, Busiata, which is handmade in Salemi. The festival takes place in the charming streets of the historic center, with local chefs preparing and serving delicious portions of Busiata. The event is accompanied by live music and entertainment, making it a perfect mix of culinary and cultural celebration.

Walking Tour of Salemi

Salemi is a picturesque town with a fascinating blend of history, culture, and stunning architecture. Here's a walking tour to help you explore its key sites:

#1. Castello Normanno-Svevo (Salemi Castle)

Begin your tour in the Piazza Alicia, where the imposing Norman-Swabian Castle dominates the landscape. Built in the 12th century, this well-preserved fortress offers panoramic views of the surrounding countryside and was once a strategic point for controlling western Sicily. The castle's towers and walls are accessible, and it's a great spot to start your exploration.

#2. Chiesa Madre- Basilica di San Nicolo di Bari (Mother Church of Salemi)

Adjacent to the castle is the Chiesa Madre, which dates back to the 13th century but has been rebuilt several times due to earthquake damage. The facade is a beautiful example of Baroque architecture, and the interior is rich with religious art.

#3. Museo Civico di Salemi (Civic Museum)

Continue your tour to the Civic Museum, which features archaeological artifacts, medieval art, and rotating exhibitions on Salemi's cultural heritage. The museum is housed in an elegant historic building.

#4. Chiesa di Sant'Agostino (St. Augustine)

A short walk from the Civic Museum is the Church of Sant'Agostino, dating back to the 14th century. It features a beautiful rose window and is one of the oldest churches in Salemi.

#5. Quartiere Arabo (Arab Quarter)

Wander through the Arab Quarter, a labyrinth of narrow, winding streets that reflect Salemi's Arabic past. This area has a distinctly different architectural style, offering a glimpse into the town's multi-cultural heritage.

#6. Museo del Pane Rituale (Ritual Bread Museum)

End your tour back near the castle at the Ritual Bread Museum, which showcases the art of making traditional breads used in Sicilian festivals, particularly for the Festa di San Giuseppe.

#7. Mafia Museum

Salemi has an interesting and complex relationship with the Mafia, particularly in the context of its history and recent efforts to confront that legacy. Located in western Sicily, Salemi, like many towns in the region, was once affected by Mafia activity, but it has also become a symbol of change in the broader effort to reclaim Sicily from its Mafia-dominated past.

During the 19th and 20th centuries, the Mafia had a significant presence in many rural areas of Sicily, including Salemi. The Mafia often exerted influence over agricultural production, local businesses, and even political power structures, particularly through intimidation and violence. Salemi's location in western Sicily placed it within an area traditionally affected by Mafia control.

Day Trip Options Near Salemi

Gibellina. 9 kilometers (5.6 miles) northwest of Salemi. 20 minutes by car from Salemi. Gibellina was destroyed by an earthquake in 1968 and was rebuilt as a modern town filled with contemporary art and architecture. The town is an open-air museum, featuring impressive works by artists such as Alberto Burri, who created the Cretto di Burri, a massive concrete installation on the ruins of old Gibellina. It's a must-visit for art lovers.

Santa Ninfa. 12 kilometers (7.5 miles) northeast of Salemi. This quiet town offers beautiful countryside and the Grotta di Santa Ninfa Nature Reserve, a protected karst landscape with caves and limestone formations. It's a peaceful spot for nature walks and exploring the geological features of the area.

Logistics

Train: The closest train station to Salemi, Sicily is Salemi-Gibellina station, located about 10 km (6 miles) from the town.

Bus: From Palermo or Trapani: AST (Azienda Siciliana Trasporti) operates bus services connecting Salemi with larger cities.

Car: Driving Directions: Salemi is accessible by car from nearby towns such as Trapani, Marsala, and Palermo. Take the A29 motorway from Palermo toward Trapani and follow signs for Salemi (exit Salemi/Segesta). The drive takes about 1.5 hours.

Parking: Parking is available at multiple points around the town. Piazza Alicia and the areas near the Civic Museum offer public parking.

Dining Recommendation

La Giummara. Address: Via G. Mazzini, 50

Known for its traditional Sicilian dishes, La Giummara offers local favorites such as pasta alla Norma, grilled meats, and seafood.

Accommodation

Hotel Baglio Borgesati. Address: Contrada Scorrione, 91018 Salemi, Italy

This hotel offers a beautiful countryside setting just outside Salemi. It's housed in a historic baglio (traditional Sicilian farmhouse) and offers comfortable rooms.

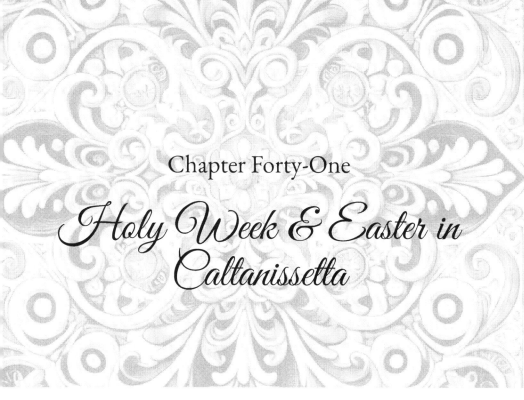

Chapter Forty-One
Holy Week & Easter in Caltanissetta

La Settimana Santa e La Pasqua

Where: Caltanissetta

When: Week leading up to Easter; dates vary by year but March or April.

Average Festival Temperatures: High: 19°C (66°F). Low 9°C (48°F).

Discover Caltanissetta: The Heart of Sicily's Interior

Nestled in the rolling hills of central Sicily, Caltanissetta stands as a testament to the island's diverse history and the resilience of its inland communities. Often bypassed by tourists heading to the coast, this provincial capital offers a true taste of Sicilian life, away from crowded areas. With its mining history, baroque buildings, and position at ancient trade crossroads, it invites visitors to discover a lesser-known side of Sicily.

The history of Caltanissetta stretches back to ancient times, with evidence of settlements dating to the Sicani and Sicels, the island's early inhabitants. The city's name is believed to derive from the Arabic "Qal'at an-Nisa" meaning "Castle of Women," hinting at its importance during the Arab domination of

Sicily.

However, it was during the Norman conquest in the 11th century that Caltanissetta gained prominence. The city flourished under successive rulers, including the Chiaramonte family in the 14th century, who left their mark on its urban fabric. The discovery of sulfur deposits in the 19th century transformed Caltanissetta into a key center of Sicily's mining industry, bringing both prosperity and social upheaval that would shape its modern identity.

Caltanissetta is in the heart of Sicily, approximately 95 kilometers southeast of Palermo and 140 kilometers northwest of Syracuse. The city is built on a series of hills at an elevation of about 600 meters above sea level, providing panoramic views of the surrounding countryside. This inland location, far from the coastal areas that dominate Sicily's tourism, has helped preserve Caltanissetta's authentic character. The landscape around the city is characterized by gently rolling hills, wheat fields, and remnants of the once-booming sulfur mines, creating a unique blend of natural and industrial heritage.

Caltanissetta has a population of approximately 60,000 residents, making it a medium-sized city by Sicilian standards. Once heavily dependent on sulfur mining, the economy has diversified in recent decades. Agriculture remains important, with the production of wheat, almonds, and olives being significant.

Holy Week and Easter

Holy Week and Easter in Sicily are times of profound cultural and spiritual significance, offering a unique experience for visitors of all backgrounds. While deeply rooted in Catholic traditions, these celebrations also showcase Sicily's rich history, art, and community spirit. Whether you're a devout Catholic, a follower of another faith, or simply a curious traveler, the spectacle and emotion of these events can be deeply moving and enlightening.

Easter week in Sicily is a glorious time, with spring sunshine warming the days and nature coming to life. While Caltanissetta serves as our focal point for exploring Easter traditions, the island offers a wealth of experiences in various towns. With a car, you can easily access several Holy Week events, each with its own local flavor and customs. However, it's worth noting that accommodations can be limited during this popular period, so planning is essential.

The Resurrection of Christ is at the heart of Easter celebrations, marking the culmination of His redemptive mission. Easter Sunday's date varies annually, falling on the first Sunday after the first full moon of spring, between March 22nd and April 25th. This moveable feast influences the timing of other religious observances, like Ascension and Pentecost. Easter Monday is also recognized as a national holiday throughout Italy and much of Europe, extending the festive period.

For Catholics, Easter is preceded by Lent, a period of fasting and reflection. While many Sicilians observe these traditions privately, visitors can witness the public aspects of the celebrations. Easter morning typically begins with Mass, followed by festive gatherings. For those interested in experiencing local customs, some agriturismi (farm restaurants) and family-run restaurants offer traditional Easter meals, featuring dishes like roast lamb and artichokes. While many shops close for the holiday, essential services and public transport usually remain operational, albeit with reduced schedules.

Holy Week, known as "Settimana Santa" in Italian, transforms Sicily into a vibrant tapestry of religious processions, ancient rituals, and community events. These ceremonies attract pilgrims and tourists from around the world, creating a unique atmosphere that blends devotion, tradition, and spectacle. Even for non-religious visitors, the historical and cultural significance of these events offers a fascinating glimpse into Sicily's heritage and the enduring power of communal traditions.

Palm Sunday Procession (Domenica delle Palme)

Here's a comprehensive overview of the events and traditions associated with Palm Sunday in Caltanissetta:

The Palm Sunday celebrations in Caltanissetta mark the beginning of Holy Week with a blend of solemn ritual and community spirit. The day begins with a special Mass at the Cathedral of Caltanissetta, where the priest blesses palm branches and olive fronds. These blessed branches, symbolizing the crowds that welcomed Jesus into Jerusalem, play a crucial role in the day's ceremonies and hold deep significance for the faithful.

The Procession

Following the Mass, a grand procession winds its way through the streets of Caltanissetta, starting from the Cathedral. This procession is a vibrant display of faith and tradition, bringing together various segments of the community. Members of local confraternities, clergy, and parishioners form the core of the parade, many carrying their freshly blessed palms. The inclusion of children and families in the procession underscores the event's importance as a unifying force within the community, bridging generations in a shared expression of devotion.

The visual spectacle of the procession is enhanced by the traditional attire worn by many participants, especially those belonging to religious brotherhoods. Their customary robes add a layer of historical and cultural richness to the event, connecting present-day observers with centuries of Sicilian tradition. As the procession moves through the city, it is accompanied by the sound of traditional music and chanting, creating an atmosphere that is both spiritual and emotionally stirring.

Throughout the procession route, there are designated stops for prayers and reflections. These pauses serve as moments of collective meditation, allowing participants to contemplate the deeper meanings of Palm Sunday and the week to come. These brief interludes of quiet reflection amidst the pageantry of the procession offer a balanced experience of communal celebration and personal spiritual journey.

The Palm Sunday celebrations in Caltanissetta thus serve as a powerful prelude to Holy Week, setting the tone for the solemn and joyous observances that will follow. They exemplify how religious tradition, community participation, and cultural heritage intertwine in Sicilian Easter celebrations, creating an experience that resonates with locals and visitors alike.

Holy Tuesday (Martedì Santo): Continuation of Devotional Activities

While there is no major procession on Holy Tuesday, local churches often hold special masses, and preparations continue for the events later in the week. It's a good day to explore the city's religious sites and observe the communities as they ready themselves for the upcoming processions.

Holy Wednesday (Mercoledì Santo): Procession of the Real Maestranza

The Real Maestranza of Caltanissetta is one of the most ancient and prestigious traditions in Sicily, deeply embedded in the city's Holy Week celebrations. Dating back to the 16th century, the guild was originally formed by various artisans and artisans who played a significant role in both the religious and social life of the city. During the Spanish rule of Sicily, these guilds were an essential part of urban society, not only representing different trades but also holding civic and religious duties such as assisting in public works and contributing to major religious events. The guild's name, "Real" (meaning Royal), was likely conferred by a Spanish monarch, acknowledging their loyalty and service to the city.

At the heart of the Holy Thursday procession, the Real Maestranza takes center stage during Caltanissetta's Holy Week, a highlight of the city's religious calendar. The members wear traditional black suits, complete with a cape, gloves, and top hat, which reflect the somber tone of the religious occasion. They also carry the insignia of their respective trades, which could represent professions such as blacksmiths, carpenters, bakers, or goldsmiths. In addition to their black attire, the members carry ceremonial swords, symbolizing their historical role as protectors of the city and the Church, and embodying their loyalty to both their craft and their faith.

Each year, a captain is elected from among the guild members, tasked with leading the procession and carrying the ceremonial sword. The Captain represents the guild in all official matters and plays a central role in the religious rituals of Holy Week. One of the most symbolic moments of the procession occurs when the Captain, in an act of humility, lays the sword at the feet of the Bishop of Caltanissetta. This gesture represents the guild's submission to the Church and its deep-rooted dedication to faith and tradition.

The Holy Thursday procession, led by the Real Maestranza, is known as the Processione della Real Maestranza. This grand procession begins at the Cathedral of Santa Maria la Nova and weaves through the streets of Caltanissetta, drawing the entire community together. The procession, accompanied by other religious groups and confraternities, returns to the cathedral for a solemn religious ceremony, marking one of the most poignant events of Holy Week.

Holy Thursday (Giovedì Santo): Procession of the Vare Statues

On Holy Thursday in Caltanissetta, visitors can expect to witness one of the most profound and visually captivating events of Holy Week: the Procession of the Vare. This procession, which has been part of the city's tradition since the 1700s, showcases 16 life-size statue groups representing different scenes from the Passion of Christ. These statues are carried through the historic streets of Caltanissetta, accompanied by emotional funeral marches performed by local and regional bands.

What to See and Experience:

The Vare Statues: These statues, made from wood, terracotta, and papier-mâché, were created by the renowned Biangardi family of Neapolitan sculptors. Each one represents a unique moment from Christ's Passion, such as the Last Supper, the Crucifixion, and the Pietà, bringing these sacred scenes to life in vivid detail. The statues are beautifully adorned with flowers and candles, and their intricate craftsmanship offers a glimpse into Sicily's artistic heritage.

The Procession Route: The procession starts at sunset and winds through the narrow, historic streets of Caltanissetta, creating a powerful visual experience against the backdrop of the city's ancient architecture. Thousands of spectators line the streets, many holding candles and observing in silence as the statues pass by. The procession is slow and deliberate, emphasizing reflection and reverence.

Music and Atmosphere: The sound of funeral marches, played by Sicilian bands, adds to the deeply somber and emotional atmosphere. The music heightens the spiritual intensity of the event and echoes throughout the city, reinforcing the reflective nature of the procession.

The Spartenza (Separation): As the night progresses, the procession reaches Piazza Garibaldi, where the final act known as the Spartenza takes place. Here, the statues are separated and returned to their respective churches or homes, symbolizing the end of the communal journey through Christ's Passion. This moment is highly symbolic, marking the conclusion of the Holy Thursday rituals.

The Holy Thursday Procession is a key part of Caltanissetta's Holy Week and offers a unique opportunity to experience the city's rich traditions, deep spirituality, and artistic heritage. Whether you are religious, the atmosphere, folklore, and history makes this an unforgettable event.

Venerdi Santo (Good Friday): Procession of the Black Christ

On Good Friday in Caltanissetta, the most important event is the Procession of the Black Christ, a deeply moving and solemn occasion. The day is characterized by silence, mourning, and reflection as the community gathers to remember the crucifixion of Jesus.

The central figure of the procession is the Black Christ, a revered wooden crucifix from the 15th century. This crucifix is said to have been discovered in a cave by two local herb gatherers, or fogliamari, and has since become one of the most venerated religious symbols in the city. During the procession, the fogliamari, dressed in purple tunics and barefoot as a sign of penitence, carry the crucifix through the streets on their shoulders. Accompanied by mournful music and lamentations in Sicilian dialect, the procession moves through the San Francesco district and winds its way across the city.

The participants include not only the fogliamari but also local craftsmen representing the Real Maestranza, alongside clergy, nuns, monks, and the public. Many of the faithful walk barefoot as an expression of devotion, fulfilling vows, or asking for divine grace. The procession is followed by sizeable crowds, and its solemnity reflects the deep spiritual connection that the people of Caltanissetta have with this centuries-old tradition.

This event is an emotionally charged and highly symbolic part of the city's Holy Week, offering visitors an opportunity to witness one of the most powerful expressions of faith in Sicily.

Holy Saturday (Sabato Santo)

On Holy Saturday (Sabato Santo) in Caltanissetta, the atmosphere remains one of reflection and anticipation as the city awaits the celebration of the Resurrection. The day is primarily marked by a somber, contemplative mood, as there are no major processions or public events during the daytime. Holy Saturday is traditionally a day of silence, prayer, and preparation in the Christian calendar, as the faithful meditate on Christ's death and burial.

In the evening, the focus shifts to the Easter Vigil, which is held at the Cathedral of Santa Maria La Nova. This service is one of the most significant in the Catholic liturgical year. The vigil begins with the blessing of the new fire and the lighting of the Paschal candle, symbolizing the light of Christ returning to the world. The service is accompanied by readings, prayers, and hymns, celebrating Christ's victory over death. This joyful event culminates with the announcement of the Resurrection, marking the transition from mourning to celebration.

Easter Vigil (Mass until midnight the night before Easter)

While Holy Saturday itself is quieter compared to the processions of the previous days, the Easter Vigil is an important spiritual event that prepares the city for the joyous celebrations of Easter Sunday. If visitors are in Caltanissetta during this time, they can take part in the vigil and experience the powerful liturgical rites that have been cherished traditions for centuries.

Easter Sunday (Pasqua)

On Easter Sunday in Caltanissetta, the atmosphere transforms from the solemnity of Holy Week into one of joy and celebration, as the city marks the Resurrection of Christ. The day begins with a solemn Mass in the Cathedral of Santa Maria la Nova, where the faithful gather to celebrate the culmination of the Easter season.

After the Mass, the highlight of the day is the Procession of the Resurrection, led by the Real Maestranza. In contrast to the somber black attire worn earlier in the week, the members of the Maestranza now wear white gloves, ties, and socks, symbolizing the joy and renewal of Easter. Accompanied by a lively marching band, they process through the streets toward the bishop's residence. The procession concludes in Piazza Garibaldi, where the bishop blesses the crowd, and doves are released into the sky, symbolizing peace and the Resurrection.

The Captain of the Real Maestranza, who plays a prominent role throughout Holy Week, formally returns the keys to the city to the Mayor, symbolizing the end of the Maestranza's ceremonial duties for the week. This event brings Caltanissetta's Holy Week to a close with a sense of renewal and spiritual triumph.

Holy Monday (Lunedì dell'Angelo, also called La Pasquetta). Holy Monday is part of the Easter Octave, which extends the observance of the Resurrection for eight days. Joy and Christ's victory over death continue to be the focus. It is a national holiday in Italy, a day Italians go out and have a picnic or celebrate with family and friends outdoors.

Easter Treats

People across Italy celebrate Easter by enjoying a variety of food traditions that vary by region, but there are several culinary delights that are commonly enjoyed. Let me give you a rundown of the most popular Easter foods in Sicily.

Colomba di Pasqua: The Colomba di Pasqua is a traditional Italian Easter cake, shaped like a dove to symbolize peace and renewal. It is made with a rich, soft dough infused with candied fruit and topped with a crunchy almond glaze, making it a popular sweet treat during Easter celebrations across Italy.

Capretto al Forno (Roast Kid): To prepare a traditional Easter dish called roast kid (young goat), people use herbs, garlic, and sometimes lemon, and they roast it until it becomes tender and flavorful.

Pizza Rustica: Also known as "Torta Pasqualina," this is a savory pie filled with a mixture of ricotta cheese, spinach or other greens, and sometimes eggs. It has a rich, buttery crust, and people frequently enjoy it as a starter or side dish.

Frittata di Agnello (Lamb Frittata): This dish features lamb, usually cooked with onions, herbs, and eggs, to make a savory frittata.

Crespelle (Sicilian Pancakes): Thin pancakes filled with various ingredients like ricotta cheese, spinach, or ham, and then baked with a tomato sauce.

Pupi cu l'Ogghiu (Puppets with Oil): Pupi cu l'Ogghiu are traditional Sicilian cookies made from a simple dough of flour, sugar, and olive oil, typically shaped into figures like animals or puppets. These cookies are popular during festive times, especially during Easter, and are often decorated with vibrant colors or hard-boiled eggs.

Lamb Dishes: Various lamb recipes, prepared with local herbs and spices, are common during Easter in Sicily, including stews, grilled lamb, and braised lamb.

Uova di Pasqua (Chocolate Easter Eggs): In modern times, chocolate Easter eggs have become a widespread tradition across Italy. However, the eggs in Italy differ from what we envision in America. You can find chocolate eggs that are as big as your purse or even your suitcase. They are hollow, and they have toys inside, stuffed animals, and almost like an Easter basket inside of an egg. They can cost 60, 100, even 500 euros. It is a unique tradition.

In Caltanissetta for Holy Week?

Consider visiting nearby Holy Week events for a deeper experience of the region's rich traditions.

These cities are nearby but offer unique experiences and events this week. You can visit four towns, visit some sites and enjoy their celebrations.

Enna: Located 34 kilometers (21 miles) from Caltanissetta, Enna is famous for its evocative Procession of the Dead Christ on Good Friday, featuring thousands of hooded members of religious brotherhoods. Its elevated position provides dramatic views and a striking backdrop for the solemn torch-lit procession.

Gela: 60 kilometers (37 miles) from Caltanissetta, Gela celebrates Holy Week with traditional processions, such as the Processione del Venerdì Santo (Good Friday Procession). This coastal town offers a unique perspective on Sicilian Easter traditions.

Caltagirone: 62 kilometers (39 miles) away, Caltagirone is known for its artistic and cultural heritage, which blends into its Holy Week traditions. The Procession of the Dead Christ: Caltagirone is known for its Baroque architecture, which serves as a stunning backdrop for the solemn Good Friday procession. During this event, a life-sized statue of Christ in a glass coffin is carried through the streets, accompanied by religious brotherhoods and townspeople dressed in traditional robes. The atmosphere is one of deep reverence and reflection, enhanced by the candlelit streets and mournful music played by local bands. This unique procession embodies centuries of tradition and provides a powerful experience for visitors.

Walking Tour of Caltanissetta

#1. Piazza Garibaldi

The central square of Caltanissetta, a focal point for local life, is an excellent place to begin your exploration. The statue of Giuseppe Garibaldi, the Italian revolutionary hero, stands prominently in the square.

#2. Duomo di Caltanisetta (Caltanissetta Cathedral)

The Caltanissetta Cathedral, dedicated to both the Immaculate Conception and Saint Michael the Archangel, is a striking example of Baroque and Neoclassical architecture. Located in Piazza Garibaldi, the cathedral was completed in 1622 and features a magnificent interior adorned with frescoes by the Flemish artist Guglielmo Borremans. Painted between 1720 and 1721, the frescoes depict scenes from the life of the Virgin Mary, including the Immaculate Conception, the Coronation of the Virgin, and St. Michael's triumph.

The cathedral's layout follows the Latin cross plan, with three aisles and 14 arches that give the space a sense of grandeur and light. Noteworthy inside the cathedral is the statue of the Immaculate Conception (1760), beautifully crafted with silver drapery, and the impressive wooden statue of St. Michael from the 17th century, symbolizing the saint's role as the city's protector.

#3. Chiesa di San Francesco d'Assisi (Church of St. Francis)

The Church of San Francesco d'Assisi in Caltanissetta is a beautiful example of Sicilian Baroque architecture. Built in the 17th century, the church features an ornate façade and a richly decorated interior. Inside, the church's most striking feature is its intricate wooden ceiling, adorned with gilded carvings and detailed artwork. The main altar is another highlight, boasting fine marble work and Baroque ornamentation, which enhances the church's serene yet grand atmosphere. Visitors are drawn to this church not only for its religious significance but also for its artistic and architectural beauty, which offers a peaceful space for reflection

#4. Via Vittorio Emanuele

Discover quaint streets like Via Vittorio Emanuele and Via Roma, where you'll find shops, cafes, and local life.

#5. Chiesa di San Sebastiano

A smaller yet historically significant church, originally built in the 16th century and later reconstructed in the 18th century. It is dedicated to Saint Sebastian and features a simple but elegant Neoclassical facade.

#6. Palazzo Moncada

The Palazzo Moncada is one of Caltanissetta's most architecturally significant and historically important noble residences. Built in the 17th century, this grand palace once belonged to the powerful Moncada family, who were influential figures in Sicilian aristocracy. The building reflects the Baroque style, characterized by elegant balconies, elaborate stone carvings, and a stately façade. The palace's ornate architecture features intricate details, including beautiful balustrades and decorative masks carved into the stone.

While today much of the interior is not fully accessible, the building is used for cultural events and exhibitions, providing visitors a glimpse into the opulent lifestyle of Sicily's noble families during the Baroque period. The Palazzo's central location also makes it an important landmark in the city's urban landscape, offering a connection to Caltanissetta's aristocratic past and architectural heritage7 End at the Public Garden (Giardini Pubblici): A peaceful park offering a relaxing space to conclude your tour. Enjoy the green spaces, fountains, and scenic views.

#7. Giardini Pubblici (Public Gardens)

The Public Garden (Giardini Pubblici), near the historic center of Caltanissetta, offers a tranquil retreat amidst the hustle and bustle of the city. Established in the early 20th century, the garden is a popular spot for locals and visitors to relax and enjoy the natural surroundings. The park is beautifully landscaped with lush green spaces, fountains, and vibrant flowerbeds, making it an ideal place for a peaceful stroll or quiet reflection. Scenic views of the surrounding hills and countryside provide a picturesque backdrop, and there are also plenty of shaded areas and benches where visitors can rest and soak in the serene atmosphere. The Giardini Pubblici is not only a place of leisure but also a venue for local festivals and outdoor events, making it a key feature of the community's social life.

Caltanissetta Festivals and Sagre Throughout the Year

Festa di San Michele (St. Michael)

September 29

The Festa di San Michele is one of Caltanissetta's most important religious celebrations, dedicated to Saint Michael the Archangel, the city's patron saint. The tradition dates back to the 17th century, when Saint Michael was credited with miraculously saving Caltanissetta from a plague outbreak. During the festival, a statue of Saint Michael, created by Stefano Li Volsi, is carried through the streets in a grand procession. The statue, dressed in armor, represents Saint Michael defeating the devil, symbolizing the victory of good over evil. Expect music, street stalls, fireworks, and lively festivities, especially in Piazza Garibaldi, where the procession starts and finishes. Locals and visitors alike gather to enjoy food, music, and entertainment that fills the city streets.

Sagra del Pomodoro (Tomato Festival)

September

The Sagra del Pomodoro is a vibrant food festival dedicated to celebrating local tomato varieties, which are a staple of Sicilian cuisine. This festival highlights Caltanissetta's agricultural heritage, especially the production of tomatoes used in local dishes like sauces and salads.

During the event, visitors can expect food tastings, cooking demonstrations by local chefs, and opportunities to buy fresh tomatoes and related products. Local vendors also offer a variety of tomato-based products, including sauces, jams, and artisan goods. It's a great way to experience the local food culture while exploring the town's community spirit.

Procession of the Three Saints

December 28

The Procession of the Three Saints is held annually to commemorate the devastating Messina earthquake of 1908, which severely affected eastern Sicily and southern Calabria but miraculously spared Caltanissetta. The three saints honored during this procession are Saint Michael, Saint Joseph, and Saint Anthony, each credited with protecting the city from the disaster.

The procession starts at the Church of Saint Michael and moves through the streets with the statues of the saints carried by local religious groups. The event is solemn yet hopeful, marking a day of remembrance and gratitude for Caltanissetta's preservation.

Day Trip Options: Nearby Sites, Cities and Towns

Riesi. 30 kilometers (19 miles) southeast of Caltanissetta. Riesi is a small, authentic Sicilian town known for its agricultural heritage and community spirit. Founded in the 17th century, it has retained much of its traditional charm and offers visitors a glimpse into everyday Sicilian life away from tourist hotspots. tes to visit:

- Chiesa Madre: The main church dedicated to Santa Maria Assunta
- Palazzo Comunale: The town hall, an interesting example of local architecture
- Local markets: Experience the vibrant atmosphere and fresh produce
- Nearby sulfur mines: Reflect the area's industrial heritage

Gela. 50 kilometers (31 miles) south of Caltanissetta. Gela is a coastal town with a rich history dating back to ancient Greek times. Founded in 689 BC by colonists from Rhodes and Crete, it was one of the most important Greek cities in Sicily. Gela is known for having the most days of sunshine in Italy annually, making it a pleasant destination year-round. Sites to visit:

- Archaeological Park of Gela: Featuring Greek fortifications and temples
- Regional Archaeological Museum: Housing important artifacts from the region
- Castello di Terranova: A 13th-century fortress overlooking the sea
- Gela's beaches: Enjoy the Mediterranean coastline

Regarding World War II significance, Gela was a key landing site during Operation Husky, the Allied invasion of Sicily in July 1943. The town saw intense fighting between Allied forces and Axis defenders, playing a crucial role in the Sicily campaign that ultimately led to the Allied victory in the Mediterranean theater.

Logistics

Trains: Caltanissetta's train station (Caltanissetta Centrale) that is part of the Trenitalia network, connecting Caltanissetta with major Sicilian cities such as Palermo, Catania, and Syracuse.

Bus: Buses operated by AST (Azienda Siciliana Trasporti) connect different parts of the town and nearby areas.

Regional Buses: AST also operates regional bus services that connect Caltanissetta with other Sicilian towns and cities, including Palermo, Catania, and Agrigento.

Car: From Catania: Take the A19 motorway toward Palermo and exit at Caltanissetta, around 110 km (68 miles) and 1 hour and 20 minutes.

Parking: Parcheggio Ex Stadio Palmintelli: Located just outside the ZTL, near the center, this parking area is free or has low rates. It is one of the largest and most convenient options. Parcheggio Via Cavour: Another option located just outside the ZTL, offering easy access to the city center on foot. Public Street Parking: There are various blue-line street parking zones (paid parking) outside the ZTL area. Be sure to pay at nearby meters and display your ticket on your dashboard.

Dining Recommendations

Piacere & Gusto. Address: Via Chiarandà 46

This charming eatery is celebrated for its wood-fired pizzas and a wide selection of Italian wines. Besides its pizzas, the menu includes a variety of traditional Sicilian dishes with a modern twist. With its friendly service and inviting ambiance, it's a glorious spot for a relaxed meal with family or friends.

Sale & Pepe. Address: Corso Umberto I, 146

Sale & Pepe is renowned for its Mediterranean-inspired menu, featuring creative dishes made with fresh, local ingredients. From delicious risottos to inventive takes on Sicilian classics, the restaurant offers something for everyone. The elegant yet relaxed setting makes it ideal for both casual meals and special occasions.

Ristorante Centro Storico. Address: Via Benintendi 133

This cozy restaurant in the heart of Caltanissetta is perfect for savoring authentic Sicilian flavors. Known for its fresh seafood and handmade pasta dishes, it's a favorite for those seeking traditional local cuisine. The warm atmosphere and attentive service make it a delightful dining experience.

Accommodation

Antichi Ricordi. Address: Via Villaglori, 45

Antichi Ricordi is a 4-star hotel in the heart of Caltanissetta's historic center. It offers elegantly furnished rooms and suites, blending modern amenities with traditional Sicilian charm. Guests appreciate its proximity to major attractions and the personalized service provided by the staff.

Hotel San Michele. Address: Via Fasci Siciliani, 6

This 4-star hotel is known for its spacious rooms and tranquil atmosphere. Located a short distance from the city center, Hotel San Michele provides a peaceful retreat with amenities such as an on-site restaurant serving local cuisine and a well-maintained garden area.

Hotel Plaza. Address: Via Berengario Gaetani, 5

Hotel Plaza is a 3-star establishment offering comfortable rooms equipped with modern amenities. Its central location makes it an excellent base for exploring the city. Guests appreciate the friendly staff and the hotel's proximity to shopping and dining venues.

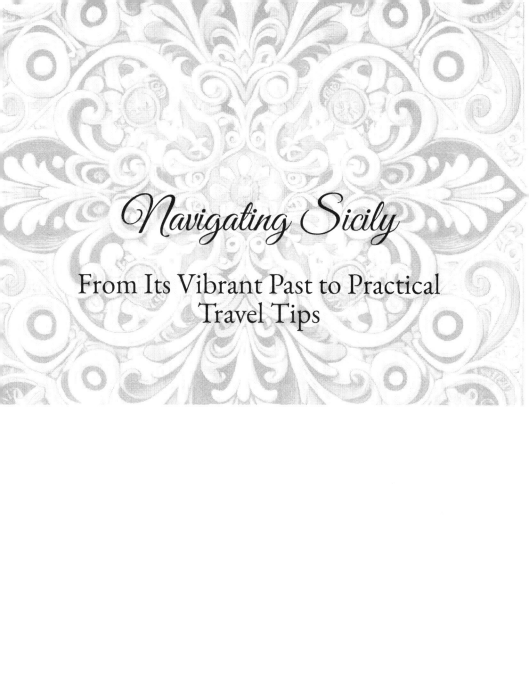

Navigating Sicily

From Its Vibrant Past to Practical Travel Tips

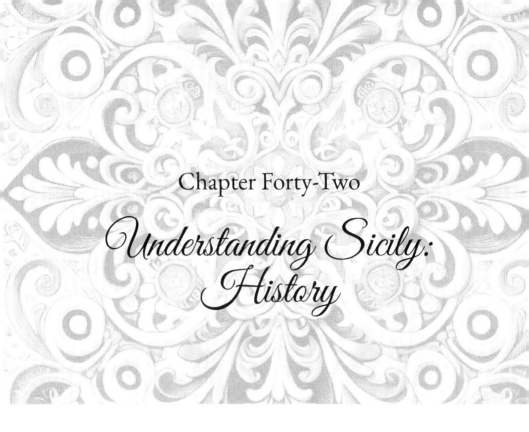

Chapter Forty-Two
Understanding Sicily: History

Discovering Sicily: A Journey Through Time and Culture

Sicily, the largest island in the Mediterranean Sea, has a rich and complex history shaped by its strategic location and natural resources. Over the centuries, this beautiful island has been a crossroads of cultures, each leaving its mark on the land and its people.

Ancient Beginnings: The Greeks and the Phoenicians

Evidence of human settlement in Sicily can be traced back thousands of years, with origins dating back to 10,000 BC. The island's recorded history began around 800 BC when the Greeks and Phoenicians established colonies along its coasts. The Greeks founded several major cities, including Syracuse, Agrigento, and Messina, which became centers of trade, culture, and learning. Greek influence remains visible today in archaeological sites such as the Valley of the Temples in Agrigento and the Greek Theater in Syracuse.

The Phoenicians, great traders from the eastern Mediterranean lands such as Lebanon, Syria, Israel, settled in the western part of Sicily, establishing cities like

Palermo and Motya. They carried with them their knowledge of navigation and trade, which helped Sicily become a vital hub for commerce in the ancient world. Starting in the 8th century BC, Greek city-states began colonizing Southern Italy and eastern Sicily. To enhance trade, agriculture, and geopolitical influence, the Greek city-states in the eastern Aegean region founded colonies along the southern coast of Italy and eastern Sicily. This colonization was part of a larger phenomenon known as Magna Graecia (Latin for "Greater Greece"), which encompassed the coastal areas of southern Italy and Sicily.

Greeks brought their artistic and architectural styles, constructing temples, theaters, and public buildings. Magna Graecia's architecture combined Greek elements with local styles, creating distinct regional variations. This area became a center of Greek culture, politics, and trade, establishing vibrant city-states that mirrored those in mainland Greece.

Ancient Greek Temple at Agrigento

As Sicily's strategic importance grew, it became the focal point of conflict between the Greeks, Carthaginians, and Romans. The island was at the center of the First Punic War between Rome and Carthage in the 3rd century BC. After years of intense battles, Rome emerged victorious, and in 241 BC, Sicily became the first Roman province outside the Italian peninsula, marking the beginning of Rome's expansion beyond Italy.

Under Roman rule, Sicily flourished as an agricultural center, known as the "granary of Rome" because of its vast wheat fields. The Romans introduced new agricultural techniques, and they also expanded Sicily's road network, with many parts of it still in existence today. The island's prosperity continued during the reign of the Romans, but it also saw periods of social unrest and slave revolts, such as the famous rebellion led by Spartacus in 73 BC.

Byzantine and Arab Periods

As the Roman Empire weakened and split, the eastern half became the Byzantine Empire, with its capital in Constantinople (modern-day Istanbul). The Byzantines, originally the eastern continuation of the Roman Empire, took control of Sicily in 535 AD, after the fall of the Western Roman Empire. Under Byzantine rule, Christianity flourished on the island, and they established many churches and monasteries. The Byzantines were known for their strong connection to Orthodox Christianity and their preservation of Roman law and culture, but their rule in Sicily was often marked by internal conflict and invasions.

In the 9th century, Arab forces from North Africa conquered Sicily, starting a period of significant transformation and prosperity. The Arabs introduced advanced agricultural techniques, including irrigation systems, and new crops like citrus fruits, sugar cane, and cotton. They also enriched the island's cultural fabric, leaving lasting influences in Sicilian language, architecture, and traditions. Many of these contributions still shape Sicilian life today, especially in architectural styles and culinary influences found across the island.

The Norman Conquest and the Kingdom of Sicily

In the 11th century, Norman adventurers from Northern Europe invaded Sicily, eventually driving out the Arab rulers. By 1091, the Normans had fully conquered the territory, establishing the Kingdom of Sicily. Under Norman rule, Sicily became a fusion of diverse cultures, blending Norman, Arab, Greek, and Byzantine influences. The Normans had a reputation for tolerating different cultures and religions, enabling Christians, Muslims, and Jews to live together peacefully. Many consider this period a golden age for Sicily, as architectural masterpieces like the Palatine Chapel and the Cathedral of Monreale showcase a fusion of Norman, Arab, and Byzantine styles.

The Swabians, Angevins, and Aragonese

After the Norman dynasty ended in the late 12th century, Sicily came under the rule of the Swabians in 1194. The Swabians were a Germanic dynasty, part of the Hohenstaufen family from the region of Swabia (in present-day southwestern Germany). Their most famous ruler was Frederick II, a highly influential emperor of the Holy Roman Empire and King of Sicily. Frederick II was known as "Stupor Mundi" (the Wonder of the World) due to his intellectual curiosity and administrative reforms. Under his rule, Sicily became a hub of cultural and intellectual exchange, blending Norman, Arab, and Byzantine influences.

Following the Swabians, the island fell under the control of the French Angevins in 1266, when Charles of Anjou was appointed by the Pope to rule over Sicily. However, the French rule was unpopular, and tensions culminated in the Sicilian Vespers in 1282, a major uprising against Angevin rule. This revolt led to the end of French dominance and the beginning of Aragonese rule. In the early 16th century, this led to Sicily becoming part of the vast Spanish Empire. This period saw the rise of powerful noble families and the entrenchment of a feudal system, which deepened social divides. Spanish rule also introduced the Inquisition, which targeted religious minorities, including the Jewish community, leading to their expulsion from Sicily in 1492.

The Val di Noto region in southeastern Sicily is renowned for its stunning Baroque architecture. The cities included in this book—Ragusa, Militello in Val di Catania, Scicli, and Noto—showcase this rich heritage. After the catastrophic earthquake of 1693, the towns of Val di Noto were rebuilt in the Baroque style, transforming the region into a treasure trove of artistic and architectural splendor. The earthquake of 1693, one of the most destructive in European history, struck on January 11th with a magnitude of 7.4. The tremors devastated over 45 towns and villages across the region, and fires and aftershocks compounded the damage. The loss of life was staggering, with estimates ranging from 60,000 to 100,000 casualties. Entire communities were uprooted, and the economic toll made recovery a slow and arduous process.

In the wake of the disaster, the cities and villages were rebuilt, giving birth to the unique style now known as Sicilian Baroque. Defined by elaborate ornamentation and the use of local stone, this architectural style is distinct for its vibrant colors and intricately detailed interiors. Many families who rebuilt their homes after the earthquake still have descendants living in the same houses and palaces today, maintaining a deep historical connection to the region.

As you explore the cities of Val di Noto, you'll notice the distinctive Sicilian Baroque churches with their three-level designs: main doors on the ground floor, decorative elements on the second, and church bells on the third. Unlike the towering bell towers of Venice, for example, those in Val di Noto remain shorter and more modest. This is a direct result of the earthquake's destruction, as bell towers toppled and caused further damage to surrounding buildings. Architects of the time observed that churches in the new Sicilian Baroque style withstood the tremors better, leading to a shift in design across the region.

The Bourbon Era and Unification of Italy

In the 18th century, Sicily fell under the control of the Bourbons, a royal family of French origin, who ruled Sicily as part of the Kingdom of the Two Sicilies (which also included mainland southern Italy). The Bourbons first came to power in 1734 when Charles of Bourbon conquered the Kingdom of Naples and Sicily, establishing the Bourbon dynasty in the region. In 1816, the Kingdom of the Two Sicilies was officially formed, uniting the Kingdom of Sicily with the Kingdom of Naples under Bourbon rule.

The Bourbons ruled intermittently through periods of war and revolution, facing opposition from both the local nobility and the general population due to their often autocratic governance. They attempted to introduce several reforms during their reign, particularly under Ferdinand II, who sought to modernize the kingdom's infrastructure and economy. However, their rule was generally marked by oppressive policies, deep social inequality, and resistance to liberal ideas. Poverty and unrest were widespread, and the failure of the Bourbons to effectively address the economic needs of the people, combined with their authoritarian tendencies, made their rule highly unpopular in Sicily.

Social Unrest and Economic Hardship

Sicily experienced growing social unrest under Bourbon rule, exacerbated by economic hardship and the repression of political movements advocating for greater autonomy or independence. The island's agricultural economy remained stagnant, and the gap between the wealthy aristocracy and the poor widened.

This discontent fueled a desire for change, setting the stage for Sicily to become a crucial part of the Risorgimento, the movement for Italian unification.

The Thousand and Garibaldi's Role

During the Risorgimento—the 19th-century political and social movement that sought to unite Italy—Sicily emerged as a key battleground. In 1860, the island played a pivotal role in the movement when Giuseppe Garibaldi, a nationalist and military leader, landed in Sicily with his force of just over 1,000 volunteers, known as the "Thousand" (I Mille). These volunteers, many of whom were young men from northern Italy, launched a campaign against the Bourbon forces, symbolizing the larger struggle for Italian unity. Although vastly outnumbered by the well-armed Bourbon troops, Garibaldi's expedition gained widespread support from Sicilians who were eager to overthrow Bourbon's rule. His force swiftly advanced through Sicily, capturing Palermo and other key cities. The success of Garibaldi's "Thousand" was due not only to his military skill but also to the backing of local populations, who saw his movement as a path to liberation from Bourbon oppression.

Unification with Italy

By 1861, Garibaldi had successfully toppled Bourbon rule in Sicily, paving the way for the island to be incorporated into the newly formed Kingdom of Italy. This marked the beginning of a new chapter in Sicily's history, as the island became part of a united Italian state, although challenges like regional inequality and social unrest would continue in the years following unification.

Modern Sicily: Challenges and Resilience

Since becoming part of Italy, Sicily has faced many challenges; however, the island has also shown remarkable resilience and adaptability. Sicily's vibrant culture, rich history, and stunning landscapes attract millions of visitors each year. Sicily continues to celebrate its diverse heritage through festivals, cuisine, and architecture. The island's historical sites, from ancient Greek ruins to Norman cathedrals, offer a window into its past, while its modern cities like Palermo and Catania blend history with contemporary life.

Chapter Forty-Three
Dining and Sicilian Specialties

Types of Italian Eateries

1. Ristorante

- The most formal dining option. Offers a full menu with a wide selection of dishes.
- Often more expensive and suitable for special occasions

2. Trattoria

- A less formal, family-run establishment. Serves traditional, home-style cooking.
- Usually offers a more limited menu than a ristorante.
- Less expensive and popular with locals

3. Osteria

- Traditionally a place serving wine and simple food. Modern osterie often offer a full menu similar to trattorias.

- Known for a casual atmosphere and reasonable prices

4. Pizzeria

- Specializes in pizza, often wood-fired, may also offer pasta dishes and salads
- Can be sit-down restaurants or take-away establishments

5. Tavola Calda

- Literally "hot table," similar to a cafeteria
- Offers pre-made hot and cold dishes
- Good for a quick, inexpensive meal

6. Bar/Caffè

- Serves coffee, pastries, and light snacks. Often stands in for breakfast spots in Italy.
- Some offer sandwiches or simple meals for lunch

7. Enoteca

- Wine bar that may also serve food. Great for wine tasting and light meals.

Traditional Structure of an Italian Meal

A full Italian meal typically comprises several courses:

1. Aperitivo

- A pre-meal drink to stimulate the appetite
- Often accompanied by small snacks

2. Antipasto

- The appetizer course can include cured meats, cheeses, olives, or small hot dishes

3. Primo

- The first course, usually pasta, risotto, or soup
- Portions are typically smaller than a main course in other cultures

4. Secondo

- The main course, typically meat or fish. Rarely includes side dishes.

5. Contorno

- Side dishes, often ordered separately. Usually vegetable-based, like salads or grilled vegetables.

6. Dolce

- Dessert course can include cakes, pastries, or gelato.

7. Caffè

- A shot of espresso to end the meal

8. Digestivo

- An after-dinner drink like grappa, amaro, or limoncello

Remember, it's unnecessary to order every course. Many Italians might only have a primo or a secondo with a contorno, especially at lunch. Order as much or as little as you like!

In Sicily, you might also encounter some unique local eateries:

- **Rosticceria:** Shops selling ready-made foods like arancini, calzones, and other Sicilian specialties.
- **Pasticceria:** Pastry shops, often doubling as cafes, where you can find traditional Sicilian sweets.

Traditional Sicilian Dishes to Try on your Trip

Sicily's cuisine is a feast for the senses, blending Italian, Greek, Arab, and Spanish influences into dishes bursting with history and flavor. Here are some iconic Sicilian creations you absolutely must savor during your visit:

1. **Arancini**

    - Golden, crispy rice balls with a molten heart of savory meat ragù, gooey mozzarella, and tender peas—a comforting bite of Sicily's soul.

2. **Pasta alla Norma**

    - A symphony of flavors in honor of Bellini's opera, this dish features al dente pasta bathed in rich tomato sauce, crowned with fried eggplant, fresh basil, and tangy ricotta salata.

3. **Caponata**

    - A tantalizing medley of sweet and sour eggplant, crunchy celery, briny olives, and capers—a versatile dish enjoyed as an antipasto or a luscious side.

4. **Pasta con le Sarde**

    - A harmonious marriage of sardines, wild fennel, pine nuts, and raisins. This dish offers a unique dance between sweet and savory that is unmistakably Sicilian.

5. **Involtini di Pesce Spada**

    - Delicate swordfish fillets rolled around a flavorful filling of breadcrumbs, pine nuts, and raisins, delivering a sophisticated taste of the Mediterranean.

6. **Parmigiana di Melanzane**

    - Layers of tender eggplant, vibrant tomato sauce, and melty cheese—Sicily's eggplant-centric take on lasagna, oozing with rustic charm.

7. **Cannoli**

    - The epitome of Sicilian desserts: crisp pastry tubes filled with velvety sweet ricotta cream, often adorned with pistachios, chocolate chips, or candied fruit.

8. **Cassata Siciliana**

    - A decadent masterpiece of sponge cake, sweet ricotta, marzipan, and jewel-like candied fruit—a dessert as vibrant as Sicily itself.

9. **Granita**

    - A refreshing semi-frozen delight in flavors like lemon, almond, or coffee, often paired with a warm, pillowy brioche for the ultimate Sicilian breakfast.

10. **Panelle**

    - Crispy chickpea fritters, beloved as Palermo's quintessential street food, perfect for a quick snack on the go.

11. **Sfincione**

    - Sicily's answer to pizza: a thick, fluffy crust topped with sweet tomato sauce, caramelized onions, anchovies, and a sprinkling of breadcrumbs.

12. **Frutta Martorana**

    - Exquisite marzipan creations sculpted and painted to resemble lifelike fruits—a whimsical and artistic treat.

13. **Pistacchio di Bronte**

    - The emerald green treasure of Sicily, these pistachios are transformed into velvety pesto, luscious desserts, or nutty pasta sauces—a must-try indulgence.

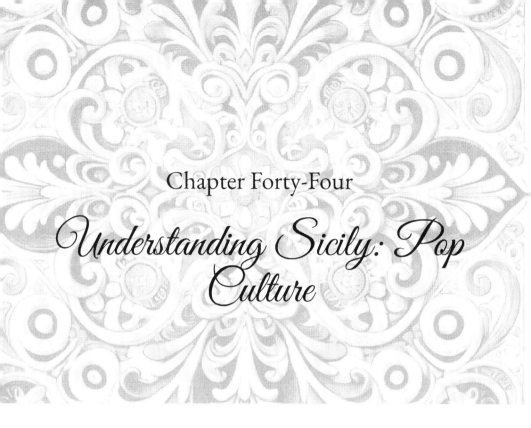

Chapter Forty-Four

Understanding Sicily: Pop Culture

1. Cinema and Television

Il Commissario Montelbano

Il Commissario Montalbano is a popular Italian television series based on the detective novels by Andrea Camilleri. The show is set in the fictional town of Vigàta in Sicily, but it's actually filmed in various locations throughout southeastern Sicily, particularly in the provinces of Ragusa and Syracuse.

Relationship to Ragusa, Scicli, and Noto:

Ragusa: Many scenes in the series are filmed in Ragusa Ibla, the old town of Ragusa. The baroque architecture and picturesque streets of Ragusa Ibla often serve as a backdrop for Montalbano's investigations. Some specific locations include:

- Piazza Duomo: Often featured in the show
- Circolo di Conversazione: Appears as Vigàta's social club

- Various streets and buildings in Ragusa Ibla

Noto: While Noto itself isn't as prominently featured as Ragusa, it's part of the broader Val di Noto region where much of the filming takes place. The show showcases the stunning baroque architecture that Noto is famous for.

Scicli: The town hall of Scicli is used as the exterior of Montalbano's police station. Scicli is also where the filming sets are still available to visit.

Other nearby locations frequently used in the show include:

- Punta Secca: The beach house of Montalbano is located here
- Modica: Another baroque town that appears in various episodes

Other TV Series Filmed in Sicily

Young Montelbano (Il Giovane Montalbano). Filmed in Ragusa, Modica and Scicli.

The Godfather Films: Explore the connection between Sicily and The Godfather trilogy. Include locations like Savoca and Forza d'Agrò, where iconic scenes were filmed.

Cinema Paradiso: Highlight the award-winning Sicilian film that portrays life, love, and cinema in a small town.

Lions of Sicily Series. Filmed in and around Palermo. Hulu.

White Lotus (Season 2, 2022). Filmed in Taormina. HBO

2. Literature

Andrea Camilleri: Include his Inspector Montalbano series, which has a cult following in Italy and abroad.

Giovanni Verga: Highlight Cavalleria Rusticana and its depiction of Sicilian life.

Luigi Pirandello: Discuss works like Six Characters in Search of an Author and his role as a Nobel Prize-winning Sicilian playwright and author.

3. Music

Traditional Sicilian Music: Highlight folk instruments like the friscalettu (flute) and marranzano (jaw harp).

Contemporary Sicilian Artists: Mention singers like Carmen Consoli, who blends modern music with Sicilian roots.

Sicilian Opera and Classical Music: Discuss the influence of Vincenzo Bellini and Sicilian opera traditions.

4. Festivals with Pop Culture Impact

Sagra del Mandorlo in Fiore (Almond Blossom Festival): Its colorful folkloric roots and influence on representations of Sicilian tradition.

Infiorata of Noto: Known for its Instagram-worthy floral carpets.

5. Sicilian Cuisine in Pop Culture

Cannoli: Made famous in The Godfather ("Leave the gun, take the cannoli").

Arancini: A dish featured in many contemporary films and TV series set in Sicily.

Chef's Table Influence: Discuss the rise of Sicilian cuisine internationally, including restaurants like Anna Tasca Lanza's cooking school.

6. Sicilian Dialect and Expressions

Language in Media: Highlight the charm of the Sicilian dialect used in films, TV, and songs.

Proverbs and Sayings: Add common Sicilian sayings that reflect the island's philosophy.

7. Visual Arts

Sicilian Cart Art: Discuss its influence on modern design, from Dolce & Gabbana to home decor trends.

Ceramics and Majolica: Link traditional pottery with contemporary art and souvenirs.

8. Influences in Fashion

Dolce & Gabbana: Highlight how the brand frequently draws inspiration from Sicilian traditions, landscapes, and culture.

Ceramic Head Motifs (Teste di Moro): A popular design element tied to Sicilian legends and fashion.

9. Sicilian Sports

Soccer Teams: Palermo FC and their influence in local pride and identity.

Traditional Sports: Mention events like the Palio di Castelbuono or historical sword tournaments.

10. Influential Sicilian Figures

Frank Sinatra: His Sicilian heritage and impact on pop culture.

Mario Puzo: Author of The Godfather, who drew from Sicilian influences.

Rita Levi-Montalcini: Nobel Prize-winning Sicilian scientist.

Chapter Forty-Five

Transportation Detail

Airports

Sicily has three major airports.

1. Catania-Fontanarossa Airport (CTA)

Location: 4.3 kilometers (2 miles) southwest of Catania

- Also known as: Vincenzo Bellini Airport
- Why it's special: The busiest airport in Sicily, handling over 10 million passengers annually
- Best for: Accessing eastern Sicily, including Taormina, Syracuse, and Mount Etna
- Fun fact: Named after Vincenzo Bellini, a famous opera composer born in Catania

2. Palermo Airport (PMO)

Location: 35 kilometers (22 miles) west of Palermo

- Also known as: Falcone-Borsellino Airport

- Why it's special: The second-busiest airport in Sicily, serving the capital city

- Best for: Exploring western Sicily, including Palermo, Cefalù, and the Egadi Islands

- Fun fact: Named after two anti-mafia judges, Giovanni Falcone and Paolo Borsellino

3. Trapani-Birgi Airport (TPS)

Location: 15 kilometers (9 miles) south of Trapani

- Also known as: Vincenzo Florio Airport

- Why it's special: A hub for low-cost carriers, making it budget-friendly

- Best for: Reaching western Sicily and the Egadi Islands

- Fun fact: Also serves as a military airport

The Supporting Cast: Other Sicilian Airports

While the big three handle most international traffic, Sicily has a few more airports worth mentioning:

1. **Comiso Airport (CIY)**: A small airport in southeastern Sicily, useful for reaching Ragusa and the southern coast.

2. **Lampedusa Airport (LMP)**: Serves the island of Lampedusa, Italy's southernmost territory.

3. **Pantelleria Airport (PNL)**: Connects the volcanic island of Pantelleria to Sicily and mainland Italy.

Choosing Your Landing Spot

When deciding which airport to fly into, consider:

- Your itinerary: Which part of Sicily do you plan to explore first?

- Flight options: International flights are more frequent to Catania and Palermo.

- Ground transportation: How will you get from the airport to your destination?

- Budget: Trapani often offers cheaper flights but may have fewer options.

Remember, Sicily isn't huge (it's about the size of Vermont in the US, slightly larger than Wales in the UK, or about half the size of Tasmania in Australia), so you're never too far from your destination, regardless of where you land. Each airport offers its own unique welcome to the island, from Catania's views of Mount Etna to Palermo's bustling energy.

So, whether you're soaring in over sparkling coasts or touching down with a view of ancient ruins, your Sicilian adventure begins the moment your plane starts its descent. Benvenuti in Sicilia!

Navigating the Island - Overview

Trains: Sicily's rail network (see list of train station in Transportation Details chapter) operated by Trenitalia, weaves through the island like iron threads in an ancient tapestry. We found the trains to be new, clean, and on time.

Bus Services: I have found the bus services in Italy easy to navigate. I like to sit in the front seat for maximum views. In Sicily, several bus companies operate to connect cities, towns, and rural areas. The primary websites you can use to check bus schedules and book tickets are:

Boats and Ferries: Being an island, Sicily naturally incorporates maritime transport into its tapestry. Ferries and hydrofoils connect Sicily to its smaller islands like Lipari and Ustica, as well as to the Italian mainland. These maritime strands offer a chance to feel the sea breeze. Booking in advance is recommended.

Car Rentals: Several well-known car rental agencies operate in Sicily, providing a range of vehicle options across major cities, airports, and tourist destinations.

Trains in Detail: Cities and Towns in Sicily with Trenitalia Stations

These are the larger stations across Sicily. We found the TrenItalia trains to be new and on time.

Website: https://www.trenitalia.com/en.html

Main Cities with Trenitalia Stations

1. Palermo – Palermo Centrale
2. Catania – Catania Centrale
3. Messina – Messina Centrale
4. Syracuse (Siracusa) – Siracusa Station
5. Trapani – Trapani Station
6. Agrigento – Agrigento Centrale and Agrigento Bassa
7. Caltanissetta – Caltanissetta Centrale and Caltanissetta Xirbi
8. Ragusa – Ragusa Station
9. Enna – Enna Station
10. Gela – Gela Station
11. Marsala – Marsala Station
12. Mazara del Vallo – Mazara del Vallo Station
13. Milazzo – Milazzo Station
14. Patti – Patti-San Piero Patti
15. Barcellona Pozzo di Gotto – Barcellona-Castroreale Station
16. Termini Imerese – Termini Imerese Station

17. Cefalù – Cefalù Station

18. Alcamo – Alcamo Diramazione and Alcamo Marina

Smaller Towns with Trenitalia Stations

1. Modica

2. Comiso

3. Caronia

4. Cammarata-San Giovanni Gemini

5. Acireale

6. Giardini Naxos (near Taormina)

7. Castelvetrano

8. Sant'Agata di Militello

9. Falcone

10. Fiumefreddo di Sicilia

11. Taormina-Giardini

12. Bagheria

13. Lentini

14. Augusta

15. Noto

16. Licata

17. Capo d'Orlando-Naso

18. Santo Stefano di Camastra-Mistretta

Additional Information

- The rail network in Sicily is primarily operated by Trenitalia. There are two main lines: the northern coast line and the southern line. For the most up-to-date and detailed information, always check with Trenitalia or local transportation authority's when planning a trip.

- Train services in Sicily can be limited compared to other parts of Italy, and in some cases, buses might be more frequent or convenient for travel between certain locations.

Ferrovia Circumetnea Stations (Selected Cities Along Mt. Etna)

The Ferrovia Circumetnea is a narrow-gauge railway that circles the base of Mount Etna, providing a more retro, scenic, and leisurely travel experience compared to modern rail systems. Its route, built in the late 19th century, is around 110 kilometers long, and it connects several small towns, vineyards, and scenic landscapes around the volcano. The trains are smaller, slower, and more traditional, giving passengers a unique, vintage feel as they traverse the countryside.

Website: https://www.circumetnea.it/

- Catania – Borgo Station (Circumetnea terminus)

- Paternò

- Adrano

- Bronte

- Randazzo

- Linguaglossa

- Riposto (also served by Trenitalia)

Buses – The Detail

Where trains don't reach, buses fill the gaps. Think of them as the flexible fibers in our tapestry, connecting smaller towns and hard-to-reach villages. Companies like AST and SAIS offer routes that criss-cross the island, often at prices that will make your wallet smile.

Bus Services: I have found the bus services in Italy easy to navigate. I like to sit in the front seat for maximum views. In Sicily, several bus companies operate to connect cities, towns, and rural areas. The primary websites you can use to check bus schedules and book tickets are:

Interbus (www.interbus.it): A major bus service covering routes between cities like Palermo, Catania, and Syracuse, as well as many smaller towns across Sicily.

AST (Azienda Siciliana Trasporti) (www.aziendasicilianatrasporti.it): AST operates many regional routes throughout the island, connecting smaller towns and rural areas to major cities.

Sais Trasporti (www.saistrasporti.it): Another popular company offering both regional and long-distance routes, including connections between Sicily and mainland Italy.

These websites allow you to check routes, timetables, and book tickets online. If you are traveling between smaller villages or more remote areas, buses are often the most convenient form of public transportation. It's also a good idea to check schedules in advance, as frequencies may vary, especially on weekends or holidays.

Ferry and Hydrofoil

Here are some websites for ferry and hydrofoil companies that operate in Sicily:

Liberty Lines (hydrofoils)

They provide high-speed services to the Aeolian Islands, Egadi Islands, and other Sicilian destinations.

https://www.libertylines.it/en/

Siremar (ferries and hydrofoils)

Siremar connects mainland Italy with Sicily and the surrounding islands, including the Aeolian and Egadi Islands.

https://www.siremar.it/

Grandi Navi Veloci (GNV) (Ferries)

GNV offers ferry services between mainland Italy and Sicily, including routes to Palermo.

Tirrenia (ferries)

Tirrenia operates ferries from mainland Italy to various Sicilian ports, including Palermo.

https://en.tirrenia.it/

Caronte & Tourist (ferries)

They offer ferry services between mainland Italy (Villa San Giovanni) and Sicily (Messina).

https://carontetourist.it/en

These companies cover various routes, making it easy to plan travel between Sicily and the surrounding islands or mainland Italy.

Rental Car Options

Several well-known car rental agencies operate in Sicily, providing a range of vehicle options across major cities, airports, and tourist destinations. Here are some popular international and local car rental companies in Sicily:

International Car Rental Agencies

1. Hertz

- Locations: Palermo, Catania, Trapani, Syracuse, Agrigento, and more.
- Known for a wide range of vehicles and flexible services.

2. Avis

- Locations: Palermo, Catania, Trapani, Syracuse, and other key cities.
- Offers various types of vehicles, including compact cars, sedans, and SUVs.

3. Europcar

- Locations: Available at major airports and cities like Palermo, Catania, Trapani, and Messina.
- Offers a large fleet, including eco-friendly options.

4. Sixt

- Locations: Primarily at major airports (Palermo, Catania, and Trapani).
- Known for premium and luxury vehicle options, as well as more budget-friendly options.

5. Budget

- Locations: Palermo, Catania, Trapani, and other popular areas.
- Focuses on affordable rentals with a wide variety of vehicle sizes.

6. Enterprise

- Locations: Available in major cities and airports in Sicily.
- Offers a range of vehicles from economy to premium.

7. Thrifty

- Locations: Primarily available at airports and major city locations.
- Offers cost-effective rental options with a straightforward service.

Local Car Rental Agencies

1. Sicily by Car

- Locations: Available throughout Sicily, including airports in Palermo, Catania, and Trapani.
- A local favorite, offering a wide selection of vehicles at competitive prices.

2. Noleggiare

- Locations: Available in main cities and airports across the island.
- Known for good customer service and a mix of vehicle options.

3. Locauto

- Locations: Major cities and airports.
- Offers a range of cars from economy to premium, with flexible terms.

4. Maggiore

- Locations: Across all major airports and cities in Sicily.
- One of Italy's oldest car rental companies, providing quality service and vehicles.

Tips for Renting a Car in Sicily

Book in advance, especially during high tourist seasons (spring to fall), to secure availability and better rates.

Check insurance options: Sicily's narrow roads and city traffic can be challenging, so ensure you're covered for accidents and damages.

Renting an automatic car: If you're not used to driving manual vehicles, request an automatic, as manuals are more common in Italy. These do cost more but make life easier for sure.

Chapter Forty-Six

Accommodation Detail

Sicily offers a wide range of accommodation options to suit every traveler's needs and budget. Here's a comprehensive guide to help you choose the perfect place to rest your head during your Sicilian adventure:

1. Hotels

Hotels in Sicily are graded with one to five stars, reflecting their amenities and service levels.

- One-star hotels: Basic accommodations with shared bathrooms.
- Two-star hotels: Simple rooms with private bathrooms.
- Three-star hotels: Comfortable rooms with additional amenities like TV and mini-fridge.
- Four-star hotels: Higher quality accommodations with room service and often a restaurant on-site.
- Five-star hotels: Luxury accommodations with full services, often including spa facilities and gourmet restaurants.

Websites: Booking.com, Hotels.com, Expedia

2. Private Rooms and B&Bs

These offer a more personal touch and often provide insights into local life. They range from spare rooms in family homes to professionally run guesthouses.

Websites: Airbnb, Booking.com, BedandBreakfast.com

3. Holiday Apartments

Self-catering apartments are great for longer stays or for those who prefer more independence. They often provide better value for families or groups.

Websites: Airbnb, Booking.com, VRBO

4. Rural Accommodations

Agriturismo

These are working farms that offer accommodation. They provide a unique opportunity to experience rural Sicilian life and often serve home-cooked meals made with farm-fresh ingredients.

Wineries

Some Sicilian wineries offer on-site accommodation, allowing you to immerse yourself in Sicily's wine culture.

Websites: Agriturismo.it, ItalyFarmStay

5. Hostels

Hostels offer budget-friendly accommodations, often with shared rooms and communal facilities. They're great for solo travelers looking to meet others.

Websites: Hostelworld, Hostelling International

6. Campsites

Sicily has many campsites for outdoor enthusiasts, ranging from basic to well-equipped sites with amenities like pools and restaurants.

Websites: Eurocampings, ACSI

References & Resources

Calendar, Alphabetical Index, Glossary, Index, and Inspirations

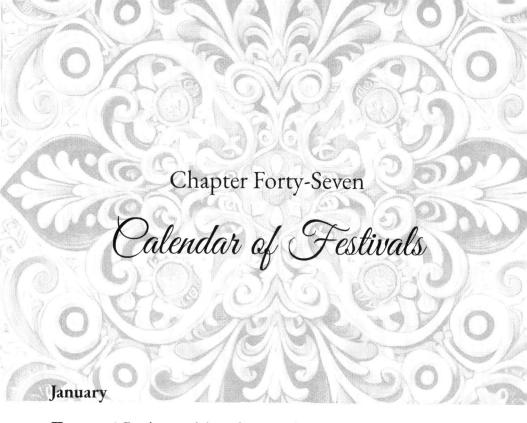

Chapter Forty-Seven

Calendar of Festivals

January

January 6: Epiphany and the Befana in Cefalu and throughout Italy

January 20: Festival of St. Sebastian (San Sebastino) in Syracusa and Acireale

February

February 3-5: Festival of St. Agatha (Sant'Agata) in Catania and Palermo

February 19: Festival of Saint Conrad (San Corrado) in Syracuse and Noto

February mid-month: Festival of the Almond Flower in Taormina

February: Carnival throughout Italy but included in Cefalu

March

March 19, Saturday closest to March 19: Ride of St. Jospeh in Scicli

March (late March): Ricotta Cheese Festival in Piana degli Albanesi

April

April 23: Feast of St George the Great Martyr in Piana degli Albanesi

April Holy Week

- Good Friday: Feast of Our Lady of Sorrows in Naro
- Good Friday: Procession of the Mysteries in Trapani
- Holy Week: Acireale and Erice
- Easter: The Joy of Easter in Scicli

May

May 1: One Day Music Festival in Catania

May 1: The Tomato and Grape Festival in Scicli

May 1-3: Feast of the Holy Crucifix in Monreale

Weekends May to July: Fish Festival in Syracuse

Fridays in May: Sicilian Cart Festival in Taormina

First Sunday in May: Feast of St. Lucy of the Quails in Syracuse

2nd weekend in May: Cannolo Festival in Piana degli Albanesi

3rd weekend in May: Infiorata of Noto

3rd weekend in May: Trapani Comix and Games Festival in Trapani

Last Saturday in May: Festival of the Madonna in Scicli

Last Sunday in May: Festival of Saint George in Ragusa

Late May and Early June: Festival of Kites in San Vito Lo Capo

Late May: Beer Catania Spring

June

June to September: Catania Summer Fest in Catania

June to September: Marranzano World Fest (Folk Music) in Catania

June 3: Feast of Saint Mary of the Letter in Messina

June 6-9: Etna Comics in Catania

June to August: Taormina Art Festival in Taormina

June 9: Feast of St. Pancras in Taormina

June 13: Feast of St. Anthony in Messina

June 15-17 Festival of St. Vito in San Vito Lo Capo

June 15-25 Feast of St. Calogero in Naro

June 18: Feast of St. Calogero in Agrigento

June 18-19: Feast of St. Calogero in Cesaro

June 24: Feast of St. John the Baptist in Ragusa and Naro

June 29: Feast of St. Peter and St. Paul in Castelbuono

June with Dates that Vary

June: Caper Festival in Lipari

June: Lemon Festival in Acireale

June: Pentacost Fair in Noto (50 days after Easter)

June on Sunday of Corpus Christi (first Sunday after Pentacost): Infiorata in Cefalu and Piazza Armerina

Late June: Strawberry Festival in Maletto

Late June for two weeks: Sicilia Jazz Festival in Palermo

End of June: Palermo Pride in Palermo

July

July 10-15 Festival of St. Rosalia in Palermo

July 16: Festival of Our Lady of Mt. Carmel in Noto

July 25-27: Festival of St. Ann in Castelbuono

July 26: Festa di St. Vanera in Acireale

July and August: Monreale Summer Festival in Monreale

July and August: The Maletto Summer Festival in Maletto

July and August: Opera Festival in Trapani

Last weekend in July: Stragusto Street Food Festival in Trapani

July with Dates that Vary

Ortygia Film Festival in Syracuse

Welcome Back Tony Scott Festival in Salemi

Festival of the Sea in Messina

August

August: Tiles of Light Festival throughout August in Scicli

August 2-6: Festival of the Crying Madonna in Cefalu

1st Saturday in August: Macaroni Festival in Librizzi

August 7: Festival of St. Albert in Trapani

August 8-11: Festivalle (Jazz Festival) in Agrigento

August 10: Festival of St. Lawrence in Piazza Armerina

August 10-14: Parade of Giants in Messina

2nd Sunday: Feast of Mary who Shows the Way in Bronte

August 12-14: Palio of the Normans in Piazza Armerina

August 15: Ferragosto, Feast of the Assumption of Mary throughout Italy and specifically in Messina

August 15: Feast of Our Lady of Victories in Piazza Armerina

August 15: Feast of Our Lady of the Chain in Librizzi

August 16: Festival of St. Mary in Trapani

August 24: Feast of St. Bartholomew in Lipari

August 29 to September 1: Festival of the Crying Madonna in Syracuse

Last week: The Feast of our Lady of Custonaci in Erice

August with Dates that Vary

Taranta Jazz Festival in Scicli

Jazz Festival in Taormina

Opera Festival in Trapani

Eggplant Festival in Messina

Festival of Bread and Wine in Lipari

Ypisgrock Festival (Music Festival) in Castelbuono

September

September 2: Feast of St. Mary Hodegetria in Piana degli Albanesi

September 2: Feast of St. Julian in Erice

September 8: Feast of the Madonna of Health in San Vito Lo Capo

September 29: Feast of St. Michael the Archangel in Maletto, Caltanisetta and Librizzi

Throughout September: Sicilian Cart Festival in Taormina

September with Dates that Vary

Castelbuono Jazz Festival in Castelbuono

Grape Must Festival in Librizzi

Grape Harvest Festival in Bronte

Tomato Festival in Caltanisetta

Festival of Madonna of the Light in Cafalu

Monreale Organ Festival in Monreale

October

1st Two Weeks: Festival of the Ficodindia (Cactus fruit) and Mostarda (Grape Must) in Militello in Val di Catania.

October 26: Feast of St. Demetrius in Piana degli Albanesi

October with Dates that Vary

Wild Boar Festival in Ragusa

Ibla Buskers Festival in Ragusa

Stairs of Taste Food Festival in Ragusa

Taormina Gourmet in Taormina

Chestnut Festival in Maletto

Mushroom Festival in Castelbuono

Festival of Knowledge in Acireale

Sagra della Scaccia Ragusana (traditional bread) in Ragusa

November with Dates that Vary

The Morgana Puppet Festival in Palermo

The Medieval Festival in Trapani

December

December 6: Festival of St. Nicholas in Messina and Bronte

December 8: Feast of the Immaculate Conception in Noto

December 28: Procession of Three Saints in Caltinasetta

Throughout December: Nativity Scenes of Palermo

Throughout December: Christmas Market Monreale

Chapter Forty-Eight

Alphabetical Index of Locations with Events

Acireale, Carnival, March	Militello in Val di Catania, Festa della Madonna della Stella, September
Aeolian Islands. Immersion Experience.	Mondello Beach. Immersion Experience.
Agrigento, Festa di San Gerlando, February	Monreale, Festa di San Castrense, February
Agrigento, Almond Blossom Festival, February	Mount Etna, 4x4 Tour. Immersion Experience
Bronte, Pistachio Festival, September	Naro, Festa di San Calogero, June
Caltagirone, Festa di Maria Santissima, August	Noto, Infiorata, May
Caltanissetta, Holy Week and Easter, March	Palermo, Palermo Jazz Festival, June
Castelbuono, Festa di San Martino, November	Palermo, Festa di Santa Rosalia, July
Catania, Festa di Sant'Agata, February	Piana degli Albanesi, Festival of the Cannolo, May
Cefalu, Epiphany and La Befana, January	Piazza Armerina, Palio Dei Normanni, August,
Cesaro, Black Pig and Porcini Festival, October	Ragusa, Festa di San Giorgio, May
Egadi Islands. Immersion Experience	Salemi, Festa di San Giuseppe, March
Erice, Summer Festival, July to August	San Vito Lo Capo, Cous Cous Festival, September
Erice, Festa di Madonna Santissima di Custonaci, August	Scala dei Turchi. Immersion Experience.
Lakes of Avola. Immersion Experience.	Scicli, Festa della Madonna delle Milizie, May
Librizzi, Macaroni Festival, August	Syracusa (Syracuse), Festa di Santa Lucia, December
Lipari, Festa di San Bartolomeo, August	Taormina, Festa di San Pancrazio, July
Magna Via Francigena. Immersion Experience.	Taormina, Taormina Art Festival, June
Maletto, Strawberry Festival, June	Trapani, Stragusto Street Food Festival, July
Messina, Parade of Giants, Ferragosto, August	Taormina, Taormina Art Festival, June
Militello in Val di Catania, Festa di Santissimo Salvatore, August	Trapani, Stragusto Street Food Festival, July

Chapter Forty-Nine

A Glossary of Key Terms

Albergo / Locanda: Hotel

Agriturismo: Agriturismo is a form of rural tourism in Italy that combines agricultural activities with hospitality services, offering travelers an immersive experience in the countryside. Derived from the Italian words agricoltura (agriculture) and turismo (tourism), an agriturismo typically involves staying on a working farm where guests can enjoy accommodations, authentic local cuisine, and activities related to rural life.

Agriturismi (plural) often highlight sustainable practices and traditions, providing opportunities for guests to engage in activities like wine tasting, olive oil production, cooking classes, or harvesting seasonal produce.

Angevin Rule: (1266 – 1282). After the defeat of the Hohenstaufens, Sicily was given to Charles of Anjou, marking the start of Angevin rule. However, Charles' reign was short-lived, as it led to the Sicilian Vespers uprising in 1282, expelling the Angevins.

Argonese Rule: (1282 – 1410). Following the Sicilian Vespers, Peter III of Aragon was invited to take control of Sicily, establishing Aragonese rule. The Crown of Aragon ruled the island as part of a larger Mediterranean empire.

Basilica: A term derived from the official building of a Greek magistrate, Basileus.

In antiquity, it was a roofed building with a double colonnade used for law courts, assemblies, or markets. In the Christian era, it meant a characteristic type of church building with a high nave and two or four aisles. Usually oriented to the west. basilicas usually have windows on the elevated part of the walls (clerestory) where the roof meets the wall. A basilica is the shape of Catholic churches since the 4th century. The Pope has given a Basilica special privileges as a major church.

Benedictines: St. Benedict of Nursia (c. 480-547) founded the oldest order of Western monks. 529AD. The Benedictine rules formed the basis of western monasticism. The primary task was to cultivate liturgy and prayer. Physical labor, scholarly and artistic work supplemented this.

Brotherhoods: The brotherhoods, or "confraternite" in Italian, are religious lay organizations that play a crucial role in preserving and celebrating local traditions of the region. These brotherhoods have deep historical roots, often dating back centuries, and are named after various saints or religious concepts.

Bourbon Dynasty: (1734-1860) The Bourbons were a European royal dynasty that ruled over various territories, including Sicily and southern Italy, during the 18th and 19th centuries. Their influence in Sicily began when Ferdinand IV of Naples (also known as Ferdinand III of Sicily) became king of the Kingdom of Sicily in 1759. The Bourbon rule in Sicily was a significant period in the island's history, particularly as part of the larger Kingdom of the Two Sicilies, which included both Sicily and the southern Italian mainland.

Byzantine architecture: This style relates to the architecture developed in the Byzantine or Eastern Roman Empire. Characterized by enormous domes, mosaics, rounded arches, and spires.

Campanile: A bell tower of an Italian church. Sometimes, a watchtower for the town, the bell tower, grew in importance during the Renaissance.

Centro Storico: The historic center of town.

Chiesa di. Church of followed usually by a saint's name.

Chiesa Madre: Mother church or the most important church in town. This is not a duomo or cathedral.

Cinquecento: A term shortened in Italian from mille-cinquecento. It means the

1500s or the 16th century.

Cistercians: The Cistercians are a monastic Catholic order that has its origins in the reformed Benedictine monastery of Citaeux founded in 1098. The new order set out to achieve fully the ideal from the Rule of St. Benedict.

Confraternite: Religious brotherhoods composed of laypeople dedicated to prayer, charity, and community service, especially within Catholic traditions. Confraternities in Italy, including those in Sicily, are often responsible for organizing and participating in religious processions during major festivals. During events such as the Festa di Santa Rosalia in Palermo, the confraternities don traditional garments—typically long tunics and capes—carrying banners and religious symbols. They play a key role in maintaining the solemnity and spiritual focus of the event, embodying centuries-old traditions of faith and devotion.

Consul: A Roman consul was one of the highest-ranking elected officials in the Roman Republic. After the overthrow of the Roman monarchy, the Romans introduced the office of consul around 509 BC. The Roman Republic elected two consuls each year to serve jointly for a one-year term. They held significant power and responsibilities.

Corso / Via: Street.

DOC: DOC stands for Denominazione di Origine Controllata (Designation of Controlled Origin) in Italian. It is a quality assurance label for Italian wines, cheeses, and other agricultural products. This classification guarantees that the product meets strict production standards and comes from a specific geographic area.

Duomo or Cattedrale: These are all referred to as the town's Cathedral but they have different significance. Cathedral means the main church of the diocese where the bishop's seat is located. Duomo is the Italian word for Cathedral, but both Duomo and Cattedrale are used when seeking the bishop's seat in Italy.

Habsburgs: A royal family originally from Switzerland that virtually monopolized the title of Holy Roman Emperor from 1438 to 1806.

Hohenstaufen Dynasty: The Hohenstaufen dynasty ruled Sicily from 1194 to 1266, following the marriage of Constance of Sicily (daughter of Roger II) to

Emperor Henry VI of the Holy Roman Empire. Under Frederick II, one of the most prominent Hohenstaufen rulers, Sicily became a center of learning, culture, and legal reform, blending Norman, Arab, and Latin influences. Frederick II was known for his progressive policies, fostering religious tolerance and intellectual exchange. The Hohenstaufen rule ended with the defeat of Manfred of Sicily by Charles of Anjou in 1266, leading to the rise of the Angevin dynasty.

Magna Grecia: Greater Greece was a land mass much larger than Greece itself, including a scattered group of Greek city-states that included the lower part of Italy and Sicily. These cities maintained a close alignment with their mother cities on the mainland of Greece, sharing the same conflicts with one another. They founded Siracusa in 734 BC.

Municipio/Comune: Town hall or city hall.

Norman Rule: The Normans, led by Roger I of Hauteville and his brother Robert Guiscard, launched a series of military campaigns starting in 1061 to conquer Sicily from the Arab rulers who had controlled the island for over two centuries. By 1091, the Normans had successfully conquered all of Sicily, marking the end of Muslim rule and the beginning of the Norman Kingdom of Sicily.

Odeon: Odeons were important cultural venues in ancient Greece, fostering the arts and serving as central locations for various forms of entertainment and public discourse.

Piazza: Square where people get together.

Reformation: A major religious movement from within the Catholic Church that began in Germany in 1517 at the instigation of Martin Luther. His challenge of the practices and doctrines of the Roman Catholic Church ultimately led to the establishment of the Protestant churches.

Romanesque: A term used to describe forms of Roman architecture such as rounded arches, columns, capitals, and vaults that were used in buildings in the early Middle Ages. The term Romanesque covers the period from about 1000 to the point when Gothic began.

Spiaggia: Beach.

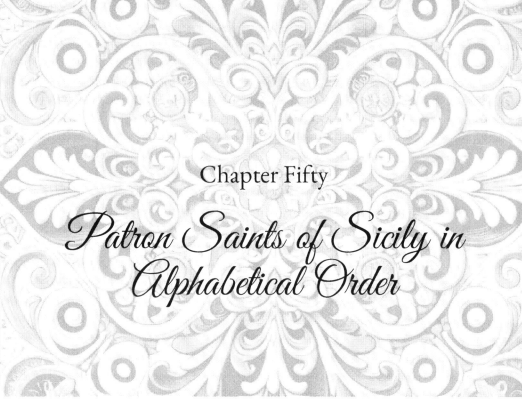

Chapter Fifty

Patron Saints of Sicily in Alphabetical Order

Sant'Agata. According to Catholic tradition, Saint Agatha was martyred during the persecutions under Emperor Decius in the third century. She is venerated as a saint, virgin, and martyr by the Catholic Church, the Orthodox Church, and the Anglican Church, which all honor her memory on February 5. She is the patron saint of Catania, the Republic of San Marino, and the island of Malta. Her principal place of worship is the Cathedral of Saint Agatha in Catania, where her relics rest. Catania dedicates a grand feast to her on February 3, 4, 5, and 6.

San Bartolomeo. St. Bartholomew, also known as Nathanael, was one of the Twelve Apostles of Jesus Christ. His story appears in the New Testament, most notably in the Gospel of John, where he is introduced by the Apostle Philip and becomes a follower of Christ. Known for his honesty and strong faith, he was described by Jesus as "a man in whom there is no deceit." His name, "Bartholomew," means "son of Tolmai" or "son of the furrows." After the Ascension of Christ, Bartholomew is said to have traveled far to spread the Gospel, likely reaching regions such as India, Armenia, Mesopotamia, and Persia.

Tradition holds that St. Bartholomew was martyred for his missionary work, especially in Armenia, where he was said to have been flayed alive and then beheaded for converting people to Christianity. Because of this, Bartholomew is often depicted in Christian art holding his own skin. His feast day is celebrated on August 24 in the Catholic Church, and he is venerated as the patron saint of various professions and places, including butchers, tanners, and leather workers. The town of Lipari in the Aeolian Islands honors him with an annual festival, as he is the island's patron saint, believed to have protected the community from natural disasters and pirate invasions.

San Calogero. San Calogero is a revered saint in Sicily, known for his association with healing and protection. Born in Constantinople in the 5th century, San Calogero is celebrated for his life as a hermit and his dedication to spreading Christianity across Sicily. His legacy in the town of Naro is significant, where he is honored during the annual festival dedicated to him.

San Castrense. San Castrense, also known as Saint Castrensis, was a 5th-century bishop from North Africa who became a revered figure in parts of Italy. During the Vandal persecutions, he and eleven other bishops were exiled by King Genseric, set adrift on a ship intended to sink. Miraculously, they survived and landed on the coast of Campania, Italy. San Castrense eventually settled in Sessa Aurunca, where he dedicated himself to pastoral work until his death.

His veneration spread across various regions, and he is honored as the patron saint of several towns, including Marano di Napoli, Castel Volturno, and San Castrese di Sessa Aurunca. In Monreale, Sicily, his relics are enshrined in the Cathedral's Chapel of San Castrense, a gift from Archbishop Alfano of Capua to King William II on the occasion of his marriage to Joan of England in 1177.

San Gerlando. Believed to be a native of Besançon, Gerland was a relative of the Norman Roger I of Sicily. After the expulsion of the Saracens from Sicily, Roger summoned Gerland in 1088 (or 1093) to serve as the first post-Saracen bishop of Agrigento, with the mission of re-establishing the church across the island. Gerland was canonized in 1159. His relics are housed in a silver urn in Agrigento Cathedral, which has been dedicated to him since its reconstruction by Bishop Bertaldo di Labro in 1305.

San Giorgio (Saint George) is one of Christianity's most venerated saints, famous for his legendary battle with a dragon, symbolizing the triumph of good over evil. Often depicted as a knight on horseback slaying the dragon, San Giorgio is the patron saint of several towns and regions in Italy, including Ragusa and Modica in Sicily. His feast day, typically celebrated on April 23, involves grand processions, reenactments of the dragon-slaying legend, and religious ceremonies.

San Giuseppe. St. Joseph, the earthly father of Jesus and the husband of the Virgin Mary, is a central figure in Christianity, celebrated for his unwavering faith, humility, and protective care of the Holy Family. Though the Gospels offer few direct accounts of his words or actions, Joseph's quiet yet powerful presence is deeply revered. He is often depicted as a compassionate and devoted father, a hardworking carpenter, and a man of profound trust in God's plan. When faced with the miraculous conception of Jesus, Joseph displayed remarkable courage and obedience by accepting his role as protector and provider, guided by dreams sent by God.

In Catholic tradition, St. Joseph is honored as the patron saint of workers, fathers, and the universal Church. His feast day, March 19, is celebrated with devotion around the world, often marked by altars adorned with bread, pastries, and symbolic foods, particularly in Italy and other Mediterranean cultures. These "St. Joseph's Tables" reflect his role as a provider and commemorate his intercession during times of famine. Through his example of selfless love and quiet strength, St. Joseph inspires believers to live lives of integrity, faith, and service to others.

Santa Lucia. Saint Lucy was killed during the great persecution of Christians under Diocletian in 304. She is venerated as a saint by both the Catholic Church and the Orthodox Church, with her feast day celebrated on December 13. Saint Lucy is one of the seven virgins mentioned in the Roman Canon and is traditionally invoked as the protector of sight because of the Latin etymology of her name (Lux, meaning light). Her mortal remains are kept in the Sanctuary of Lucy in Venice. The principal place of worship is the Church of Santa Lucia al Sepolcro in Syracuse.

Madonna della Stella. The festival is called Madonna della Stella (Madonna of the Star) because it is dedicated to the Virgin Mary under the title "Our Lady of the Star." This title reflects a specific devotion to the Virgin Mary, emphasizing her role as a guiding light and protector, much like a star serves as a guiding point in the night sky.

The title "Stella" or "Star" is often used in Marian devotion to symbolize Mary's role in guiding Christians towards Jesus, much like the Star of Bethlehem guided the Wise Men. In many traditions, Mary is referred to as the "Star of the Sea" (Stella Maris), a title that highlights her as a spiritual guide and protector for those navigating the hardships of life.

In Militello in Val di Catania, the devotion to Madonna della Stella is deeply embedded in the local culture and religious practices. The specific association of the Madonna with a star may also have historical or legendary origins particular to the region, reflecting the local community's reverence and the special significance they attribute to this aspect of Marian devotion.

Madonna delle Milizie. The origins of the Madonna delle Milizie date back to the period when Sicily was a contested territory between the Christian Normans and the Muslim Saracens. According to legend, in the year 1091, Scicli was under threat from a Saracen invasion. The local population, fearing destruction, prayed fervently to the Virgin Mary for protection.

During the ensuing battle, the legend states that the Madonna miraculously appeared on horseback, wielding a sword and leading the Christian Normans to a decisive victory against the Saracens. This miraculous intervention was a sign of divine favor, and the Madonna was subsequently honored with the title "Madonna delle Milizie," symbolizing her role as a protector of the town and its people.

San Pancrazio. Pancras, also known as Pancratius (Greek: Παγκράτιος, Pankratios; Italian: Pancrazio), is an Italian saint associated with Taormina and venerated as a Christian martyr. According to legend, Pancras was born in Antioch in Cilicia (modern Adana). He traveled to Jerusalem with his parents during Jesus' ministry, and the family was later baptized in Antioch. Pancras retreated to a cave in Pontus, where he was discovered by Saint Peter, who sent him to Sicily in the year 40 to become the first Bishop of Tauromenium (modern Taormina). He was eventually martyred by stoning by pagan opponents.

Santa Rosalia. Rosalia Sinibaldi (Palermo, 1130–Palermo, September 4, 1170) is venerated as a saint by the Catholic Church. She is the patron saint of Palermo, and her veneration is widespread throughout the city and all of Sicily. The traditional Feast of Santa Rosalia, celebrated in her honor, attracts hundreds of thousands of people from across Sicily. Her relics are preserved in the Cathedral of Palermo, which is dedicated to her and the Virgin of the Assumption.

Chapter Fifty-One

Photo Credits

FestaFusion Taormina. Taormina Teatro Greco: y Radek Kucharski from Warsaw, Poland - Sunset at Greek theater of Taormina, CC BY 2.0, https://commons.wikimedia.org/w/index.php?curid=114368404

Immersion Experience-Wild Swimming and Tranquil Escapes in the Laghetti d'Avola: By Simona Di Salvo - Fonte, CC BY-SA 2.0, https://commons.wikimedia.org/w/index.php?curid=77536737

FestaFusion Piazza Armerina. Villa Romana Mosiac Bikini Girls: by Kenton Greening - Own work, Public Domain, https://commons.wikimedia.org/w/index.php?curid=27300169

Santa Lucia in Procession. La Statua di Santa Lucia durante la festa religiosa della santa patrona siracusana: By Salvo Cannizzaro - www.panoramio.com, CC BY-SA 3.0, via Wikimedia Commons, https://commons.wikimedia.org/w/index.php?curid=27562294

Candelora of the Festa di Sant'Agata Catania. Festa di Sant'Agata (Catania) 04 02 2020 05. by Effems - Own work, CC BY-SA 4.0, https://commons.wikimedia.org/w/index.php?curid=86843282

FestaFusion Taormina. Taormina Teatro Greco: y Radek Kucharski from Warsaw, Poland - Sunset at Greek theater of Taormina, CC BY 2.0, https://commons.wikimedia.org/w/index.php?curid=114368404

Immersion Experience-Wild Swimming and Tranquil Escapes in the Laghetti d'Avola: By Simona Di Salvo - Fonte, CC BY-SA 2.0, https://commons.wikimedia.org/w/index.php?curid=77536737

FestaFusion Piazza Armerina. Villa Romana Mosiac Bikini Girls: by Kenton Greening - Own work, Public Domain, https://commons.wikimedia.org/w/index.php?curid=27300169

Santa Lucia in Procession. La Statua di Santa Lucia durante la festa religiosa della santa patrona siracusana: By Salvo Cannizzaro - www.panoramio.com, CC BY-SA 3.0, via Wikimedia Commons, https://commons.wikimedia.org/w/index.php?curid=27562294

Syracuse from above. Syracusa from Above. By Agostino Artnoir Sella - Ortigia, CC BY-SA 2.0, https://commons.wikimedia.org/w/index.php?curid=31922549

Candelora of the Festa di Sant'Agata Catania. Festa di Sant'Agata (Catania) 04 02 2020 05. by Effems - Own work, CC BY-SA 4.0, https://commons.wikimedia.org/w/index.php?curid=86843282

Chapter Fifty-Two
Thank You & Please Leave a Review

Thank you for reading the *Ultimate Festival and Travel Guide Sicily*. It is the first in the Travel Italy Series.

If the guide enhanced your travel planning, I'd greatly appreciate it if you could leave a review on Amazon. Your feedback not only helps other travelers, but also supports this book's success.

Scan Here to link to the Book on Amazon

I sincerely hope you have enjoyed this tour through Sicily via its festivals. I would love to hear about your own festival adventures! Connect with me on Instagram, where I share hundreds of videos from the festivals of Sicily and Italy—perfect for a sneak peek before your trip.

For even more travel inspiration, visit my blog for deeper dives into Sicily's stunning beaches and off-the-beaten-path gems, which are not covered extensively in this guide. https://katerinaferrara.com/blog/

Thank you for being part of this journey, and I look forward to hearing about yours!

Wishing you the safest and happiest travels!

Katerina Ferrara

Connect with Me

Free Italy Travel Resources and More

Newsletter / Travel News

Sign up for my newsletter and stay updated with insider secrets about Italy's charming towns, vibrant festivals, and mouthwatering food—things you won't find in any travel guide. Stay updated with the latest on festivals, tours, podcasts, and special insights that go beyond the book!

Link to KaterinaFerrara.com

Immersion Travel by Katerina Ferrara Blog

Looking for even more hidden gems in Italy? My blog is packed with insider tips, from secret beaches tucked away on Italy's lesser-known coastlines to self-guided walking tours that take you off the typical tourist path. Whether you're planning a relaxing escape or an adventurous exploration, you'll find everything you need to create unforgettable Italian journeys. Subscribe at for exclusive travel insights and start uncovering Italy's best-kept secrets! www.katerinaferrara.com

Stay Connected

Follow me on social media to see the festivals of Italy as they come to life every day of the year and tag me in your posts when you visit Rome.

Instagram: @KaterinaFerraraAuthor

Festival Enthusiasts - Immersion Travel Italy offers one-of-a-kind experiences for travelers seeking to connect deeply with Italy's culture. We organize small-group journeys to discover Italy's most vibrant festivals and sagre, explore charming towns, and embark on unforgettable adventures. Whether you're savoring local delicacies at a food festival or taking part in centuries-old traditions, our personalized trips allow you to experience the heart and soul of Italy like a local. Join us for an immersive travel experience you'll treasure forever!

Corrections / Updates / Suggestions Oops!

Even the best of us can make mistakes. I would appreciate your help to make my content better. Please visit the book page here: https://katerinaferrara.com/choose the book, and scroll down to the book feedback button.

About the Author: Katerina Ferrara

Katerina Ferrara is a published author and the founder of Immersion Travel Italy, a company dedicated to creating unforgettable travel experiences in Italy. With over 25 years of exploring Europe, Katerina has developed a deep love for immersing herself in the diverse cultures, traditions, and culinary delights of the places she visits. Fluent in Italian, she effortlessly connects with locals and travelers alike, bringing an insider's perspective to her travel writing.

Katerina jokes that she lives her life on a perpetual diet—not for vanity, but to prepare for the next irresistible festival in Italy. Her ultimate dream is to inspire **Festival Followers**—travelers who prioritize experiencing incredible festivals first and then explore the surrounding sites while immersing themselves in local traditions. She believes festivals offer a unique lens into a region's heart and culture, making them the perfect starting point for any adventure.

About the Author: Katerina Ferrara

An avid hiker and fitness enthusiast, Katerina incorporates her passion for staying active into her travels, often seeking out scenic trails, walking tours, and outdoor adventures that connect her to the natural beauty of a destination (while making room for just a little more gelato).

When she's not exploring new destinations or writing, Katerina enjoys sharing her travel insights and tips with fellow adventurers, inspiring them to delve deeper into the cultural richness of the places they visit—and maybe even discover their own favorite festival.

Chapter Fifty-Three

Select Bibliography

Ackerman, James. The Architecture of Michelangelo. Chicago: University of Chicago Press, 1961 (Pelican 1971).

Benjamin, Sandra. Sicily. Three Thousand Years of Human History. Steerforth Press. Hanover, New Hampshire. 2006.

Borsi, Franco. Bernini Architetto. Milan: Electa, 1980.

Burke, Peter. The Italian Renaissance: Culture and Society in Italy. Princeton: Princeton University Press, 1986.

Burckhardt, Jacob. The Civilization of the Renaissance in Italy. Barnes and Noble Books, 1999.

Giorgi, Rosa. Saints. A Year in Faith and Art. Abrams New York. 2005.

Lanciani, Rodolfo. Golden Days of the Renaissance. Boston: Houghton Mifflin, 1906.

Murray, Peter. The Architecture of the Italian Renaissance. New York: Schocken Books, 1920, 1986.

Nicholson, Peter. Encyclopedia of Architecture. New York: Franklin Watts, 1988.

Made in the USA
Middletown, DE
31 July 2025